Perspectives on

Teaching

Connected Speech

to Second Language Speakers

Perspectives on Teaching Connected Speech to Second Language Speakers

edited by
JAMES DEAN BROWN
KIMI KONDO-BROWN

series editor
RICHARD SCHMIDT

NATIONAL FOREIGN LANGUAGE RESOURCE CENTER
University of Hawai'i at Mānoa

Manufactured in the United States of America

The contents of this Technical Report were developed under a grant from the U.S. Department of Education (CFDA 84.229, P229A020002). However, the contents do not necessarily represent the policy of the Department of Education, and one should not assume endorsement by the Federal Government.

ISBN(10): 0–8248–3136–5
ISBN1(3): 978–0–8248–3136–3

∞™ The paper used in this publication meets the minimum requirements of the American National Standard for Information Sciences–Permanence of Paper for Printed Library Materials.   ANSI Z39.48–1984

book design by Deborah Masterson • cover photo by Bob Chinn

About the
National Foreign Language Resource Center

THE NATIONAL FOREIGN LANGUAGE RESOURCE CENTER, located in the College of Languages, Linguistics, & Literature at the University of Hawai'i at Mānoa, has conducted research, developed materials, and trained language professionals since 1990 under a series of grants from the U.S. Department of Education (Language Resource Centers Program). A national advisory board sets the general direction of the resource center. With the goal of improving foreign language instruction in the United States, the center publishes research reports and teaching materials that focus primarily on the languages of Asia and the Pacific. The center also sponsors summer intensive teacher training institutes and other professional development opportunities. For additional information about center programs, contact us.

Dr. Richard Schmidt, Director
National Foreign Language Resource Center
University of Hawai'i
1859 East-West Road #106
Honolulu, HI 96822–2322

e-mail: nflrc@hawaii.edu
http://nflrc.hawaii.edu

NFLRC Advisory Board

Contents

How should
connected
speech
be tested?

What do we know so far?

Introducing Connected Speech

JAMES DEAN BROWN
KIMI KONDO-BROWN
University of Hawai'i

This chapter introduces the notion of connected speech covered in this book in three steps: First, the chapter describes what connected speech is, including the different phonological phenomena that fall under this general term (word stress, sentence stress and timing, reduction, citation and weak forms of words, elision, intrusion, assimilation, juncture, and contraction); second, it discusses a number of reasons for why we should teach connected speech in language classrooms; and third, it describes what this particular book has to offer with regard to the theory and practice of teaching connected speech in five sections that each address a different question (What do we know so far about teaching connected speech? Does connected speech instruction work? How should connected speech be taught in English? How should connected speech be taught in Japanese? and, How should connected speech be tested?). This chapter should be of interest to all readers interested in connected speech.

What is Connected Speech?

In order to fully explain how we are using the term *connected speech* in this book, we will need to address three questions:

1. What does the term *connected speech* mean?
2. What are all the different aspects of connected speech?
3. Why label all these phenomena "connected speech"?

Hopefully, answers to those three questions will add up for the reader to a fuller understanding of just exactly what we mean by connected speech.

What does the term *connected speech* mean?

In one way or another, all of the articles in this book are about connected speech.[1] So we will begin by explaining what we mean by connected speech. Crystal (1980) defines connected speech as:

---

[1]   Editors' note: Apparently, in the related literature on connected speech in the Japanese language, a further distinction is also made between fast speech and casual speech (see chapter 10 for much more on this distinction).

Brown, J. D., & Kondo-Brown, K. (2006) Introducing connected speech. In J. D. Brown, & K. Kondo-Brown, (Eds.), *Perspectives on teaching connected speech to second language speakers* (pp. 1–15). Honolulu, HI: University of Hawai'i, National Foreign Language Resource Center.

A term used by linguists to refer to spoken language when analysed as a continuous sequence, as in normal utterances and conversations. Its significance lies in the contrast implied with studies of linguistic units seen in isolation, such as an individual sound, word or phrase, which were the subject matter of traditional linguistic enquiry. It is now realized that important changes happen to these units when they are used in connected speech, as demonstrated by such processes as assimilation and elision, e.g., *and* becoming /n/ in such phrases as *boys and girls*. (p. 81)

Crystal's definition works well for the purposes of this book, except that we will expand the list of processes involved to include word stress, sentence stress and timing, reduction, strong and weak forms of words, elision, intrusion, assimilation, transition (juncture), liaison, and contraction.

The general topic of this book, then, is connected speech, but the individual processes involved have the different names listed in the previous sentence (as well as many variations of those names). In addition, the forms themselves, that is, the phonological forms used to accomplish connected speech, are often referred to as *reduced forms* or *reductions*. Thus, the two reductions that might be written as *I'm* and *Whatcha say?* are parts of connected speech, one accomplished by contraction and the other by assimilation, and at the same time, they are two different reduced forms.

What are all the different aspects of connected speech?

Clearly then, in order to explain connected speech, we must first define the central processes involved: *word stress, sentence stress and timing, reduction, citation and weak forms of words, elision, intrusion, assimilation, juncture,* and *contraction*. Let's examine these processes one at a time.

Word stress. According to Crystal (2003) the *stress* in word stress is: "A term used in phonetics to refer to the degree of force used in producing a syllable. The usual distinction is between *stressed* and *unstressed* syllables, the former being more prominent than the latter (and marked in transcription with a raised vertical line, ['])" (p. 435). Put another way, *word stress* can be more simply defined as the organization of stressed syllables in a word (which is in turn, the smallest distinctive unit of meaning that can stand on its own in speaking or writing) in terms of prominence.

Sentence stress and timing. We will define *sentence stress* simply as the stress or pattern of stress groups in a sentence (or utterance, since they are typically oral). We will define *sentence timing* as the pattern of stress or syllable timing in the stress groups in a sentence (or utterance) of the language. Languages are sometimes categorized in one of two ways:

> *Syllable timed languages* (i.e., those that tend to give each syllable approximately the same prominence), e.g., Japanese (wherein *arigatoo gozaimasu* "thank you very much" is broken up into the following syllables, or *mora*,[2]: *a ri ga to o go za i ma su* each with approximately the same weight) and French (wherein an utterance like *Il est très fatigué* "He is very tired" would be pronounced in six syllables of approximately equal weight as follows: *Il est très fa ti gué*);
> *Stress timed languages* (i.e., those that tend to give each stress group approximately the same weight), e.g, English (wherein the utterance *When'll*

---

[2]   Note: Both linguists and Japanese language teachers in general call the timing unit a *mora* rather than syllable; nevertheless, the concepts appear to be similar, the *mora* is generally defined as a CV or V and is thought of as a unit of timing.

'Tom be coming 'back? would be timed in two stress groups: *When'll 'Tom* and *be coming 'back?* [Note that we use the word *tend* to qualify our definitions. We do so because such definitions only hold under certain conditions and because such definitions are not necessarily exactly the same across languages that may be characterized as one or the other (see Crystal, 2003, p. 436; Dauer, 1983).]

Reduction. *Reduction* is a process that occurs in connected speech, in which phonemes of the language are changed, minimized, or eliminated in order to facilitate pronunciation. For example, in North American English (NAE), vowels in unstressed syllables are often reduced to schwa /ə/[3] or incorporated into a syllabic consonant like /n̩/, for example, the word *television*, when pronounced very clearly, would be /ˈtɛlaˌvɪʒɪn/, but at least four other pronunciations with reduced vowels would be acceptable in connected speech: /ˈtɛlaˌvɪʒən/, /ˈtɛləˌvɪʒən/, /ˈtɛləˌvɪʒn̩/, and even a three syllable version /ˈtɛlˌvɪʒn̩/.

Citation and weak forms of words. Some words in a language may be pronounced one way when they are prominent or stressed and another way (or other ways) when they are not prominent or stressed. For instance, when a word in English is stressed or prominent, as when it is pronounced in isolation, we call that the *citation form*, which may be pronounced quite differently from the weak form of the same word found in an unstressed position. For example, the citation form for *and* is /ænd/ in NAE. However, the same word can appear in a *weak form* or several weak forms in addition to the citation form depending on the meaning being expressed, the phonological environment, and level of formality involved. For example, the *and* in *bread and butter* can be pronounced /æn/ or /n̩/ in connected speech (i.e., /brɛdænbʌɾɾ/ or /brɛdn̩bʌɾɾ/); the *and* in *you and I* can be pronounced in even more divers ways in connected speech: /ˈjuənˈdai/, /ˈjun̩ˈdai/, /ˈjuənˈai/, and /ˈjun̩ˈai/.

Elision. *Elision* is a process of elimination or dropping of phonemes (vowels or consonants) that would be present in the citation form of a word or phrase. For example, in citation form, *chocolate* is pronounced /tʃakələt/, but in connected speech, NAE speakers would be much more likely to drop the middle vowel in *chocolate* /ˈtʃaklət/. Elision can also occur at word boundaries as in the last consonant in the word *old* in *He's a good ol' boy* where it is pronounced /ol/, while in citation form it would be /old/. Indeed, elision is a common process in continuous speech, especially in the numerous weak forms of the (mostly function) words.

Intrusion. A process that is the opposite of elision involves inserting phonemes within or between words. This process will be called *intrusion* here. In English, within words for example, many NAE speakers insert a /t/ between the /n/ and /θ/ in *month* /mʌntθ/, or between /n/ and /ʃ/ as in *bunch* /bʌntʃ/, or between /l/ and /s/ as in *false* /falts/; or they insert a /p/ between /m/ and /f/ as in *comfort* /kʌmpfərt/; or they insert a /k/ between /ŋ/ and /st/ as in *gangster* /geŋkstər/ or between /ŋ/ and /θ/ as in *length* /lɛŋkθ/. Between words, insertion of /r/ is common in some dialects of English after the vowel /a/ at the end of one word and before a vowel at the beginning of another word. For example, *China and Japan* would be pronounced in some NAE dialects with the /a/ in *China* changed to /ə/ and an intrusive /r/ as /tʃainərəndʒəpæn/, something like *Chin'r and Japan*. In French, an intrusive /t/ is

---

[3]   This book assumes basic knowledge of IPA phonetic transcription conventions, which are used uniformly where appropriate in the following chapters. For a quick review or overview of these conventions, see the IPA website at http://www.arts.gla.ac.uk/ipa/ipachart.html

added (and even spelled) when *Il a…* "He has" is inverted to form a question as in *A-t-il…?*

Assimilation. *Assimilation* is a process whereby one phoneme is changed into another because of the influence of a nearby phoneme. For example, in Japanese, the place name made up of the two words *shin* and *bashi* is pronounced (and even spelled in Roman characters) as *Shimbashi*. In this case, the /n/ phoneme changes to a bilabial /m/ phoneme because of the influence of the bilabial /b/ phoneme that follows it. In a sense, the lips are preparing to form the /b/ as they pronounce /m/. Another example, in English this time, is the influence of the voiceless /t/ on the pronunciation of *s* as a voiceless /s/ in *cats*, as compared to the influence of voiced /g/ on the pronunciation of *s* as a voiced /z/ in *dogs*.

Assimilation can occur in several ways depending on the direction in which phonemes influence each other. *Anticipatory assimilation* (sometimes called *regressive assimilation*) occurs when a phoneme is influenced by the phoneme that follows it, as was the case in the Japanese example above of the /n/ in *shin* becoming /m/ in anticipation of the bilabial /b/ in *bashi* when they are combined in *Shimbashi*. Notice that very similar anticipatory /n/ to /m/ assimilation occurs in words like *sunbeam* /sʌmbim/ in English. *Progressive assimilation* (sometimes called *lag* or *perseverative assimilation*) involves a phoneme being influenced by the phoneme that precedes it, as was the case in the English example above of the voiceless /t/ on the pronunciation of *s* as a voiceless /s/ in *cats*, as compared to the influence of voiced /g/ on the pronunciation of *s* as a voiced /z/ in *dogs*. The last category, *reciprocal assimilation* (sometimes called *coalescent assimilation*) occurs when two phonemes mutually influence each other. For example, the /t/ phoneme combines with /j/ across word boundaries to become a third sound /tʃ/ as in the English phrase *That you?* in NAE connected speech.

Transition (juncture). *Transition* refers to the ways that neighboring phonemes are connected. *Close transition* refers to those pronunciations wherein there is close connection between successive sounds, whereas *open transition* refers to pronunciations where there is a slight break in the continuity of pronunciation. For example, consider the two pronunciations *nitrate* and *night rate*. The connection between /t/ and /r/ is different in the two; the former demonstrates a close transition and the latter an open transition. Some analysts use the term *juncture* (including open and close forms) when others would apply *transition*.

Liaison. *Liaison* refers to one specific type of transition, wherein a sound is introduced at the end of one word if the following word begins with a vowel. For instance, in French, the plural article *les* is typically pronounced /le/ with the *s* silent when the following word begins with a consonant as in *les parents* (the parents) pronounced /leparã/. However, when the following word begins with a vowel as in the word *enfants* (children), the *s* is pronounced as a /z/ creating a liaison to the next word with the ensemble pronounced /lezãfã/

Contraction. A *contraction* is a way of showing the reduced characteristics of spoken language in written language (often used to write dialogue in a way that shows its spoken flavor). Examples include *can't, I've, she's, they'll, we're,* and *you'd*.

Why label all these phenomena *connected speech*?

One reason we feel the need to be very clear about defining connected speech is that a number of other terms have all been used to describe this overall topic. Indeed, aspects of this topic have been discussed for a number of years in the language teaching field in a rather disjointed and scattered manner under headings like *casual speech, colloquial speech, fast speech, informal speech, reduced forms, reduced speech, reductions, relaxed speech,* and *sandhi variation.* Some teachers also refer to them as *lazy, sloppy, careless, slack, slipshod, slovenly, substandard, low-class,* or *low-status* speech. None of those labels works 100% well.

Five of the labels describe when connected speech is used, that is, during *casual speech, colloquial speech, fast speech, informal speech,* and *relaxed speech.* It is easy to understand how such labels could come into being given that continuous speech is most prominent and obvious in these more laid-back sorts of language use. In one very important sense, such labels are misleading because they imply that the issues at hand only apply in certain registers or styles of language. The truth is that connected speech is commonly used in all registers and styles. Even the most formal pronunciation of a language will typically contain some aspects of these phenomena. For example, *transition* is applied even in the most formal of speech in English. Otherwise, the words would be pronounced separately and the speech would sound disconnected and unnatural.

Four other labels describe some aspects of connected speech, but not all of them: *Reduced forms, reduced speech, reductions,* and *sandhi variation* are each aspects of connected speech but do not themselves include all aspects of connected speech (i.e., word stress, sentence stress and timing, reduction, strong and weak forms of words, elision, intrusion, assimilation, transition/juncture, liaison, and contraction). The remaining labels, *lazy, sloppy, careless, slack, slipshod, slovenly, substandard, low-class,* or *low-status* speech, are generally negative and judgmental stereotypes which have no place in this academic discussion.

The bottom line is that connected speech encompasses a variety of phenomena that are found in all registers of a language, but to varying degrees depending on the register and style involved.

Why Should We Teach Connected Speech?

A number of reasons underlie our belief that language teachers should teach connected speech. Consider the following:

- Connected speech is a very real part of language.
- Students need to learn more than the traditional grammar, vocabulary, and pronunciation that many language teachers present; connected speech is an important subset of the new information they need to learn.
- Students need to be able to adjust their styles and registers in using language; the ability to understand and use connected speech is essential for making such adjustments.
- Connected speech is not just lazy, sloppy, careless, or slovenly language; rather, it occurs in all levels of speech, including the most formal manners of speaking.
- In all levels of formality, connected speech takes on what Gimson (2001, p. 249) describes as an important "accentuation" function; the understanding of connected speech can therefore help language learners understand aural language input and produce spoken language output that is more comprehensible.
- Research indicates that language learners do indeed have problems in understanding and producing connected speech (Bley-Vroman & Kweon, 2002;

Bowen, 1976; Brown & Hilferty, 1986a, 1986b; Henrichsen, 1984; Ito, chapter 6 of this book; Kim, 1995; Kweon, 2000;).

- Research also indicates that connected speech can be taught to non-native speakers of English (Brown & Hilferty, 1986a, 1986b).
- Our experience is that students enjoy learning about reduced forms because it is mostly new information that they find interesting.

What Does This Book Contribute?

One of the problems with connected speech as a discipline is that it isn't a discipline or even a sub-discipline. True, connected speech has interested some teachers and researchers over the past 30 years (see e.g., Bowen, 1975a, 1975b, and the many other citations in this book), but only a few people have worked systematically on connected speech and those few have done so only sporadically. In the meantime, teachers continue to teach the phonemes of their language of focus and later wonder why their students' pronunciation is still inadequate, that is, why their students cannot put the phonemes together in anything even approaching a native-like manner. Inquisitive teachers go in search of help with this issue and find a hint here and a brief explanation there about stress, contraction, assimilation, and so forth, but they do not find any single body of information that systematically addresses the ways the phonemes that they teach are connected. That is, they don't find any systematic treatment of connected speech.

This book is an attempt to kick-start interest in systematically researching and teaching connected speech. To that end, it collects together 14 (mostly recent) articles on various aspects of connected speech. In other words, our goal is to revitalize and create interest in the areas of researching and teaching connected speech by assembling key articles on the topic in one place. More formally, the purposes of the book are two-fold: to facilitate and promote research on connected speech in applied linguistics and to stimulate and encourage the teaching of connected speech in language classrooms around the world.

Because of the nature of the work to date on connected speech, such a book will necessarily cover a wide range of related topics in addressing the above purposes. Some of these topics will be interesting to teachers, others to researchers, and still others to materials developers. Since we also aim to show that continuous speech is not just an issue in ESL/EFL teaching, we also have included articles that address continuous speech in another language, Japanese in this case. Thus this book also contains articles that may be primarily of interest to Japanese language teachers, researchers, and materials developers. The last chapter of the book is on continuous speech in language testing (with examples in English, French, and Japanese) which should certainly be of interest to language testers, but will also probably be of interest to teachers, researchers, and materials developers in both ESL/EFL and Japanese (and perhaps French). Table 1 illustrates which audiences we feel will be most interested in each of the chapters.

Notice in Table 1 that the first and last chapter will probably be of interest to virtually all readers. Other chapters may only be of interest to some of the groups: three groups in the cases of chapters 2 and 3, four groups for chapters 4 through 9, and five groups for chapters 10 through 13. Table 1 also shows that this book will serve some groups better than others. For instance, applied linguistics researchers and language testers should find most of the chapters interesting, while EFL/EFL teachers and materials developers are likely to find 10 chapters of interest, and Japanese language teachers, researchers, and materials developers may find that only six chapters are interesting to them.

Table 1.　Who will be most interested in these chapters?

			primary audiences						
chapter	section		ESL/EFL teachers	applied linguistics researchers	ESL/EFL materials developers	Japanese teachers	Japanese researchers	Japanese materials developers	language testers
What do we know so far?									
1	*Introducing connected speech* Brown & Kondo-Brown		X	X	X	X	X	X	X
2	*The significance of reduced forms in L2 pedagogy* Ito		X	X	X				X
3	*What do textbooks have to offer to teachers of connected speech?* Brown		X	X	X				
Does connected speech instruction work?									
4	*The effectiveness of teaching reduced forms for listening comprehension* Brown & Hilferty		X	X	X				X
5	*Comprehension of English reduced forms by Japanese business people and the effectiveness of instruction* Matsuzawa		X	X	X				X
6	*Effect of reduced forms on input-intake process* Ito		X	X	X				X
How should connected speech be taught in English?									
7	*Don'cha know? A survey of ESL teachers' perspectives on reduced forms instruction* Rogerson		X	X	X				X
8	*Teaching reduced interrogative forms to low-level students* Cahill		X	X	X				X
9	*Visualizing English speech reductions using the free phonetic software package WASP* Varden		X	X	X				X

continued…

Table 1.   Who will be most interested in these chapters? *(cont.)*

chapter	section	ESL/EFL teachers	applied linguistics researchers	ESL/EFL materials developers	Japanese teachers	Japanese researchers	Japanese materials developers	language testers
					primary audiences			
How should connected speech be taught in Japanese?								
10	*On casual speech: How it differs from fast speech* Hasegawa		X		X	X	X	X
11	*Pedagogical issues related to teaching listening to oral Japanese with a focus on reduced forms* Toda		X		X	X	X	X
12	*Use of CAI learning materials for teaching sound changes in spoken Japanese* Sakai & Igashima		X		X	X	X	X
13	*Why second language learners of Japanese need to learn difficult minute sounds in connected speech* Hirata		X		X	X	X	X
How should connected speech be tested?								
14	*Testing students' abilities to understand and used connected speech* Brown & Kondo-Brown	X	X	X	X	X	X	X

Notice also that Table 1 is broken up into five sections each headed by a question: (a) What do we know so far about teaching connected speech? (b) Does connected speech instruction work? (c) how should connected speech be taught in English? (d) How should connected speech be taught in Japanese? And, (e) How should connected speech be tested? Each of the 14 chapters will now be described under the subheadings, which are the questions that guide each of the five main sections of this book.

What do we know so far about teaching connected speech?

One salient feature of the literature on connected speech is that there is not much available. Clearly, much less is written on connected speech than on just about any other topic in applied linguistics. Indeed, it might be most accurate to characterize the literature on connected speech as being made up of a bit here and a bit there over a great many years. A few authors have made modest efforts to explain a few features of connected speech and to explore ways to teach the various topics involved (e.g., Brown & Hilferty, 1989, 1995, 1998; Celce-Murcia, Brinton, & Goodwin, 2004; Dauer, 1993; Gilbert, 1984, 1993; Gimson, 1962, 1970, 1975, 1989, 2001; Grant, 1993; Hill & Beebe, 1980; Morley, 1987; Pennington, 1996; Sheeler & Markley,

1991). However, most of those authors have only touched on connected speech as one small portion of a larger treatment of pronunciation or listening comprehension improvement. Notable exceptions include Griffee (1993), Griffee and Hough (1986), Hagen (2000), Hough (1995), Kobayashi and Linde (1984), Rost and Stratton (1978, 1980), and Weinstein (1982, 2001), all of which provided student texts with coverage focused on connected speech. The first section of this book seeks to introduce the basic concepts involved in the teaching of connected speech including basic terminology and to briefly review the bits and pieces that have been covered in the literature to date.

This chapter introduces the book. We began by defining the general notion of *connected speech*. Then, we described the different phonological phenomena that fall within the general definition (thereby further defining the term), which included *word stress, sentence stress and timing, reduction, citation and weak forms of words, elision, intrusion, assimilation, juncture,* and *contraction*. Next, we discussed the various reasons why language teachers should teach their students connected speech. Finally, in this section, we are describing what the chapters of this particular book have to offer in terms of the theory and practice of teaching connected speech.

In chapter 2, Yasuko Ito provides a literature review of the work to date (including some of the other articles in this book) on reduced forms in language teaching. Ito's goal is to explain why reduced forms are important in L2 teaching and explore some of the approaches that can be used in teaching reduced forms. The author begins by describing the nature of reduced forms. Then, she discusses several studies about ESL learners' reduced forms performance. The author continues by explaining the relationship between the notions focus-on-form instruction and the teaching of reduced forms. Ito ends by suggesting useful directions that reduced-forms instruction might take in the future.

In chapter 3, J. D. Brown reviews the resources to which teachers can turn if they want better understanding of connected speech to help them teach the topics involved. Brown identifies resources in two basic categories. First, there are teacher training resources with some coverage of connected speech, which includes books for training linguists, books for training applied linguists and language teachers, articles for training applied linguists and language teachers, and miscellaneous professional resources. Second, there are ESL/EFL student books with coverage of connected speech, which includes both ESL/EFL student books that have some coverage of connected speech and ESL/EFL student books that focus primarily on connected speech. The books in this last category of student books (those focused primarily on connected speech) are examined and compared in some depth.

Does connected speech instruction work?

Concrete primary research on topics related to connected speech is very difficult to track down. Some studies are reported in Bowen (1975b, 1976, 1977), Henrichsen (1984), Brown and Hilferty (1986a, 1986b), Anderson-Hsieh, Riney, and Koehler (1994), Kim (1995), Kweon (2000), Ito (chapter 6 of this book), as well as Bley-Vroman and Kweon (2002).

Henrichsen (1984) was the first to explore the differential effects of the presence or absence of sandhi-variation (what we are calling connected speech here) on the listening comprehension scores of native speakers and ESL students. He argued that sandhi-variation reduced the perceptual saliency of spoken English and hypothesized that there would be no significant differences for presence or absence in the scores of the native speaker group, but significant differences for the ESL participants. He did indeed find statistically significant differences between the two groups and between the two conditions (i.e., the presence or absence of sandhi-variation), as well as a significant interaction effect (apparently caused by the lack of difference for native speakers between the presence and absence conditions in contrast to the large differences found for the ESL students). Clearly, Henrichsen demonstrated important effects for connected speech on ESL students' comprehension.

The second section of this book extends Henrichsen's research by presenting three studies that address the question of whether or not connected speech can be taught. Clearly, the three projects were conducted in three very different settings (i.e., two in EFL settings in the People's Republic of China and Japan, and one in an SLS setting in Hawai'i in the USA), but all come to the same conclusion: Teaching connected speech appears to be worth the effort.

More specifically, in chapter 4, J. D. Brown and Ann Hilferty (first published as Brown & Hilferty, 1986b[4]) provide the first research report on the effectiveness of teaching reduced forms for listening comprehension. The 32 EFL participants were randomly assigned to control and treatment groups. They then received five 10-minute lessons per week for 4 weeks: The control group learned how to recognize minimal pairs (the authors felt that this was the equivalent of a placebo) while the treatment group learned how to understand reduced forms. Three tests (each counterbalanced in two forms) were administered to all participants at the beginning and end of the four weeks: two forms of Bowen's IGT, retired versions of the UCLA ESLPE listening subtest, and reduced-forms dictations (based on the reduced forms that had been taught to the treatment group). At the end of the study, the treatment group's scores were higher than the control group's scores on all the three measures, though the differences were only statistically significant for Bowen's IGT and the reduced-forms dictation. The authors concluded that reduced forms can be taught and that such instruction appears to improve listening comprehension ability.

In chapter 5, Takashi Matsuzawa addresses the issue of why Japanese speakers of English have so much difficulty with listening comprehension. The author hypothesizes that Japanese do not recognize some of the crucial differences that arise when trying to understand written and spoken language. He proposes that a mixture of reduced forms and sound changes interfere with their listening comprehension. Matsuzawa explores the hypothesis that reduced forms do, in fact, impede comprehension while also investigating the effect of explicit instruction of reduced forms. His results indicate that a serious deficiency does occur in comprehending reduced forms; he also finds that explicit instruction leads to improvements in recognizing and comprehending reduced forms.

In chapter 6, Yasuko Ito investigates the influence of reduced forms on input/intake. She also examines differences in the reduced form type and sentence complexity in the test she is using. Her participants were 18 ESL students and nine native speakers of English at the University of Hawai'i at Mānoa (UHM). They took two versions of a dictation test. Like Henrichsen (1984), she found statistically significant listening-comprehension score differences between proficiency levels and between two experimental conditions: the presence or absence of reduced forms. In addition,

---

[4]   This article is reproduced by permission of the authors (*RELC Journal* was appropriately notified).

a statistically significant interaction effect was found for proficiency and the type of reduced form, but not for proficiency and the presence or absence of reduced forms. Her study supports the notion that reduced forms influence listening comprehension. However, her results also indicate that different types of reduced forms may influence learners' listening comprehension differently.

How should connected speech be taught in English?

As pointed out above (and in chapter 3 of this book), over the years, some books have provided scattered information for language teachers on ways to teach connected speech (Avery & Ehrlich, 1992; Bowen, 1975a; Celce-Murcia, Brinton, & Goodwin, 2004; Dalton & Seidlhofer, 2001; Gimson, 1962, 1970, 1975, 1989, 2001; Kelly, 2003; Kenworthy, 1987; Kreidler, 1997; Pennington, 1996; Prator & Robinett, 1995; Roach, 2004; Teschner & Whitley, 2004; and Underhill, 1994). Other books have offered a smattering of materials (in amongst other pronunciation instruction) that can help language instructors teach connected speech (Dauer, 1993; Gilbert, 1984, 1993; Grant, 1993; Henrichsen, Green, Nishitani, & Bagley, 2002; Hewings, 1993a, b; Hewings & Goldstein, 1998; Lane, 2005; Laroy, 2003; Morley, 1987; Orion, 1988; Prator & Robinett, 1995; Rogerson & Gilbert, 2001; and Sheeler & Markley, 1991).

Over the years, nine books (see chapter 3 for much more information on these books) have directly addressed connected speech with lessons specifically designed to teach various aspects of connected speech (Griffee, 1993; Griffee & Hough, 1986; Hagen, 2000; Hough, 1995; Kobayashi & Linde, 1984; Rost & Stratton, 1978, 1980; Weinstein, 1982, 2001). In this section, we expand the quest for ways to teach continuous speech by exploring what teachers think about teaching such content, as well as some ideas for teaching continuous speech both in the classroom and through the use of a computer program called WASP that can help students visualize reduced speech.

More specifically, in chapter 7, Moana Rogerson surveys the views of a group of ESL teachers on reduced forms instruction. In the process, she deals with three issues: the familiarity of ESL instructors with reduced forms in oral English; their views about teaching reduced forms for listening comprehension; and the challenges they face in teaching reduced-forms. She concludes with a call for more research on reduced forms and their importance in language learning, as well as a call for more systematic and effective reduced forms teaching materials. Indeed those are issues that the present book is designed to foster and respond to.

In chapter 8, Robert Cahill begins by discussing the concepts of *teacher talk, motherese,* and *foreigner talk,* and shows how they are related to reduced speech. He then provides examples of how reductions have been treated in the literature and discusses the variety of terminology used in such treatments. After settling on *reductions* or *reduced forms* as his labels for the processes involved in informal enunciation, he states that the purposes of his chapter are to recognize the importance of reduced forms and to propose guidelines to help teachers prepare efficient exercises to teach such reduced forms (as part of existing courses). He begins the main body of the chapter by describing the context in which he teaches at Yokohama Shoka Daigaku High School. He contends that communicative elements should be used to complement a structural syllabus like the one in which he finds himself and offers ways to present elements of communicative competence as well as phonological consciousness raising. He then deals with pedagogical issues associated with reduced forms and describes what he calls "efficient aural processing." Next, he focuses on teaching interrogative reduced forms to students with limited experience in three steps: (a) contractions, (b) *yes/no* questions, and (c) *wh*-questions. Cahill's goal is to get students to move from controlled to automatic processing.

In chapter 9, J. Kevin Varden illustrates how a phonetic software program called WASP (downloaded free from http://www.phon.ucl.ac.uk/resource/sfs/wasp.htm) can be used to promote the learning of NAE reduced forms. He begins by discussing the basic information provided by the various WASP graphs and showing numerous examples of the various types of sounds in NAE pronunciation. He then discusses several types of reductions (schwa reduction, flapping, coalescent assimilation, and elision) and shows how WASP represents them. His abundant use of examples and his discussion of the difficulties instructors may encounter in using software for pronunciation training both provide teachers with the information and warnings they will need to start a computer-supported NAE reduced forms pronunciation training program.

How should connected speech be taught in Japanese?

In the field of teaching Japanese-as-a-second language (JSL), there is also considerable interest in teaching spoken Japanese as connected speech. During the last decade, a number of studies have investigated how best to assist JSL learners in developing their oral communication skills to comprehend and produce connected speech.[5] In developing oral communication skills, teachers' incorporating *naturalistic* or *authentic* language use is encouraged (e.g., Brown, 2001; Omaggio Hadley, 2001). Recent JSL studies have indeed raised the issue of authentic language use in developing learners' communication skills and examined the effect of pedagogical activities where JSL learners (a) orally interact with native speaker guests (Mori, 2002; Yorozu, 2001), (b) are exposed to authentic audio/visual materials such as videotaped Japanese TV commercials (e.g., Ohara, Saft, & Crookes, 2001), and (c) exchange email messages with native speakers (e.g., Yamada & Moeller, 2001), where spoken language forms of Japanese may be used in written messages.

Despite growing interest in naturalistic language use in communicative JSL classrooms, little research has examined how best to instruct the reduced forms that occur in colloquial Japanese. Negishi's (1999) work, which was based on native speakers' views of nonnative speakers' use of contracted forms in Japanese, was perhaps one of the pioneering studies that advocated the need of establishing a methodological framework for teaching reduced forms in Japanese. Negishi's study suggests that native speakers tend to feel that the non-native speakers' use of causal speech without contracted forms sounds unnatural, and so we should probably consider teaching beginning-level and advanced-level JSL learners to use contracted forms in causal speech.

More recently, Byun (2004) examined how Korean learners of Japanese living in Japan produce high vowel devoicing and suggests that mere exposure to reduced

---

[5]   For example, recent JSL-related studies have dealt with the issues of developing oral communication skills with a focus on sociolinguistic competence (e.g., Cook, 2001; Ohta, 1999; Saito & Beecken, 1997; Siegal, 1996; Yoshimi, 2001), discourse competence (e.g., Watanabe, 2003), and strategic competence (Kim & Alajpro, 1997). Pedagogical concerns for teaching Japanese for oral communication have also been discussed in terms of task designs (Iwashita, 2001; Mori, 2002), native perceptions of non-native performance (Okamura, 1995; Watanabe, 2005), performance evaluations (Kondo-Brown, 2004), and affective issues (Kitano, 2001; Kurahashi, 1996; Machida, 2001).

forms in "natural" environments may not be sufficient for JSL learners to acquire them. Instead, learners need to be made aware of phonological changes that occur in Japanese connected speech through formal instruction on reduced forms.

Popular JSL language textbooks, especially in intermediate- and advanced-level texts, do include a variety of reduced forms as target grammatical items (see Negishi, 1999). However, few textbooks seem to provide systematic and comprehensive accounts of sound changes in naturalistic spoken Japanese as well as meaningful and communicative tasks that require the use of such changes (with the notable exceptions of Toda, 2004, and Tomisaka, 1997). As our interest in developing JSL learners' oral communication skills via use of naturalistic Japanese grows, we need more work to examine which reduced forms should be taught, at what level, and how.

Reduced forms instruction may be particularly important for teaching Japanese-as-a-heritage-language (JHL) students, who have typically been using colloquial Japanese at home before beginning to learn Japanese formally in the classroom. Many of these JHL students may write Japanese as they speak including a variety of reduced forms discussed in this section because they are not aware of the difference between the unfamiliar written Japanese and the familiar colloquial Japanese (Kondo, 1998). Although there is unprecedented interest in instruction for heritage students in the United States (see, for example, Kondo-Brown, 2003, 2005), there have been few investigations of the advantages and disadvantages that JHL students may have in terms of the use of reduced forms in connected speech.

The four chapters in this section will provide not only systematic accounts for phonological changes in Japanese connected speech but also offer useful examples that may help teachers carry out form-focused instruction with a focus on sound changes in Japanese connected speech.

More specifically, in chapter 10, Nobuko Hasegawa discusses sound changes in Japanese connected speech by examining casual speech processes in comparison with fast speech processes. Hasegawa demonstrates that, while phonological changes in fast speech (e.g., "high vowel devoicing," "vowel degemination and lengthening") are merely determined by phonological environments related to the rate of speech, casual speech processes are indifferent to the speed of speech. According to Hasegawa, casual processes (e.g., "nasal syllabicization," "vowel fusion," "less sonorant vowel deletion," "phrase final reduction") apply only to specific lexical items and are highly sensitive to sociological factors in a given speech context such as politeness, intimacy, gender, and so forth. Therefore, causal speech processes may not be triggered unless the resulting phonological changes match with the given speech context determined by other grammatical components of the sentence.

In chapter 11, Takako Toda begins by examining sound changes in Japanese connected speech using some categories of reduced forms defined earlier: *elision* (e.g., "vowel elision" [see "less sonorant vowel deletion" in Hasegawa's chapter]), *contraction* (e.g., "consonant palatalization," "vowel coalescence" [see "less sonorant vowel deletion" in Hasegawa's chapter]), *assimilation* (e.g., "*museika*/devoicing" [see "high vowel devoicing" in Hasegawa's chapter], "rendaku/ sequential voicing," "sokuon-ka/consonant gemination," and "hatsuon-ka/moraic nasalization" [see "nasal syllabicization" in Hasegawa's chapter], and finally *transition* (e.g., *liaison* and *close transition*). While Hasegawa (see chapter 10 of this book) discusses some of these sound changes in connected speech in terms of fast versus casual speech, Toda examines such changes in comparison with European languages such as English or

French. She emphasizes that, like European languages, Japanese sound changes are triggered by ease of articulation. She also emphasizes the notion that the *mora* plays an important role in the categorization of Japanese reduced forms. Toda recommends that explicit form-focused instruction of Japanese reduced forms, where the students are encouraged to connect the target reduced form to meaning, should be encouraged in teaching JSL. In the second part of her chapter, Toda demonstrates how Japanese language teachers can do that with various examples.

In chapter 12, Takako Sakai and Yu Igashima (like Toda) recommend explicit form-focused instruction in teaching sound changes in Japanese connected speech. Sakai and Igashima specifically recommend the use of computer-assisted language learning (CALL) because it can effectively cope with individual differences in general and cognitive learning styles in particular, all of which may influence phonological information processes. Sakai and Igashima show several examples of CALL materials that they have developed based on previous empirical research. These example materials focus on three phonological changes (also discussed in Hasegawa's and Toda's chapters): "moraic nasal" [N] (e.g., /ganbaNnasai/ "do your best"), "word coalescing" (e.g., /tabechatta/ "ended up eating"), and "vowel devoicing" (/uts(u)k(u)shii/ "beautiful").[6] Sakai and Igashima show that student evaluations of the CALL materials are positive.

Thus, chapters 10, 11, and 12 emphasize the importance of teaching Japanese sounds in connected speech contexts from the perspective of systematic phonological changes that occur in such contexts. In contrast, chapter 13 by Yukari Hirata emphasizes the importance of teaching connected speech in terms of the increased difficulty that JSL learners have in distinguishing the length of Japanese vowels and consonants in connected speech and in isolated words. As Hirata points out, traditionally, teachers present paired words such as 町/machi/ "town" vs. マッチ/mattchi/ "match," ビル/biru/ "building" vs. ビール /biiru/ "beer" as isolated words. However, Hirata's first experimental study shows that JSL students have more difficulty in perceiving Japanese vowel and consonant length in connected speech than in isolation. Hirata's two other experimental studies explore alternative explanations for this difficulty. First, Hirata argues that the duration of Japanese vowels spoken by native speakers varies considerably with speaking rate and that this variation, in turn, creates significant overlaps between short and long vowel sound lengths at various speech rates. Second, she demonstrates that even native speakers of Japanese often fail to identify the vowel length accurately (a) when listening to the original target word containing the vowel in cases where it is excised from its connected speech carrier sentence and (b) when listening to the word edited with a mismatched vowel length even in the connected speech carrier sentence.

How should connected speech be tested?

Bowen (1975b, 1976) was the first researcher to focus on testing connected speech forms with the development of the Integrative Grammar Test (IGT). He designed a test to measure students' abilities to listen to sentences "pronounced in normal,

---

[6]   Editorial notes: We have decided to leave the authors' choices in describing pronunciations as they are. For example, in transcribing Japanese in Roman letters, in Toda's and Sakai & Yu's chapters, the more phonetic ヘボン式 (hebon-shiki) is used, while in Hasegawa's chapter, 訓令式 (kunrei-shiki), which stresses one-on-one correspondence with the Table of basic *kana* system, is used. Additionally, the devoiced vowels are marked by parentheses ( ) in Sakai and Igashima's chapter (e.g., /uts(u)s(u)kushii/), dots underneath the vowels in Hasegawa's chapter (e.g., /uṭụkụshii/), and underlines in Toda's chapter (e.g., /uts̲u̲ku̲shii/).

informal, conversational English" (p. 31; with the first two words in each involving a reduced form of English) and demonstrate their comprehension by writing down the full form of the second word in each sentence in the blank. Two other researchers, Brown and Hilferty (1982, 1986a, 1986b, also see chapter 4 of this book) developed what they called reduced-forms dictations for their research.

Since then, most other researchers have used variations of the Bowen's IGT. Henrichsen (1984) used single independent sentences to test sandhi-variation in one form of his test, in which the students heard 15 sentences with reduced forms (selected from Bowen's IGT); the students were required to write down the full forms of the words (in blanks that were provided) when they heard each sentence. Just like the IGT, the first two words in each of these sentences were reduced. Matsuzawa (chapter 5 in this book) required the examinees to write down all words they heard in listening to 30 sentences in each of his two test forms. In this case, a wider range of different reduced forms was tested and the item format was different (i.e., the spaces in which the students were to write were provided in parentheses). Ito (chapter 6 of this book) asked students to listen to 20 sentences and write the sentences in their full forms in blanks that were provided. Two of the words, which were near but not at the beginning of each sentence, were contracted or blended together (half were lexical reductions and half were phonological reductions).

In addition, Ito (in chapter 2 of this volume) points to a number of "classic activities such as dictation (e.g., Norris, 1995), read-aloud exercises (e.g., Celce-Murcia, Brinton, & Goodwin, 2004; Dauer, 1993), cloze exercises (e.g., Hewings & Goldstein, 1998; Kobayashi & Linde, 1984; Norris, 1995), and listen-and-repeat exercises (e.g., Gimson, 1975; Kobayashi & Linde, 1984), all of which could be used for testing purposes.

In chapter 14, J. D. Brown and Kimi Kondo-Brown give a great deal more detail with examples of each of the types of tests described in the previous three paragraphs. In the process, they discuss classical activities that can be used to test reduced-forms (including examples of reduced-forms read-aloud tests, reduced-forms cloze exercises, reduced-forms listen-and-repeat tests) and other reduced-forms testing ideas (including examples of partial reduced-forms dictations, reduced-forms dialog comprehension, reduced-forms dialog dictocomp, testing sentence stress, minimal contrast tests, etc.). The authors also raise the issue of whether similar tests can be developed for other languages, which they answer with examples of connected speech tests for both French and Japanese. The chapter also explores the requirements for using communicative activities to test reduced-forms (including the characteristics of such tests) as well as some ideas for other alternative forms of assessment (including portfolios, conferences, and peer-assessments or self-assessments).

‎

2

NFLRC
monographs

The Significance of
Reduced Forms in L2 Pedagogy

YASUKO ITO
University of Hawai'i

One purpose of this chapter is to examine the currently available literature on continuous speech and discuss why reduced forms are important in L2 pedagogy. Another purpose is to explore approaches that could be used to teach reduced forms. To those ends, the chapter describes the nature of reduced forms. Then, the chapter reviews a number of studies that involve ESL learners' performance on reduced forms. And finally, it suggests future directions that reduced forms instruction might profitably develop. Thus, this chapter will probably be of most interest to language teachers, researchers, testers and materials developers who want to understand, teach, and develop materials or tests for teaching reduced forms.

In the process of learning an L2, learners experience a number of difficulties. One commonly heard complaint from learners of English as an L2 is that "native speakers talk too fast" (Gilbert, 1995, p. 97). Although the current trend of L2 teaching methodology emphasizes the use of authentic materials in classrooms, learners often find themselves being unable to understand the language outside the classroom where they encounter the real use of the language. The question is, why do they feel that way? Gilbert claims that this is due to "the lack of training in the way spoken English systematically uses such mechanisms as reduction and intonational marking for emphasis and thought grouping" (p. 97). This mechanism of reduction is often referred to as *reduced forms, sandhi-variation, weak forms,* or *connected speech.* These terms collectively refer to phonological phenomena such as reduction, assimilation, contraction, linking, deletion, and so forth, which occur in spoken English (Brown & Hiferty, 1986b; Celce-Murcia, Brinton, & Goodwin, 2004). These phenomena, which will be referred to as "reduced forms" in this chapter, are very common in spoken English regardless of the speed and formality of the speech (Kaisse, 1985). Despite the apparent nature of spoken English, many learners of English as an L2 are not trained to deal with "real" English and are shocked when they go outside the classroom where they are unable to comprehend what native speakers are saying.

Difficulties caused by unfamiliarity with reduced forms are not limited to listening comprehension skills. Learners' pronunciation is also affected as Celce-Murcia, Brinton, & Goodwin (2004) point out. They note that "learners often attempt to

Ito, Y. (2006) The significance of reduced forms in L2 pedagogy. In J. D. Brown, & K. Kondo-Brown, (Eds.), *Perspectives on teaching connected speech to second language speakers* (pp. 17–25). Honolulu, HI: University of Hawai'i, National Foreign Language Resource Center.

pronounce each individual word so clearly that they fail to blend words within a single thought group smoothly. This can cause their speech to sound choppy" (p. 165). The learners' unfamiliarity with reduced forms in English is, therefore, one major source of difficulties in their listening comprehension as well as in their pronunciation skills.

Despite these problems, reduced forms have received little attention in research on L2 acquisition and pedagogy. The purpose of this chapter is to examine the literature that is currently available, to discuss why reduced forms are important in second language (L2) pedagogy, and to explore approaches that can be used in teaching them. First, I will describe the nature of reduced forms. Then, in the following section, several studies will be reviewed that involve ESL learners' performance on reduced forms. Finally, I will explore future directions for the instruction of reduced forms.

Reduced Forms in Spoken English

In speaking events, "speakers often like to convey their meaning with the least articulatory effort" (Ladefoged, 2000, p. 250). This produces reduced forms in spoken language. Ladefoged contends that:

> Except when they [i.e., speakers] are striving for clarity of articulation, they tend to produce utterances with a large number of assimilations, with some segments left out, and with the differences between other segments reduced to a minimum. Producing utterances in this way requires a speaker to follow a principle of *ease of articulation*.   (p. 251)

Thus, reduced forms occur for the speakers' sake.

However, this does not mean that reduced forms occur freely or randomly. There are systematic rules that determine which forms (or sounds) are reduced. To recognize those rules, it is necessary to understand the nature of the English language first. English is generally categorized as a stress-timed language, in which stressed syllables stand out while other syllables are weak (Kreidler, 1989). In contrast, French, for instance, is a syllable-timed language in which every syllable receives the same prominence. Kreidler provides the following two sentences to describe these two characteristics (p. 160):

(1) a. Sue bought nice, fresh, warm, sweet rolls.
    b. A group of black and white ducks were swimming in the pond.

Notice that (1a) has a "staccato rhythm" (Kreidler, 1989, p. 160). This is so because every word (or syllable in this case) receives the same prominence for the following reason: Every word in (1a) is a monosyllable as well as a content word (i.e., noun, verb, adjective, adverb). Thus, (1a) represents syllable timing, just like French. In contrast, (1b) contains polysyllabic words and function words such as articles, prepositions, conjunctions, and auxiliary verbs (Kreidler, 1989). This makes the reading of (1b) distinct from that of (1a); In (1b) those syllables that receive stress stand out while the others remain weak. This variation in the degree of stress governs the system of reduced forms in English in that those syllables that are weak generally get reduced.

Given that unstressed syllables are reduced in English, which elements, at the word level, receive stress and which do not? English words can be divided into two categories: content words (e.g., nouns, verbs, adjectives, adverbs, *wh*-words, and demonstratives) and function words (e.g., articles, prepositions, auxiliaries, pronouns, conjunctions, and relative pronouns). Content words are usually stressed whereas function words are usually unstressed (Avery & Ehrlich, 1992, p. 75). Since (1b) given above contains some function words, which are unstressed, the rhythmic pattern of the sentence is different from that of (1a). The unstressed words generally involve some phonological adjustments, such as contraction, linking, assimilation, vowel reduction, and deletion (Avery & Ehrlich, 1992; Celce-Murcia et al., 2004). Examples of these phenomena include I *will* becoming *I'll*, *his* being pronounced as [ɪz] without [h] at the beginning, *did you* becoming *didja*, and *should have* changing to *shoulda* (Weinstein, 1982).

Reduced forms are often assumed to occur only in fast and casual speech. However, Zwicky (1972) points out that casual speech need not be fast, and that fast speech need not be casual. Sound reductions are observed even in slow speech (Shockey, 2003). Thus, reduced forms are not limited to fast or casual speech. In other words, spoken English in general involves reduced forms.

Reduced forms are widely used in spoken English regardless of the speed or the register of speech. Therefore, L2 learners need to become familiar with them in order to comprehend English, their L2.

Research on Reduced Forms in L2 English

As mentioned at the beginning of the previous section, reduced forms occur to increase ease of articulation for the speakers. Conversely, reduced forms may boost the listener's burden because, while speakers try to speak with minimum articulatory effort, listeners expect "sufficient perceptual contrast between sounds" to allow them to comprehend the speakers' intent (Ladefoged, 2000, p. 253). This listening burden may be even heavier in the case of L2 learners.

Despite the potential difficulties in listening comprehension that reduced forms may contribute, they have not been explored very much in the research on L2 acquisition and pedagogy. This section reviews several studies currently available that investigated reduced forms in relationship to L2 speakers. The studies can be grouped into two categories: reduced forms in listening comprehension on the one hand and those in pronunciation on the other. After reviewing these studies, the relationship between the two skills, that is, listening comprehension and pronunciation, will be discussed.

Among many factors that can affect L2 learners' listening comprehension, one obvious factor is reduced forms (Shockey, 2003). Henrichsen (1984) examined the effect of presence/absence of reduced forms, or what he called "sandhi-variation," on ESL learners' listening comprehension skill. He administered two dictation tests (in which sentences were presented with and without reduced forms) to nonnative speakers from different levels of English proficiency and native speakers. The results showed a statistically significant interaction between proficiency level and the presence/absence of reduced forms. This finding led him to conclude that the presence of reduced forms affected the learners' listening comprehension. Ito (chapter 6 in this volume) further explored this issue by adding two variables to Henrichsen's basic design: modifications of sentence complexity in the dictation test and the effects of different types of reduced forms. Two versions of a dictation test were given to native speakers as well as to nonnative speakers from two different English proficiency levels. As in Henrichsen's study, the nonnative participants in Ito scored statistically significantly higher on the dictation test when reduced forms were absent than when they were present, while native speakers' scores did not differ for the two conditions. This finding, together with that in Henrichsen (1984), suggests that L2 learners' listening comprehension is affected by the presence of reduced forms.

As these studies show, the presence of reduced forms in the input can negatively affect learners' listening comprehension skill. The next question is whether instruction can help them improve their listening comprehension skill. Brown and Hilferty (1986a and chapter 4 in this volume) explored this question. They provided a treatment group with instructions on reduced forms for 4 weeks, and compared their pretest and posttest scores with those from a control group that did not receive such instruction. There were three tests given as a pretest and a posttest: the Bowen Integrative Grammar Test, a multiple-choice listening test, and a dictation test. The results showed that the treatment group's posttest scores on the grammar test and the dictation test were significantly higher than the control group's. This finding indicates that instruction on reduced forms can improve L2 learners' listening comprehension skill. Matsuzawa's study (chapter 5 in this volume) also suggests positive effects of instruction on reduced forms on the improvement of learners' listening comprehension, though his study did not have a control group to compare with the treatment group.

While these studies are concerned with reduced forms in listening comprehension, another group of studies examined reduced forms in L2 learners' pronunciation. Anderson-Hsieh, Riney, and Koehler (1994), for instance, studied Japanese ESL learners' connected speech modifications in English. They collected speech data from intermediate- and high-proficiency Japanese learners of English as well as from native speakers of English, using sentence reading and spontaneous speech tasks. Four types of connected speech modifications were investigated in this study: alveolar flapping, linking, vowel reduction, and consonant cluster simplification. They found that the proficiency level had an effect on the degree of modifications in that the high-proficiency learners' modifications were closer to the native speakers'. Furthermore, native language transfer was also observed in the Japanese learners' connected speech modifications.

Among various types of connected speech modifications, some researchers focused on flapping by ESL learners (e.g., Ito, in press; Šimáčková, 1997, 2000; Young-Scholten, 1994). These studies show that ESL learners experience difficulties in producing flapping, depending on phonological contexts. Celce-Murcia et al. (2004) also claim that most ESL learners are unaware of flapping and that this lack of awareness can make their speech sound nonnative. They add that this lack of awareness can cause difficulties in listening comprehension.

While the studies reviewed here approach reduced forms as important knowledge in either listening comprehension or pronunciation independently, Gilbert (1995) attempts to connect the two skills by proposing pronunciation practice of reduced forms to promote learners' listening comprehension. Other pronunciation materials also include developing listening comprehension skills as one of their objectives (e.g., Dauer, 1993; Kobayashi & Linde, 1984).

However, the question of which comes first, perception or production ability, is a separate issue explored in other research. Although, in L1 acquisition, many theorists claim that perception precedes production (Sheldon & Strange, 1982), some L2 studies provide evidence that this is not always true in L2 acquisition (e.g., Goto,

1971; Sheldon & Strange, 1982). These studies have shown that some learners can produce certain L2 sounds while they cannot perceive them.

Despite the debates about which comes first, perceptive or productive skill, researchers as well as material developers who are interested in pronunciation teaching usually attempt to link listening comprehension and pronunciation skills. Morley (1991) also contends that one principle guiding current pronunciation teaching is "a focus on the link between listening and pronouncing/speaking and a need to expand the nature and the range of pronunciation-oriented listening activities" (p. 494). It may be more promising to approach both listening comprehension and pronunciation together, rather than separate them, when we teach reduced forms to ESL learners.

As revealed in these studies, L2 learners experience difficulties when they encounter reduced forms in both listening comprehension and pronunciation. Accordingly, reduced forms should be a part of the language teaching curriculum, and yet they have received little attention in practice. In the next section, I will discuss what should be done in instruction of reduced forms to remedy the current situation.

Future Directions in the Reduced Forms Instruction

Before proposing approaches to instruction of reduced forms, I should first examine possible reasons why language teachers are less likely to teach reduced forms even though studies have clearly suggested that reduced forms are one factor causing difficulties in L2 learning. One possible, and probably major, factor is teacher unfamiliarity with reduced forms. Although recently published teachers' guides for teaching English pronunciation cover reduced forms (e.g., Avery & Ehrlich, 1992; Celce-Murcia et al., 2004; Hewings, 1993a, 1993b), it is unknown to what degree they are covered in actual teacher training, or to what extent the teachers are paying attention to them. Rogerson's study (chapter 7 in this volume), in which she investigated various perspectives of ESL teachers on reduced forms, revealed that the level of teachers' familiarity with reduced forms varied. Of the 45 ESL teachers surveyed in her study, 13 responded they were *very familiar* with reduced forms, 26 rated themselves as *somewhat familiar*, and 6 answered *not very familiar* or *not at all familiar* (p. 89 of this volume). This variation in terms of familiarity was reflected in the teachers' perceptions of reduced forms in language instruction. For example, while more than 50% of *very familiar* respondents answered that reduced forms were "very important to teach" (nearly 80%) and "very helpful" (slightly above 60%) in ESL listening comprehension, only about 30% of *somewhat familiar* and *not very/not at all familiar* respondents considered reduced forms very important or very helpful. Rogerson also points out that the teachers tend to present common examples of reduced forms, instead of focusing on "the systematic linguistic and pragmatic constraints of reduced form," when they teach the forms (p. 91 of this volume). Rogerson attributes this tendency to the teachers' limited knowledge of such constraints. Another challenge experienced by ESL teachers is that they do not have sufficient time and adequate materials for teaching reduced forms. Furthermore, 40% of the respondents in Rogerson's study said that reduced forms were not in their curriculum. These findings suggest a need of teacher training in reduced forms. This may be a more serious concern in the EFL context, where the majority of English teachers are nonnative speakers, since as nonnative speakers, those teachers may not even be aware of the existence of reduced forms.

Another factor that affects instruction on reduced forms is the availability of materials. As the ESL teachers surveyed in Rogerson's study commented, there are not adequate materials for teaching reduced forms. Those textbooks that sometimes include reduced forms as an element of study are typically focused on pronunciation. While there are a few textbooks that focus entirely on reduced forms (e.g., Kobayashi & Linde, 1984; Weinstein, 1982), most pronunciation textbooks simply include reduced forms as one aspect to be covered (e.g., Dauer, 1993; Gilbert, 1984, 1993; Grant, 1993; Hewings & Goldstein, 1998; Morley, 1987; Sheeler & Markley, 1991).[1] Rogerson (chapter 7, this volume) also points out that one of the problems with ESL texts is that "these texts rarely develop the systematic linguistic and pragmatic constraints of reduced forms, rather focusing solely on common examples" (p. 91 of this volume). Rogerson partly attributes teachers' failure in teaching reduced forms to this characteristic of ESL materials.

One general problem regarding materials is that, as Jones and Ono (2000) found in their comparison of textbook dialogues and real conversational interactions, "textbook dialogues do not reflect the ways in which real talk is produced in actual interactions" (p. 12). Although the use of authentic materials is encouraged in language teaching nowadays (Carter, Hughes, & McCarthy, 1998; Dunkel, 1995), textbooks do not necessarily present dialogues or interactions that take place in real conversations. This trend is more apparent in materials for elementary levels, "due to the learners' limited knowledge of the language and also out of a desire to introduce certain grammatical items and/or vocabulary" (Jones & Ono, p. 4). Thus little attention is paid to reduced forms in such materials.

Specific remedies for these problems are beyond the scope of this chapter, but clearly they are important issues in L2 English pedagogy. Keeping these issues in mind, I would now like to turn to approaches that may be useful for promoting the teaching of reduced forms.

The first step is to raise teachers' awareness about reduced forms, not only familiarizing them with the system of reduced forms, but also helping them to realize the effectiveness of instruction on reduced forms. Although explanations of reduced forms are more commonly found in pronunciation textbooks, teaching them also enhances learners' listening comprehension as previous studies suggest (e.g., Brown & Hilferty, 1986a, 1986b; Matsuzawa, chapter 5 in this volume). Hewings (1993a, 1993b) argues that we must be concerned more about listening to connected speech than producing it since learners can still make themselves understood without connected speech. However, as discussed above, the link between listening comprehension and pronunciation may be important, though the issue of which comes first, the perceptive or productive skill, is still open to debate. This suggests that even though Hewings might be right in saying that learners can still make themselves understood without relying on connected speech, practice in the pronunciation of connected speech may enhance their listening comprehension. All of this suggests that instruction on reduced forms should be developed not only in pronunciation-focused or listening-focused classes, but also in more general oral communication classes that involve both speaking and listening skills.

Once teachers become aware of the significance of teaching reduced forms, what can they do in classrooms to actually teach these forms? To answer this question, we should consider larger issues relevant to language pedagogy. One of the major issues

---

[1]   Editors' note: Also see chapter 3 of this book, which lists additional resources for teachers.

to consider here is learners' attention. Schmidt (1990, 1995) claims that attention is required in L2 acquisition. To examine the relationship between attention and connected speech, Kim (1995) conducted an experiment investigating what elements Korean ESL learners attended to in English oral input. He administered a listening comprehension test using two types of texts, one read with a normal rate of speech and the other with a slower rate of speech. He also had a retrospective interview immediately after the listening comprehension task to elicit answers from the learners about what elements they had attended to while listening. The results included the finding that learners were more likely to attend to phonetically prominent elements, which received primary or secondary stress in the intonational phrasing. Although the listening comprehension scores did not significantly differ between the two conditions (i.e., listening to a text of normal speed and listening to a text of slower speed), the number of elements that the learners attended to differed between the two. The general pattern was that those who listened to slower recordings were able to attend to more words than those who listened to recordings at normal speed. More specifically, the degree of identifying structural elements (e.g., prepositional phrases, noun phrases, etc.) in addition to key words in test sentences was slightly higher for the group that listened to texts read at a slower speed than the group listening to texts read at normal speed. Since the difference was not statistically significant, the claim is tentative at best. However, this result indicates the following:

> ...by increasing the quantity and clarity of accessible speech elements [i.e., reading at a slower rate of speech], the listener might be encouraged to move from a more lexical mode, in which she relies on several key words for comprehension, to a more syntactic mode in which she encodes structural elements as well as more lexical elements in the speech.   (p. 78)

This finding tells us that those forms that are reduced in connected speech are less likely to be attended to by L2 learners. If attention is necessary for L2 acquisition to take place (Schmidt, 1990, 1995), directing learners' attention to such unattended forms may become important.

However, this raises another issue for language pedagogy, which is how to direct learners' attention. To address this issue in the field of instructed SLA, an approach called "focus on form," as compared to "focus on forms," has been proposed (Long, 1991). While focus on forms can be exemplified by such methods as Grammar Translation and the Audiolingual Method in which learners are presented with and practice "a series of linguistic items, or forms" (Long & Robinson, 1998, p. 16), focus on form draws "students' attention to linguistic elements as they arise incidentally in lessons whose overriding focus is on meaning, or communication" (Long, 1991, p. 46). Since L2 acquisition involves the acquisition of both form and meaning, not just one of them, focus on form has been recognized as an effective method in L2 instruction.

Taking into consideration these aspects in language teaching, classic activities such as dictation (e.g., Norris, 1995), read-aloud exercises (e.g., Celce-Murcia et al., 2004; Dauer, 1993), cloze exercises (e.g., Hewings & Goldstein, 1998; Kobayashi & Linde, 1984; Norris, 1995) and listen-and-repeat exercises (e.g., Gimson, 1975; Kobayashi & Linde, 1984) that have often been proposed in instruction on reduced forms may be restricted in terms of their effectiveness in that they do not involve any meaningful communication. However, they are still commonly used as a part of language teaching, and we should reexamine the effectiveness of using such activities in reduced forms instruction.

As repeated several times earlier in this chapter, reduced forms play an important role in both listening and speaking (or pronunciation). In this sense, we can easily implement interactional activities to teach reduced forms. For example, we can design a task in which listeners must rely on specific reduced forms to comprehend the speaker's meaning. If the listener fails to understand the reduced forms, communication breakdown will occur and lead to the failure to achieve the task. This type of task could also be used in research examining the relationship between reduced forms and listening comprehension. In some previous studies, dictation tests were used exclusively (e.g., Henrichsen, 1984; Ito in chapter 6 of this volume). However, as Ito observes, dictation may not be a valid measure for listening comprehension given that meaning may have a very small role in dictation. Nonetheless, researchers need to operationalize the listening-comprehension construct. Since a communicative task such as the one described here engages learners in both form and meaning, it would seem to measure listening comprehension more accurately than a dictation.[2]

Students may also benefit more from the teaching of systematic knowledge about reduced forms than from individual isolated examples of such forms (see Rogerson in chapter 7 of this volume). To accomplish this, we could have students analyze several reduced forms so that they can hypothesize the system through which reduced forms work (e.g., function words are reduced, whereas content words are not; e.g., Avery & Ehrlich, 1992). Another related activity would be to have students keep listening journals, which would allow them to attend to the reduced forms used in real communication outside the classroom (Norris, 1995). However, the materials they listen to must be carefully selected to suit the learners' proficiency levels, needs, purposes, and so on. Self-monitoring of their own use of reduced forms could also be used to raise their awareness of reduced forms in the speaking skill. Through these activities, learners' attention would be directed to reduced forms that might otherwise go unnoticed in the normal speech they hear around them.

Reduced forms are crucial not only in listening and speaking skills in general. They also play an important role in the area of morphosyntactic acquisition. Reduced forms often involve function words, whose major role is to express grammatical relations (Celce-Murcia et al., 2004). Such relationships are usually examined by scholars whose interests lie mostly in the acquisition of morphosyntax. One representative study, which investigated the acquisition of reduced forms from a syntactic standpoint, is Kweon (2001). Her study explored the question of whether Korean ESL learners were able to distinguish subject extraction questions (e.g., *Who do you want to/wanna kiss Mary?*) and object extraction questions (e.g., *Who do you want to/wanna kiss?*) with respect to *wanna* contraction. Her results indicate that the learners tended to permit ungrammatical contraction, that is, *Who do you wanna kiss Mary?* This suggests that learners face challenges in the acquisition of *wanna* contraction, and perhaps in the acquisition of reduced forms in general. For instance, there may be a variety of factors that cause difficulties in the acquisition of contraction phenomena, but directing learners' attention to the particular form in an appropriate way may enhance their acquisition of *wanna* contraction. One recently published pronunciation textbook actually discusses such syntactic constraints in reduced forms (Teschner & Whitley, 2004).

---

[2] Editors' note: For more on this topic, see the discussion on designing communicative testing of reduced forms in chapter 14 of this book.

Once we identify what approaches to take in considering such issues as attention and the way to direct learners' attention, the kinds of materials we design will naturally follow. As discussed earlier, lack of materials is a problem that makes instruction of reduced forms difficult. Although there are pronunciation textbooks that cover some aspects of reduced forms, most of the activities designed in those materials are classic ones such as dictation, read-aloud exercises, cloze exercises, and listen-and-repeat exercises. Many language teachers may still be employing focus on forms instruction in their classrooms, but more and more practitioners have started recognizing the significance of communicative tasks in language teaching. It is now generally agreed that focus on forms is not effective in that they do not enable learners to use an L2 in communicative contexts. Since language teachers expect learners to be able to use an L2 in real communication, designing tasks and materials that go along with the tasks must follow the principle of focus on form.

Furthermore, designing materials that incorporate both speaking and listening skills, rather than separating them, appears to be important. Here, what I mean by "speaking" is beyond merely practicing pronunciation of words and sentences, that is, it involves the speaking skills that are required for meaningful communication. Similarly, what I mean by "listening" is not "listen and fill in the blank," but is the skill that learners need in order to communicate effectively.

The use of authentic materials has become increasingly common in language teaching, and authentic listening materials inevitably contain a large number of reduced forms. It would be unfair to expect learners to comprehend the materials without appropriately directing their attention to the reduced forms. Since research indicates that reduced forms can hinder listening comprehension in an L2, we should consider reduced forms more seriously in L2 pedagogy.

Conclusion

In this chapter, I discussed the importance of instruction on reduced forms and approaches that we should take to teach reduced forms. Clearly, research on reduced forms in ESL is extremely limited. To learn more about the role of reduced forms in L2 learning, more research should be conducted in the future. This will enable teacher trainers, language teachers, and material writers to understand the nature of reduced forms in L2 teaching, and hence, language teachers will be encouraged to teach reduced forms in their classrooms.

It seems apparent that specific teaching approaches interact with other challenges that teachers face, for instance their unfamiliarity with reduced forms and lack of materials to teach them. Thus, future instruction on reduced forms should take these factors into consideration as well.

3

Teacher Resources for
Teaching Connected Speech

JAMES DEAN BROWN
University of Hawai'i

*The purpose of this chapter is to review the accessible resources that language
teachers, researchers, and materials developers can turn to if they want to
understand, teach, and adopt or develop materials for connected speech
instruction. A number of such resources have been identified that can help
language teaching professionals understand and teach the various topics
involved in connected speech. These resources fall into two main
categories: (a) teacher training resources with some coverage of connected
speech (including books for training linguists, books for training applied
linguists and language teachers, articles for training applied linguists
and language teachers, and miscellaneous professional resources) and
(b) ESL/EFL student books with coverage of connected speech (including
ESL/EFL student books that have some coverage of connected speech
and ESL/EFL student books that focus on connected speech).*

Introduction

This chapter is about existing resources that can help teachers understand and teach
connected speech.[1] A number of resources exist that can help language teachers
understand and teach the various topics involved in connected speech. These
resources include (a) teacher training resources with some coverage of connected
speech and (b) ESL/EFL student books with coverage of connected speech. Let's
briefly consider each of these categories in turn, then take a closer look at the student
books that focus exclusively on the issues involved in connected speech.

Teacher Training Resources with Some Coverage of Connected Speech

A number of teacher training books have been published over the years that include
some coverage of the topics involved in connected speech. Some of these have been
written from the perspective of training linguists and others take the perspective of
training applied linguistics or language teachers. Still other resources can be found in
various journal articles aimed at applied linguists or language teachers. And finally, in
my wanderings through the topics involved in connected speech, I have found a few

---

[1] Editors' note: See chapter 1 for a definition of this term and related concepts, and chapters 1
and 2 for related literature reviews.

Brown, J. D. (2006) Teacher resources for teaching connected speech. In J. D. Brown, & K. Kondo-Brown, (Eds.),
Perspectives on teaching connected speech to second language speakers (pp. 27–47). Honolulu, HI: University of Hawai'i,
National Foreign Language Resource Center.

"miscellaneous" professional resources that are very helpful with regard to understanding and teaching connected speech. Let's consider each of these sorts of teacher training resources in turn.

Books for training linguists

Over the years, a large number of books have been published that describe the pronunciation of English from various perspectives. Of those, only a few provide any depth of linguistic coverage of the topics involved in connected speech and most of those provide spotty coverage at best. For example, some coverage is provided in Gussenhoven and Jacobs (2003), Gussman (2002), Hyman (1975), Jones (1972), Ladefoged (2000), and Sommers (1977). Of these generic phonology books, Ladefoged provides the best coverage. One other book not previously listed is Obendorfer (1998), which focuses fairly narrowly but provides considerable depth in its treatment of the issues involved in the strong and weak word forms of modern English.

Books for training applied linguists and language teachers

Of the books aimed at training applied linguists and language teachers, at least some coverage related to the topics involved in connected speech is found in Avery and Ehrlich (1992), Bowen (1975a), Celce-Murcia, Brinton, and Goodwin (2004), Dalton and Seidlhofer (2001), Gimson (1962, 1970, 1975, 1989, 2001), Kelly (2003), Kenworthy (1987), Kreidler (1997), Pennington (1996), Prator and Robinett (1995), Roach (2004), Teschner and Whitley (2004), and Underhill (1994). Of these, Avery and Ehrlich, Celce-Murcia, Brinton, and Goodwin, and any of the editions of Gimson provide the most coverage.

Articles for training applied linguists and language teachers

Aside from the articles that form the chapters of this book, very few articles on connected speech have been published in the applied linguistics literature. Chronologically, these include Brown and Hilferty (1982), Dauer (1983), Henrichsen (1984), Brown and Hilferty (1986a, 1986b, and chapter 4 of this volume), Dauer and Browne (1992), Anderson-Hsieh, Riney, and Koehler (1994), Kim (1995), Kweon (2000), and Bley-Vroman and Kweon (2002). In addition, Hill and Beebe (1980) provides a short, concise, yet fairly comprehensive overview on contraction in English. In addition, Bowen (1975b, 1976) and Brown and Hilferty (1989, 1995, 1998, and chapter 4 of this volume) illustrate ways to practice/assess the ability to comprehend connected speech in listening (see also chapters 5–9 of this book).

Miscellaneous professional resources

I have found a number of other books very useful in my explorations of the topics related to connected speech. For example, Nilsen and Nilsen (1973) proved useful because it supplies long lists of minimal pairs for the key consonant and vowel contrasts in English pronunciation. In each case, minimal pairs are provided for word initial, medial, and final position. IPA (2001) also proved useful for detailed information on the international phonetic alphabet. I also found the information and downloadable fonts available at the IPA website (IPA, 2005) very useful. And finally, Cordry (1997), a dictionary of NAE pronunciations, was very useful for trying to cure my own hopelessly *expatois* pronunciation system.

ESL/EFL Student Books with Coverage of Connected Speech

A number of student books have also been written that include material for teaching connected speech. Some of these texts have fairly sparse coverage of the topics, while others focus entirely on the issues involved.

ESL/EFL student books that have some coverage of connected speech

For exercises to help in teaching language students the subtopics related to connected speech, parts of the following student pronunciation textbooks may prove useful: Dauer (1993), Gilbert (1984, 1993), Grant (1993), Henrichsen, Green, Nishitani, and Bagley (2002), Hewings (1993a, 1993b), Hewings and Goldstein (1998), Lane (2005), Laroy (2003), Morley (1987), Orion (1988), Prator and Robinett (1995), Rogerson and Gilbert (2001), and Sheeler and Markley (1991). The Gilbert and Henrichsen, Green, Nishitani, and Bagley books seem to have the best overall coverage. While the Gilbert book is not focused solely on connected speech, in amongst lessons on pronunciation and listening comprehension, it does provide lessons on stress, rhythm, and other reduced forms topics that may prove useful for teachers interested in teaching reduced forms. Similarly, digging through the material in Henrichsen, Green, Nishitani, and Bagley will unearth considerable material that can help in teaching the various types of reduced forms.

ESL/EFL student books that focus on connected speech

Over the years, other student textbooks have made a more concerted effort to address the issues involved in connected speech: Griffee and Hough (1986), Griffee (1993), Hagen (2000), Hough (1995), Kobayashi and Linde (1984), Rost and Stratton (1978, 1980), and Weinstein (1982, 2001). Each of these textbooks will be covered briefly in more-or-less chronological order (and, as it turns out, in increasing degrees of coverage) in five groups according to the authors involved. After briefly describing each textbook, I will compare them all in terms of their characteristics and coverage.

Rost and Stratton (1978, 1980)

The 143 page Rost and Stratton (1978) book, as the title *Listening in the Real World: Clues to English Conversation* (Lingual House) suggests, was designed "to bridge the gap between the formally enunciated language of the ESL classroom and the informal language that the student is likely to encounter beyond the classroom setting" (p. 3). This textbook is organized into three separate parts: presentations, situational dialogs, and activation exercises. The 36 presentations on reductions are based mostly on comparison examples between "long" (written or citation) versions of sentences and parallel "short" (reduced) versions. The 200 "situational dialogs" organized into 12 sets provide blanks where "reductions" are heard. Students are then required to write the full forms in the blanks to demonstrate that they heard and understood them. An additional 12 sets of activation exercises, which are based on the situational dialogs, encourage students to use the reductions. There are no illustrations in this book. Appendix A gives answers to the presentation lesson exercises and Appendix B provides complete scripts for all the dialogs in the book. A cassette tape is available to go along with the book—perhaps an important add-on for some teachers who are not native English speaking teachers.

The purpose of the 141 page Rost and Stratton (1980) book, entitled *Listening Transitions: From Listening to Speaking* (Lingual House), was "to present many necessary skills in integrated units, with the units always being directed toward a transition to language production" (p. 5). Instead of being organized into three major parts like their previous book, this one is organized into 25 lessons each of which covers a major communicative function like "making conversation," "getting directions," interrupting," and so forth. Each lesson includes a variety of different activities/exercises in exactly the same order: a preview of vocabulary, a pronunciation exercise ("long" and "short" form contrasts like the previous book), a taped dialog, dialog comprehension questions, a fill-in dialog, and fill-in transition dialogs (with multiple situations transitioning to productive language use). After every five lessons, there is a set of review dialogs that consist of five three-sentence exchanges. This book has one black and white drawing per lesson. Appendix A gives answers for Exercise a activities (listen to the questions about the dialog and write your answers); Appendix B gives sample summaries for Exercise B activities; and Appendix C provides answers for the fill-in listening dialogs. All of the activities in this book are based on a cassette tape that is available separately.

Kobayashi and Linde (1984)

Kobayashi and Linde is an 83 (plus ix) page book entitled *Practice in English Reduced forms* (Sanshusa) that was designed to introduce and teach reduced forms, with "the most common reductions, which are in many cases the most difficult, toward the beginning" (p. v). This text is organized into 36 lessons each of which covers a particular reductions topic from a phonological point of view. Many of the lessons (mostly the odd numbered ones) are based on weak forms like "and, you, do, [t + consonant]," "are, to, verb-ing, [d + i]," "that, is, your, [t + j]," and so forth. The other lessons (mostly the even numbered ones) are based on phonological transitions like "[p,b,t,d, + vowel]," "[p + p], [k + k], [s + s], [s + ʃ]," "[f + j], [s + i]," etc. Each chapter includes some form of presentation, either a 12-sentence "listen and repeat" drill (one reduction is underlined in each sentence) or a listen-to-the-dialog-and-repeat drill. Then each lesson also has a "listen and fill in the blanks" reduced forms dictation. After every two lessons, there is what is called a "Listening Comprehension," which consists of a listen-and-repeat dialog, a true-false self-check exercise, and a reduced forms dictation. After every two "Listening Comprehension" sections there is a test (for a total of seven tests) that consists of 25 fill-in blanks in a dialog dictation, and a "partial dictation" with longer blanks. Three supplementary lessons are also provided along with a list of 82 reduced forms with the strong and weak forms given for each word. There are no illustrations in this book. However, a cassette tape is available.

Griffee and Hough (1986), Griffee (1993), Hough (1995)

While chronologically these three books were published as Griffee and Hough, Griffee, Hough, it is clear that, in order of difficulty, Hough is the lowest (or first) level book, Griffee and Hough is the middle (or second) book, and Griffee is the highest (or third) book. I will review them in chronological order here.

The 121-page Griffee and Hough (1986) book, entitled *HearSay: Survival Listening and Speaking* was designed to "teach survival skills in a listening mode with emphasis on reduced forms" (p. iv). The 18 lessons of this textbook are organized around different types of conversations, or more precisely around different speech acts (e.g., "May I have your name?", "Could I have your phone number?", "I'm sorry, I don't understand.," etc.). The 18 presentations on reductions are based mostly on comparison examples between phonetic explanations of examples for "slow," "fast," and "faster" speech. Each lesson has 10 or so activities and a couple of "Bonus" activities. The activities are generally of three types: listen-and-fill-in-the-blank dialogs, listen-and-circle (multiple-choice) exercises, or listen-and-fill-in-the-missing-turns dialogs. The "Bonus" activities include one "open dialog (listen and fill in the blank turns) and one role play (using "key words"). Unlike the Rost and Stratton (1978, 1980) books, this one places considerable emphasis on the gradations of reduction that students may encounter in "slow," "fast," and "faster" speech (e.g., for I *am*, slow [aɪ æm], fast *I'm* [aɪm], and faster *I'm* [am]; or for *what do you*, slow [wɑt du yu], fast [wədəyə], and faster [wətʃə]). In addition, this book has some illustrations, two black and white drawings per lesson to be exact. A tape is also available to go along with the book.

The 98 (plus vi)-page Griffee (1993) is entitled *More HearSay: Interactive Listening and Speaking* and was designed to teach speaking and listening for communication in English and understanding "natural spoken English" (p. iv). The 15 units are organized around different types of conversations, or more precisely around different sorts of speech acts (e.g., "My first name is …," "How much is the bus for downtown?", "It looks good on you," etc.). The 15 presentations on reductions are based on comparisons between phonetic explanations of examples for "slow," "fast," and "faster" speech. Each lesson has five or six activities (labeled "tasks") and a set of review questions that are to be answered in pairs. The activities are generally of the listen-and-fill-in-the-blank dialogs, listen-and-circle (multiple-choice) exercises, pair/group work activities, and lesson review questions. Like Griffee and Hough (1986), this book places considerable emphasis on the gradations of reduction that students may encounter in "slow," "fast," and "faster" speech (e.g., for *want to*, slow [want tu], fast [wantə], and faster [wanə]). In addition, this book has at least one full-page color drawing per lesson, with a few other color drawings used in exercises. A tape is also available for this book.

The 179 (plus ix) page Hough (1995) book, entitled *Before HearSay: Basic Listening for the Classroom*, was created to teach listening for real classroom communication in English (p. vii). The 22 lessons are organized around classroom skills like the following: "Listen and write," "How many pieces of paper do you have?," "Write the date in the upper right-hand corner,"and so forth. The 22 presentations on reduced forms are based on comparison examples between phonetic explanations of examples for "slow" and "fast" speech. Notice that, unlike the other two books in this series, this one only differentiates between "slow" and "fast" speech. Each lesson has 10 activities (labeled "tasks") and a set of pair work dictation sentences/questions. The activities are generally listen-and-point cartoon dialogs, listen-and-repeat exercises, listen-and-circle activities, listen-and-match exercises, listen-and-fill-in-the-blank activities, and pair work (dictate to your partner) exercises. In addition, each lesson in this book has at least one cartoon dialog based on black and white drawings, and some lessons have other cartoon-like drawings. A tape is also available for this book.

Weinstein (1982, 2001)

Weinstein (1982) is one of the earliest books dedicated to the teaching for reduced forms. This book had 68 (plus xi) pages and was entitled *Whaddaya Say? Guided Practice in Relaxed Spoken English* (ELS Publications). It was designed to teach listening "to help students understand the relationships between carefully articulated English and its more informal, relaxed counterpart" (p. viii). The 20 lessons are organized around different relaxed speech patterns like the following:

gotta → *got to*, hafta → *have to*, hasta → *has to*

yer → *your, you're*, yers → *yours*

cha → /t/ + you, cher → /t/ + your, you're

-in' → -ing

The presentation of reduced forms is accomplished by having the students listen to contrasting careful (slow) and relaxed (fast) pronunciation of 10 sentences. The students can then practice the reduced forms through activities with the following sorts of directions: While reading along, listen to the pronunciation contrasts in the slow and fast pronunciation sentences, listen to the contrasts without reading, and fill-in the full forms in the following dialog dictation. The book has one black and white drawing per lesson. It also includes an answer key and has an accompanying cassette tape available.

Weinstein (2001) is a much-improved second edition entitled *Whaddaya Say? Guided Practice in Relaxed Speech* (second edition; Longman). This book has 119 (plus viii) pages and was designed to teach "the most common reduced forms (wanna, gonna, gotta, etc.) needed to understand natural spoken English" (p. vii). The 30 lessons are organized around conversation topics and different relaxed speech patterns like the following:

Let's go shopping: *-ing endings* → *-in'*

What are you doing this weekend? *what do you, what are you* → *whaddaya*

I want to have a hamburger: *want to* → *wanna*

Can you see the stage? *can* → *kin, can't* → *kant*

In contrast to the previous edition of this book, the reduced forms are presented by having the students listen to contrasting careful (slow) and relaxed (fast) pronunciation of 10 *dialogs*. The students can then practice the reduced forms through activities with directions like the following: While reading along, listen to the pronunciation contrasts in the dialog, answer comprehension questions, listen to the contrasts without reading, answer comprehension questions, fill-in the full forms in this dialog dictation, and have a small group discussion of....The book has two black and white drawings per lesson. It also includes 10 self-tests, self-test transcripts, an answer key for Part 2, a self-test answer key, and an "alternate levels of reduction" chart. An accompanying cassette tape is also available.

Hagen (2000)

The last book reviewed here is Hagen, entitled *Sound Advice: A Basis for Listening Comprehension* (second edition; Longman). This 183 (plus vii) page book is designed for teaching "the key features of spoken English which are essential for the comprehension of authentic, natural speech—what English language learners regularly refer to as 'fast speech'" (p. vi). The 11 lessons are organized around features of reduced speech like the following:

Introduction to linking: linking with vowels, linking identical consonants

Special sound changes: the flap, *-ty/-teen* (e.g., *thirty/thirteen*), *-nt* reduction, the glottal stop, *can/can't, of,* linking *of* with vowels,

Silent h: function words beginning with *h,* questions beginning with *have/has,* pronoun summary

Each chapter contains one to three highlighted (with a blue border) boxes that hold explicit explanations with examples of each reduced forms teaching point. The exercises include listen-and-underline/mark/chose/check exercises, listen-and-fill-in-the-blanks activities, listen-and-fill-in-the-blanks dialogs, and compare-answers-with-a-partner activities, along with self-tests and TOEFL listening self-tests. Each chapter has one or two sets of blue-and-white (the print is dark blue in my copy) drawings per lesson. The book also includes three TOEFL practice listening tests, an explanation of pronunciation of past -ed and -s, a tapescript, and an answer key. Like all of the other books reviewed in this section, this one has a cassette tape available.

Comparison of characteristics

Table 1 provides a summary comparison chart for the nine books reviewed here. Each row compares a different characteristic: title, publisher, purpose of the book, number of pages, skill focus of the book, organization of the lessons, types of explanations for reduced forms, types exercises provided for practicing the reduced forms, number and types of illustrations, other miscellaneous features, and the availability of a cassette tape.

Comparison of coverage

With the exception of the Weinstein and Hagen books, the chapter headings for the books reviewed here are not very useful for knowing what reduced forms are actually being taught in each book. Table 2 provides a listing of which reduced forms are covered in each chapter of each book. There is remarkable variation in the topics included in these books. The similarities and differences among these topics would itself form a basis for an interesting study. However, for the moment, this chart can serve as a guide for teachers looking for reduced forms topics to cover with students, and/or teachers who are looking for materials that cover particular topics. As Yoda might put it, "useful topics these are."

Looking at Tables 1 and 2, it is clear that making choices among these nine books is not a simple task. All nine books explicitly focus on helping students learn reduced forms. All nine books provide numerous exercises and taped material to help teachers present various aspects of continuous speech to their students, and most of them focused exclusively on using knowledge about reduced forms to help students with listening comprehension. As Table 1 shows three of the texts *claim* to prepare students to also use the reduced forms in listening in preparation for using them in speaking. However, the types of exercises available in each book may be more telling: Three of the books (not necessarily the same three making the claim in the previous sentence) actually offer pair work and group work exercises. Those books would seem to me to be the most useful if the goal is to get the students to actually use reduced forms.

Overall, if I had to choose one of the nine books to use in teaching reduced forms, I would select the Hagen (2000) because of its explicit, though limited, explanations of a relatively large number of continuous speech topics and because of its wealth and variety of exercise types. The focus in Hagen's book on TOEFL practice tests would be of less use to me. Note, however, that my preference for Hagen may be based on a residual, and perhaps old fashioned, need to teach things explicitly, rather than to rely on student discovery learning, the strategy that seems to underlie the other eight books. Given the wide variety of reduced forms topics covered, all nine books may prove useful, in one way or another, for any teacher looking for reduced forms topics and exercises; as such, they are all recommended.

Table 1. Summary comparison chart for the nine books reviewed here (part 1)

	Stratton & Rost (1978)	Stratton & Rost (1980)	Kobayashi & Linde (1984)	Griffee & Hough (1986)	Griffee (1993)
title	Listening in the Real World: Clues to English Conversation	Listening Transitions: From Listening to Speaking	Practice in English Reduced Forms	HearSay: Survival Listening and Speaking	More HearSay: Interactive Listening and Speaking
publisher	Lingual House	Lingual House	Sanshusha	Addison-Wesley Japan	Addison-Wesley Japan
purpose	link formal listening to informal reductions of real spoken English	transition to productive language through integrated skills	introduce and teach the most common reductions	teach survival skills in a listening mode with emphasis on reduced forms	teach speaking and listening for communication in English and understanding natural spoken English
number of pages	143 pages	141 pages	ix+83 pages	121 pages	vi+98 pages
skill focus	listening→speaking	listening→speaking	mostly listening comprehension	mostly listening comprehension	listening→speaking
organization	3 separate parts: 36 presentation lessons; 200 situational dialogs organized into 12 sets; 12 sets of activation exercises	25 Lessons organized by major communicative functions	36 lessons organized by reductions topics defined by weak forms and phonological transitions	18 lessons organized around different types of conversations	15 units organized around different types of conversations
types of explanations for reduced forms	pairs of contrasts with and without reductions are presented; students listen and repeat, then practice exercises: listen and select whether it is the "long" or "short" form, or listen and fill in the blank	pronunciation exercises are used to present contrasts between "long" (written or citation) versions of sentences and their "short" (reduced) spoken equivalents	listen and repeat drills (with reduced words underlined) and listen to the dialog and repeat drills are used to introduce students to reduced forms	listen, phonetic explanation, examples for "slow," "fast," and "faster" speech	listen, phonetic explanation, examples for "slow," "fast," and "faster" speech

exercise types	situational dialogs with blanks students must fill in with reductions; speaking exercises that could be done individually, in pairs, or in groups	pronunciation exercises ("long" and "short" form contrasts), taped dialogs, dialog comprehension questions, dialog summary exercise, fill-in dialogs, fill-in turns transition dialogs (to promote productive language use)	exercises include listen and fill in the blanks reduced forms dictations, listen and repeat dialogs; true-false self-checks are used in the lessons and in the "Listening Comprehension" sections; the tests consist of reduced forms dialog dictations (partial or full)	listen and fill in the blank dialogs, listen and circle (m-c), listen to "open" dialog and fill in turn	listen and fill in the blank dialogs, listen and circle (m-c), pair/group work activities, lesson review questions
illustrations	none	1 B&W drawing per lesson	none	2 B&W drawings per lesson	1 full-page color drawing per lesson
other features	answer key for presentation lesson exercises, compete dialogs	answer keys for the dialog comprehension questions, dialog summaries exercise, fill-in dialogs	7 tests, 3 supplementary lessons, list of English reduced forms		
cassette tape available?	yes	yes	yes	yes	yes

Table 1. Summary comparison chart for the nine books reviewed here (part 2)

	Hough (1995)	Weinstein (1982)	Weinstein (2001)	Hagen (2000)
title	*Before HearSay: Basic Listening for the Classroom*	*Whaddaya Say? Guided Practice in Relaxed Spoken English*	*Whaddaya Say? Guided Practice in Relaxed Speech (2nd ed.)*	*Sound Advice: A Basis for Listening Comprehension (2nd ed.)*
publisher	Addison-Wesley Japan	ELS Publications	Longman	Longman
purpose	teach listening for real classroom communication in English	teach listening "to help students understand the relationships between carefully articulated English and its more informal, relaxed counterpart" (p. viii)	teach "the most common reduced forms (wanna, gonna, gotta, etc.) needed to understand natural spoken English" (p. vii)	teach "the key features of spoken English which are essential for the comprehension of authentic, natural speech—what English language learners regularly refer to as 'fast speech'" (p. vi)
number of pages	ix+179 pages	xi+68 pages	viii+119 pages	vii+183 pages
skill focus	mostly listening comprehension	mostly listening comprehension	mostly listening comprehension	mostly listening comprehension
organization	22 lessons organized around classroom skills	20 lessons organized around different relaxed speech patterns	30 lessons organized around conversation topics and different relaxed speech patterns	11 lessons organized around features of reduced speech
types of explanations for reduced forms	listen, phonetic explanation, examples for "slow" and "fast" speech	listen to contrasting careful (slow) and relaxed (fast) pronunciation of 10 sentences	listen to contrasting careful (slow) and relaxed (fast) pronunciation of 10 turn dialogs	1–3 highlighted, explicit explanations with examples of each teaching point per lesson

exercise types	listen and point (cartoon dialogs), listen and repeat, listen and circle, listen and match, listen and fill in the blank, pairwork (dictate to your partner)	while reading along listen to the pronunciation contrasts in the slow and fast pronunciation sentences, listen to the contrasts without reading, fill-in full forms in dialog dictation	while reading along, listen to the pronunciation contrasts in the dialog, answer comprehension questions, listen to the contrasts without reading, answer comprehension questions, fill-in full forms in a different dialog dictation, small group work discussion	listen and underline/mark/chose/check, listen and fill-in the blank, listen and fill in the blank dialog, compare answers with a partner, self-test, TOEFL listening self-test
illustrations	1 or 2 sets of B&W drawings per lesson	1 B&W drawing per lesson	2 B&W drawings per lesson	1 or 2 sets of blue & white drawings per lesson (the print is dark blue)
other features		answer key	10 self-tests, self-test transcripts, answer key for part 2, self-test answer key, alternative levels of reduction chart	3 TOEFL practice listening tests, explanation of pronunciation of past -ed and -s, tapescript, answer key
cassette tape available?	yes	yes	yes	yes

Table 2. Reduced forms covered in each chapter of each book (part 1)

lesson	Stratton & Rost (1978)	Stratton & Rost (1980)	Kobayashi & Linde (1984)	Griffee & Hough (1986)	Griffee (1993)
1	reduced forms: and & or	just got back, went there, must have been, did you do, & most of the time	and, you, do, [t + consonant]	your name, could you, first name, last name	is that your, have a, and your, let me
2	contrast: a & the	picked up a, put them away, spice shelf, cans of, & with the	[p,b,t,d + vowel]	what is your, could I, 13, 14, 15, 16, 17, 18, 19, 30, 40, 50, 60, 70, 80, 90	it will, can I, is it, can take a, did you
3	reduced forms: prepositions	how long have you, back east, used to it, west side, & don't like	are, to, verb-ing, [d + i]	what did you say? I did not, I did not understand, could you	for a, or, they are, do too
4	contractions: be and pronouns	can you, won't you, which way, that's right, & go to	[p + p], [k + k], [s + s], [s + ʃ]	is this, is that, are these, are those	here is your, do not understand, like them, I would like
5	contractions: be with nouns/question words here/there/that	take long, taking you, wanted to talk, what can I, & could I	that, is, your, [t + j]	this one, that one, one of, want you will	I have, this will, have to, I will, you will
6	contractions: will	going to, did it have any, left it, sure it's, & why did you	[f + j], [s + i]	what do you, it is, and, have it	to, you had, want to, that will be
7	contractions: have/has in present perfect	help you, is there, there are, what does it, & if we	did, the, his, [vowel + t + vowel]	some, I am, we are, do not understand, a cup of	did not, does he, does she, is your, have you got a, they are
8	contractions: would	must be, would you, about yourself, worked as a, & all of my	[k + j], [θ,s + vowel]	want to, go to, what is the, one is, that will be	aren't you, going to, where do you, you could
9	contractions: had past perfect/had better	haven't, car is still, can you, got about, & calling about	has, he, her, [tʃ,f + vowel]□	where is the, in the middle of, on the right, on the left	looks like, should have, of, look at
10	contractions: not	want to be, just two, but I, one of them, & in the front of the plane	[d + consonant], [g,k + vowel]□	let me, off at, I'll let you, when to get off	may I, going to, when is he, when is she, could you

11	contrasts: isn't and wasn't	who was it, where's he, what's he, I met him, & about his	as, she, him, [d + ð]	[es][ef][er si ef][er si es], first, second, third, fourth, fifth, come on out, down the hall	do you want me to, should I, I am looking for, you have got to
12	contrasts: aren't and weren't	how did you, let me, it's easy, what else, & it's really	[m + j], [p + j]	have change for, how do you, want it, 1, 2, 3, 4, 5, 6, 7, 8, 9, 10, ones, twos, threes, fours, fives, sixes, sevens, eights, nines, tens	have you ever been to, it is, it's…isn't it, on the, it would be
13	reduced forms: words beginning with aspirated "h"	than, little bit, meter and a, kind of, & it was	who, of, them, [d + j]	isn't this, you've got the, just a, you have, would you, do not have a, we will, I had	it's not, were you
14	contrasts: them and him	have to, is there, out of town, have you, & is that	[n + j], [v + j]	for next, would be, I'd like to, days of the week	do not know, don't you, what is, how about
15	reduced forms: verb-ing	you're asking, think about it, aren't any, more than, & lot of	was, can, going to, [z + j]	and a, can you, what is it, pick it up, that'll be, it will be	I have got to, what do you, come on, it is not, his, her
16	reduced forms: going to/want to/have to	got a, what did he, says he, doesn't he, & wouldn't	[n + ð], [z + j]	do I/do you, can I/can you, put your, and your/and now	
17	reduced forms: be in questions (present tense)	ought to, haven't, what have you, see her, & do you	were, from, want to, [ŋ + j]▢	kind/kinds, kind of, do/to, we've got, I'll take	
18	reduced forms: be in questions (past tense)	look at it, send it back, tell them about it, it might take, & half of the	[s + j], [z + t]▢	what, at/it, a/the, there is	
19	contrasts: be in wh-questions (present tense)	this isn't, shouldn't, told me, don't you, & not at all	have, would, their, your're, you'll▢		
20	reduced forms: be in wh-questions (present tense)	want to, can, don't we, if you're, & need to	you've you'd (had)▢		
21	reduced forms: be in wh-questions (past tense)	what's in it, let's see, I'd rather, what's it, & written	been, could. our, he'll, she'll▢		

continued…

Table 2. Reduced forms covered in each chapter of each book (part 1) *(cont.)*

lesson	Stratton & Rost (1978)	Stratton & Rost (1980)	Kobayashi & Linde (1984)	Griffee & Hough (1986)	Griffee (1993)
22	contrasts: be in wh-questions (present and past tense)	haven't I, didn't you use to, working, I've always been on, & what's your	he's (has, is), he'd (had, would), she's (has, is), she'd (had, would)]		
23	reduced forms: don't/doesn't/didn't in statements	I want to, not in, would you, must have made, & is there	than, should, -n't, it's (is, has)		
24	reduced forms: do/does in questions	it isn't, I've got to, why would you want to, but you, & ask your	that's (is, has), it'd (would, had), that'd (would, had)		
25	reduced forms: did in questions	thinks it's a, when does the, aren't you going to be, it's really, & guess it's better	had, for, my, I'm, we're		
26	contrasts: do/does and did in questions		I've, I'll, I'd (would, had), we'd (would, had)		
27	reduced forms: do/does in wh-questions		us, a (an), some, they're		
28	reduced forms: did in wh-questions		they've, they'd (would, had), they'll		
29	contrasts: do/does and did		does, am, used to, here's		
30	reduced forms: be in negative questions		there'll, it'll, that'll, we'll, we've		
31	reduced forms: do in negative questions		or, must, have to, who'll		
32	reduced forms: has/have in questions		who's (is, has), who'd (had, would)		

33	reduced forms: has/have in statements	will, ought to, at, do (does, did)…?
34	reduced forms: modals in questions	where's (is, has), where'll, there's (is, has)
35	reduced forms: modal perfect in statements	but, has to, don't (doesn't, didn't) …?
36	deletion: initial verb forms in questions	what's (is, has), what'll

Table 2. Reduced forms covered in each chapter of each book (part 2)

lesson	Hough (1995)	Weinstein (1982)	Weinstein (2001)	Hagen (2000)
1	and, don't	ya→you	your, you're→yer	reductions: syllable stress, ellipsis, function words, more ellipsis (dropping initial sounds), going to/want to/have to, and/or
2	ABC, DEF, GHI, JKL, MNO, PQR, STU, VWX, UVW, XYZ	whaddaya→what do you, what are you	yours→yers	introduction to linking; linking with vowels, linking identical consonants
3	letters, capital, small	wanna→want to	for→fer	special sound changes: the flap, -ty/-teen (e.g., thirty/thirteen), -nt reduction, the glottal stop, can/can't, of, linking of with vowels,
4	in the, write the, listen and	gonna→going to	of→a	silent h: function words beginning with h, questions beginning with have/has, pronoun summary
5	first, second, third, next, last	donno→don't know	you→ya	advanced linking: linking similar consonants, linking with -ed endings, assimilation with y
6	what is, it is	ta→to	-ing endings→-in'	focus on function words: listening for unstressed function words, a/an, our/are/or
7	question, answer	gotta→got to, hafta→have to, hasta→has to	what do you, what are you→whaddaya	contractions: negative contractions, common contractions with personal pronouns, contractions with "wh" words, other contractions with will, that "'s" contraction, contractions with it/that

#				
8	yer→your, you're, yers→yours	20, 30, 40, 50, 60, 70, 80, 90	want to→wanna	endings and beginnings: -s/-es endings, -en ending, adjective endings, prefixes, comparative and superlative endings
9	cha→/t/+you, cher→/t/+your, you're		going to+verb→gonna	grammar challenges: understanding tag questions, infinitives (to+verb) and gerunds (verb+ing), negative comparisons, talking to vs. talking about
10	-in'→ing		can→kin, can't→kant	grammar challenges ii: past tense modal reductions, expressing conditions with should and had
11	whacha→what do you, what you		get→git	special aspects of intonation and stress: statements as questions, tag endings, contrastive stress, indicating surprise with yes/no questions, using rhetorical questions to show sarcasm
12	ja→/d/+you, jer→/d/+your		to→ta	TOEFL practice I
13	er→or		to after a vowel sound→da	TOEFL practice II
14	'e→he, 'is→his, 'im→him, 'er→her, 'em→them		got to→gotta, have to→hafta, has to→hasta	TOEFL practice III
15	'n→and		used to→useta, supposed to→supposta	
16	kin→can		he→'e, his→'is, him→'im, her→'er, them→'em	
17	a→of		and→'n'	
18	before participle: shoulda→should have, coulda→could have, woulda→would have, musta→must have, maya→may have, mighta→might have		or→er	

Table 2. Reduced forms covered in each chapter of each book (part 2) *(cont.)*

lesson	Hough (1995)	Weinstein (1982)	Weinstein (2001)	Hagen (2000)
19		da→to after a vowel sound	don't know→donno	
20		fer→for	/t/+you→cha, /t/+your, you're→cher	
21			/d/+you→ja, /d/+your→jer	
22			deletion of initial /h/: *wh*-question words+have→'ave, *wh*-question words+has→'as, *wh*-question words+had→'ad	
23			deletion of initial /h/: subject+have→'ave, subject+has→'as, subject+had→'ad, subject+haven't→'aven't, subject+hasn't→'asn't, subject+hadn't→'adn't	
24			before past participle: should have→shoulda, could have→coulda, would have→woulda, must have→musta, may have→maya, might have→mighta, shouldn't have→shouldna, couldn't have→couldna, wouldn't have→wouldna	
25			very informal reduction: what are you→whacha	
26			very informal reduction: let me→lemme, give me→give me	
27			deletion of syllables: about→'bout, because→'cause, come on→c'mon	

28	deletion of words in questions: do you want some…→want some…, are you going to see…→gonna see…, would you like to…→like to…, have you seen the…→seen the…
29	unusual contractions: what are→what're, what will→what'll, where are→where're, where will→where'll, why are→why're, why will→why'll
30	unusual contractions: who are→who're, who will→who'll, when are→when're, when will→when'll, how are→how're, how will→how'll

Conclusion

In this chapter, I have examined what must be at least a majority of the resources available to language teachers interested in teaching connected speech including teacher-training resources with some content related to connected speech, ESL/EFL student books with some material helpful for teaching connected speech, as well as student books that focus entirely on helping students to learn connected speech.

With only a few exceptions the teacher training books for budding linguists and language teachers have only sparse coverage of the topics related to connected speech like word stress, sentence stress and timing, reduction, strong and weak word forms, elision, intrusion, assimilation, transition (juncture), liaison, and contraction. The "few exceptions" that I mentioned in the previous sentence would be three books (Avery & Ehrlich, 1992; Celce-Murcia, Brinton, & Goodwin, 2004; and Gimson, 1962, 1970, 1975, 1989, or 2001), each of which provides interesting explanations of some aspects of connected speech, but none of which can be said to be comprehensive on the topic of connected speech.

Similarly, ESL/EFL student textbooks for pronunciation have relatively sparse content on connected speech. Of these, Gilbert (1984, 1993) and Henrichson, Green, Nishitani, and Bagley (2002) offered the most, though that coverage was scattered in and amongst other information about the pronunciation of English and/or listening comprehension.

The nine books reviewed most carefully in this chapter were those that explicitly focused on helping students learn reduced forms. Of those, I recommended Hagen (2000) because of its explicit explanations of a relatively large number of connected speech topics and because of its wide variety of exercise types. However, I also pointed out that, given the variety of exercise types offered and the diversity of reduced forms topics covered, all nine books may prove useful for any teacher looking for new reduced forms topics and exercises.

I should add that the book you are currently reading was conceived with the purpose of adding to the available teacher training materials on connected speech and reduced forms by pulling together and synthesizing the perspectives of a number of different researchers on the topics involved. In addition, Brown (forthcoming) is designed to synthesize and add to what is known about connected speech topics and communicate that information to teachers. It will also provide ideas for implementing reduced forms instruction.

Good pronunciation in English must include much more than just a mastery of the citation forms of the consonant and vowel sounds of English. ESL/EFL students also need to understand and use the processes underlying connected speech if they are ever going to be able to understand native speech and themselves combine the consonant and vowel sounds into meaningful words and utterances in something approaching real spoken English. In short, students need to understand how the individual sounds fit together through processes of strong and weak word forms, word stress, sentence stress and timing, elision, intrusion, liaison, reduction, transition, assimilation, and contraction, as well as how those processes combine and interact. To those ends, teachers will themselves need to understand how those concepts work so they can help their students learn connected speech, and they will also need materials to use in teaching reduced forms. I hope this book in general will help teachers understand the overall concepts and that this chapter will help teachers find and select materials they can profitably use in teaching connected speech to their students.

Does connected speech instruction work?

4

NFLRC
monographs

The Effectiveness of
Teaching Reduced Forms for
Listening Comprehension[1]

JAMES DEAN BROWN
University of Hawai'i

ANN HILFERTY
Harvard University, Massachusetts

The research reported in this chapter investigates the effectiveness of teaching reduced forms (e.g., "gonna" for "going to") for improving listening comprehension among EFL students in the People's Republic of China. A randomly selected experimental group (n = 16) received 30 lessons of approximately 10 minutes each on reduced forms. This was part of their regular course work. At the same time a control group (n = 16) received "placebo" lessons of 10 minutes on minimal pairs in pronunciation. Three measures of listening comprehension were used to pretest and posttest the students. The results indicate that teaching reduced forms does aid listening comprehension, but this is reflected to varying degrees in the three measures. The discussion explores causes for these differences, as well as solutions to some of the problems encountered in small classroom research.

Introduction

This chapter will probably be of most interest to language teachers, researchers, testers and materials developers who want to understand, teach, and develop materials or tests for teaching reduced forms.

The literature over the last three decades contains only a handful of advocates of teaching reduced forms in the ESL classroom. Kingdon (1950) encourages the teaching of what he terms "weak forms" and attempts to classify and describe these forms grammatically by tabulating what he considers the 50 most common according to word class. He also includes phonetic transcriptions of each word in its various

---

[1]   This chapter originally appeared as Brown, J. D., & Hilferty, A. (1987). The effectiveness of teaching reduced forms for listening comprehension. *RELC Journal, 17*(2), 59–70. It is reprinted by permission of the authors, and RELC in Singapore has been appropriately notified. The article appears as it did in the original with minor changes to correct typographical errors and bring it in line with the formatting conventions of this book.

sentence environments and a few teaching suggestions. The classification seems less than comprehensive with only 38 selected function words and 12 miscellaneous ones (some of which are "Sir," "Madam," and "Saint"). However, this Kingdon article stands almost alone during the fifties except for two additional works of his own (1958a, 1958b).

Bowen (1975a) classifies, explains, and illustrates informal speech: (a) reduction, or usually the dropping of strong vowels when a syllable is weak-stressed, (b) assimilation, or usually the changing of adjacent or nearby consonants to resemble each other, and (c) contraction, or specific sets of words where assimilations occur whenever specific sounds are brought together in sequence. Bowen's detailed description of each phenomenon along with numerous examples and teaching exercises provide useful resources to support his encouragement of teachers to include reduced forms in their courses. This same information is presented in compressed form and from another perspective in Madsen and Bowen (1978). They advocate the teaching of "realistic pronunciation" and provide teaching resources in an abbreviated version of Bowen's earlier treatment accompanied by illustrations and sample exercises.

Also in 1978 (a and b), Odlin presents quite a different set of reasons for studying reduced forms. He suggests that there is a correlation between the frequency and variety of ESL students' contractions and their proficiency in ESL, and therefore a number of possible stages in the acquisition of contraction rules. A study of the language of six ESL students provides data that indicate that (a) contraction frequency correlates with general proficiency in English as measured by CELT, (b) that more advanced students reduce vowels more frequently than the less advanced, and (c) that more advanced students contract with a greater number of preceding words. Although the individual students' contraction patterns are idiosyncratic, there do seem to be evolutionary stages related to levels of proficiency. Odlin sees evidence that the perception and use of reduced forms are crucial to aural comprehension and general ESL proficiency and ends his article (1978b) with a call for clear attention to contractions and, quoting Kingdon, "weak forms."

Labov (1969) who had generally influenced Odlin, found that whatever forms can be contracted in standard English can be deleted in negro dialect and vice versa; similarly, whatever cannot be contracted in the first cannot be deleted in the second, and the reverse. He went on to explore the rules for standard English contraction and found the following: (a) contraction in standard English has both phonological and lexical constraints, (b) contraction and deletion are separate but similar rules, and (c) there is variation in the use of contractions among individuals and groups which may represent basic mechanisms of language development. Labov's work provides a number of possibilities for further study of contractions: (a) he provides a set of rules which can be further tested, (b) he uses both linguistic description and statistical methods of analysis, and (c) the study can serve as a model for conducting future research.

The questions left open by four ESL writers, Kingdon, Bowen, Madsen, and Odlin, and those suggested by Labov are not easy to answer. It is only with difficulty and sometimes flights of fancy that the would-be teachers of reduced forms can find resources other than those described above to use in planning class materials or further classroom research projects. For a number of reasons, available sources of language analysis do not seem to provide information that can be easily adapted. The problem can be illustrated with examples from widely differing sources.

In such early works on pronunciation as Pike (1945), examples are written according to the conventions of written English, that is, without acknowledging reduced forms except the small number of allowable written contractions. In Bolinger (1965), as in grammar references, only a laborious, close reading or an interpretive search through the index will turn up a few nuggets concerning reduced forms.

Works on transformational grammar and phonology do not provide simple or quick answers to the inquiries of the would-be materials developer or researcher, either. For example, in Chomsky and Halle (1968), the terms "contraction," "assimilation," and "reduction" are used in highly technical senses in the service of abstract analyses of individual words. Applications of such detailed descriptions of the phonological processes to teaching materials or classroom research design would necessarily presuppose the analysis of discourse using units of measurement and operational definitions much more suitable to the needs of the ESL teacher.

In spite of the general lack of appropriate background materials, a few recent ESL textbooks have included materials for reduced forms. Notable among these are Morley (1979), Trager (1982), Weinstein (1982), and Gilbert (1984). Morley includes, along with many other exercises in the first unit, lessons in reduced syllables, reduced words, and two-word contractions, elisions, and assimilations. Traeger devotes an entire section to what she terms, "relaxed pronunciation patterns." Designed with emphasis on recognition rather than pronunciation for intermediate through advanced speakers, part VII of the book provides brief explanation and exercises in listening to, and then reproducing in writing, the full forms of three broad areas of relaxed pronunciation patterns (which the author terms "contracted forms," "the dropping of sounds," and "sound changes"). Weinstein provides a simpler treatment. The goal is to help beginning students understand relationships between carefully articulated English and the English of quick, relaxed, informal speech. Using language patterns which include fewer than three dozen base words, the author provides exercises in listening, following and listening, and "translating" into carefully articulated speech, as well as listening and identifying, and filling in the full forms. She does not point out distinctions among kinds of reduced forms, and provides little supplementary information about phonetic, syntactic, and social constraints. Gilbert presents only one chapter on reductions. This covers the disappearance of the "h" sound, for example, Did (h)e go?, and those forms of "be" and "have" which are normally contracted in writing, for example, he's, I've. One other related chapter briefly explains the linking of words in pronunciation. None of the four sources discussed here can be said to fully treat reduced forms.

The review of the literature done for this study[2] indicates that there is a clear need for much further work on reduced forms from every perspective: linguistic and sociolinguistic analysis, the acquisition process, the acts of perceiving and producing, and the development of teaching strategies and materials.

This chapter describes a study based on classroom research in which limited resources were used to teach reduced forms. Our specific purpose here was to investigate the effectiveness of teaching reduced forms in the Guangzhou English Language Center (GELC) program. To this end, the following research questions were posed:

---

[2]   Editors' note: Recall that this study was originally published in 1986. However, note that the more up-to-date literature reviews provided in chapters 1 through 3 of this book also indicate a clear need for much more work in this particular area of phonology.

- Do reduced forms lessons significantly increase students' abilities in integrative grammar as measured by the Bowen Integrative Grammar Test (IGT, Bowen, 1976)?

- Do such reduced forms lessons significantly increase students' overall English listening abilities as measured by a norm-referenced multiple-choice listening test?

- Do 10-minute daily lessons on reduced forms significantly increase students' abilities to understand reduced forms as measured by reduced forms dictations?

Null hypotheses of no significant mean differences were constructed and tested for each of these questions. The alpha level was set at .05 for all statistical tests.

Method

Participants

The participants ($N = 32$) in this study were all Chinese graduate students. They were predominantly experienced scientists studying at the Guangzhou English Language Center (GELC) to improve their English so that they could go abroad as visiting scholars. There were 29 males and three females in this random sample drawn from the larger population of all intermediate (B level) students at GELC during the spring quarter of 1981. Their major fields were engineering (56%), biology (13%), English (9%), agriculture (6%), mathematics (6%), physics (6%), and chemistry (3%). While all of the participants spoke standard Mandarin Chinese, they came from a variety of first dialect backgrounds including Shanghai dialect (34%), Cantonese (28%), Beijing dialect (13%), and a number of other dialects represented by only one person each (25%). The mean age for theses participants was 38.5 years (with a standard deviation of 5.3).

The participant pool was divided into two randomly assigned groups: an experimental group ($n = 16$), who received the reduced forms treatment, and a control group ($n = 16$), who received what we viewed as a placebo of pronunciation minimal pairs practice instead of reduced forms.

Materials and procedures

Selected reduced forms from American English (as collected and agreed upon by the experimenters, one from Boston and one from Los Angeles) were listed and categorized before the course began. These were broken down into four weeks of daily lessons (five to ten reduced forms each), which were to be presented such that the students would learn to understand rather than produce them. Each daily lesson was to last no more that 10 minutes and to involve presentation of these forms with students responding individually or collectively to questions built from them. Aside from this plan, the teachers did not consult on how to teach these short lessons.

In addition to presenting the reduced forms, seven dictations were developed which included twenty to forty-six previously covered reductions each. The students were required to write out the full forms of all words in these dictations and only those words actually involved in reduction were scored. The purpose of these dictations was to encourage the students to review the reduced forms periodically and to give them further practice in comprehending the forms. Both the reduced forms lessons and dictations were presented only to the treatment group.

The control group, on the other hand, received daily 10 minute drills in discriminating minimal pairs drawn from Trager and Henderson (1956). The belief here was that 10 minutes per day drilling on individual phoneme contrasts for 4 weeks would not have much effect on any aspects of the students' listening comprehension abilities. All of the consonants of English were covered in these lessons, as well as the major consonant clusters. In addition, brief lessons on intonation, stress, and rhythm were presented.

Three measures were used in this study: the Bowen (1976) Integrative Grammar Test (divided into two forms of 50 items each), outdated versions of the UCLA English as a Second Language Placement Examination (ESLPE) listening comprehension subtest (combined and divided into two approximately equal subtests of 25 items each), and reduced forms dictations (sampling all of the reduced forms presented for a total of 45 points possible on each form).[3]

Classroom research is often very difficult to accomplish for three reasons: (a) adequate sampling procedures are often impossible, (b) controlling for testing effect is difficult, and (c) controlling for differences in teaching style and/or ability among the teachers in an experiment is problematic. The design developed here is suggested as a way to circumvent each of those problems and actually do classroom research.

Sampling is often a problem in classroom research, either because we have no control of students' assignments to courses or sections of those courses, or because students themselves decided which class they want to take. At GELC, this problem evaporated because students are randomly assigned to sections within each level. In other words, students in level B, the intermediate level at GELC, are randomly assigned to the sections of the level. As a result, we have randomly assigned students to classes that we can designate as treatment or control groups as the need arises in classroom research.

Controlling for testing effect (i.e., the effect of having taken a given test on the results of subsequent administrations of the same or similar tests) was more problematic. In this four-week study, the three tests (with two forms each) described above were administered to both the treatment and control groups at the beginning and end of the experiment. Thus, any testing effect could reasonably be expected to be equal for both groups. Nevertheless, in order to minimize this effect, if not eliminate it, the tests were counterbalanced in the administrations such that no student took exactly the same form of any test twice and such that half (random) of each group took each form of each test at each administration (see Table 1). This counter balancing also served to nullify any differences there might have been between the two forms of each test.

Controlling for differences in teaching style is a problem when teacher A teaches the control group and teacher B teaches the treatment group. The results of such a study might show that, indeed, the treatment group was much better in some way or other. The problem is that the treatment group might be better because teacher B is a better teacher overall rather than because of the treatment itself. To circumvent this problem, the teachers in this experiment were rotated between the treatment and control groups on a weekly basis such that each group had each teacher for a total of 2

---

[3]   Editors' note: For other ideas of ways to test or assess reduced forms, see chapter 14 of this volume.

weeks. Any differences in teaching effectiveness were therefore equally distributed between both groups.

Table 1.   Counterbalancing of the three tests and two groups

test	treatment group		control group	
Bowen IGT				
form A	Ss 1–8	Ss 9–16	Ss 17–24	Ss 25–32
form B	Ss 9–16	Ss 1–8	Ss 25–32	Ss 17–24
UCLA ESLPE listening				
form A	Ss 9–16	Ss 1–8	Ss 25–32	Ss 17–24
form B	Ss 1–8	Ss 9–16	Ss 17–24	Ss 25–32
Reduced Forms Dictation				
form A	Ss 1–8	Ss 9–16	Ss 17–24	Ss 25–32
form B	Ss 9–16	Ss 1–8	Ss 25–32	Ss 17–24

Analysis

The pretest results were used in this study simply as a means for checking the initial equivalence of the two randomly assigned groups. The analysis itself was a posttest only design.

The posttest results on all three tests were investigated using two-way repeated measures analysis of variance. Then, the means for the two groups on each test were examined for simple main effects.

It should be noted that in such a study the statistics are much simpler if only one posttest is used. In a one-test two-group study, a simple t-test can easily be calculated by hand (Guilford & Fruchter, 1973, pp. 149–162) to determine the significance of mean differences. This would be a much more practical approach for the neophyte to this type of research.

Results

At the outset of the study, we were interested in whether or not the randomly assigned treatment and control groups were equivalent as indicated in sampling theory. To determine this, we examined the two groups' means (M) and standard deviations (S) on the three tests at the beginning of the study (see Table 2). The differences which appear between the means of the two groups were not found to be significant (using Fisher's t), even at the liberal .25 level and even though we were violating degrees of freedom rules (which would favor finding unwarranted significant differences) by making such multiple t comparisons.

The posttest results described in Table 2 also indicate that the means on all three tests were higher for the treatment group. But only the means on the Integrative Grammar Test and the reduced forms dictation were found to be significantly different (see Tables 3 and 4).

Table 2.   Descriptive statistics for treatment and control groups

test	statistic	pretest		posttest	
		treatment group	control group	treatment group	control group
Bowen IGT	M	3.19	3.06	3.56	2.25
	S	2.43	1.28	1.99	1.57
	n	16	16	16	16
UCLA ESLPE listening	M	12.63	11.94	17.25	14.81
	S	3.79	3.13	3.53	4.09
	n	16	16	16	16
Reduced Forms Dictation	M	16.38	14.19	30.56	15.87
	S	4.66	5.18	7.76	4.62
	n	16	16	16	16

Table 3.   Repeated measures ANOVA for groups and tests

source	SS	df	MS	F
groups	906.51	1	906.51	32.70*
subjects/groups (error)	813.56	30	27.72	
tests	6789.58	2	3394.79	219.87*
groups x tests	880.59	2	440.30	28.52*
tests x subjects/groups	926.50	60	15.44	
total	10334.74	95		

note: $p<.01$

Table 4.   Simple main effects for groups on each test

test source	SS	df	MS	F
groups on IGT	13.78	1	13.78	4.27*
groups on ESLPE	47.53	1	47.53	3.26
groups on reduced forms dictation	1725.78	1	1725.78	42.31*

note: $p<.05$

Discussion

In answer to the initial research question, it was found that there was a significant difference in the mean performance of the two groups on Bowen's IGT. This indicates that the observed difference in means was probably due to other than chance factors. It should be noted that the means (when doubled to approximate Bowen's 100 item versions) reported here are considerably lower than those reported by Bowen himself (1976). This may be due to differences in tape quality or playback equipment. It could also be a result of unfamiliarity or frustration with this type of test on the part of our students. Or perhaps, there is something about mainland Chinese' learning/study styles, which makes this test more difficult for them. In any case, 4 weeks of reduced forms lessons did seem to have an effect on performance on this test.

In response to the second research question, a significant difference was found between the means of the two groups on the reduced forms dictations. The difference was not only statistically significant (i.e., it probably did not occur by chance alone) but also meaningful because it was large. Whereas the treatment group was able to correctly identify and write down the full forms for an average of 68% of the words involved in reduced forms, the control group could manage only 35%. While this difference may be due in part to the treatment group's practicing this type of dictation, it nevertheless seems to indicate that the exposed group was understanding reduced forms better and able to demonstrate this understanding through reduced forms dictations. Therefore, 4 weeks of reduced forms lessons did seem to have a marked effect on performance on the reduced forms dictations.[4]

The key elements in the approach to classroom research used here were the random sampling procedure, the controlling of the testing effect, and the controlling of differences in teacher style/ability. There are no doubt innumerable individual variables going on in any given language classroom. These variables are extremely difficult to identify, much less control. Nevertheless, based on statistical sampling theory, such differences should equal out over two groups if those groups are randomly selected from the larger population and randomly assigned to the two groups. Using random sampling in connection with controls for testing and teacher effects should therefore provide a fairly strong experimental design. Nevertheless, each situation is different and the classroom researcher should always be asking what variables, internal or external to the study, could have an effect on the study. Once identified, every effort should be made to control any such variables. In fact, a perceptive reader should be asking at this point if there are any crucial variables that were forgotten in this study.

One that might come immediately to mind is a variable called practice effect. In the case of the reduced forms dictations in this study, they were both pretest and posttest measures, as well as part of the treatment itself. Hence any difference between the control and treatment groups might be due entirely to the difference in the amount of practice on this novel type of exercise. There are two reasons that this was viewed as a relatively minor problem here. First, there was also a significant difference between the means on the Bowen IGT (which also tests the ability to comprehend and write down reduced forms). And second, the difference between the means on the reduced forms dictation was not only significant, but also meaningfully large, almost 15 points. Whether this doubling of the average score was partially due to practice effect or not was of little concern considering the degree to which the students had clearly increased their ability to comprehend and write down reduced forms.

Doing and/or evaluating such a research project can often raise additional questions. Some of those that occurred to us are provided here in the hope that someone will find them interesting enough to pursue.

- Would the same, or similar, results be obtained at other institutions, especially in ESL settings, where students are more likely to be exposed to reduced forms in daily life?
- What is the relationship of reduced-forms dictations to regular dictations and to other types of language tests?
- To what degree do standardized listening tests (e.g., TOEFL) involve reduced forms? Why or why not?
- What categories do reduced forms fall into and how can they logically be systematized?
- What are the rules governing all types of reduction?

---

[4]   Editors' note: As readers will see, chapters 5, 6, and 8 further support the notion that reduced forms can be taught in ESL/EFL settings.

5

Comprehension of English Reduced Forms by Japanese Business People and the Effectiveness of Instruction[1]

TAKASHI MATSUZAWA
Temple University, Japan

Why do Japanese speakers of English have so much difficulty with listening comprehension? Language teachers, researchers, testers, and materials developers need to know so they can better understand, teach, and develop materials or tests for teaching reduced forms. This author's hypothesis is that Japanese do not understand some of the critical differences between understanding written texts and spoken discourse. Various reduced forms and sound changes are factors that interfere with good listening comprehension. The study reported in this chapter tests the hypothesis that reduced forms do interfere with students' comprehension and investigates the effect of explicit instruction of reduced forms. The results show not only a serious lack of comprehension of reduced forms among participants but also an improvement in their listening comprehension after explicit instruction in recognizing and understanding reduced forms.

Recognizing the importance of reduced forms in ESL/EFL listening, educators (Avery & Ehrlich, 1992; Celce-Murcia, Brinton, & Goodwin, 2004) have discussed various types of reduced forms that teachers should be aware of, namely assimilation, palatalization, contractions, deletion, and linking.[2] In addition, I would like to extend the definition of reduced forms in this chapter to cover other sound-change phenomena that can occur in spoken discourse of North American English at natural speed. All these phenomena can cause changes in the pronunciation of a word spoken alone (i.e., its citation form). The added phenomena are weak forms of function words, high frequency phrases (Avery & Ehrlich, 1992), for example, *gonna* (going to), and the sound changes of flapping, glottalized /t/, and linked /nt/ reduction. The terms *connected speech* and *sandhi variation* are also used in the field of

---

[1] A preliminary analysis of this study was presented at the Fourth Temple University Japan Applied Linguistics Colloquium held in Osaka on February 17, 2002.

[2] Editors' note: A substantial amount of literature review was edited out of this chapter because very similar material was covered in other chapters. See the definitions in chapter 1 of this volume as well as the literature reviews in chapters 1 through 3 for this sort of information.

Matsuzawa, T. (2006) Comprehension of English reduced forms by Japanese business people and the effectiveness of instruction. In J. D. Brown, & K. Kondo-Brown, (Eds.), *Perspectives on teaching connected speech to second language speakers* (pp. 59–66). Honolulu, HI: University of Hawai'i, National Foreign Language Resource Center.

teaching pronunciation but because of the focus on sound changes in this chapter, *reduced forms* is the most appropriate term for these pronunciation phenomena here.[3]

In this study, I wanted to (a) investigate the extent to which Japanese business people can comprehend the reduced forms of North American English and (b) determine whether reduced forms instruction results in improved listening comprehension. As supplemental information, after all the activities are completed I also survey the participants to find out if they knew about the existence of reduced forms. I was unable to locate any other research that has investigated these questions in the context of Japanese learning English.

Method

Participants

Sixteen male and four female Japanese business persons, aged 23 to 41 (average age 30) participated in this study.[4] They were all college graduates with TOEIC scores ranging from 380 to 850 (average 613), and they had volunteered to participate. This study did not have a control group because the primary purpose was to give reduced forms instruction to all participants. As a result, the study was conducted as a counterbalanced pretest-posttest only design (Brown, 1988). For testing, three sentences were created for each of 10 reduced forms, for a total of 30, and these were randomly ordered as a set. This step was repeated three times to create three sets of 30 sentences, 90 sentences in total. Then the three sets, A, B, and C, were recorded on cassette tape by native speakers (NSs) of North American English; each person recording one of the sets A, B, and C, as well as practice sentences provided by me.

At the beginning, participants were randomly assigned to two groups. One group of 10 participants took a dictation test (pretest) with one tape (hereafter, tape A) and the other group of 10 took this dictation with another tape (hereafter, tape B).[5]

Materials

An answer sheet was provided, on which blank parentheses were printed corresponding to the number of words of each sentence. The participants were asked to write down all words in the parentheses as they listened to each sentence. I decided to apply this procedure so that the participants would not just focus on reduced forms but on the comprehension of the sentence. However, only word(s) with a target reduced form were evaluated for correctness. For example, for palatalization, the italicized words in parentheses two and three were evaluated.

(Where) (*did*) (*you*) (go) (Friday)?

---

[3]   Editors' note: For definitions of the above terminology see chapter 1 or the glossary of this book.

[4]   Editors' note: Because the sample size of 20 in this study is very small, readers should interpret the results very cautiously.

[5]   The sentence "*What are you* up to?" was selected for palatalization in tape A. However, the tape was recordeded with flapping (['wʌɾəju]). So tape A contained four flapping sentences and two palatalization sentences instead of three each. Test B erroneously included a flapping sentence, "It doesn't *matter* (['mæɾər]), I think" instead of a linked /nt/ reduction sentence. So there were four flapping sentences and two linked /nt/ reduction sentences instead of three of each. Because these sentences also contained correct reduced forms of flapping, the comprehension of these sentences was included in the quantitative analyses of reduced form comprehension and the effectiveness of the instruction.

Also, only exact spellings were counted correct even if the sound was seemingly understood. For example, the answer *cats* instead of *cat's* in "My cat's been sick since Monday" was considered incorrect. This rule was to ensure that the participants had understood not only the sound of a reduced form but also the grammatically correct meaning of the utterance.[6]

Procedures

After the pretest, a total of seven lessons covering the 10 reduced forms were conducted in Japanese during lunch breaks or after working hours over a period of one month. Each lesson was designed to last 30 minutes so the total time spent on this course was about 4 hours (excluding pre- and posttest time) including a sample test, which was based on the third sentence set (tape C) at the final class.

In the first lesson, a brief explanation was provided concerning top-down and bottom-up processing of listening as well as the rhythm and stress of English. Then, instruction on the weak forms of function words was given. Some lessons covered two categories of reduced forms when they were considered easy to learn. The instruction consisted of an explanation of the reduced forms: the definition, when it could occur, and what the samples were, using handouts developed by me. With the exception of the first lesson, each lesson began with a review exercise about the previous lesson, then the main lecture, which was in turn followed by listening exercises. The most common listening exercises involved listening to short sentences either taped by NSs of North American English or spoken by me and filling in reduced forms in blank parentheses for each sentence on paper. There were some exercises where the participants discussed and predicted in which part a reduced form could happen. I developed all lecture materials and exercise handouts. However, I borrowed many exercises from Hagen (2000). The following is an example of a lesson (treatment).

Lesson 3: Linking

> *Review exercise:* contractions (10 questions)
>
> *Lecture on linking:* C+V, C+C, V+V, V + semi-V
>
> *Exercise:* 1) Listen to seven short sentences (by an NS) and fill in the blanks.
>
> 2) Discuss with the neighbor how linking would occur on the 10 sentences provided.
>
> 3) Listen to six short sentences (spoken by me), select a correct word from the list and fill in the parenthesis.
>
> (based on Hagen, 2000, pp. 16, 18)

After all the lessons were finished, a posttest was conducted using tapes A and B again with the two participant groups.

Results and Discussion

The pretest result indicated that the participants correctly wrote down about half of the reduced forms ($M = 14.95$, $SD = 4.43$). Twenty-five reduced forms out of 60 (tapes A and B) had less than 50% comprehension (see Appendix). So, in answering the research question (a), it may be said that the participants had difficulty in

---

[6]   Editors' note: For other ideas on ways to test or assess reduced forms, see chapter 14 of this volume.

comprehending reduced forms. Among these 25 reduced forms, there were five for flapping; four contractions; three each for glottalized /t/, high frequency phrases, and weak forms of function words; two each for linking, linked /nt/ reduction, and deletion; and one for palatalization. All assimilation of nasals had more than 50% comprehension. Flapping was apparently the most difficult for participants to understand. However, the difficulty may have been due to factors other than the existence of reduced forms. I will discuss this below.

I did not expect that contractions and weak forms of function words would be among the major comprehension obstacles because they appear in almost all spoken discourse of English. About contractions, "*They've* finished eating" had no one answer correctly among the 10 participants.[7] The suffix -*ve* was not recognized. This may be because the sounds /v/ and /f/ are both labiodentals, and thus /v/ is "shortened when it is before [the] identical consonant" (Ladefoged, 2001, p. 60) and only the word *finished* was recognized. "My *cat's* been sick since Monday" had only one correct answer, here several participants recognized the sound and wrote *cats* instead. This may imply that the participants were not used to listening to the contracted form of *has* with a noun and thus not able to understand that the sound /s/ connotes an auxiliary *has* even if followed by *been*. "He *hasn't* left the office yet" had one correct answer and seven participants heard it as *has* instead, a phenomenon like Celce-Murcia, et al. (2004) cited using the sample of *can*. "He'd never seen it before" had three correct answers. This is a case of what Ladefoged (2001, p. 47) explained as follows: "Final stops are unexploded when the next word begins with a nasal." So /d/ sounded weak and as both /d/ and /n/ were alveolar, /d/ was not recognized. For weak forms of function words, "Have you seen *him* (/ɪm/) today?" had three correct answers out of ten participants; both "Would you like cream *and* (/ən/) sugar?" and "Where did *he* (/i/) go Thursday?" had four each. These involved the problem Avery and Ehrlich (1992, p. 81) commented on as follows: "The fact that function words in English are generally unstressed and reduced makes them almost unrecognizable to beginning ESL students." This comment seems applicable to many of the participants in this study.

The fact that high frequency phrases were listed high in the difficulty ranking would seem to indicate that they need attention in teaching listening. "We are never *going to* (/gənə/) make it" had one correct answer, "It's *going to* rain tonight" had two, and "When are you *going to* arrive?" had one correct among 10 participants. There were some *gonna* and *gone a* answers. Hence, I concluded that most of the participants did not know that *gonna* was used to connote *going to* in spoken discourse.

About flapping, other factors than reduced forms may have impaired listening comprehension. "I found this box in the attic (['ærɪk])" had no correct answers among 10 participants. There was one answer of *atic*, one *adic* and all others were blank. It is possible that many participants did not know this word, which is not common in a Japanese context as few houses in Japan have attics. The word was chosen as it typically contained flapping articulation but, in retrospect, lexical considerations should have excluded it. "*What are you* (['wʌɾəju]) up to?" for flapping had no correct answer out of 10. This sentence contained a combination of flapped /t/ in *what are*, and *you* connected to it and it may not have been appropriate to use a complex sentence like this for this study. As noted in footnote 5, this study

---

7   Due to the counterbalancing, the other ten participants were given a different tape of 30 sentences.

contained two extra flapping sentences (total eight instead of the planned six) and five for both palatalization and linked /nt/ reduction instead of six each, a fact that may have emphasized the difficulty with flapping.

The posttest results showed an improvement ($M = 18.65$, $SD = 5.34$), which was statistically significant (t (19) $= 4.485$, $p < 0.005$) with a paired t test. So the answer to research question (b) was positive. Because the participants took different tests for pre- and posttests, confirmation was required to show that tapes A and B were not different in difficulty. Based on the assumption that the English ability of the two participant groups were similar, an independent t test of the two tapes was conducted and showed that they could be considered as having approximately the same difficulty (tape A: $M = 15.80$, $SD = 4.38$ and tape B: $M = 14.10$, $SD = 4.32$ with t (18) $= 0.874$, $p > 0.05$).

The next step was to conduct two correlation analyses using Microsoft Excel 2002; to understand (a) if there was any relation between participant English proficiency (as expressed by TOEIC scores) and the reduced-form comprehension (as measured by the pretest) and (b) if the comprehension improvement (difference between their pre- and posttest scores) occurred only for participants of specific proficiencies. The correlation between English proficiency and reduced-forms comprehension was high ($r = 0.716$) indicating that participants with higher English proficiency tended to comprehend more reduced forms than those with lower proficiency. The correlation between English proficiency and improvement in reduced-form comprehension was nearly zero ($r = 0.097$) indicating that the improvement did not relate to any specific English proficiency, that is, all participants benefited about equally from the instruction.

The posttest showed that 15 reduced-form sentences out of 60 had less than 50% comprehension; four for contractions; two each for flapping, linking, glottalized /t/, and linked /nt/ reduction; one each for deletion, high frequency phrases, and weak forms of function words. As for contractions, the previously discussed four sentences had zero (My *cat's*...), 1 (*They've*...), 2 (*He'd*...), and 3 (*He hasn't*...) correct answers out of 10, showing little improvement. Weak forms of function words still remained problematic. In the posttest, three participants correctly understood *him* (/ɪm/); both *he* (/i/) and *and* (/ən/) were answered correctly by only half of the participants.

There were cases where comprehension seemed to have become better through the instruction. For example, out of 10 posttest participants, "I don't like it *because* (/'kʌz/) that's wrong" resulted in eight correct answers as opposed to three at the pretest. "I *miss your* (/'mɪʃuər/) phone calls" for palatalization resulted in eight correct answers versus three. "When are you *going to* arrive?" resulted in five correct answers posttest versus one pretest.

After the course a survey (in Japanese) was conducted. In it, 10 participants (50%) replied they had not known about the existence of reduced forms. Nine participants replied they knew of the existence of reduced forms somewhat: five from experience and four from classes (one at high school, one at college, the others privately). All 20 participants expressed the view that the lessons were useful.

Conclusion

This study had limitations in that there was no control group, no consideration of other English dialects, and a small number of participants, and the results cannot be generalized to the wider Japanese EFL environment. However, the results of the study demonstrated that (a) reduced forms generally present barriers to listening comprehension for the participants, 20 Japanese business people in this case, and (b) short lessons can result in improvement in the comprehension of reduced forms.[8] Additionally, the results suggest that, from a teaching viewpoint, contractions and weak forms of function words may deserve special attention.

This study was designed on the basis of a pedagogical categorization of reduced forms and thus contained phonetically different mechanisms of articulation in one category group. So one had high comprehension among the participants and another in the same reduced-form category had low comprehension. As a follow up to this study, it would be worthwhile to categorize reduced forms by phonetic mechanism and see which pose difficulties and which do not. The availability of such information should help teachers to teach reduced forms to EFL students more effectively.

Even if the fundamentals of reduced form comprehension are better understood, the extent to which the teacher should make the learner comprehend them is another important issue. Lessons suggested for North American English by Brown and Hilferty (1995) include *Jawanna* (Do you want to) and *Whaja* (What did you), and Hagen (2000) lists such phrases as: "*Dze* (does he) know that?" and "*A-vi* (have I) done it O.K.?" All these are hybrids of multiple categories of reduced forms. For example, *jawanna* includes palatalization of *do you* and the high frequency phrase of *wanna* in one articulation. Obviously, there is a proficiency gap between the participants in the present study and the target students for the lessons suggested in this paragraph.

Acknowledgements

I would like to thank J. D. Brown for his guidance and consultation, and David Beglar, Jana Marvel, Denise Mouch, Hanako Okada, and Carolyn Pieroway for recording test and practice tapes. I would also like to thank anonymous reviewers of JALT Journal for their insightful feedback, and Torkil Christensen and Mary Lee Field for their help in revising the chapter.

---

[8]   Editors' note: Further support for this contention is presented in chapters 4 and 6.

Appendix: Reduced forms comprehension results

target reduced form	pretest comprehension (%)	posttest comprehension (%)	category	sentence ID	sentence
attic	0.0	0.0	flapping	A–16	I found this box in the *attic*.
fair enough	0.0	0.0	linking	B–9	I think it's *fair enough*.
fattening	0.0	0.0	glottalized /t/	B–15	This food is *fattening*.
they've	0.0	10.0	contraction	B–7	*They've* finished eating.
mutton	0.0	30.0	glottalized /t/	B–8	*Mutton* is sheep meat.
what are you	0.0	50.0	flapping*	A–27	*What are you* up to?
county	0.0	70.0	linked /nt/ reduction	B–10	He lives in Orange *County*.
cat's (cat has)	10.0	0.0	contraction	A–18	My *cat's* been sick since Monday.
butter	10.0	10.0	flapping	A–5	Use *butter* for this cooking.
hasn't (has not)	10.0	30.0	contraction	A–26	He *hasn't* left the office yet.
gonna (going to)	10.0	50.0	high freq. phrase	A–29	When are you *going to* arrive?
she's on	10.0	50.0	linking	B–26	*She's on* the phone right now.
Peter	10.0	60.0	flapping	B–4	This is *Peter* Watson.
gonna (going to)	10.0	60.0	high freq. phrase	B–25	We are never *going to* make it.
postman	20.0	30.0	deletion	A–11	He's a *postman* for 10 years.
gonna (going to)	20.0	30.0	high freq. phrase	A–14	It's *going to* rain tonight.
he'd (he had)	30.0	20.0	contraction	A–10	*He'd* never seen it before.
him	30.0	30.0	weak form of func. word	A–3	Have you seen *him* today?
enter	30.0	30.0	linked /nt/ reduction	A–19	Stop! Don't *enter*!
certain	30.0	50.0	glottalized /t/	B–24	Are you *certain* this is true?
miss your	30.0	80.0	palatalization	B–22	I *miss your* phone calls.
because	30.0	80.0	deletion	B–23	I don't like it *because* that's wrong.
and	40.0	50.0	weak form of func. word	B–21	Would you like cream *and* sugar?
he	40.0	60.0	weak form of func. word	B–1	Where did *he* go Thursday?
city	40.0	100.0	flapping	B–13	I live in a *city* suburbs.
if it's	50.0	30.0	linking	A–22	*If it's* OK, I'm leaving.
won't go	50.0	50.0	assimilation (nasal)	B–29	We *won't go* there. We will stay.
on my	50.0	60.0	assimilation (nasal)	A–7	There's nothing *on my* plate.
past	50.0	60.0	deletion	B–12	His father is a *past* president.
mountains	50.0	70.0	glottalized /t/	A–2	My hobby is to climb *mountains*.
and	50.0	70.0	weak form of func. word	A–23	He goes to school now *and* then.

Appendix: Reduced forms comprehension results (*cont.*)

target reduced form	pretest comprehension (%)	posttest comprehension (%)	category	sentence ID	sentence
dentist	50.0	90.0	linked /nt/ reduction	B–17	I have a *dentist* appointment.
identity	60.0	20.0	linked /nt/ reduction	A–8	I think that's her *identity*.
center	60.0	50.0	linked /nt/ reduction	A–25	That's the Medical *Center*.
wanna (want a)	60.0	60.0	high freq. phrase	A–9	Do you *want a* cup of coffee?
dunno (don't know)	60.0	70.0	high freq. phrase	B–2	They *don't know* if it's true.
am I	60.0	90.0	linking	B–3	*Am I* late? There was a heavy traffic.
have	70.0	70.0	weak form of func. word	B–19	The men *have* finished.
can't go	70.0	90.0	assimilation (nasal)	A–15	I'm busy so I *can't go*.
about	70.0	90.0	deletion	A–30	How *about* going for lunch?
can't believe	70.0	90.0	assimilation (nasal)	B–14	I *can't believe* it.
gonna (going to)	70.0	100.0	high freq. phrase	B–20	She is *going to* leave soon.
can go	80.0	70.0	assimilation (nasal)	A–24	He *can go* to the store but she can't.
what's up	80.0	80.0	linking	A–1	You look very tired. *What's up?*
matter	80.0	80.0	flapping**	B–30	It doesn't *matter*, I think.
waiting	80.0	90.0	glottalized /t/	A–17	I'm *waiting* for the bus.
can't	80.0	90.0	contraction	B–27	She *can't* hear me, I think.
pretty	80.0	90.0	flapping	B–28	That's a *pretty* doll.
next	80.0	100.0	deletion	A–6	I'll do it *next* month.
what's	80.0	100.0	contraction	B–16	*What's* the problem, John?
stop trying	90.0	50.0	linking	A–12	Don't *stop trying*. We are helping you.
this year	90.0	80.0	palatalization	A–20	I went there *this year*.
little	90.0	90.0	flapping	A–28	She speaks French a *little*.
did you	90.0	90.0	palatalization	B–5	Where *did you* go Friday?
please yourself	90.0	90.0	palatalization	B–18	*Please yourself*.
can go	90.0	100.0	assimilation (nasal)	B–6	If things are OK, I *can go*.
of	100.0	90.0	weak form of func. word	A–13	I need a cup *of* coffee.
would you	100.0	100.0	palatalization	A–4	*Would you* mind if I come?
important	100.0	100.0	glottalized /t/	A–21	That's not *important*.
kindness	100.0	100.0	deletion	B–11	Thank you for your *kindness*.

notes: * This sentence was selected for palatalization in tape A. However, the tape was recorded with flapping.[5]

   ** This flapping sentence was erroneously included instead of linked /nt/ reduction sentence in tape B.[5]

NFLRC
monographs

The Comprehension of English Reduced Forms by Second Language Learners and Its Effect on Input-Intake Process[1]

YASUKO ITO
University of Hawai'i

Corder (1967) first proposed the distinction between input and intake. Whether or not target language input becomes intake is determined by various factors, one of which is perceptual saliency. The language phenomenon called reduced forms, which is observed in informal spoken languages, decreases perceptual saliency, and is thus believed to influence the input-intake process in SLA. Henrichsen (1984) examined how the presence and absence of reduced forms influence ESL learners' input-intake process. The purpose of the study reported in this chapter was to further investigate the influence of reduced forms on the input-intake process, by modifying two aspects of Henrichsen's study: (a) sentence complexity in the test and (b) differences in reduced form type. The data were collected from 18 ESL learners and nine native speakers at the University of Hawai'i at Mānoa using a dictation test. Two two-way repeated measures ANOVAs indicated that the presence of reduced forms, students' language proficiency, and the type of reduced form (lexical vs. phonological forms) affected the learners' listening comprehension. The interaction effect was also found to be statistically significant between the type of reduced form and proficiency, but not between the presence of reduced forms and proficiency. This chapter provides further understanding, not only of whether or not reduced forms influence listening comprehension, but also of which types of reduced form can influence learners' listening comprehension more than others. Thus, this chapter should be of most interest to language teachers, researchers, testers, and materials developers who want to understand, teach, and develop materials or tests for teaching reduced forms.

Effect of Reduced Forms on ESL Learners' Input-Intake Process

The distinction between input and intake, first proposed by Corder (1967), has been widely discussed by SLA researchers. Whether or not target language input becomes

---

[1]   This chapter was presented as a paper at the Pacific Second Language Research Forum (PacSLRF) 2001 in Honolulu, Hawai'i. This is a revised version of a paper that appeared in *Second Language Studies* (Working Papers in the Department of Second Language Studies, University of Hawai'i at Mānoa; 2001, 20, 99–124).

Ito, Y. (2006) The comprehension of English reduced forms by second language learners and its effect on input-intake process. In J. D. Brown, & K. Kondo-Brown, (Eds.), *Perspectives on teaching connected speech to second language speakers* (pp. 67–81). Honolulu, HI: University of Hawai'i, National Foreign Language Resource Center.

intake is thought to be determined by various characteristics of the target language, one of which is perceptual saliency. The language phenomenon *reduced forms*,[2] which is observed in informal spoken languages, lessens perceptual saliency and is thus believed to influence the input-intake process in SLA (Larsen-Freeman, 1976).

Henrichsen (1984) investigated how the presence and absence of *sandhi-variation*, another term referring to reduced forms, influence ESL learners' comprehension of input. He found a statistically significant interaction between proficiency level and the learners' test scores for presence/absence of sandhi-variation. This supported his hypothesis that "there would not be significant differences between presence and absence scores for the native speakers but that there would be for the ESL learners" (p. 117).

Henrichsen's finding is significant and thus contributes to the understanding of the input-intake process in SLA; however, his study was limited in several ways. The study reported in this chapter further investigates the influence of reduced forms on the input-intake process, modifying two aspects of Henrichsen's study: (a) sentence complexity in the test and (b) differences in reduced form type. Reexamining the influence of reduced forms on listening comprehension, and consequently on the input-intake process, with these changes should provide further understanding, not only of whether reduced forms influence listening comprehension, but also of which type of reduced form influences learners' listening comprehension more than others.[3]

Input-Intake Process

As mentioned above, the input-intake distinction was first made by Corder (1967). In his report, Corder claims:

> The simple fact of presenting a certain linguistic form to a learner in the classroom does not necessarily qualify it for the status of input, for the reason that input is "what goes in" not what is *available* for going in, and we may reasonably suppose that it is the learner who controls this input, or more properly his intake.   (p. 165)

However, there has been some confusion about the definition of intake. Reviewing research on intake, Kumaravadivelu (1994) provides two views: intake as product and intake as process. In the product view, intake is a subset of input "*before* the input is processed by learners" (p. 35), whereas in the process view, intake is "what comes *after* psycholinguistic processing" (p. 36). In other words, in the product view, intake is input that is unprocessed language, while in the process view, it is a part of the learner's interlanguage system and is thus processed language. Recognizing flaws in both views, Kumaravadivelu redefines the concept of intake as follows: "an abstract entity of learner language that has been fully or partially processed by learners, and fully or partially assimilated into their developing system" (p. 37).

SLA researchers have postulated various factors that may influence the input-intake process, in other words, factors that determine which input becomes intake. For

---

[2]   The term *reduced forms* is taken from Brown and Hilferty (1986b, also see chapter 4). Other researchers use different terms to refer to this phenomenon: Celce-Murcia, Brinton, and Goodwin (1996) use the term *reduced speech forms*; *sandhi forms* is another term commonly used (Crystal, 1997).

[3]   Editors' note: For much more on the literature associated with connected speech and reduced forms, see chapters 1–3 of this book.

example, Kumaravadivelu (1994) suggests the following learner-internal and learner-external factors as *intake factors*:

Individual factors: Age and anxiety
Negotiation factors: Interaction and interpretation
Tactical factors: Learning strategies and communication strategies
Affective factors: Attitudes and motivation
Knowledge factors: Language knowledge and metalanguage knowledge
Environmental factors: Social context and educational context   (p. 39)

It is generally agreed that comprehensible input is necessary (but not sufficient) for SLA to occur. Comprehensibility of input is determined not only by some of the factors listed above, but also by linguistic factors such as language complexity, frequency, and perceptual saliency. Several researchers have suggested that "perceptual saliency makes certain features of the input more comprehensible and thus more liable to become intake" (Henrichsen, 1984, p. 106). Hakuta (1976) recognized perceptual saliency as one of the factors determining which forms are acquired. However, perceptual saliency is largely affected by the presence of reduced forms: When reduced forms are present, perceptual saliency lessens, thereby chances of the input becoming intake decrease (Larsen-Freeman, 1976).

A claim has been made that attention to input is necessary for input to become intake (Schmidt, 1990; Tomlin & Villa, 1994). Schmidt suggests various factors that influence noticeability. These include expectations, frequency of occurrence, perceptual salience, skill level, and task demand. Having L2 learners listen to normal and slow L2 speech, Kim (1995) examined speech elements that L2 learners attend to when they listen to L2 speech. The results revealed that phonetic prominence of elements contributed to the noticing of particular elements.

Listeners with greater knowledge of the language system can use the knowledge "to compensate for the loss or reduced saliency of portions of the input" created by reduced forms, but listeners with less knowledge cannot (Henrichsen, 1984, pp. 117–118). Thus, such listeners with less knowledge are forced to depend more on signals to comprehend input. A decrease in perceptual saliency, therefore, can affect those listeners who have less knowledge of the language system to a greater degree than those who have more knowledge.

The purpose of the study reported in this chapter is to reexamine the effect of reduced forms on input-intake process by modifying Henrichsen's study (1984). As briefly mentioned above, two aspects of Henrichsen's study are improved upon in the current study: (a) sentence complexity in the test and (b) differences in reduced form type. Henrichsen pointed out that sentences used in his test may have been so complex as to affect the scores of low-proficiency learners; therefore, simpler sentences were used in the present study. Secondly, Henrichsen did not analyze his results according to the type of reduced form. Reduced forms may be categorized into several different types, for example, reduction, assimilation, and contraction. Another approach is to classify them into two categories according to the derivation of the forms. In this study, those categories are labeled as phonological or lexical forms. Phonological forms are those that were derived as a result of the application of phonological rules: for example, *take them* → *take 'em*. Lexical forms, in contrast, are those that are not derived based on phonological rules, but tend to be memorized as one lexical item: for example, *will not* → *won't*; *do not* → *don't*. In the present study, the second method of categorization—phonological versus lexical forms—is considered.

Thus, in this study, the following three research questions were investigated:

1. Does the presence of reduced forms affect L2 learners' listening comprehension?
2. Does the effect of reduced forms on learners' listening comprehension vary according to their language proficiency?
3. Is the listening comprehension of L2 learners affected by the type of reduced form?

In his study, Henrichsen (1984) hypothesized that there would be no significant difference between native speakers' listening comprehension scores for the presence and absence of reduced forms whereas learners would score significantly differently, scoring higher in the absence of reduced forms than in the presence of reduced forms. His results confirmed this hypothesis; therefore, in this study, it was also hypothesized as follows:

Hypothesis 1. The presence of reduced forms will affect L2 learners' listening comprehension: Learners will score higher in the absence of reduced forms than in the presence of reduced forms, while native speakers will score similarly in both conditions.

One finding in Henrichsen's study contradicted his hypothesis, in that the difference between the scores for the lower proficiency learners for the presence and absence conditions was smaller than that for the higher proficiency learners, despite the lower proficiency learners' more limited knowledge of the language system. However, Henrichsen explained that this contradiction was due to the difficulty in comprehending sentences even when reduced forms were "absent." Therefore, following Henrichsen's initial hypothesis, I hypothesized as follows:

Hypothesis 2. The effect of reduced forms on learners' listening comprehension will vary according to their language proficiency: The difference between the test scores for the absence of reduced forms and those for the presence of reduced forms will be larger for learners with lower proficiency than learners with higher proficiency.

Reduced forms that appear as lexical forms seem to be more salient to learners than those that appear as phonological forms because learners cannot derive the lexical forms through phonological rules and are thus required to store those reduced forms as lexical items. Therefore, the following was predicted.

Hypothesis 3. Learners' listening comprehension will be affected by the type of reduced form: Those more salient to learners—lexical forms—will be less difficult for them to comprehend than those less salient to learners—phonological forms.

Method

Participants

The participants in this study were 30 nonnative speakers enrolled in the ESL programs at the University of Hawai'i at Mānoa and 13 native speakers of English. Out of the 30 nonnative speakers, 5 were removed from the data because of extremely low proficiency levels compared to the other participants or due to technical problems that arose during the data collection. An additional 7 nonnative speakers were randomly omitted from the data in order to balance the number of participants in the two groups. Consequently, data from 18 nonnative speakers were analyzed in this study.[4] They were from two different levels of listening/speaking classes in an ESL program at the university: nine from the advanced listening/speaking classes (henceforth referred to as NNS-upper), and nine from the intermediate listening/speaking classes (henceforth referred to as NNS-lower). The students' placement into these two levels was based on their TOEFL scores upon their admission to the university, or their placement test scores given prior to, or at the beginning of, the semester. There were three males and six females in the NNS-upper group, and four males and five females in the NNS-lower group. The upper-level[5] learners' ages ranged from 19 to 32 with a mean of 24.13, and the lower-level learners ranged from 18 to 33 with a mean of 26.00. Their L1 backgrounds also varied, but all of them had Asian languages as their L1. The languages (with number of learners for each language in parentheses) were as follows: Japanese (8), Korean (4), Chinese (3), Vietnamese (2), and Thai (1). Their participation was voluntary.

All the native speakers, except one, were enrolled in a graduate program in the Department of Second Language Studies at the same university. The other native speaker was an instructor in an ESL program at the university. Four out of the 13 native speakers were randomly removed from the data to get the same sample size as each of the NNS groups. There were five males and four females in this native speaker group (henceforth referred to as the NS group). Their ages ranged from 25 to 44 with a mean of 31.78. All of them spoke American English as their L1.

Materials

A dictation test consisting of sentences with reduced forms was administered to measure listening comprehension following Henrichsen's method of measurement. To improve upon Henrichsen's methodology, 20 sentences with lower syntactic complexity were prepared, based on Azar (1996). All the grammatical rules and vocabulary contained in the sentences appeared in the grammar book for beginning level learners (see Appendix A for the list of sentences).

As for the other modification to Henrichsen's study, two different types of reduced forms were incorporated into the 20 sentences: 10 sentences used lexical forms and 10 used phonological forms. The lexical forms used in the sentences were as follows: *isn't, wasn't, weren't, don't,*[6] *doesn't, won't, hasn't,* and *haven't.* The phonological forms, on the other hand, were as follows: *he's* (derived from *he is*), *she's* (derived from *she is*), *they're, I've, he's* (derived from *he has*), *she's* (derived from *she has*), and *they've.* Such phrases as I *think that* and I *know that* were added to sentences with phonological reduced forms in order to prevent the target reduced forms from appearing at the beginning of the sentences. This was done to ensure that participants would not miss words merely because they were not ready for listening.

---

[4]   Editors' note: Because of the small sample size of 18, readers are advised to interpret the results cautiously.
[5]   One participant from the NNS-upper group did not report her age and therefore her age was not included in the calculation of the age for the group.
[6]   Among the lexical forms listed here, *don't* and *won't* are purely lexical whereas the others— *isn't, wasn't, weren't, doesn't, hasn't,* and *haven't*—are rather lexical. When *do* and *not* are contracted, the pronunciation of each individual word completely changes: /du nɑt/ becomes /dount/. Similarly, the pronunciation of *will* and *not* changes when they are contracted: /wɪl nɑt/ becomes /wount/. In contrast, pronunciation of rather lexical reduced forms partly changes: for example, /ɪz nɑt/ becomes /ɪznt/, keeping the pronunciation of /ɪz/.

Using these 20 sentences, two versions of a dictation test (Version A and Version B) were prepared, both of which contained the same 20 sentences, but in different orders. Out of the 20 sentences in each version, 10 sentences were read with reduced forms (presence of reduced forms), while the other 10 sentences were read without reduced forms (absence of reduced forms). Those sentences that were read with reduced forms in one version were read without reduced forms in the other. Both the test instructions and sentences were read by a female native speaker of American English and tape-recorded in advance (see Appendix B for the taped instructions).

To calculate the dictation test scores, only the target reduced forms, that is, the lexical and phonological forms listed above, were considered. The score given to each participant was a total score for both versions. Four types of scores were calculated for each individual: an absence score when reduced forms were absent, a presence score when reduced forms were present, a phonological score when phonological reduced forms were involved, and a lexical score when lexical reduced forms were involved.

The validity of the tests was demonstrated by the baseline data of NSs' test scores. Their absence mean score was 39.89 out of a maximum of 40, with a standard deviation of 0.33; the presence mean score was also 39.89 with the same standard deviation; the phonological mean score was 19.89 out of a maximum of 20, with a standard deviation of 0.33; and the lexical mean score was 20 with a standard deviation of zero.

The reliability of the tests was calculated for the NNSs using Cronbach alpha. The value of Cronbach alpha was .78 for both test versions combined.[7]

Procedure

Before the test administration, participants were asked to read and sign a consent form, which also asked them to provide background information. After completion of the consent form, they took the first dictation test, either Version A or B. In the dictation test, the participants first read the instructions written on the answer sheet then listened to the taped instructions. After that, they listened to the recorded sentences and wrote down what they heard (see Appendix C for the answer sheet). Each sentence was played only once, and 15 seconds were given between sentences to allow participants to write down the sentence they had just heard. Those who took Version A first, took Version B second, and vice versa, so that the order of test administration would be counterbalanced. In between the two dictation tests, a crossword puzzle was given to the participants as a distracter. The whole process took approximately 30 minutes. The taped instructions and answer sheets were taken directly from Henrichsen's study with a few modifications.

Analyses

The dependent variable in this study was the total score on the two dictation tests. The independent variables were the presence of reduced forms with two levels (absence or presence), type of reduced form with two levels (lexical or phonological), and students' language proficiency with two levels (NNS-upper and NNS-lower). The NS data were used as baseline data and were not included in the statistical analyses.

---

[7]   Editors' note: For other ideas of ways to test or assess reduced forms, see chapter 14 of this volume.

The overall alpha level of this study was set at .05. To investigate the effect of presence of reduced forms and proficiency level on test scores for research questions 1 and 2, a two-way repeated-measures ANOVA, using a 2 x 2 design, was applied with the alpha level set at .025. Similarly, in order to investigate the effect of reduced form type and proficiency level on test scores for research question 3, a two-way repeated-measures ANOVA, using a 2 x 2 design, was applied with an alpha level of .025. The alpha level was set at .025 based on the Bonferroni adjustment. Although Henrichsen (1984) also used ANOVA, he did not use a repeated-measures design, though he could have done so in his data analysis. Therefore, the statistical analysis can be regarded as another aspect that was improved upon in this study.

The assumptions for these ANOVAs were also considered. As the values of skewedness and kurtosis given in Tables 1 and 2 show, the assumption of normal distribution was not met. However, since ANOVA is known to be robust to violations of this assumption, this violation was not considered a serious problem (Kirk, 1968; Shavelson, 1996). The assumption of equal variances, on the other hand, was met as revealed by a non-significant result in the Levene's Test of Equality of Error Variances. The assumption of independence for the between-subjects variable was also met because each participant belonged to only one of the proficiency groups.

Table 1. Descriptive statistics for the dictation test scores displayed separately for the absence and presence of reduced forms

	absence		presence	
	NNS-upper	NNS-lower	NNS-upper	NNS-lower
n	9	9	9	9
M	35.89	35.22	34.78	29.00
SD	2.37	3.23	3.46	1.73
skewedness	0.02	1.12	−1.42	−0.19
SES	0.72	0.72	0.72	0.72
kurtosis	0.08	1.66	3.13	−2.07
SEK	1.40	1.40	1.40	1.40

note: maximum score=40

Table 2. Descriptive statistics for the dictation test scores displayed separately for types of forms within presence of reduced forms

	phonological		lexical	
	NNS-upper	NNS-lower	NNS-upper	NNS-lower
n	9	9	9	9
M	15.67	10.33	19.11	18.67
SD	3.28	1.94	0.78	1.12
skewedness	−1.62	−0.21	−0.22	−0.54
SES	0.72	0.72	0.72	0.72
kurtosis	4.33	−1.61	−1.04	−0.80
SEK	1.40	1.40	1.40	1.40

note: maximum score=20

In addition to ANOVA, correlational analyses were also conducted using the Pearson product-moment coefficients for all possible pairings of absence scores, presence scores, lexical scores, phonological scores, and learners' proficiency.

Results

The results are given here for each of the original hypotheses. The first hypothesis in this study was that the presence of reduced forms would affect L2 learners' listening comprehension. Following Henrichsen's (1984) hypothesis, it was hypothesized that learners would score higher in the absence of reduced forms condition than in the presence of reduced forms, while native speakers would score similarly in both conditions. Table 1 shows the descriptive statistics for the absence and presence scores. According to the ANOVA results shown in Table 3, a statistically significant effect was found for presence of reduced forms on NNSs' dictation test scores. As mentioned earlier, NSs' absence and presence mean scores were the same, that is, 39.89. Figure 1 shows the same NNSs' result graphically. Based on these results, the first hypothesis that the NNSs' absence score would be higher than their presence score, while NSs' would not differ, was confirmed.

Table 3.   ANOVA on test scores for proficiency level and absence/presence of reduced forms

source	SS	df	MS	F	$\eta 2$	power
between subjects						
proficiency	200.69	1	200.69	19.73*	.55	.97
error	162.78	16	10.17			
within subjects						
reduced forms	42.25	1	42.25	7.93*	.33	.64
reduced forms x proficiency	10.03	1	10.03	1.88	.11	.17
error	85.22	16	5.33			

note: $p < .025$

The second hypothesis was that learners' language proficiency would influence the effect of reduced forms on their listening comprehension. Table 3 shows that there was a statistically significant main effect for proficiency level on their test scores. A *t-test* comparing presence scores between NNS-upper and NNS-lower revealed that their presence scores were significantly different ($t(16)=4.48$, $p=.000$). However, the interaction effect between the presence of reduced forms and the proficiency level was not statistically significant. Similarly, a *t* test comparing the NNS-upper's and NNS-lower's mean difference between the presence and the absence scores did not show a statistically significant result ($t(16)=-1.37$, $p=.189$). Therefore, this result did not confirm the second hypothesis, which examined the interaction effect.

The third hypothesis was that the type of reduced form would affect learners' listening comprehension. In the present study, lexical and phonological forms were examined, and it was hypothesized that learners would have less difficulty in listening to lexical forms than phonological forms. Table 2 and Figure 2 show the learners' performance on each type of reduced form. According to Table 4, which shows the ANOVA results for the effect of reduced form type and proficiency level on test scores, the learners' performance on the dictation test was significantly affected by the

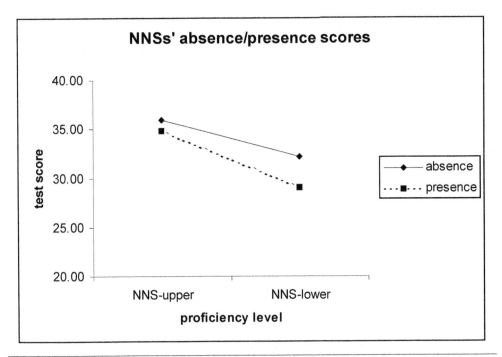

Figure 1.   Dictation test scores for the absence and presence of reduced forms.

type of reduced forms. While native speakers scored the same on both types as mentioned earlier, nonnative speakers scored lower on phonological forms than on lexical forms. Furthermore, the interaction effect between the type of reduced form and proficiency was also found to be statistically significant. This interaction effect was further investigated using t tests comparing phonological and lexical scores within each proficiency group with an alpha level of .0125 for the Bonferroni adjustment.[8] The effect of the type of reduced form was statistically significant for NNS-lower group ($t(8)=9.45$, $p=.000$); however, it was not statistically significant for NNS-upper group ($t(8)=3.15$, $p=.014$).

Table 4.   ANOVA on test scores for proficiency level and phonological/lexical forms

source	SS	df	MS	F	$\eta2$	power
between subjects						
proficiency	75.11	1	75.11	20.10*	.56	.97
error	59.78	16	3.74			
within subjects						
types of forms	312.11	1	312.11	70.23*	.81	1.00
types of forms x proficiency	53.78	1	53.78	12.10*	.43	.83
error	71.11	16	4.44			

note: $p<.025$

---

[8]   Editors' note: When interpreting the results here, readers should keep in mind that the Bonferroni adjustment is only an approximate correction that helps to account for the problem of multiple comparisons; it is not exact.

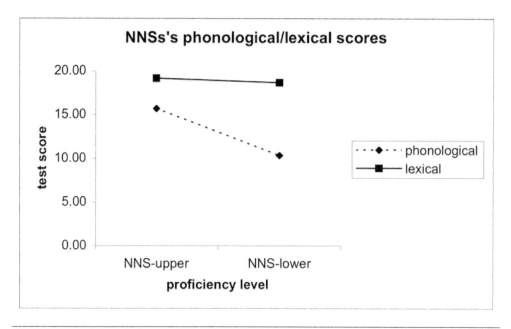

Figure 2.   Dictation test scores for lexical and phonological forms.

Results of the correlational analyses are summarized in Tables 5, 6, and 7. All the tables show that the presence score and the phonological score are highly correlated across the two proficiency levels of NNSs. Based on the coefficients of determination (i.e., the squared correlation coefficients), which can be interpreted as the proportion (or percent) of variance shared by two variables, 94.09%, 67.24%, and 94.09% of the presence score can be accounted for by knowing the phonological score within the NNS-upper group, the NNS-lower group, and the group of both NNS-upper and NNS-lower combined, respectively.

Table 5.   Correlations between each pair of test scores of NNS-upper participants

	1	2	3	4
absence	—	.55	.28	.51
presence		—	.33	.97
lexical (presence)			—	.11
phonological (presence)				—

note: $n=9$, $p<.01$

Table 6.   Correlations between each pair of test scores of NNS-lower participants

	1	2	3	4
absence	—	.07	–.19	.17
presence		—	.13	.82
lexical (presence)			—	–.46
phonological (presence)				—

note: $n=9$, $p<.01$

Table 7. Correlations between each pair of test scores of NNS participants and their proficiency level

	1	2	3	4	5
proficiency	—	−.57	−.75	−.24	−.72
absence		—	.59	.11	.60
presence			—	.32	.97
lexical (presence)				—	.08
phonological (presence)					—

note: *n*=18, *p*<.01

Discussion

The results can be summarized as follows: (a) While NSs scored identically on both conditions, NNSs scored statistically significantly higher in the absence of reduced forms than in their presence; (b) the effect of reduced forms on learners' listening comprehension did not vary according to their proficiency level; and (c) while NSs' scores were the same on both reduced form types, NNSs scored lower on phonological than lexical forms. Accordingly, the presence of reduced forms and the type of reduced form affected the learners' listening comprehension as measured by the dictation test. Likewise, the main effect of learners' proficiency level on their listening comprehension, regardless of the presence of reduced forms, was found to be statistically significant. The interaction effect was also found to be statistically significant between types and proficiency level, but not between the presence of reduced forms and proficiency level. The general trend towards a language proficiency effect on listening comprehension, as shown by the main effect of learners' proficiency as well as the result of a *t* test comparing the presence score between the two proficiency levels, is similar to what was observed in Henrichsen's study (1984). Thus, listeners with a greater knowledge of the language system seem to be able to compensate for reduced saliency.

The results showing differential performance on two types of reduced forms should be examined further. Although learners scored lower on phonological than lexical forms, the reasons for this difference in performance are unclear, that is, the type of reduced form might have affected listening comprehension as predicted here, but the inherent difference in syntactic complexity between the two types of reduced forms may also have affected their performance. As explained earlier, the syntactic structures used in the sentences in this study all appeared in a grammar book for beginning level learners. Moreover, all the reduced forms chosen as targets in this study share the same characteristic: They are contracted forms. However, even within the same reduced form type, there is a difference in syntactic complexity. Having reduced forms with the same syntactic complexity for both lexical and phonological forms would have been ideal. Although this was attempted at the stage of selecting target reduced forms, it could not be achieved. Other lexical forms might exist, but the lexical forms chosen for this study were negative contractions. In contrast, the phonological forms used in this study included the present tense of copula and present perfect forms.

Several limitations in this study should also be noted. First, a larger sample size might have helped in meeting the assumption of normal distribution as well as in achieving greater power in the statistical analysis. Second, learner characteristics should also be considered. Exposure to natural English with reduced forms is important, but participants in Henrichsen's study were experiencing a lack of exposure to "normal" input because of their learning environment. Although I assume that learners in the present study have more exposure to English spoken by native speakers than those in Henrichsen's study, the participants in this study may still have had less exposure to native speaker English than similar learners on the mainland of the United States. Third, some gains were observed in scores from the first administration of the test to the second. Although the participants did a crossword puzzle between the two administrations, the time spent on the puzzle and/or its complexity may not have been sufficient to allow participants to forget what they had written down during the first administration.

Moreover, whether a dictation test is appropriate for measuring listening comprehension is questionable. A dictation test can easily measure whether participants understood reduced forms correctly. However, it may not measure their listening comprehension ability accurately. Another limitation is sentence length. Adding phrases I *think that* and I *know that* resulted in longer sentences, and thus the length of sentence varied across the two types of reduced forms. Sentences with phonological forms turned out to be longer than those with lexical forms. This might have affected learners' performance on the dictation test. Only the target reduced forms were scored to obtain scores, but the learners were expected to write down a whole sentence. Thus, longer sentences might have produced a heavier memory load, which could potentially have affected participants' performance on those long sentences. With these limitations taken into consideration, further investigation of the effect of reduced forms on listening comprehension is desirable.

Conclusions and Implications

The results obtained in the present study support Henrichsen's claim that reduced forms affect the input-intake process. In an attempt to acquire a second language, learners may experience more difficulty in comprehending the input if it contains more reduced forms, with the result that less input becomes intake.[9] Henrichsen suggested the necessity for further input in a different mode, for instance, written English. Foreigner talk, in which input is modified to facilitate learners' understanding, is another mode of input he suggests. With the findings in my study, as well as in Henrichsen's study, the effectiveness of using authentic materials in second language classrooms becomes questionable. Since authentic listening materials (e.g., TV broadcasts) are produced for native speakers, the input in such materials contains a large number of reduced forms. Thus learners may need extra input to help in order for the authentic input to become intake. The extra input could be written input, for example (Henrichsen, 1984).

Improving upon several aspects of Henrichsen's study, I attempted to examine not only whether or not reduced forms influence listening comprehension, but also what types of reduced form influence learners' listening comprehension more than others. The findings of this study showed that learners comprehended lexical reduced forms better than phonological reduced forms. As mentioned earlier, this performance difference could be attributed to the difference in syntactic complexity between the two types of reduced forms. However, this finding suggests that learners' listening

---

[9]   Editors' note: Indeed, the results of this study and the input-intake interpretation may provide an explanation for the results reported in chapters 4 and 5.

comprehension is influenced by different types of reduced forms, and thus requires further investigation.

Acknowledgements

I would like to thank Dr. Michael Long for his guidance throughout the study and Dr. J. D. Brown for his help with statistical analyses. I am also grateful to Dr. Patricia Donegan for her advice on the phonological aspects in this chapter. Lastly, I would like to express my appreciation to Linda Woo who helped me in the data collection, Nicola J. D. Bartlett, Martyn Clark, Steve Jacques, and Ken Urano who proofread earlier drafts and gave me insightful comments, and all those who sincerely agreed to participate in this study.

Appendix A: Sentences with lexical and phonological reduced forms

Sentences with lexical reduced forms

1. He *does not* work very hard at home.
2. We *will not* go out to dinner with our friends.
3. They *do not* have dictionaries on their desks.
4. She *has not* taught biology at the school.
5. I *have not* spoken to my teacher.
6. She *is not* writing a letter to her parents.
7. They *were not* attending the conference at the school.
8. I *was not* working in the office.
9. We *do not* eat breakfast in the cafeteria.
10. I *will not* call my sister in New York.

Sentences with phonological reduced forms

1. I think that I *have* never lived in a small town.
2. I know that *he has* never worked at an automobile factory.
3. I think that *she has* been a good friend of mine.
4. I think that *they have* stayed at a hotel in this city.
5. I know that *they have* been to the zoo in Hawai'i.
6. I think that *he is* working at a wonderful restaurant.
7. I think that *she is* teaching English class at the school.
8. I think that *he is* playing soccer with his friends.
9. I know that *they are* having a secret dinner at a Hawaiian restaurant.
10. I think that *they are* buying tickets at the theater.

Appendix B: Taped instructions for test

In a moment you will hear 20 sentences. After you hear each sentence, write it down in the appropriate space on your paper. Use the full form of each word even though some of the words you hear may be contracted or blended together. For example, if you hear the sentence "What'd ja do yesterday?" you should write down "What—did—you do yesterday?" even though the first few words were contracted and reduced to "What'dja."

You should rely on your knowledge of English sentence structure as well as on the sounds you hear. Think, and write quickly. The pauses between sentences will not be too long. If you do not have time to write the full sentence or you cannot remember all of it, write as much as you can—even if it is only the first few words. Each sentence will be spoken only once and none of the sentences will be repeated.

If you have any questions about what you are supposed to do, raise your hand and ask us.

Appendix C: Answer sheet

1   2   A   B

name _____ date _____

nationality _____ native language(s) _____

Instructions

When the tape begins, you will hear 20 sentences. There will be a short pause after each sentence. During the pause, write the sentence you hear on the line provided on the next page.

When you write, use full (normal) words only. Do *not* use contractions even though some of the words you hear may be contracted or blended together.

All the spoken sentences are grammatically correct, so your written sentences should also be grammatically correct.

If you do not have time to write the full sentence or you cannot remember all of it, write as much as you can—even if it is only the first few words.

Think and do your best. Each sentence will be spoken only once and none of the sentences will be repeated.

If you have any questions about what you are supposed to do, raise your hand and ask the teacher now.

example: _*What did you do yesterday?*_____

1. _____
2. _____
3. _____
4. _____
5. _____
6. _____
7. _____
8. _____
9. _____
10. _____
11. _____
12. _____
13. _____
14. _____
15. _____
16. _____
17. _____
18. _____
19. _____
20. _____

How should connected speech

be taught in English?

NFLRC
monographs

Don'cha Know?
A Survey of ESL Teachers' Perspectives
on Reduced Forms Instruction[1]

MOANA ROGERSON
University of Hawai'i

The perceptual saliency of spoken English is often reduced creating variation in the way English is spoken in very formal contexts from more naturally occurring English. Reduced forms refer to basic elements of this naturally occurring spoken English, integral and pervasive elements of spoken English that are seriously neglected in both research and materials development. Reduced forms occur in all registers and styles of speech with pragmatic and syntactic constraints inherent in their use. The study reported in this chapter provides an overview of the current literature and a survey of ESL teachers' perspectives on reduced forms instruction. The chapter also calls for more research into the role of reduced forms and the development of more authentic teaching materials that support the teacher in a systematic and effective approach to reduced forms instruction. Thus, this chapter will probably be of most interest to language teachers, researchers, testers and materials developers who want to understand, teach, and develop materials or tests for teaching reduced forms.

Introduction

Language teaching has developed from a time when grammar translation and drills were the norm to a more communicative process, with an emphasis on meaningful and authentic materials considered the most effective way of teaching. Despite this new emphasis on authenticity and communication, language learners still face difficult challenges when it comes to understanding natural native speaker conversations.

It's a common and frustrating experience that many second language learners can relate to. Students are taught grammar and vocabulary, and practice conversations and dialogues to learn a new language. Language teachers speak clearly and provide listening materials that are full of clearly pronounced and articulated speech. Language learners develop their listening and speaking skills based on this adapted English speaking style. Then they arrive at the host country and are shocked and

---

[1] An earlier version of this chapter appeared in the working papers of the Department of Second Language Studies at the University of Hawai'i as Rosa, M. (2002). Don'cha know? A survey of ESL teachers' perspectives on reduced forms instruction. *Second Language Studies, 21*, 49–78.

Rogerson, M. (2006) Don'cha Know? A survey of ESL teachers' perspectiveson reduced forms instruction. In J. D. Brown, & K. Kondo-Brown, (Eds.), *Perspectives on teaching connected speech to second language speakers* (pp. 85–97). Honolulu, HI: University of Hawai'i, National Foreign Language Resource Center.

dismayed to find that native speakers don't actually speak in the way the language is written or in the ways their teachers and listening materials represent the language. The language outside of the classroom seems unfamiliar and fast, and the students are unable to decipher word boundaries or recognize words or phrases. Students who do not receive instruction or exposure to this type of *real*, naturally occurring language, are "going to have a very rude awakening when he [*sic*] tries to understand native speech in natural communicative situations" (Ur, 1987, p. 10).

All languages have this type of variation from written to spoken texts: "It results from a simple *law of economy*, whereby the organs of speech, instead of taking a new position for each sound, tend to draw sounds together with the purpose of saving time and energy" (Clarey & Dixson, 1963, p. 12). With English, this process of assimilation is combined with contractions, elision, and reduction to produce the connected speech commonly referred to as "reduced forms" (Brown & Hilferty, 1989). Naturally occurring English conversation, whether formal or informal, fast or slow, is full of these reduced forms. This creates a serious challenge for English as a second language (ESL) students who have little or no exposure to reduced forms.

Studies on this widely occurring aspect of English are very limited, yet those that are available are enlightening in that they reveal the complexity of spoken English as well as the dearth of research and materials available to teachers. Based on a broad range of theories on how reduced forms should be taught, various types of instruction have been suggested. Although the focus of instruction may vary due to proficiency level, all of the exercises and instructional approaches that have been suggested can be adapted for any proficiency level in order to, at the very least, raise learners' attention to the presence of reduced forms in spoken English. Openly discussing and identifying common reduced forms and increasing students' exposure to reduced forms with authentic listening materials is a common suggestion for introducing reduced forms and awareness-raising practices (Brown & Hilferty, 1989; Guillot, 1999; Koster, 1987; Rost, 1991; Snow & Perkins, 1979). Included in these awareness-raising activities are exercises that have students writing in their journals about their personal listening experiences with reduced forms and practicing self-monitoring (Avery & Ehrlich, 1992; Norris 1993, 1995; Rost, 1991). With an increased awareness of reduced forms, practice with reduced forms is valued over study of reduced forms, "letting foreign language students listen frequently to the spoken language with all the characteristics of connected speech is no doubt more important than familiarizing them with the theoretical aspects of, for instance, assimilation...practice is much more important than theory" (Koster, 1987, p. 143).

This focus on practice with authentic materials is supported by many other researchers and authors (e.g., Brown & Hilferty, 1989; Buck, 1995; Prator & Robinett, 1995; Rost, 1991). Some of the exercises suggested to promote practice include cloze tests and dictation (Avery & Ehrlich, 1992; Brown & Hilferty, 1989; Norris, 1993, 1995), analyzing spoken and written texts for stress and rhythm (Guillot, 1999; Norris 1993, 1995; Prator & Robinett, 1995), and read aloud exercises (Moh-Kim Tam, 1997; Prator & Robinett, 1995). Meaningful, purposeful, communicative task-based exercises to provide this practice must also be a factor incorporated into these activities (Brown, A., 1995; Buck, 1995; Moh-Kim Tam, 1997; Norris 1993, 1995; Snow & Perkins, 1979).

These exercises and suggestions can be very helpful for teachers, but only in a day-to-day way, when what would really benefit teachers and students would be a more thorough understanding of the relationship between listening and pronunciation and the rules and constraints (linguistically and pragmatically) of using reduced forms. This deeper, more systematic knowledge of reduced forms does not need to take away from meaningful and authentic practice with reduced forms. Rather, with a more systematic understanding of how reduced forms work, teachers will be better equipped to guide their students' practice and can promote the development of more authentic and effective teaching materials.

In reviewing the literature[2] on reduced forms, how they come about, and how they should be taught, the lack of relevant research becomes very evident. Obviously, more research is needed in all areas of reduced forms. Many have cited raising the awareness of learners as an integral factor in improving both learners' comprehension and pronunciation of reduced forms. I believe that teachers and researchers also need to raise their own awareness of the role of reduced forms in language learning. Future research should seek to clarify the ways in which reduced forms are used. The focus and approach of teaching reduced forms should also be further researched. It would be helpful to analyze the current treatment of reduced forms in available teaching materials as well as a general survey into teachers' attitudes and practices when it comes to reduced forms. It is only through more research and more awareness of the systematic and pervasive role of reduced forms in spoken English and in language learning that we will begin to answer some of these pertinent questions and be able to provide language students with a systematic framework and practice with which to learn.

In order to understand more clearly the current situation in the classroom with regard to reduced forms and English teaching, a survey of ESL teachers was conducted. The purpose of the survey was to investigate the perspectives of ESL instructors toward reduced forms and English teaching as well as to understand their familiarity with the role of reduced forms in spoken English. The three primary research questions were the following:

1. How familiar are ESL instructors with the role of reduced forms in spoken English?
2. What are ESL teachers' perspectives on the role of reduced forms in teaching listening comprehension?
3. What challenges do ESL instructors face with respect to reduced forms instruction?

Method

Participants

A total of 52 survey questionnaires were distributed to ESL instructors throughout the island of Oahu. This included nine surveys that were distributed directly to ESL teachers at the Hawai'i TESOL Conference held in February, 2003 in Honolulu, 16 surveys delivered to all the ESL teachers at the Hawai'i English Language Program (HELP) at the University of Hawai'i at Mānoa (UHM), 17 surveys delivered to all the ESL teachers at the English Language Institute (ELI) at UHM, and 10 surveys sent to ESL teachers at Brigham Young University Hawai'i (BYUH). All the surveys, except those that were done at the TESOL Conference, were delivered to the teachers' school mailboxes. Teachers were able to return the surveys to one volunteer

---

[2]   Editors' note: To avoid redundancies between chapters in this book and for reasons of overall book length, this literature review was shortened considerably. For more on the reduced forms literature, see chapters 1–3.

teacher at their school who collected them, or to the researcher's mailbox directly. Of these surveys, 13 out of 16 were returned completed from HELP, 15 out of 17 were returned completed from ELI, and 8 out of 10 were returned completed from BYUH. All nine of the surveys administered at the TESOL conference were completed and returned on the same day.[3]

Of the 45 respondents, ESL teaching experience ranged from half a year to 35 years. Thirty-four of the teachers were native speakers of English, and 11 of the teachers were non-native speakers of English, with first languages including Japanese, Korean, Chinese, and Portuguese. Thirty-seven of the teachers also spoke a second, and often third or fourth language, including Japanese, Korean, Chinese, Spanish, Portuguese, German, French, Russian, Hebrew, Tongan, Vietnamese, and Nepali. The teachers predominantly were involved in intensive English programs as well as English for academic purposes. Two of the teachers were teaching at the high school level, while the remaining 43 were teaching at the university or adult levels. Forty of the 45 teachers had experience teaching reduced forms, five had never taught reduced forms.

Materials

The survey used in this study was developed from an original pilot study involving 17 ESL/EFL teachers enrolled in the UHM Second Language Studies Department graduate program in ESL. Based on this pilot study, and after much feedback and multiple revisions, the final version of the survey was developed (see Appendix). The resulting survey is two pages long and includes 17 questions. Teachers reported that the survey took an average of about 5 minutes to complete.

The survey began with a short introduction, stating the purpose of the study and a very brief explanation of what exactly the phrase "reduced forms" refers to. There were also three questions directed towards the biographical data of the respondents, including how long they have taught ESL, what languages they speak, and the type of program with which they are involved. Fifteen of the 17 questions were closed-response items, offering either Yes or No options, Likert scales, or checklists in which teachers could check as many elements as were applicable. The items were first aimed at establishing the amount of knowledge and familiarity teachers have with the role of reduced forms in English, followed by items focused on their own experiences and perspectives with teaching reduced forms, and finally on the challenges they face in teaching reduced forms. Two open-ended questions finished out the survey by asking teachers what they would like to see in the future with regard to reduced forms and asking for any further comments the teachers might have.

Like most survey instruments, it should be noted that, despite the multiple revisions of the survey, some teachers found that a few of the closed-response items on the survey did not fully represent their opinions. The most common occurrence of this was in item eight, in which teachers were asked to identify how much time they typically devote to reduced forms instruction in any typical class. Six of the 40 teachers who had experience teaching reduced forms chose not to answer this as they noted it depended on a multitude of factors and they could not provide a generalization. Despite some of these difficulties with a closed-response format, for the most part, teachers were able to complete the survey successfully without too much (written) disapproval.

---

[3]   Editors' note: In interpreting the results of this study, readers should keep in mind that the sample was one of convenience, rather than a random or even stratified random sample.

Procedure

The survey was developed over a period of 4 months and distributed personally to the office mailboxes of all ESL teachers involved in the ELI and HELP. They were also distributed directly to the office mailboxes of ten ESL instructors at the BYUH campus. The surveys distributed at the TESOL Conference were completed on site. All of the TESOL conference surveys were completed and returned to the researcher the day of the conference. Of the teachers who received their surveys in their office mailboxes, teachers had the option of returning the survey directly to the researcher, dropping the survey off in the researcher's office mailbox, or dropping the survey off with a co-operating teacher involved in their personal ESL program. The teachers were primarily chosen to take part in this survey because of their current involvement in ESL instruction and their involvement in local ESL programs.

The return rate was quite high, with 87% of the total surveys distributed being returned completed. I believe there are two possible reasons for this high return rate. First, all of the teachers involved were active in ESL teacher training and development, as they were working in programs connected with university ESL programs or taking part in the local TESOL conference. Secondly, the format of the survey was clear and the items were brief.

The completed surveys were coded and the results tabulated. First the overall results were analyzed for general trends among all the teachers. This was followed by an analysis of the results when teachers' answers were organized by specific groups, for example, comparing the responses of teachers with fewer than 3 years teaching experience to those with three to 10 years of experience and those with over 10 years experience.

Results[4]

Of the 45 teachers surveyed, 47% (21 teachers) had taken courses on teaching listening comprehension; 20 of these teachers had received instruction on the role of reduced forms in teaching ESL listening comprehension. Only 20 of all 45 teachers had received any training in reduced forms instruction. Twenty-five of the teachers learned about reduced forms from ESL textbooks. Twenty-six of the teachers felt that they were *somewhat familiar* with the role of reduced forms in English, while 13 teachers felt they were *very familiar* with reduced forms in spoken English, and six chose *not very familiar* or *not at all familiar*.

Teachers' self-assessed familiarity with reduced forms

Those 13 teachers who chose *very familiar* in regard to the role of reduced forms in spoken English also had more training in teaching reduced forms, including taking courses on teaching ESL listening comprehension in which reduced forms instruction was covered, as well as other teacher training that covered reduced forms and information from ESL textbooks. Although over 90% of all the teachers were familiar with linking, deletions, and contractions, and over 80% were familiar with assimilation and the English vowel sound of schwa, these teachers who considered themselves *very familiar* consistently had higher than average familiarity with these listed aspects of reduced forms. The most significant difference was in the stress-timed

---

4   Editors' note: The results in this study are reported using only descriptive statistics. Readers should note that, without further statistical analyses like chi-square in this case, we have no way of knowing which of the differences in frequencies and percentages observed here may have occurred by chance alone and which probably did not.

aspect of English. These teachers were much more familiar with the stress-timed aspect of English, with 69% of these teachers marking this option, compared to 46% for those who chose *somewhat familiar* and none for those who chose *not at all familiar*.

Another aspect that differentiated these teachers was in item number three which asks teachers to best identify the role of reduced forms instruction. Option one described reduced forms as most often occurring in "fast spoken English." Option two described reduced forms as most often occurring in "casual, informal spoken English." Option three described reduced forms as occurring in "all types of spoken English." Fifty-eight percent of all teachers chose option three, considering reduced forms to be a part of all types of English. Sixty-nine percent of those who considered themselves *very familiar* with the role of reduced forms chose option three, compared to 58% of those that had marked they were *somewhat familiar*, and only 33% of those who had marked that they were *not very familiar* or *not at all familiar*.

Teachers' experience with reduced forms instruction

Forty of the 45 teachers had experience teaching reduced forms. Of these 40, 73% had addressed reduced forms in class when they have come up in context and 58% had explicitly taught reduced forms. Fifty-three percent of the teachers had addressed reduced forms with respect to listening comprehension, while 49% of the teachers had addressed reduced forms with respect to pronunciation.

The group of teachers who had explicitly taught reduced forms (58% of total teachers) had slightly more teaching experience on average, with similar amounts of teacher training dealing with teaching reduced forms. This group considered reduced forms to be *very important* in teaching ESL listening comprehension, with 58% choosing this option in response to the item "Do you consider reduced forms to be an important element to teach in ESL listening comprehension?" Those who had not taught reduced forms explicitly were more likely to consider reduced forms instruction to be *somewhat important* in teaching reduced forms instruction (63%). It is important to note that 42 of the 45 teachers considered reduced forms instruction *somewhat* to *very important*, with those who had experience explicitly teaching reduced forms more often choosing *very important*. Forty-three of the 45 total teachers considered it *very helpful* to *somewhat helpful* to teach reduced forms (19 and 24, respectively), again with those teachers with experience teaching reduced forms more often explicitly supporting this. It is also interesting to note that those teachers who had explicitly taught reduced forms report on average that their students seem more interested in the instruction compared to teachers who had not explicitly taught reduced forms.

Teachers' use of linguistic and pragmatic systems with reduced forms instruction

Twenty percent of the teachers often taught reduced forms as a system of linguistic rules and constraints; 48% often taught reduced forms as a system of pragmatic rules and constraints; and 75% often taught reduced forms within context, using common examples. Teaching reduced forms as a linguistic system of rules and constraints was the least common response, with 53% of the teachers choosing *never* to the statement "I teach reduced forms as a system of linguistic rules and constraints." Only 12% of the teachers chose *never* to the statement "I teach reduced forms as a system of pragmatic rules and constraints." Seven percent of the teachers chose *never* to the statement "I teach reduced forms with in context, using common examples."

The teachers who most often taught linguistic systems when teaching reduced forms were those teachers who considered themselves *very familiar* with the role of reduced forms, who most often considered reduced forms to occur in all types of spoken English, and were also most aware of the stress-timed concept of spoken English. The teachers who seldom taught reduced forms using linguistic systems, or never taught using linguistic systems, wanted to increase the role of reduced forms instruction in their classrooms. These teachers cited *not enough experience teaching* of reduced forms as one of the main challenges in their instruction. None of the teachers who used linguistic systems in their instruction cited this as a challenge to their instruction, rather most often citing *not enough time* (62.50%) as the main challenge of instruction. Another challenge cited in reduced forms instruction was *not enough material*. Fifty-seven percent of the teachers that *never* taught reduced forms using linguistic systems marked this option, 45% of those who *seldom* used linguistic systems in instruction marked this option, and only 25% of those who *often* used linguistic systems in the instruction of reduced forms marked this option.

Challenges and needs of teachers

Most teachers typically spend 10% or less of any typical class session on reduced forms instruction. Forty-two percent of the teachers cited *not enough material* and *not enough time* as the primary challenges they face in reduced forms instruction, as well as 40% of the teachers citing *not in the curriculum*. Forty-four percent of the teachers would like to see the role of reduced forms instruction increasing in their classroom, while 56% were satisfied with the amount of reduced forms instruction in their classrooms.

In response to the open ended item, "What would you like to see in the future with regard to reduced forms instruction?," 35 teachers responded. Fifty-four percent of those who responded called for more materials on reduced forms. Twenty percent of the teachers called for more instruction and materials available that address the pragmatic aspects of reduced forms. One respondent wrote, "Social attachment (meaning) in use of reduced forms is very difficult to explain/teach to students No correct pragmatic rules and explanation pragmatically" [sic]. Another respondent stated, "More emphasis on how the use of reduced forms varies. For example, understanding/comprehending reduced forms is important, but students who will use English as a lingua franca with other NNSs might become less comprehensible if they use too many reduced forms. They need to be aware of this." Fourteen percent of the respondents would like to see more teacher training with respect to reduced forms. Other answers ranged from a focus in all four skill areas to those who would like a focus on authentic materials for listening or speaking.

Discussion

Clear trends emerged from the survey, providing answers to the three research questions as well as suggesting areas for the development of pedagogical application and further research.

1. **How familiar are ESL instructors with the role of reduced forms in spoken English?**

ESL instructors consider themselves familiar with the role of reduced forms in spoken English, though teachers have little specific training in reduced forms instruction, with most information stemming from ESL texts. These texts rarely develop the systematic linguistic and pragmatic constraints of reduced forms, rather focusing solely on common examples. Those teachers that received more training in reduced forms instruction were also those who more often explicitly taught reduced forms, including the linguistic systems of reduced forms. A majority of the teachers were familiar with most of the elements involved with reduced forms except for the element of stress-timing in spoken language. This may explain why instructors tend to teach in context, with common examples, rather than through the system of linguistic rules and constraints.

Fifty-eight percent of the teachers identified reduced forms as occurring in all types of language, while 42% chose reduced forms as occurring in casual, informal spoken English. This 42% identifies with the role of reduced forms that is most often supported by current ESL textbooks, which typically supply common examples of reduced forms in casual, informal English conversation with little information about the systems in place that produce them. So while there was little direct training in reduced forms instruction, the majority of teachers felt familiar with the role of reduced forms in spoken English and had some experience teaching them. Possibly due to this lack of specific training, very little time is spent on reduced form instruction, and when it is taught, it is typically taught using common examples. This occurs despite the fact that most teachers (especially those who explicitly teach reduced forms) report their students seem *very* or *somewhat interested* in reduced forms.

In response to this trend, more materials must be developed both for teachers and students that go beyond supplying common examples of reduced forms. These materials should provide teachers, and consequently their students, with more information about the role of reduced forms in spoken English and the systems in place that produce and affect them.[5]

2. What are ESL teachers' perspectives on the role of reduced forms in teaching listening comprehension?

Almost all of the teachers considered reduced forms to be an important and helpful aspect of a learner's listening comprehension, yet most teachers typically spend 10% or less of any typical class session on reduced forms instruction. Moreover, more than half of teachers believed reduced forms occur in all types of spoken English, which would seem to further strengthen its important and beneficial role in ESL instruction, yet these perspectives do not change the small amount of instruction learners receive on reduced forms in spoken English.

Although the majority of teachers felt reduced forms occur in all types of spoken English, when reduced forms were taught, most of the teachers covered only the common examples found in context, rather than explicitly teaching reduced forms within their linguistic and pragmatic systems. The 18 teachers who had taught reduced forms explicitly were those who had the most training, felt the most familiar with reduced forms, recognized the stress-timed element of English more, and more often taught the linguistic systems of reduced forms. These teachers were also those who on average rated their students interest in reduced forms instruction the highest.

Almost all of the 45 teachers reported that the overwhelming majority of their students seemed *somewhat* to *very interested* in reduced forms instruction. The students' apparently high level of interest in this topic not only shows the teacher how helpful and important reduced forms instruction is, but also reaffirms to the

---

[5]   Editors' note: See chapter 3, for a review of existing materials, and chapter 8 for example materials and ideas developing reduced forms materials, as well as chapter 14 for ideas on developing quizzes and tests for reduced forms.

teacher that reduced forms are indeed a valid and integral aspect of spoken English. One teacher commented that the teacher's perception of their students' interest was "not relevant." I argue that students' interest is directly related to student motivation and needs. The students are interested in those aspects of English that affect them (e.g., reduced forms, which occur throughout all spoken English). Furthermore, the attitude of the students towards this aspect of spoken English must affect the teacher's own perspectives on reduced forms instruction.

The final item on the survey was an open response item, asking teachers for any insights or opinions that were not covered by the survey that they felt were important. Three of the comments exemplify the range of perspectives on reduced forms instruction. One teacher, who had not had specific training in reduced forms, but did consider reduced forms to be in all types of spoken English, and had taught reduced forms in context, wrote,

> In most (but certainly not all) cases, teaching formal usage and yes, even *formal* [italics added] pronunciation serves students best. Reduced forms are a real part of the language, but they can be learned without heavy emphasis.

Another teacher, who felt that reduced forms most often occur in casual, informal English, and addressed reduced forms only in context, wrote,

> So much depend on the purpose of their English classes. If the purpose is just *conversational* [italics added] English, it is much more important than *academic, formal* [italics added] English, where it is less important to stress.

The final example comes from a teacher who had specific training in teaching reduced forms in each training context given in the survey. This teacher also identified reduced forms as occurring in all types of spoken English, and wrote,

> I have had students (who never were exposed to R.F.) [sic] tell me that for the first time, they felt they were truly learning, plus, the confidence factor is relevant. I'd see student faces after I talked with other native speakers, their confidence could be shattered. We didn't use textbook English.

All of these teachers spoke from personal experience. Yet, it is interesting that the first two examples, which de-emphasize the role of reduced forms instruction, use the terms *formal* and *conversational* (or rather, "*just*" *conversational*) and *academic*, while the third teacher described two native speakers (NS) talking in front of a non-native speaker (NNS). It seems as though the first two, while possibly raising valid points about the value of needs analysis, seem to ignore the fact that in formal and academic, as well as conversational, language two NSs will not speak in "textbook English," but rather will use reduced forms, or connected speech. The more the NNS students are aware of these phenomena, the more they will be able to successfully comprehend and communicate in all areas of communication, including academic and formal settings.

Along with the development of more materials for teachers and students, more teacher training with respect to reduced forms instruction is necessary in order to more closely tie teachers' mostly positive perspectives on reduced forms instruction with their actual in-class experiences.

3. **What challenges do ESL teachers face with respect to reduced forms instruction?**

    The question arises, then, if teachers feel, in general, that reduced forms instruction is important and helpful, and that reduced forms occur in all types of spoken English, and that their students seemed to be *very* to *somewhat interested* in reduced forms, why is there such a limited focus on reduced forms in the classroom? Forty-two percent of the teachers cited *not enough material* and *not enough time* as the primary challenges they face in reduced forms instruction, and 40% of the teachers cited *not in the curriculum*. The primary concern of the five teachers who had not taught reduced forms at all was *not enough available material*.

    In the open-ended responses, 35 teachers provided answers to the item, "What would you like to see in the future with regard to reduced forms instruction?" Nineteen of the 35 teachers called for more material to be developed. Seven specifically mentioned materials for pragmatics and five called for teacher training. While lack of time is a challenge for teachers, lack of material is what may in fact keep teachers from more instruction. Teachers themselves would like more material that promotes reduced forms instruction beyond what is now available.

Conclusions

As with any research, there are limitations to this study. To begin with, the survey instrument itself could have been improved to provide more options on the Likert scales. Also some questions were possibly not clear enough, for example, item eight which asked how much time in general a teacher may spend on reduced forms. Sixteen of the 45 teachers felt uncomfortable with the available choices and wrote in an alternative answer, commented on the answer they chose, or skipped this item all together.

The survey also did not delve into specifics of instruction that may have been of interest for materials development or future research. For example, the survey failed to ask any questions related to different proficiency levels and instruction. The survey also did not differentiate enough between reduced forms instruction with respect to listening comprehension and pronunciation. Despite these limitations, the survey did provide an insightful summary of ESL instructors' knowledge, perspectives, and challenges when teaching (or not teaching, as more often is the case) reduced forms in spoken English.

This chapter has attempted to provide an overview of the current literature on reduced forms and an analysis of ESL teachers' opinions and perspectives on teaching reduced forms. It has become clear throughout this process that reduced forms are an integral and pervasive aspect of spoken English that is seriously neglected in both research and materials development. Without further research into the role and systematic nature of reduced forms in English, and the effects of teaching reduced forms, little will change. Materials must also be developed that answer the needs of the teachers.[6] Furthermore, these materials must be developed in a systematic way, which not only introduces common examples, but the linguistic and pragmatic systems that go along with these forms. Along with these materials, teachers should have the opportunity for teacher training in the role of reduced forms in spoken English, and the effects of reduced forms instruction. Hopefully, with the importance of authentic materials becoming more and more the fashion of English listening and speaking materials, the importance and significance of reduced forms as a major aspect of communication will increase in the awareness of researchers, teachers, materials developers, and students.

---

[6] Editors' note: See chapter 8 for a number of ideas for reduced forms materials.

Appendix

UH Mānoa MA survey
Spring 2003
All information will remain confidential and anonymous.

The purpose of this survey is to investigate the opinions, perspectives, and attitudes of ESL instructors towards the teaching of reduced forms. Reduced forms refer to a common aspect of spoken English. Another name for reduced forms could be "connected speech." (For example, some common reduced forms are "*gonna*" for "going to" or "*couldja*" for "could you.")

How long have you taught ESL? _____

first language? _____ other languages? _____

type of program _____

1. Have you taken courses on teaching ESL listening comprehension?__ yes __ no

    If so, were teaching reduced forms covered in these courses?   __ yes __ no

    Were reduced forms covered in any of your teacher training?   __ yes __ no

    Did you learn about reduced forms from ESL textbooks?   __ yes __ no

2. How well do you understand the role of reduced forms in spoken English?
    _____ very well _____ somewhat familiar _____ not very familiar _____ not at all

3. Which description *best* reflects your view of the use of reduced forms? (Please check one.)
    _____ Reduced forms occur most often in fast spoken English.
    _____ Reduced forms occur most often in casual, informal spoken English.
    _____ Reduced forms occur in all types of spoken English.

4. Please check all the following aspects of reduced forms with which you are familiar:
    _____ assimilation of sounds
    _____ linking of sounds
    _____ deletions of sounds
    _____ contractions
    _____ stress-timed languages
    _____ identifying content words and structure words
    _____ the English schwa sound
    _____ other _____
    _____
    _____

5. Do you consider reduced forms to be an important element to teach in ESL listening comprehension?
    _____ very _____ somewhat _____ not very _____ not at all

6. How helpful do you feel reduced forms instruction might be for your students' listening comprehension?
    _____ very _____ somewhat _____ not very _____ not at all

7. Have you taught reduced forms in your classes? (Please check all that apply.)
    _____ I have explicitly taught reduced forms in my class.

____ I have addressed reduced forms in my class when they have come up in context.

____ I have addressed reduced forms with respect to student's pronunciation.

____ I have addressed reduced forms with respect to student's listening comprehension.

____ I have never taught reduced forms in my classes.

____ other _____

_____

_____

If you have never taught reduced forms, please skip to question 14.

8. In any given class session (for example one 50-minute class period), how much time do you typically devote to reduced forms instruction?

____ 100% ____ 80% ____ 60% ____ 40% ____ 20% ____ 10% ____ 0%

9. With respect to reduced forms instruction, what percentage of your students seem to be:

____% very interested

____% somewhat interested

____% not very interested

____% not interested at all

____ other _____

_____

_____

10. I teach reduced forms as a system of linguistic rules and constraints.

____ often ____ seldom ____ never

11. I teach reduced forms as a system of pragmatic (appropriate social contexts) rules and constraints.

____ often ____ seldom ____ never

12. I teach reduced forms within context, using common examples.

____ often ____ seldom ____ never

13. What are the challenges you face when teaching reduced forms: (Please check all that apply)_____

____ not enough time available in the course

____ not identified as a need by the students

____ not enough available material

____ not in the curriculum

____ not enough experience teaching reduced forms

____ other _____

_____

_____

14. Even if you have not yet taught reduced forms, what challenges do you think you might face: (Please check all that might apply)

____ not enough time available in the course

____ not identified as a need by the students

____ not enough available material

____ not in the curriculum

____ not enough experience teaching reduced forms
____ other _____
_____
_____

15. Would you like to see the role of reduced forms in your own ESL classroom in the future
____ increasing ____ staying the same ____ decreasing

16. What would you like to see in the future with regard to reduced forms instruction?

17. Are there any insights or perspectives about reduced forms not covered by this survey that you think are important or valuable?

Thank you for your time and cooperation. The results of this survey will be written up as a scholarly paper at UH Mānoa ESL Department. If you have any questions or concerns, you can reach me at imoana@iwon.com. If you would like a copy of the results of this paper, please provide your e-mail address.

8

Teaching Reduced Interrogative Forms to Low-Level EFL Students in Japan

NFLRC
monographs

ROBERT CAHILL
Yokohama Shoka Dai High School, Japan

This chapter begins with a brief overview of the concepts of teacher talk, motherese, and foreigner talk. It then turns to examples of previous pedagogical treatments of reductions and the various sorts of terminology used in those treatments. The chapter focuses on reductions or reduced forms with the purposes recognizing the importance of reduced forms and providing guidelines to help teacher prepare efficient reduced forms exercises to supplement existing courses. The chapter proceeds with a description of the author's teaching context at Yokohama Shoka Daigaku High School, which is followed by a discussion of the importance of using communicative elements to complement a structural curriculum as well as ways to introduce elements of communicative competence and raise phonological consciousness. Then, pedagogical issues relating to reduced forms are covered (i.e., the intrinsic influence of reductions on spoken English, phonetic alphabet vs. standard orthography, processing vs. production of reduced forms, and potential obstructions when teaching reductions). The chapter turns next to the issues involved in teaching interrogative reductions in a three-step process: (a) contractions, (b) yes/no questions, and (c) wh-questions. The goal is to help students to shift from controlled to automatic processing. This chapter should be of particular interest to language teachers, researchers, testers and materials developers who want to understand, teach, and develop materials or tests for teaching reduced forms.

Introduction

Teacher talk, motherese, and *foreigner talk* are all strategies for simplifying input in order to facilitate comprehension for non-native speakers. In the classroom, teacher talk undoubtedly serves a useful purpose by making input more comprehensible to students. However, over-reliance on simplification strategies tends to misrepresent the target language and disaffirm the purpose of fluency-oriented instruction. As students progress, the teacher should encourage them to remove the training wheels and try to process natural discourse. Failure to address features that are masked by discourse adjustments is a dereliction of duty by the teacher, and it will eventually leave students with serious communicative deficiencies.

Ellis (1985) reviews several investigations into both foreigner talk and teacher talk, and he divides the observed input modifications into three categories: pronunciation,

Cahill, R. (2006) Teaching reduced interrogative forms to low-level EFL students in Japan. In J. D. Brown, & K. Kondo-Brown, (Eds.), *Perspectives on teaching connected speech to second language speakers* (pp. 99–125). Honolulu, HI: University of Hawai'i, National Foreign Language Resource Center.

lexis, and grammar. Exaggerated pronunciation, reduced speed, and unnaturally distinct word boundaries are three of the five most common phonological alterations mentioned by Ellis (the other two are heavier stress and increased volume). Although rate of speech and clarity of pronunciation have some bearing on my discussion, my main focus will be on reduced forms commonly found in natural-speed discourse. Reduced forms here will be defined as non-suprasegmental, phonological alterations that cannot be represented by standard orthography.

Reductions have often been overlooked in ELT (English Language Teaching) classrooms, and many students have been left to figure them out for themselves. Naiman (1992) states that a large percentage of reduced forms occurs in interrogatives. In this chapter, I will explore a systematic approach to teaching reduced forms by exploiting patterns that exist in common *yes/no* questions and *wh*-questions. Due to the methodological nature of instruction, reductions can be taught in a relatively short time, and because of the frequency of questions in a language classroom, natural-speed interrogative forms can be taught at an early stage with review occurring every time a question is asked. However, before this pedagogical procedure is discussed, I will examine several textbooks to see how other ELT authors have chosen to teach reduced forms. I will also introduce my teaching situation, examine several issues that are inextricably connected to the teaching of reduced forms, review the methodology that will be used in the presentation of reductions, and briefly consider potential effects that instruction will have on students' aural processing.

Examples of Previous Pedagogical Treatment of Reductions

In the EFL literature, various terms have been used to describe the phenomena in which phonemes and syllables are reduced or deleted. Hill and Beebe (1980) contrast spoken "blendings" with written "contractions." Pennington (1990) uses the terms "linkings" and "assimilations" to describe processes in which word boundaries become indistinct in streams of speech. Brown and Hilferty (1989) refer to the components of connected speech as "contracted forms," "elisions," "liaisons," and "reductions." Rost and Stratton (1978) use the terms "assimilations," "glides," and "coarticulations;" Brown (cited in Ur, 1987) calls reduced forms "blurred" utterances; Weinstein (1982; 2001) labels them "relaxed forms;" Prator and Robinett (1995) borrow the Sanskrit term "sandhi" which means "coming together." Hagen (2000) differentiates between "ellipses," "deletions," "nonreleased final consonants," "reductions," "linkings," "flap pronunciation," "glottal stops," and "contractions."[1] For the sake of simplicity, I will refer to the process of informal enunciation as *reductions* or *reduced forms* and only elaborate on their components when necessary.

In spite of meticulous attention to their taxonomy and the salient influence that they have on most forms of oral production, reduced forms are generally ignored in textbooks. The absence of reductions could easily mislead students into believing that spoken and written English are much more similar than they really are. In reality, reduced forms and unreduced forms often bear little resemblance to one another. And, because of the fundamental role that reductions play in spoken language, they can even cause confusion in some of the most basic sentences that students will encounter (e.g., What did you do? → Whadja do?).

---

[1]   Editors' note: For definitions of the above terms see chapter 1 or the glossary of this book.

Porter and Roberts (1987) point out that, even if teachers do not explicitly teach all the micro-skills inherent in authentic language, they must at least expose students to them. By allowing students to try to process the real thing, teachers help them to come up with their own strategies for coping with it. Three relevant micro-skills that Richards (1983) deems necessary for conversational listening are the ability to understand indistinct word boundaries, reduced forms of words, and a variety of speech rates. Porter and Roberts consider the absence of these genuine linguistic features to be a serious shortcoming of most ELT listening texts. There are, however, some textbook authors who have chosen not to ignore reductions. An examination of several dozen textbooks turned up nine that focus almost entirely on reduced forms.[2]

Certainly, teachers seldom want to base a whole course on reductions, nor do they want to choose a textbook merely because it incorporates reductions. The purpose of this chapter is instead to acknowledge the importance of reduced forms and to suggest guidelines for preparing efficient exercises to complement existing courses.

Situational Considerations

Most teachers have a limited amount of time and an assortment of micro-skills to teach. Because teachers must use their class time as judiciously as possible, they can generally only devote a small percentage of their time to phonological concerns. Fortunately, this should prove to be adequate. Brown and Hilferty (1986a, 1986b, also see chapter 4 of this book) were able to substantially improve their students' ability to process reduced forms by focusing on them for 5–10 minutes in the beginning of each class. I have also found the use of carefully graded mini-lessons to be of considerable value.

Yokohama Shoka Dai High School

Before discussing the content of the mini-lessons in detail, I will first introduce the context in which they are to be taught. The school in which I teach is called Yokohama Shoka Daigaku High School. Our school offers two courses of study: a general course for the majority of students and a commercial section for students who want a business background. Since almost all of our students will go to college or vocational school, the main emphasis of our curriculum is on preparing students for higher education. However, about 15 percent of our students will go on a four-week home stay in the United States, so there is some interest in teaching communicative ability at our school. The home stay program began 12 years ago, and more than a 100 second-year students have gone to America every year since 1989. Although there is a 10-hour home-stay class before their trip, the focus of these sessions is on providing comprehensible input rather than attending to specific micro-skills.

Yokohama Shoka Dai High School has several English clubs and an annual speech contest, but for most students, consideration of aural/oral skills is limited to their first year in high school. Since the first native-speaking English teacher came to our high school in 1978, all of our first-year students have been required to take either a language lab or an English conversation course. These classes have been prescribed instead of the usual grammar course. Language lab and conversation lessons are held twice a week and meet for about 60 or 70 hours each year. All of the students are male, and almost all of the first-year students are either 15 or 16 years old. This year, there are 14 first-year classes, and each has either 53 or 54 students. About two-thirds

---

[2]   Editors' note: Textbooks for teaching reduced forms are reviewed in depth in chapter 3 of this book.

(37) of the students are in the language lab section, and slightly less than one-third study conversation.

Using communicative elements to complement a structural curriculum

Although there are two native speakers who teach English conversation at Yokohama Shoka Dai High School, our approaches to the course are quite different, so I will only discuss my class. The typical high school English class in Japan focuses almost exclusively on accuracy, relies heavily on L1, and requires almost no aural/oral skills in the target language. In order to complement these other classes, it is necessary to provide ample opportunities for comprehensible input and output; to activate bottom-up, top-down, and interactive listening processes; and to help students to bridge gaps in their communicative competence.

The textbook that I chose for my class, *Fifty-Fifty* (Wilson & Barnard, 1992), helps to facilitate these goals. This is a communicative textbook with 15 chapters: 12 of the chapters each center around a linguistic function, and three chapters (every fifth one) are for review. There is plenty of comprehensible input that often qualifies as optimal, and there are many opportunities for comprehensible output. There is a listening activity in each chapter, which, although probably scripted, sounds as natural as any ELT tape that I have ever heard. These listening exercises were designed to develop both top-down and bottom-up skills, and the students found them interesting and sufficiently challenging. Although the speed of delivery and the vocabulary sound genuine, the word boundaries are more distinct than you would expect in normal speech. This is one of the main reasons that I have chosen to highlight reduced forms in mini-lessons.

Fifty-Fifty also includes an information-gap activity in each chapter. Since my classes have either 16 or 17 students, there is only a limited amount of time for me to interact with each student. Therefore, it is necessary to find methods of increasing the amount of time that students have for exchanging information and negotiating meaning. Information-gap activities and other assignments that require students to work together allow them to maximize the time that they have for accomplishing these goals. Information-gap activities, by nature, require students to engage in communicative interchange. The tasks in *Fifty-Fifty* encourage the negotiation of meaning by suggesting phrases for repairing communicative breakdowns.

Introducing the elements of communicative competence

Phrases for repairing breakdowns, like this, would generally be considered components of strategic competence. According to Swain (1983), strategic competence is one of four components of communicative competence (the other three are grammatical competence, discourse competence, and sociolinguistic competence). Because students generally have poorly developed conversational skills and few opportunities to negotiate meaning, the teaching of strategic competence would seem to have special significance in a Japanese high school. Terrell (cited in Swain) stresses the importance of compensatory and meaning-enhancing strategies, particularly for beginners. D'Anglejan (cited in Ellis, 1985) maintains that grammar-translation courses lack opportunities for real-life communicative patterns. This is especially true in Japanese high schools in which L1 is almost always used to clear up ambiguities. In order to avoid the code switching that is so prevalent in Japanese high school classrooms, it is necessary to teach students strategies for avoiding the use of Japanese. Strategic competence will largely be promoted by formulaic sentences, by the teacher's example, and by calling attention to communicative-enhancing and corrective strategies in texts and in classroom situations. Lyons (cited in Ellis, 1985) states that formulaic sentences are "expressions which are learned as unanalysable wholes and employed on particular occasions..." (p. 167). In my experience, having students memorize the most commonly used classroom expressions (e.g., I *beg your pardon. May I ask a question?* or *How do you say _____ in English?*) leads to significantly less L1 use and considerably fewer prolonged pauses.

Since grammatical competence is the only aspect of communicative competence that generally receives any attention in Japanese high school classes, explicit attention to this linguistic aspect will rarely be necessary. Sociolinguistic and discourse competence, on the other hand, usually receive scant consideration. Although there is not enough time to attend to either of these thoroughly, it is possible to use mini-lessons to illuminate some of the areas in which students are weak. Mini-lessons are 5–15 minute exercises that will allow the teacher to include linguistic elements that would not normally be incorporated into the syllabus.

Although elements of discourse and sociolinguistic competence will usually be encountered in a broader context, mini-lessons allow the accentuation of specific features of both that are fundamental in the early development of communicative competence. Discourse competence will be addressed in skeleton dialogues in which students are given key words and expected to construct coherent and cohesive sentences. I will also use cloze exercises that require students to supply non-specific reference words (e.g., pronouns and locative words such as *here* and *there*) in order to complete a text. One sociolinguistic exercise that I will do involves describing a situation and requiring students to choose a phrase (e.g., one of the many translations of the Japanese word *dozo*[3], i.e., *please, here you are, help yourself,* or *after you*) that is appropriate). Tanaka (1988) suggests another sociolinguistic shortcoming that Japanese students often have. She states that Japanese people often use overly formal or informal expressions, which often make them seem either unfriendly or rude. Registers can be altered and underscored in almost all dialogues, and the same can even be done in formulaic sentences.

Phonological consciousness raising

Mini-lessons will also be used to touch upon phonological features of English. Since only limited time is available, I will only be able to deal with many of the more prominent phonological constituents (i.e., intonation, rhythm, and stress) expeditiously. I will try to spend a little more time helping students to distinguish between phonemic dichotomies that exist in English, but not in Japanese. Since such ELT authors as Ellis (1985) and Murphy (1991) indicate that word-level practice can be beneficial, minimal pair drills will be used in addition to more contextualized exercises. One such contextualized exercise that I will use is the "maximal pair" exercise (see Pennington, 1990). Maximal pair exercises involve listening to a sentence and then selecting it from a group of three or four similar-sounding sentences.

These particular phonological features will be included in the mini-lessons, but they will probably only receive cursory attention. Murphy (1991) states that, "improvement in pronunciation depends upon significant commitments in both time and energy from learners themselves" (p. 49). Time constraints, in addition to a broad

---

[3]   All Japanese words in this chapter are transcribed using the Hepburn system.

agenda, will mean that expectations for proficiency gains in phonological production will be modest. Pennington (1990) notes that Japanese pronunciation generally employs the blade of the tongue, whereas English makes much greater use of the tip of the tongue. She also briefly discusses the phonetic mutations that are made to English words as they are adopted into Japanese. Making students aware of some of the ways that their production differs from native speakers is a realistic goal of these exercises.

Pedagogical Issues Relating to Reduced Forms

The intrinsic influence of reductions on spoken English

As has already been mentioned, the main objective of the mini-lessons will be to familiarize students with reduced forms found in natural discourse. Bowen (1975a) confirms the need to teach reductions stating that:

> Students who have been shielded from these normal weak-stressed reductions in the belief that such pronunciations are sloppy, careless, and so forth, are practically crippled when first exposed to normal English in real contexts. It is crucially important for any second-language student of English who will ever deal with the oral aspect to have at least the experience of hearing and practicing reduced forms as a means of developing an acceptance of these morphophonemic alterations. (p. 224)

Temperly (1987) warns that failure to teach reductions at an early stage is a missed opportunity in "combating the students' tendency to learn language as individual isolated words with one pronunciation for each word" (p. 66). This admonition is particularly relevant in Japanese high school classrooms in which students memorize word lists and almost always employ a bottom-up approach when trying to extract meaning from a message.

Bowen (1975a) estimates that as many as 35% of all words can be reduced in normal discourse. Prator and Robinett (1995) maintain that 10 one-syllable words (i.e., *the, of, and, to, a, in, that, it, is,* and *I*) make up 25%of all spoken and written English. Since almost all of these words are frequently reduced, it is quite possible that Bowen's appraisal is conservative in many situations. In Brown and Hilferty's (1989) reduced-forms dictation exercise, 46 of the 85 words in the dialogue were reduced. This kind of informal, question-and-answer conversation, which contains many *wh*-words, auxiliary verbs, and pronouns, is exactly the kind of discourse that I will soon be analyzing.

Phonetic alphabet versus standard orthography

Having discussed the importance of reductions and their prevalence, I will now briefly examine some of the pedagogical issues and techniques that are involved in teaching them. The first issue that I will address is whether or not a phonetic alphabet should be used to represent reduced forms. Two textbooks, *Hearsay* and *Listening Transitions* (see chapter 3 for more on these), use a phonetic alphabet. *Hearsay* (Griffee & Hough, 1986) is a text that is best suited for beginners, and, for this reason, it is also important to be careful in using symbols with which many students will probably be unfamiliar. Rost and Stratton's first textbook (1978) *Listening in the Real World* uses standard orthography to represent reduced forms. Their second book, *Listening Transitions* (Rost & Stratton, 1980), which followed 4 years later, uses a phonetic alphabet. Both of these books are aimed at intermediate students, but the authors do not explain the reason for changing the phonemic representation. One possible reason for the change is that they found the need to express sounds more precisely. Another possible reason that Hill and Beebe (1980) point out is that the mixture of standard and non-standard spelling can easily confuse students.

In spite of these potential drawbacks, several authors that create teaching materials have chosen to use standard orthography to symbolize the results of the reduction process. In addition to Rost and Stratton (1978, 1980), other authors who have elected not to use the phonetic alphabet include Brown and Hilferty (1989), Weinstein (1982), and Hagen (2000). Hagen has written a listening text for advanced learners which focuses on very meticulous phonetic details; however, she states that the standard alphabet is more accessible and less time consuming. My students are supposed to have studied the International Phonetic Alphabet, but their understanding of it is generally very limited. Gunterman (1985) points out that, since the phonetic alphabet is not a part of Japanese college examinations, students have little motivation to learn it. I have been using the standard alphabet for several years, and the students have always found it easy to understand. Furthermore, by clearly delineating between standard and non-standard spelling, it is possible to avoid the kind of confusion that Hill and Beebe (1980) claimed to have. Using asterisks like Weinstein, or simply underlining the non-standard spelling, can remove any negative influence that it may have.

Processing versus production

Another topic that should be addressed is the purpose of teaching reduced forms. Should teachers focus all their attention on processing reduced speech, or should they also help students to produce reduced forms? Bowen (1975a), Porter and Roberts (1987), Temperly (1987), and Ur (1987) emphasize that processing reductions is a stronger priority than producing them. Porter and Roberts point out that many students who are proficient in the classroom have trouble transferring their knowledge to situations outside of it. They then state that this kind of student has far more trouble listening than speaking. Adams (cited in Pennington, 1990) states that the inability to produce reductions is one of the easiest ways to recognize a non-native speaker. Not being able to properly enunciate reduced forms may give someone away as a non-native speaker, but this problem can much more readily be compensated for than the inability to comprehend reductions in streams of speech. Native speakers of English readily understand slow speech with unnaturally distinct pronunciation, but students should not rely on native speakers to speak slowly with unnaturally distinct pronunciation for them.

Teacher talk is delivered by teachers who generally have experience simplifying input so that it can become comprehensible. *Foreigner talk*, on the other hand, is a simplification strategy which may, or may not, be employed by individuals who may, or may not, have any knowledge about, or practice in, providing simplified input. Students who only receive simplified input in the classroom cannot expect to always be pampered this way in the real world. Even when they are fortunate enough to be exposed to foreigner talk, there is no guarantee that it will be as comprehensible as the teacher talk to which they are accustomed.

Because the oral aspect of reductions will not be stressed as much as the aural component, this does not mean that it should be ignored altogether. Brown and Hilferty (1986a, 1986b, also see chapter 4 of this book) focused on aural comprehension of reduced forms, and they succeeded in bringing about significant proficiency gains in this area. However, when reflecting upon their experiment, they questioned the validity of putting too much emphasis on aural proficiency and not enough on production skills. In my discussion of the importance of processing reduced forms, I referred to Pennington's (1990) assertion that a speaker's failure to include reductions would often give them away as a non-native speaker. However, only an extremely small percentage of teachers will be fortunate enough to have students who are almost indistinguishable from native speakers. The majority of teachers will just be trying to nudge, shove, bribe, or bully their students in order to help them progress further along the inter-language continuum.

Even if most teachers will not be using the production of reduced forms to help bridge one of the few remaining gaps in their students' fluency, this does not mean that they cannot find a valuable role for them. Ur (1987) suggests that students be allowed to practice reductions in the early stages of second-language instruction. She proposes a repetition exercise that can stress either processing or production depending upon how it is followed up. The teacher either speaks or plays a tape in which reductions are featured. If the students are required to translate the utterance into its unreduced form, the exercise is process-oriented. One the other hand, if the students attempt to imitate the reduced form of the statement, then the task helps to develop both processing and production skills.

Hill and Beebe (1980) argue that the pronunciation of reduced forms should be encouraged even if the goal is aural discrimination. They state that, in their experience, production is a crucial element in the development of receptive skills. If I accept this premise, which seems to be quite reasonable, then I am obliged to have my students practice enunciating reductions no matter what my purpose is. Furthermore, if I have arrived at this conclusion, I must determine how different situational elements will influence the amount of time that is spent on production. Students' ages, their levels of proficiency, and the methods of instruction to which they have been exposed are all relevant avenues of inquiry, as is the teacher's target-language ability and what he or she perceives the goal of the class to be.

If the goal is native-like production of reduced forms, it would probably be best if the students were either very young or very proficient. Because there is no research (known to me) that specifically addresses the effect that age or proficiency has on the acquisition of reduced forms,[4] I can only speculate on the advantages that can be derived from targeting either group. Children under the age of 10 apparently have the ability to acquire accurate pronunciation faster than other age groups (see Ellis, 1985; Leather & James, 1991), and it's probably safe to assume that this ability would apply to reduced forms. Advanced students, on the other hand, will probably benefit from producing reductions for another reason. I have already noted that the production of reduced forms is one of the last phonological distinctions that will exist between highly skilled students and native speakers, so getting these students to articulate the more informal patterns of speech will almost undoubtedly be a worthwhile endeavor. However, according to Hill and Beebe (1980), it is not necessary to overdo it. Hill and Beebe distinguish between "normal speed blendings" and "fast speed blendings,"

---

[4]   Editors' note: As of the publication of this book, Cahill's contention that there is a lack of research that "specifically addresses the effect that age or proficiency has on the acquisition of reduced forms" no longer holds 100%. Ito's study in chapter 6 of this book does take proficiency into consideration, though the studies in chapters 4 and 5 do not. Nonetheless further research on the roll of proficiency in reduced forms learning would certainly be useful, and any research on the effects of age would be useful.

and they state that nonnative speakers only need to be able to produce those that occur in the former.

Potential obstructions when teaching reductions

Another matter that is of particular relevance to the target audiences is the methods of ESL instruction to which they have been exposed. Students in Japanese high schools and junior high schools are almost always required to do intensive reading in English and to be able regurgitate a multitude of grammatical structures. Any pronunciation practice that they do is almost always at the word level. Pennington (1990) states that this kind of accuracy-based training usually results in an inability to produce features that are inherent in reduced speech (e.g., linking and eliding). Gradually increasing the degree of contextualization that is used while teaching reduced forms might help to counterbalance an overemphasis on a bottom-up approach to oral skills.

One potential stumbling block to teaching reductions to Japanese students is that, by the time that they reach high school, they have already made a strong correlation between the spelling of English and the corresponding unreduced pronunciation of the words. Another potential drawback in many situations is that most non-native English speakers who teach English in Japan cannot accurately reproduce informal reductions. The main obstacle that prevents production of reduced forms in my situation is a lack of time. Because of this limitation, the production of reduced forms will most often be practiced in choral response. Individuals will be encouraged, but not required, to try to use some of the most common reduced forms (e.g., *you* → *ya*, *and* → *n*, *want to* → *wanna*) in production.

The reduced forms of articles, conjunctions, and prepositions will be taught as they occur in context, but mini-lessons (except for cloze dialogues) will generally be reserved for *wh*-words, modal/auxiliary verbs, and pronouns. In order to keep the focus on reduced forms and not on new lexical items, I will limit the scope of the mini-lessons to include 21 words (26 with first- and third-person modal/auxiliary variations) with which students are already familiar. This group incorporates seven *wh*-words (i.e., *who, what, where, why, when, which,* and *how*), seven auxiliary/modals and their alternate forms (i.e., *did, can, will, do/does, have/has, were/was,* and *are/is/am*), and seven pronouns (i.e., *I, you, he, she, it, we,* and *they*). Theoretically these three categories can exponentially create 343 reduced *wh*-questions and 49 reduced *yes/no* questions. The inclusion of negative modal/auxiliaries would appear to double this number. However, although all *yes/no* questions are often asked in both the negative and affirmative, *why* is the only *wh*-question that is used in a negative context often enough to warrant explicit attention. The fact that *I, she, we,* and *they* rarely undergo significant modification in informal speech also decreases the number of patterns that will need to be considered.

In classes for highly competent students, or classes that are specifically concerned with phonology, it might be advantageous to expound upon the various processes that contribute to the broad term *reductions* (e.g., elisions, linkings, and schwa vowels). However, in classes with less proficient students, little time, or a broader focus, it might be wiser to avoid too much attention to details and use a more inductive approach. Letting students discover recurring features for themselves is potentially less time-consuming, more process-oriented, and more suitable for lower-level students. Nevertheless, as Hill and Beebe (1980) and others point out, a brief description of the sociolinguistic and phonological restraints regarding reduced forms will probably also be necessary in order to let students know that their use is sometimes inappropriate. Earlier I mentioned two examples of situations in which reductions are unallowable: one instance would be in formal speaking situations, and the other would be when individual words are stressed.

Methodology

Using L1 examples and contractions to activate background knowledge

When introducing reductions, it would probably be helpful to put them into some kind of context with which students are already familiar. Japanese words generally do not lose much of their character because of sentence-level influences, but certain phonemic differences between written and spoken Japanese can nonetheless be found at the word level. Japanese vowels are often altered at the end of adjectives (e.g., the /i/ sound in *abunai* turns into an /a/ sound in *abunei*), and they are sometimes elided when adjacent consonant sounds are enunciated (e.g., *desuka* [the interrogative form of the Japanese verb *to be*] is pronounced *des'ka*, and the same past tense form of the same word, *deshitaka*, is pronounced *desh'taka*). In addition, Japanese secondary school students should be familiar with all of the most basic contractions in English. Consequently, the first phase of instruction will involve reviewing contractions, and then I will proceed to *yes/no* questions and *wh*-questions.

Hill and Beebe (1980) point out that most ELT textbooks introduce contractions, but ignore reduced forms. They condemn this deficiency; they note that reductions are more common than contractions; and they suggest that contractions be used to introduce reduced forms. One reason for this recommendation is that they are "committed to the principle that orthographic clues should be maximally exploited in the teaching of pronunciation" (p. 306). Another reason that Hill and Beebe give for the early introduction of contractions is that many contractions are among the most basic lexical items in English.

Even though Hill and Beebe (1980) favor using contractions before reductions, their support is not without cautionary advice. They warn teachers to make it very clear to students that contractions only represent a small proportion of all reduced forms. They also caution teachers to make sure that students do not try to contract all reductions. Hill and Beebe also point out that contractions are subject to numerous phonological, grammatical, and sociolinguistic constraints that are potentially confusing. They then propose a series of symbols and charts to explicitly teach students these exceptions (e.g., the inappropriacy of I *ain't* or the impossibility of contracting *this is* or *there are*). While this kind of accuracy strategy may be suitable for some situations, other teachers may be limited by time or a desire to focus on fluency.

Even though students in my classes seldom make errors with contractions, there could be a valid reason for this besides proficiency. Since there is no obligatory occasion in which contractions are necessitated, the use of uncontracted forms could be a result of avoiding a relatively unfamiliar structure. Using the safest avenue of expression is an effective form of simplification that falls under the communication-enhancing half of Canale's (1983) strategic competence dichotomy. Chaudron (1983) would label this type of circumvention as a form of "restrictive" simplification rather than "elaborative" simplification. In my classes, this kind of production strategy is most prevalent with, but not limited to, the contracted form of *will not*. Forcing students to use contractions denies them the use of a legitimate compensatory technique, and it also contradicts the purpose of fluency-oriented instruction. As was mentioned earlier, it is probably best to insure that lower-level students can process phonetically shortened forms and to let then make their own decisions about when to start production of these features.

Although I mentioned earlier that Japanese students are introduced to contractions in junior high school, many have never encountered them in an aural/oral environment. The value of reexamining contractions is that students are allowed to use something familiar as a bridge to more radical reductions. Hill and Beebe (1980) point out that there are only 10 words that can be contracted (*am*, *is*, *are*, *has*, *have*, *had*, *would*, *will*, *not*, and *us*). Two of these contractions (*would* and *had*) are only present in relatively difficult structures, so it is unnecessary to use then in lower-level classes like mine.

Another reason to start with contractions is that their earlier exposure to contractions does not guarantee they acquired them. One way to be certain that students have a good grasp of contractions is to give them a list of uncontracted forms and see if they can come up with their contracted equivalents. Although this may be a simple method of gauging students' competence vis-á-vis contractions, it will probably not be the best way to impart them in a Japanese high school class. If students have a problem understanding contractions, it is almost certainly because they failed to acquire the contractions when they were presented deductively. The grammar-translation method is the prototypical, deductive approach, and it is almost always used in Japanese secondary schools. Hartnett (cited in Krashen, 1987) concluded from research that some people learn structures better when they have the rule spelled out for them, and other people benefit more from inducing the rule. Hammerly (cited in Krashen, 1987) suggests that some features are more easily taught by an inductive approach while others are more conducive to deductive instruction. No matter what the cause of the student's ignorance, it would probably be helpful to reinforce contractions in a variety of contexts.

My exercises will initially only require students to determine if they have heard a contracted or an uncontracted utterance within a sentence (see Appendix 1.1). The next kind of exercise (see Appendixes 1.2 & 1.3) requires students to choose the contraction that they have heard from a group of four or five possibilities. Another exercise (see Appendix 1.4) that I will include resembles both the tasks that I just mentioned and the maximal pair exercises that I discussed earlier. This exercise involves choosing the sentence that one has heard from a group of similar-sounding sentences that include both contractions and reductions. Lastly, I will give students a list of contractions from which they must choose in order to correctly complete sentences which have one missing component (see Appendix 1.5).

The reduced forms of yes/no questions

The next phase of instruction will involve teaching the reduced forms of modal/auxiliar verb-pronoun combinations that occur in *yes/no* questions. These kinds of reduced forms are one of the most commonly found types of reductions, and almost all authors who discuss reduced forms advocate their inclusion. Peterson (1991), Brown & Hilferty (1989), Hagen (2000), Gunterman (1985), and Ur (1987), in addition to all the textbook writers that I have discussed, include examples of reduced modal/auxiliaries and pronouns. Two texts (Rost & Stratton, 1978, and Weinstein, 1982) devote large portions of their books to these features. In fact, Host and Stratton often dedicate entire chapters to the reduced forms of either one pronoun or one modal/auxiliary verb. While this much attention to a single word certainly makes students aware of its reduced form, it is doubtful that this much consideration is necessary. It would certainly seem to be much more efficient to introduce patterns of reductions as comprehensively as possible rather than trying to teach isolated words or limited combinations. As I mentioned before, the essential elements of most basic *yes/no* and *wh*-questions can be encompassed in 21 words (26 with variations). In addition to saving time by teaching these components together, it becomes much easier to accentuate their similarities and differences.

The first thing that I will do when teaching reductions in *yes/no* questions is to familiarize the students with the reduced forms of some common pronouns and modal/auxiliary verbs. Students will be provided with a list of frequently used modal/auxiliary-pronouns in both their reduced and unreduced states (see Appendix 2.1). I will give model pronunciations for both types and the students will imitate these in choral response. These modal/auxiliary verb-pronoun compounds will be presented and practiced in both their affirmative and negative manifestations. When doing this, it will be necessary to confirm that students recognize that the questions *Can you swim?* and *Can't you swim?* require the same answer. In Japanese, these kinds of affirmative and negative interrogatives require different answers; and, in my experience, students frequently employ negative transfer when answering *yes/no* questions.

One thing that will not be necessary is practicing the pronunciation of the reduced forms of *we*, *she*, *they*, and *I*. This is because these pronouns are not as drastically transformed in context as the other three that I will now explain. After pronouncing the various forms of each of the other three pronouns (*you*, *he*, and *it*), there will be a simple exercise in which students are supposed to circle the auxiliary/modal that the teacher has used in a question (see Appendix 2.2). The memorization of the most significantly reduced pronoun *you* will be facilitated by a simple mnemonic device. In negative questions *you* generally changes to *cha*, and it becomes *ya* in an affirmative question. *Cha* and *ya* are Japanese readings of two commonly used Chinese characters that can be combined to form *chaya*, the Japanese word for *teahouse*.

Next, I will turn my attention to two different exercises in a fill-in format in order to practice reduced forms in *yes/no* questions. The first one will consist of between 15 and 20 questions with the first two words missing (see Appendix 2.3). Students will listen to the teacher read each question, and they will attempt to decipher and record the initial modal/auxiliary verb-pronoun combination. Each sentence should be read several times with the teacher gradually decreasing the speed of the utterance, but maintaining the reduced forms as Ur (1987) recommends. The next kind of exercise that that I will do, closely resembles the one that I just explained, and it is similar to the ones that Burns (1992) and Avery and Ehrlich (1992) suggest (see Appendix 2.4). These are pairs of sentences that differ only by a single sound. After using these types of exercise in mini-lessons a couple of times, I will situate the modal/auxiliary components in the broader context of cloze dialogues (see Appendix 2.5). In addition to creating a more natural medium for the questions, these dialogues will also allow incorporation of affirmative and negative declaratory statements. It will also provide a chance to review reductions that have already been encountered in class. In order to give students sufficient time to complete this task, it would probably be advisable to let them hear the dialogue at least three times as Brown and Hilferty (1989) suggest. The first and third times the dialogue will be read as it would in a normal conversation, but the second playing of the dialogue will require the teacher to insert pauses.

The reduced forms of *wh*-questions

After teaching the reduced forms of *yes/no* questions, continuing with *wh*-questions seems to be a logical progression. *Wh*-questions often contain the same initial lexical sequences that appear in *yes/no* questions (Will you go there? →Why will you go there?, When will you go there?, etc.), and they are necessary for some of the most fundamental informational exchanges in English. Although I provide a chart that includes all 343 possible *wh*-word and auxiliary/modal-pronoun combinations (see Appendix 3.1), it is not practical to have students repeat all of them. I instead try to focus on the pronunciations of common *wh* -questions (see Appendix 3.2) with which I practice choral response at both the phrasal and sentence levels. As with *yes/no* interrogatives, it is not the first word of the question that undergoes the most drastic metamorphosis in a natural context, but instead the succeeding word or words (e.g., Where did you go? →Where ja go?). Therefore, there will be a strong emphasis on the various ways in which auxiliary/modals and pronouns blend in informal speech.

The next exercise, which both Burns (1992) and Ur (1987) recommend, has students write down the number of words that are in short, unsimplified sentences read by the teacher (see Appendix 3.3). Burns and Ur both point out that both the degree of the reduction and the length of the sentence can be adjusted to suit the target audience. The last two exercises (see Appendix 3.4 & 3.5) will be minimal pair sentences and cloze dialogues like the ones that I mentioned when I was discussing drills for practicing *yes/no* questions. As students become more proficient in processing interrogative forms, it is a good idea to have them use these questions in circumstances which more closely resemble real-life communicative situations. These might include having students do information gap activities or having them do guided activities in which they must ask each other about their experiences and plans.

Towards More Efficient Aural Processing

These exercises will, presumably, help students to move from controlled to automatic processing. According to Nagle and Sanders (1986), controlled processing is used when the listener is trying to decode new linguistic features. They also state that too much dependence on controlled processing can divert attention from other legitimate avenues of perception, or even result in a total breakdown of communication. Nagle and Sanders also maintain that sufficient training will allow students to shift from controlled processing to automatic processing of target input. Automatic processing requires no conscious attention to linguistic details, and it permits the listener to concentrate on top-down processing and paralinguistic cues that will enhance comprehension.

Schneider and Detweiler (cited in Schmidt, 1992) assert that the transition from controlled to automatic processing is a five-step operation. In any case, the initial tasks will attempt to, at the very least, help students to increase the speed with which they process the first two or three words in interrogative patterns. Later tasks should help learners to further automatize these features and give teachers a chance to introduce students to these forms in a variety of situations. According to Gatbonton and Segalowitz (1988), rehashing the same material leads to the automatization of larger chunks of discourse. They state that focusing on semantically related speech, rather than structurally related language, is how teachers can help students to automatize chunks of closely related functional language. Peterson (1991) states that, if learners can chunk functionally related patterns, memorization will be greatly facilitated.

Learning formulaic sentences and doing the information-gap activities and guided exercises that were discussed earlier will allow for repeated practice of high-frequency sentences and functions in the classroom.

Conclusion

The focus of this chapter has been on teaching interrogative reductions to students who have had limited experience in processing or producing English. I used a three-step process (i.e., 1. contractions, 2. *yes/no* questions, and 3. *wh*-questions) to encompass virtually all interrogative forms, and I focused attention on other high-frequency reductions as they are encountered in context. Although I focused on what I consider to be a standard American accent, it is probably best for each teacher to create materials with which he or she feels comfortable. Other decisions that a teacher will have to make are whether or not to encourage the production of reductions and whether or not to use a phonetic alphabet. These decisions will partially be determined by the students' levels of proficiency, the method or methods of instruction to which they have been exposed, and the amount of time that the teacher can devote to phonological elements. In my case, time and proficiency limitations meant that my classes used standard orthography and primarily concentrated on the processing of reduced forms. Increasing students' ability to aurally process reduced forms should actually be the minimum amount of attention that teachers should pay to this important, but all-too-often overlooked aspect of spoken English.

Appendix 1.1

Listen to the following sentences and circle "U" if it is uncontracted or "C" if it is contracted.

1. U I am tired.
   C I'm tired.
2. U She cannot come.
   C She can't come.
3. U We were not there.
   C We weren't there.
4. U They will go by bus.
   C They'll go by bus.
5. U He has been to Canada twice.
   C He's been to Canada twice.

6. U You did not know her, did you?
   C You didn't know her, did you?
7. U It does not snow much here, does it?
   C It doesn't snow much here, does it?
8. U He is a good baseball player.
   C He's a good baseball player.
9. U I will watch a movie tonight.
   C I'll watch a movie tonight
10. U You have seen this movie, have you not?
    C You've seen this movie, haven't you?

Appendix 1.2

Listen to the sentence and then circle the correct word or words that you hear.

1. I'm / I'm not / I was / I wasn't _____ hungry.
2. He's / He's not / He isn't / He was / He wasn't _____ there.
3. She's / She's not / She isn't / She was / She wasn't _____ studying.
4. It's / It's not / It isn't / It was / It wasn't _____ difficult.
5. Mr. Abe's / Mr. Abe's not / Mr. Abe isn't / Mr. Abe was / Mr. Abe wasn't _____ driving.
6. That's / That's not / That isn't / That was / That wasn't _____ right.
7. We're / We're not / We aren't / We were / We weren't _____ going to go.
8. You're / You're not / You aren't / You were / You weren't _____ late.
9. They're / They're not / They aren't / They were / They weren't _____ happy.
10. Mr. Jones and I are / and I aren't / and I were / and I weren't _____ eating.

Appendix 1.3

Listen to each sentence and circle the phrase that you hear.

1. I'll / I won't / I'm going to / I'm not going to – go home by train.
2. You'll go / You won't go / You're going / You're not going /You aren't going – there tomorrow.
3. He'll go / He won't go / He's going / He's not going / He isn't going – to calligraphy class.
4. It'll / It won't / It's going to / It's not going to / It isn't going to – rain today.
5. She'll go / She won't go / She's going / She isn't going /She's not going – by herself.
6. This'll / This won't / This is going to / This isn't going to – get cheaper.
7. That'll / That won't / That's going to / That's not going to/ That isn't going to – get hotter.
8. We'll go / We won't go / We're going / We're not going / We aren't going – to science class.
9. They'll go / They won't go / They're going / They're not going / They aren't going – to Tokyo this week.
10. These'll / These won't / These are going to / These aren't going to – get colder.
11. Those'll / Those won't / Those are going to / Those aren't going to – get more expensive.

Appendix 1.4

Please listen to the following sentences and circle the correct phrase.

1. I liked / I like / I'll like—the new school.
2. They won't go / They want to go / They went—to Disneyland.
3. He looked / He looks / He'll look—at the pictures.
4. She won't go / She wants to go / She went—swimming.
5. We lived / We live / We'll live—in Kyoto.
6. I won't go / I want to go / I went—shopping.
7. They learned / They learn / They'll learn—that in school.
8. He won't go / He wants to go / He went—skiing.
9. She lent / She lends / She'll lend—it to my brother.
10. We won't go / We want to go / We went—bowling.

Appendix 1.5

Student's copy

Please write the contraction or pronoun-contraction combination that you hear.

example: *He isn't* there.

1. ____ ____ raining.
2. ____ ____ want to go.
3. ____ ____ call you tomorrow.
4. ____ ____ know the answer.
5. ____ ____ like the movie.
6. ____ ____ corning today.
7. ____ ____ play tennis.
8. ____ ____ a good singer.
9. ____ ____ know until tommorrow.
10. ____ never been to Kyoto.
11. ____ ____ hit the ball.
12. ____ ____ coming here.
13. ____ ____ cut her hair again.
14. ____ ____ going by train.

Teacher's copy

Teacher should read:

example: *He isn't* there.

1. *It wasn't* raining.
2. *He doesn't* want to go.
3. *I'll call* you tomorrow.
4. *She doesn't* know the answer.
5. *We didn't* like the movie.
6. *He's not* coming today.
7. *She can't* play tennis.
8. *I'm not* a good singer.
9. *You won't* know until tomorrow.
10. *They've* never been to Kyoto.
11. *I haven't* hit the ball.
12. *They weren't* coming here.
13. *She's cut* her hair again.
14. *We're not* going by train.

Appendix 2.1

The following examples are in non-standard spelling.

ya			cha	
can you	kenya		can't you	can-cha
did you	did-ya	did-ja	didn' t you	din-cha
will you	will-ya		won't you	woon-cha
do you	d'ya	ja	don't you	doan-cha
are you	are-ya		aren't you	aren-cha
were you	were-ya		weren't you	weren-cha
have you	have-ya		haven't you	haven-cha
can he	kenny		can't he	can-nee
did he	diddee		didn't he	din-nee
will he	willie		won't he	woo-nee
does he	duzzy		doesn't he	duzzinee
is he	izzy		isn't he	izzinee
was he	wuzzy		wasn't he	wuzzinee
has he	hazzy		hasn't he	hazzinee
can it	kennit		can't it	can-nit
did it	diddit		didn't it	din-nit
will it	willit		won't it	woo-nit
does it	duzzit		doesn't it	duzzinit
is it	izzit		isn't it	izzinit
was it	wuzzit		wasn't it	wuzzinit
has it	hazzit		hasn't it	hazzinit

Appendix 2.2

Please listen to each sentence and circle the word that you hear.

you		he		it	
1. Are Were	you going there?	1. Is Was	he going there?	1. Is Was	it going there?
2. Don't Won't	you speak Chinese?	2. Doesn't Won't	he speak Chinese?	2. Doesn't Won't	it work?
3. Did you Can you	hear us?	3. Did Can	he hear us?	3. Did Can	it hear us?
4. Haven't Don't	you cut her hair?	4. Hasn't Doesn't	he cut her hair?	4. Hasn't Doesn't	it move?
5. Have Did	you put it on?	5. Has Did	he put it on?	5. Has Did	it put out the fire?

Appendix 2.3

Student's copy

Please listen carefully to the teacher and write the first two words of each question.

1. _____ _____ speak Korean?
2. _____ _____ come to school by train?
3. _____ _____ go to work by car?
4. _____ _____ play tennis?
5. _____ _____ rain today?
6. _____ _____ hungry this morning?

7. _____ _____ ?
8. _____ _____ drunk coffee today?

9. _____ _____ smoke cigarettes?
10. _____ _____ ?
11. _____ _____ get to school before eight-thirty?

12. _____ _____ go to college?
13. _____ _____ ?
14. _____ _____ a Hanshin Tigers fan?

15. _____ _____ a baseball fan?
16. _____ _____ snow a lot in Yokohama?

Teacher's copy

Please listen carefully to the teacher and write the first two words of each question.

1. *Can you* speak Korean?
2. *Did you* come to school by train?
3. *Does he* go to work by car?
4. *Can't you* play tennis?
5. *Will it* rain today?
6. *Weren't you* hungry this morning?
   (Teacher's tapescript only) – How about your mother?
7. *Was she* ?
8. *Have you* drunk coffee today?
   (Teacher's tapescript only) – How about your homeroom teacher?
9. *Do you* smoke cigarettes?
10. *Does he* ?
11. *Didn't you* get to school before eight-thirty?
    (Teacher's tapescript only) – How about your two best friends?
12. *Won't you* go to college?
13. *Will they* ?
14. *Are you* a Hanshin Tigers fan?
    (Teacher's tapescript only) – How about your father?
15. *Isn't he* a baseball fan?
16. *Doesn't it* snow a lot in Yokohama?

Appendix 2.4

Your teacher will read one of the following pairs of sentences. Please listen carefully and circle the letter in front of the sentence that you hear.

1. a. Did she like your present?
   b. Didn't she like your present?
2. a. Are you going home?
   b. Were you going home?
3. a. Has he gotten here yet?
   b. Hasn't he gotten here yet?
4. a. Doesn't she study every day?
   b. Doesn't he study every day?
5. a. Can't we use your desk?
   b. Can we use your desk?
6. a. Was it raining?
   b. Is it raining?
7. a. Don't you have a car?
   b. Won't you have a car?
8. a. Have I already asked you?
   b. Haven't I already asked you?
9. a. Don't they want to come with us?
   b. Didn't they want to come with us?
10. a. Isn't he really tired?
    b. Wasn't he really tired?

Appendix 2.5

Student's copy

As you listen to the following dialogues, please write the unreduced forms of the missing words that you hear.

Jim: _____ _____ ask you a few questions?

Ken: Sure. What do you _____ _____ know?

Jim: _____ taking a survey about lifestyles.

Ken: Okay.

Jim: _____ _____ smoke?

Ken: No, but I _____ _____ smoke a lot.

Jim: When did you quit?

Ken: Last week, _____ _____ _____ smoked a couple today.

Jim: I see. _____ _____ drink a lot?

Ken: That depends upon what you mean by a lot.

Jim: _____ _____ drink anything last night?

Ken: _____ _____ _____ But only about six or seven beers.

Jim: I see. "Only" six or seven. _____ _____ _____ _____ drink tonight?

Ken: _____ _____ _____ It's my poker night. _____ _____ probably drink a lot.

Jim: _____ _____ drive to your poker game?

Ken: Yeah, of course. _____ _____ a few blocks away, but my neighborhood's not safe.

Jim: Just a few more questions. _____ _____ ever exercise?

Ken: _____ _____ .

Jim: _____ _____ watch what you eat?

Ken: _____ _____ really.

Jim: One more question. How long do you _____ _____ live?

Ken: Hmm … In my neighborhood? _____ _____ long.

Teacher's copy

Prepare an audio tape with this dialogue on it and play it three times for the students. The first and third times you play the tape, don't stop it during the dialogue. When playing the tape for the second time, please pause after each line.

Jim: *Can I* ask you a few questions?

Ken: Sure. What do you *want to* know?

Jim: *I'm* taking a survey about lifestyles.

Ken: Okay.

Jim: *Do you* smoke?

Ken: No, but I *used to* smoke a lot.

Jim: When did you quit?

Ken: Last week, *but I have* smoked a couple today.

Jim: I see. *Do you* drink a lot?

Ken: That depends upon what you mean by a lot.

Jim: *Did you* drink anything last night?

Ken: *Yeah, I did.* But only about six or seven beers.

Jim: I see. "Only" six or seven. *Are you going to* drink tonight?

Ken: *Yeah, of course.* It's my poker night. *So, I'll* probably drink a lot.

Jim: *Will you* drive to your poker game?

Ken: Yeah, of course. *It's only* a few blocks away, but my neighborhood's not safe.

Jim: Just a few more questions. *Do you* ever exercise?

Ken: *No, never.*

Jim: *Do you* watch what you eat?

Ken: *No, not* really.

Jim: One more question. How long do you *expect to* live?

Ken: Hmm ... In my neighborhood? *Not very* long.

Appendix 3.1: 343 possible *wh-* word and auxiliary/modal-pronoun combinations

wh-	pronouns	did		do/does		will
what	I	whaddideye	whateye	whaddo-I		whattle-eye
	you	whaddidya	whadja	whaddaya	what-cha	whattle-ya
	he	whaddidee	whadee	whaduzzy	what-see	whattle-ee
	she	whaddidshe	wachee	whaduzshe	what-she	whattle-she
	it	whaddidit	whadit	whaduzzit	what-sit	whattle-it
	we	whaddidwe	whadwe	whaddawe		whattle-we
	they	whadthey	whaddidthey	whaddathey		whattle-they
how	I		howdeye	howdo-I		howell-eye
	you	howdidya	howdja	howdaya		howell-ya
	he		howdee	how-duzzy	howzee	howell-ee
	she		howdchee	how-duzshe	howz-she	howell-she
	it		howdit	how-duzzit	howzit	howell-it
	we		howdwe	how-dawe		howell-we
	they		howdthey	howda-they		howell-they
when	I		whendeye	when-da-eye		whennel-eye
	you		whenja	whendaya		whennel-ya
	he		whendee	when-duzzy	whenzee	whennel-ee
	she		whendshe	when-duzshe	whenz-she	whennel-she
	it		whendit	when-duzzit	whenzit	whennel-it
	we			when-da-we		whennel-we
	they			whendathey		whennel-they
why	I		wide-eye	why-da-eye		why-ull-eye
	you	why-didya	wide-ja	why-da-ya		why-ull-ya
	he		wide-ee	why-duzzy	wize-ee	why-ull-ee
	she		wideshe	why-duzshe	wize-she	why-ull-she
	it		wideit	why-duzzit	wize-it	why-ull-it
	we		widewe	why-da-we		why-ull-we
	they		widethey	why-da-they		why-ull-they
which	I			which-da-eye		which-ull-eye
	you	whichdidja		which-da-ya		which-ull-ya
	he	whichdiddee		which-duzzy		which-ull-ee
	she			which-duzshe		which-ull-she
	it			which-duzzit		which-ull-it
	we			whichda-we		which-ull-we
	they			whichda-they		which-ull-they

continued…

wh-	pronouns	did	do/does		will
who	I	hude-eye	hoodoo-eye		hooleye
	you	hude-ja	hooda-ya		hoolya
	he	hude-ee	hoo-duzzy	hoo-zee	hoolee
	she	hudeshe	hoo-duzshe	hooz-she	hoolshe
	it	hude-it	hoo-duzzit	hoozit	hoolit
	we	hude-we	hooda-we		hoolwe
	they	hudethey	hooda-they		hoolthey
where	I	wheredeye	where-da-eye		where-ull-eye
	you	wheredja	where-da-ya		where-ull-ya
	he	wheredee	where-duzzy	where-zee	where-ull-ee
	she	wheredshe	where-duzshe	where-she	where-ull-she
	it	wheredit	where-duzzit	where-sit	where-ull-it
	we	wheredwe	whereda-we		where-ull-we
	they	wheredthey	whereda-they		where-ull-they

wh-	pronouns	am/is/are		was/were	has/have		can
what	I		whaddam-eye	wha-wasseye		whattave-eye	wha-kenneye
	you	whadda-ya	what-cha	wha-wereya		whattave-ya	wha-kenya
	he	whaddizzee	what-see	wha-wazzee	whattazzee	what-see	wha-kenny
	she	whadizshe	what-she	wha-waz-she	whattaz-she	what-she	wha-kenshe
	it	whaddizzit	what-sit	wha-wazzit	whattazzit	what-sit	wha-kennit
	we		whatter-we	wha-werewe		whattavewe	wha-kenwe
	they		whatter-they	wha-werethey		whattavethey	wha-kenthey
how	I		howmeye			how've-eye	
	you		how-erya			how've-ya	how-kenya
	he	how-izzee	howzee	how-wereya	how-hazzee	howzee	how-kenny
	she	how-is-she	howz-she	how-wazzee	howhaz-she	howz-she	
	it	how-izzit	howzit	how-wazzit	how-hazzit	howzit	how-kennit
	we		how-erwe			how've-we	
	they		howerthey			how've-they	
when	I		whennem-eye			when-uv-eye	
	you		whenerya	when-wereya		when-uv-ya	when-kenya
	he	when-izzee	whenzee	when-wazzee	when-hazzee	whenzee	when-kenny
	she	wheniz-she	whenz-she	when-wazzit	when-haz-she	whenz-she	when-kennit
	it	whenizzit	whenzit		when-hazzit	whenzit	
	we		whenner-we			when-uv-we	
	they		whenner-they			when-uv-they	

wh-	pronouns	am/is/are		was/were	has/have		can
why	I		whime-eye			wive-eye	
	you		why-er-ya	why-wereya		wive-ya	why-kenya
	he	why-izzee	wize-ee	why-wazzee	why-hazzee	wize-ee	why-kenny
	she	why-iz-she	wize-she	why-wazzit	why-haz-she	wize-she	
	it	why-izzit	wize-it		why-hazzit	wize-it	why-kennit
	we		why-er-we			wive-we	
	they		why-er-they			wive-they	
which	I	which-um-eye			which-uv-eye		
	you	which-er-ya		which-wereya	which-uv-ya		which-kenya
	he	which-izzee		which-wazzee	which-azzee		which-kenny
	she	which-iz-she			which-azshe		
	it	which-izzit		which-wazzit	which-azzit		which-kennit
	we	which-er-we			which-uv-we		
	they	whicher-they			wichuv-they		
who	I	hoomeye	hoomeye		hoove-eye		
	you	hoo-er-ya	hoo-er-ya	hoo-wereya	hoove-ya	hoo-zee	hoo-kenya
	he	hoo-izzee	hoo-zee	hoo-wazzee	hoo-hazzee	hooz-she	hoo-kenny
	she	hoo-iz-she	hooz-she		hoo-haz-she		
	it	hoo-izzit	hoozit	hoo-wazzit	hoo-hazzit	hoozit	hoo-kennit
	we	hoo-er-we	hoo-er-we				
	they	hoo-er-they	hoo-er-they				
where	I		where-my				
	you	where-erya	where-ya	where-wereya			where-kenya
	he	where-izzee	where-zee	where-wazzee	where-azee	where-zee	where-kenny
	she	whereizshe	where-she		where-azshe	where-she	
	it	where-izzit	where-sit	where-wazzit	where-azit	where-sit	where-kennit
	we	where-erwe	where-we				
	they	where-erthey	wherethey				

Appendix 3.2: Common *wh*-questions and how they are pronounced

what	what did I	whadeye	whadeye say?
	what do you	whaddaya	whaddaya want?
	what will he	whattle-ee	whattle-ee do?
	what is she	what-she	what-she doing?
	what was it	wha-wazzit	wha-wazzit called?
	what have we	whattave-we	whattave-we bought?
	what can they	wha-kenthey	wha-kenthey do?
how	how can I	how-kenneye	how-kenneye get there?
	how did you	howdja	howdja know?
	how does he	how-duzzy	how-duzzy like it?
	how will she	howell-she	howell-she do it?
	how is it	howzit	howzit coming?
	how were we	how-were-we	how-were-we supposed to know?
	how have they	howve-they	howve-they been?
who	who have I	hoove-eye	hoove-eye met?
	who can you	hoo-kenya	hoo-kenya ask?
	who did he	hude-ee	hude-ee talk to?
	who does she	hoo-duzshe	hoo-duzshe think she is?
	who will it	hoolit	hoolit go to?
	who are we	hoo-er-we	hoo-er-we gonna meet?
	who were they	hoo-were-they	hoo-were-they calling?
why	why was I	why-wuzzeye	why-wuzzeye so tired?
	why have you	wive-ya	wive-ya come?
	why can he	why-kenny	why-kenny go home?
	why did she	wide-she	wide-she ask you?
	why does it	why-duzzit	why-duzzit always rain on sunday?
	why will we	why-ull-we	why-ull-we go there?
	why are they	why-er-they	why-er-they leaving now?
why not	why aren't I	why-aren-neye	why-aren-neye invited?
	why weren't you	why-weren-cha	why-weren-cha there?
	why hasn't he	why-hazzinee	why-hazzinee called?
	why hasn't she	why-canshee	why-canshee ever be on time?
	why didn't it	why-din-nit	why-din-nit leave earlier?
	why don't we	why-doan-we	why-doan-we go ta lunch?
	why won't they	why-woon-they	why-woon-they fix it?

Appendix 3.3

Student's copy

Please listen to the following sentences, and write the number of words that are in the unreduced version of each (contractions = one word). There will be contractions, yes/no questions, and "wh" questions.

example:
__4__ ['Whereja go'→
        Where (2) did (3) you (4) go?]

A _____ Where did he go?

B _____ It's cloudy today.

C _____ I don't know.

D _____ Do you like coffee?

E _____ He has to go home.

F _____ Is it blue or green?

G _____ Can't she speak Japanese?

H _____ What are you doing?

I _____ When do you want to go?

J _____ That's your grandfather, isn't it?

K _____ I want a cup of tea.

L _____ Give it to her brother.

M _____ I'm going to play tennis.

N _____ Are you tired?

O _____ How will we get there?

Teacher's copy

Please read the following sentences at natural speed and have students write the number of words that are in the unreduced version of each (contractions = one word)

example:
__4__ ['Whereja go'→
        Where (2) did (3) you (4) go?]

A __4__ Where did he go?

B __3__ It's cloudy today.

C __3__ I don't know.

D __4__ Do you like coffee?

E __5__ He has to go home.

F __5__ Is it blue or green?

G __4__ Can't she speak Japanese?

H __4__ What are you doing?

I __6__ When do you want to go?

J __5__ That's your grandfather, isn't it?

K __6__ I want a cup of tea.

L __5__ Give it to her brother.

M __5__ I'm going to play tennis.

N __3__ Are you tired?

O __5__ How will we get there?

Appendix 3.4

Your teacher will read one of the following pairs of sentences. Please listen carefully and circle the letter in front of the sentence which you hear.

1. a How did he know?
   b How will he know?

2. a Why did you get up early?
   b Why do you get up early?

3. a What are they doing?
   b What were they doing?

4. a Where has she gone?
   b Where is she going?

5. a Who will we hear?
   b Who did we hear?

6. a What am I to do?
   b What can I do?

7. a How do you do it?
   b How will you do it?

8. a Who was going there?
   b Who is going there?

9. a What has it done?
   b What is it doing?

10. a When is she going there?
    b When is he going there?

11. a Which do you like the best, ham, spam or lamb?
    b Which did you like the best, ham, spam or lamb?

12. a Why can he go?
    b Why can't he go?

Appendix 3.5

Student's copy

Please listen to the following conversations. Please write two or more separate words on each line.

Carl: _____ going to do on Sunday?
Dave: Nothing much. Why?
Carl: We're going to the beach. _____ want to come?
Dave: Sounds good. _____ going to go with?
Carl: Joey and Tim.
Dave: _____ get there?
Carl: Joey's car.
Dave: That little thing? _____ take my van?
Carl: You don't mind?
Dave: No, not at all. _____ meet you?
Carl: I'll have Tim and Joey come over to my house.
Dave: _____ be there?
Carl: How's nine-thirty?
Dave: That's early. I like to sleep a little bit on Sunday morning.
Carl: Okay. _____ want to make it?
Dave: _____ a quarter to eleven?
Carl: Great. See you then.

Teacher's copy

Prepare an audio tape with this dialogue on it and play it three times for the students. The first and third that you play the tape don't stop it during the dialogue. When playing the tape for the second time, please pause after each line.

Carl: <u>Whaddaya</u> going to do on Sunday?
Dave: Nothing much. Why?
Carl: We're going to the beach. <u>Ya</u> want to come?
Dave: Sounds good. <u>Hoo-er-ya</u> going to go with?
Carl: Joey and Tim.
Dave: <u>Howell-we</u> get there?
Carl: Joey's car.
Dave: That little thing? <u>Why-doan-we</u> take my van?
Carl: You don't mind?
Dave: No, not at all. <u>Where-ull-eye</u> meet you?
Carl: I'll have Tim and Joey come over to my house.
Dave: <u>Whennel-they</u> be there?
Carl: How's nine-thirty?
Dave: That's early. I like to sleep a little bit on Sunday morning.
Carl: Okay. <u>What-time-da-ya</u> want to make it?
Dave: <u>Howz</u> a quarter to eleven?
Carl: Great. See you then.

9

Visualizing English Speech Reductions Using the Free Phonetic Software Package *WASP*

J. KEVIN VARDEN
Meiji Gakuin University, Tokyo/Yokohama, Japan

This chapter explores the use of the free phonetic software package WASP for use in pronunciation training with a focus on the speech reductions found in North American English. The chapter discusses the basic information provided by the WASP displays and provides examples of the different types of sounds found in English. The chapter then discusses several types of common reductions—schwa reduction, flapping, coalescent assimilation, and elision. By presenting and explaining WASP graphs of the reductions and warning of the difficulties that can be encountered in using software for pronunciation training, the chapter provides motivated instructors with the information they will need to initiate a training program focusing on naturally reduced North American English speech. Thus, this chapter will probably be of interest to language teachers, researchers, testers, and materials developers who want to understand, teach, and develop materials or tests for teaching reduced forms.

CALL software has shown remarkable progress in recent years, from the simple fill-in-the-blanks grammar typing exercises I used studying French in college to visually rich multimedia titles (e.g., the Rosetta Stone family of products, 2005) and titles containing video clips that allow the learner to see and hear native speakers in action (e.g., *101 Languages of the World*). They have continued to evolve with the advent of intelligent CALL systems that allow the instructor to customize the software without the need for programming skills (Tokuda, 2002) and the Web-assisted language learning discussed in Ruipérez (2001).

The same is true for CALL software that provides visual feedback for computer-assisted pronunciation training (CAPT; e.g., Neri, Cucchiarini, Strik, & Boves, 2002). The use of visual feedback for pronunciation training goes back some 40 years to oscilloscopes that displayed a shape corresponding to a single, sustained vowel (James, 1976; Vardanian, 1964; see also de Bot, 1980). It has evolved into more sophisticated software and hardware systems used for pronunciation practice for a wide variety of purposes, especially rhythm and intonation (Anderson-Hsieh, 1992, 1996; Cranen, Weltens, de Bot, & Van Rossum, 1984; de Bot, 1983; de Bot & Mailfert, 1982; Dowd, Smith, & Wolfe, 1998; Gitlits, 1972; Hirata, 2004a, see also

Varden, J. K. (2006) Visualizing English speech reductions using the free phonetic software package *WASP*. In J. D. Brown, & K. Kondo-Brown, (Eds.), *Perspectives on teaching connected speech to second language speakers* (pp. 127–165). Honolulu, HI: University of Hawai'i, National Foreign Language Resource Center.

chapter 13 of this book; Lambacher, 1999; Molholt, 1990; Nishi & Kewley-Port, 2005; Richmond, Barrett, & Kraul, 1976; Stenson, Downing, Smith, & Smith, 1992).

One area less well explored in the CAPT literature is the teaching of speech reductions such as *wanna* from *want to* (Brown & Hilferty, 1986a; Ur, 1987; see Brown & Hilferty, 1989 for a large list of these reductions). Thus the focus of this chapter is on teaching speech reductions commonly found in North American English (NAE) using the free phonetics software *WASP*.

At this point, it is appropriate that I state my position clearly: speech reductions are not lazy or sloppy language. They are an essential part of natural spoken English, and to treat them as anything less severely handicaps the language learner's ability to understand the most basic spoken conversations (Norris, 1993, 1995).[1] The position is controversial (Henrichsen, 1984; also see Ito's study which is chapter 6 of this book). However, the concern that reduced speech input is not readily available for student uptake can be answered with the contention that this is primarily due to insufficient exposure to reduced speech combined with a lack of instructor confidence and training in reduced forms (see Rogerson's study which is chapter 7 of this book). If not introduced to a sufficient quantity of naturally reduced speech from the outset so that they can begin the acquisition process of the language's sound system that forms the basis of all other naturalistic language learning (as opposed to learning about the language), the student will be incapable of understanding the simplest of everyday conversations (Ur, 1987). This is a frustrating experience for any student who tries to use his language outside of the classroom. Also, as noted in James (1976) and others, in English, rhythm and intonation are often more important for intelligibility than production of individual sounds, and reductions are an essential part of a natural English rhythm.

Another good reason to use visualization of speech is that it provides learners with a sensitivity to speech that their ears cannot hear and they cannot readily feel (de Bot, 1983; de Bot & Mailfert, 1982). This is particularly true in light of recent work on what are called *magnet* vowels (Kuhl, 1991, 1992; Kuhl, Andruski, Chistovich, Chistovich, Kozhevnikova, and Ryskina, 1997), to be discussed further later in this chapter. Simply put, when we listen to our native language, we rely on specialized knowledge we acquired along with the language. Until we have enough experience with a foreign language, we hear it in terms of our native language(s). This is transparent in the katakana-like pronunciation of many Japanese learners of English—they are not pronouncing English poorly, but are instead pronouncing Japanese words that have been borrowed from English. Using computer displays to visualize what is happening in their mouths can help students become more sensitive to the target language's sounds, sound changes, and the muscle movements that produce them, just as visualizing movements helps athletes improve their performance.

Unfortunately, truly interactive pronunciation tutoring software is still not widely available. This is primarily due to the limitations of speech recognition software and the highly variable nature of pronunciation. The more manageable task, and the approach used by most commercial titles, is to simply supply learners with a visual representation of a native speaker model pronunciation and let them record their

[1] The history of the attitude of English speech reductions as lazy would make for an interesting sociolinguistic study. Do French language instructors characterize French liaison as lazy because the spelling no longer reflects pronunciation?

voices and try to match it. The speed of modern personal computers now makes it possible to do so with very little delay. Many language lab facilities now have PCs available for student use, and there is now free software available (also known as *freeware*). The use of software for pronunciation training is therefore within the grasp of many language learners and facilities.[2]

The problem with using this freeware to match pronunciations is, of course, that it puts the burden of learning on the instructor and the student. It necessarily involves learning how to use a personal computer, the speech analysis software being used, and a microphone for recording one's voice into the computer. Just this much is no small task. At universities like the author's, where all freshman students enroll in a compulsory computer literacy course, basic computer use is not an issue, but at institutions where this level of support is not available computer familiarity must also be covered at some level. Although no easy task, the rewards for both the instructor and student can be great.

The organization of this chapter is as follows. First, I will introduce the software displays used by the software program used throughout this chapter. I will then cover the basic visual representations of the various speech sounds, since to practice speech reductions using visual information requires the learner to be familiar with what the unreduced forms look like. This will be followed by the basic use of the speech analysis software *WASP* for pronunciation practice purposes. The chapter then contains a selected sample of English speech reductions and their visual representations. Finally, a brief summary of the chapter is provided.

WASP and Its Displays

The program chosen for demonstration purposes in this chapter is *WASP*, a phonetic voice analysis program authored and maintained by Professor Mark Huckvale at University College London. There are other free or inexpensive titles that could be used, but despite its being free *WASP* offers the necessary functions for pronunciation training and is very easy to install and learn to use. An image-rich introduction to *WASP* written for students of lower-level English ability can be downloaded from the following URL: http://www.meijigakuin.ac.jp/~varden/vsr/. Basic use of the PC and Windows will not be covered here; the reader is referred to his computer manual if necessary. Once *WASP* is installed on the PC, the instructor and student are faced with the task of familiarizing themselves with the visual representations of speech that *WASP* provides.

Waveform display

The most basic display is the *waveform*.[3] The waveform is a graphic representation of the sound waves that move through the air as we speak, like water waves over the surface of a pond. The sound waves travel into the microphone and cause part of it (the diaphragm in most microphones) to wiggle back and forth—the stronger the sound wave, the larger the movement. That movement is turned into an electric signal, and the electric signal is turned into a string of numbers. The computer

---

[2]   Many of the obstacles encountered in earlier interactive systems (lack of hard disk space for storing sound files; processor speed for producing computer displays; see, e.g., Stenson, et al., 1992, pp. 14–15) have been removed with the advent of the affordable yet powerful personal computer. This is not to trivialize the problems of those areas in the world where technology is not readily available, a separate problem which needs addressing.

[3]   Editors' note: Definitions of the various terms used in this chapter to discuss acoustic phonetics are also given in the glossary of this book.

program draws those numbers on the screen for us, and we can see the stronger and weaker sound waves as recorded by the microphone. A waveform of the recording of the word *apa* that is included with *WASP* is shown in Figure 1, with the individual sounds labeled. The two groups of waves in Figure 1 are the first and second vowels [ɑ] of [ɑpɑ]; the white gap in between is the consonant [p]. The waveform can be useful for practicing English stress, since loudness (the relative height of the waves in the waveform) is associated with stress in English. It can also be useful for practicing intonation, rhythm, and syllables.

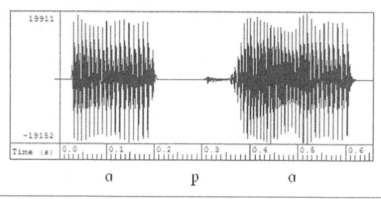

Figure 1.   **Waveform display of the word *apa*.**

Pitch trace

One of the most widely used displays in pronunciation training is the *pitch trace*. The pitch trace is a graph of the pitch of the speaker's voice as it goes up and down. Figure 2 shows the same waveform as above, together with a pitch trace. Looking at the scale on the left side of Figure 2, you can see from the pitch trace that the frequency of this speaker's voice fell from about 120 Hertz (Hz) to about 100Hz during the first vowel; it rose up to about 160Hz at the beginning of the second vowel and then fell again to about 100 Hz. Notice that only the vowels have a pitch trace associated with them. This is because pitch trace only tracks voicing; any sound that is voiceless has no voicing from which to draw a trace.

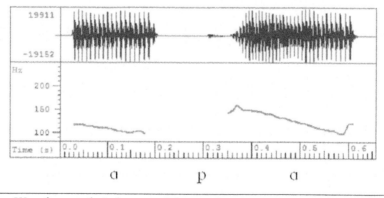

Figure 2.   **Waveform and pitch trace of the word *apa*.**

Pitch traces can be of great help in training English intonation, since the ups and downs of the pitch trace can directly show us not only word stress (higher pitch is generally associated with English stress[4]), but also can be used for teaching sentence-level intonation and rhythm.[5] To limit the scope of this chapter, teaching suprasegmentals using the pitch trace will not be covered here (see Anderson-Hsieh, 1992, 1996, for discussion and examples). Again, the message of James (1976) is worth keeping in mind: Good intonation can be much more important for intelligibility than the pronunciation of individual sounds.

Spectrograms

The other display commonly used in speech research is the *spectrogram*.

A spectrogram combines the information presented by the waveform and pitch trace. The waveform shows us how the loudness of the sound (the y-axis) changes over time (the x-axis), while the pitch trace shows us how the frequency (the y-axis) changes over time (the x-axis). The spectrogram presents all of this information at once using a third axis, the darkness of the picture (the z-axis); it shows us how the frequency (the y-axis) and loudness (the z-axis, or darkness) both change over time (the x-axis).

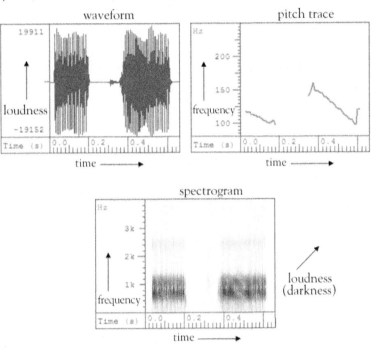

Figure 3.   Comparison of the information provided by the waveform, pitch trace, and spectrogram displays.

The spectrogram gives us a great deal of information about a speaker's pronunciation. We can get information about positions of the tongue and lips from the positions of the dark horizontal bands in the spectrogram and how they change. We can also see how the relative strength of the sounds change—the stronger portions are darker, and

---

[4]   I was somewhat surprised to learn that my stressed vowels generally drop in pitch; they are usually louder, longer, and slightly lower in pitch. Instructors need to be ready for individual variation in all aspects of pronunciation.

[5]   An interesting recent development in speech research is the idea that stress prominence in American English is based on jaw opening and closing (Erickson, 2003, 2004). For students having trouble producing clearly stressed vowels, the instructor may want to have them exaggerate their jaw opening.

the weaker portions are lighter. There are two types of spectrograms; each gives us different information.

Narrow-band spectrograms. The *narrow-band spectrogram* can clearly show us the different frequencies that a sound contains. It is especially useful when we are looking at the harmonics of a sound. The harmonics in the sample sound file apa.wav can be seen clearly in Figure 4. The bottom-most horizontal line is the pitch of the speaker's voice (the voicing of their vocal cords), and the other horizontal lines going up from the bottom of the figure are the harmonics of that frequency. You can clearly see variation in the pitch of the harmonics as the pitch of the speaker's voice changes. However, for the purposes of practicing sounds or speech reductions, the wide-band spectrogram (WBS) is generally more useful.

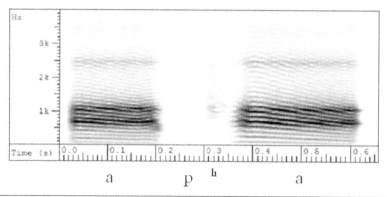

Figure 4.   A narrow-band spectrogram of the word *apa*.

Wide-band spectrograms. In contrast to narrow-band spectrograms, the WBS shows us very clearly when something starts and stops. This can be seen in Figure 5, where the vertical stripes are caused by the speaker's vocal cords clicking together. Besides being able to see the voicing clearly, we can also tell when individual sounds (like the [p] in the middle) start and stop.

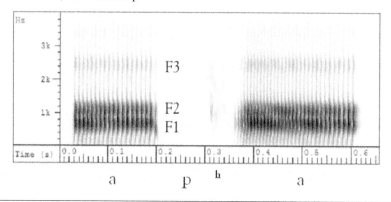

Figure 5.   A wide-band spectrogram of the word *apa*.

WBSs have one other very useful feature: the dark horizontal bands that are marked F1, F2, and F3. These are the *formants* of the vowels, the frequencies of sound that are resonating in the mouth. You can see by comparing Figures 4 and 5 that even though the pitch of the voice and all its harmonics drop over the course of both vowels (the falling, narrow horizontal lines), the formants don't fall in pitch; they stay almost perfectly horizontal. This and other characteristics of formants will be discussed further in the next section.

Visual Characteristics of Speech Sounds

We'll now turn to the visual characteristics of the most common North American English (NAE) speech sounds as seen in the *WASP* displays. Note that this introduction is necessarily brief; the reader is referred to chapter 7 of Borden, Harris, and Rapheal (1994), chapter 4 of Kent and Read (1996), or Ladefoged (2001) for further figures and background information. Also, this chapter uses the International Phonetic Alphabet (IPA) (IPA, 2001) for discussion purposes; IPA charts of the NAE simple vowels, diphthongs, and consonants are therefore provided in the appropriate sections. And perhaps the most important thing to note is the wide variability in pronunciation that you can find among speakers, even those from the same dialect. Both the instructor and student need to be flexible and patient, with the instructor playing the very important role of judging when the student's pronunciation is close enough.

Simple vowels[6]

I will begin with examples of the common NAE simple vowels. Although the number and quality of vowels vary by dialect, the simple NAE vowels are generally [i ɪ ɛ æ ʌ ɑ ɔ ʊ u], as in the words *heed, hid, head, had, hut, hot, caught, hood,* and *who'd,* respectively. (Note that not all dialects distinguish between *cot* [kɑt] and *caught* [kɔt]; see Ladefoged, 1993, p. 82). These are shown in the vowel chart in Figure 6. The position of the vowel symbols in Figure 6 are the relative positions of the top of the tongue when producing that vowel; that is, when we say an [i], our tongue is bunched up relatively high and front in the mouth. See Ladefoged and Maddieson (1996, pp. 284–285) for drawings of the actual tongue positions for these and other vowels.

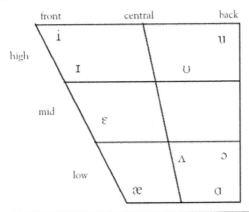

Figure 6.   The simple NAE vowels, adapted from Ladefoged (1993).

Whether or not we are consciously aware of it, we pronounce a vowel by holding the mouth and tongue in a certain position while letting the air out with *voicing,* that is, with the vocal cords vibrating. For example, to pronounce the [u] of *through* we pull the tongue fairly far back and towards the roof of the mouth, and slightly round the lips. We then pronounce the vowel with voicing. Voicing is what gives a vowel its

---

6   Editors' note: Definitions of the various phonological terms used in this chapter are also given in the glossary of this book.

power; what gives it its distinctive sound is the many different sound waves that resonate in the mouth while pronouncing it. Let's take a closer look at this process in order to understand what we're seeing in the upcoming discussion.

The vocal cords in our voice-box, or larynx, vibrate at a certain frequency during speech[7]; this is the pitch of our voice. For the average man, this is about 120 Hz, the average woman 225 Hz, and the average child 300 Hz, although the pitch of the voice varies widely between people and during speech (Kent & Read, 1992, p. 18). The vocal cords vibrate at one frequency when we hold the pitch steady (as in singing a fixed note), but like any musical instrument the vibration produces many harmonics at the same time. These harmonics of the vocal cord vibration are what give the richness to speech—as they travel out of the mouth and nose, some of them resonate within the mouth and nose. When we change the shape of our tongue and lips, the frequencies that resonate in the mouth and nose change as well. The changing resonating frequencies are what allow us to hear different vowels.

The narrow-band spectrogram shows us the harmonics of the voicing clearly. Figure 7 shows a narrow-band spectrogram of the NAE simple vowels listed above as produced by the author, a speaker of General American English. Again, the many lines going up each column in the display are the harmonics produced during each vowel; the darker the line, the stronger that harmonic frequency is resonating. The bottom-most line is the voicing, the vibration of the vocal cords; for this speaker, about 100 Hz. All of the lines above the voicing are the harmonics of the voicing frequency (e.g., the frequency of the voicing x 2, x 3, etc.).

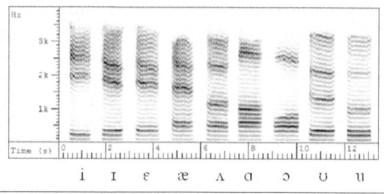

Figure 7.   Narrow-band spectrogram showing the harmonics of the simple NAE vowels.

Although useful for understanding what is happening, the narrow-band spectrogram is of limited use for pronunciation training. We talk about tongue and lip positions in pronunciation training—how we move the mouth to produce different sounds. The WBS is the more useful display for indicating these movements. To draw a WBS, the software blends the stronger adjacent harmonics together into formants. The formants for each vowel can be seen clearly in the following WBS of the simple NAE vowels, where the first two formants, F1 and F2, have been marked with line segments for clarity. By comparing Figures 7 and 8 you can see how the software blended the individual harmonics together to create the formants. Again, each vowel has its own characteristic formant pattern; if it didn't we wouldn't be able to distinguish between them.

---

[7]   An easy way to feel the vibration of the vocal cords is to put several fingers on your voice-box, and then say *sssszzzzsssszzzz*. You can feel the vibration, or voicing, during the [z].

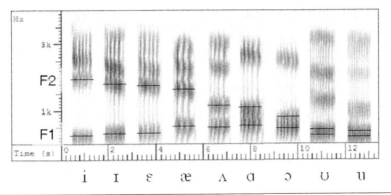

Figure 8.   Wide-band spectrogram showing the formants of the simple NAE vowels.

A useful way to think about formants is to equate them with musical notes. Each formant is very much like one note played on a piano. Each vowel, then, can be thought of as a chord of three or four notes—the dark bands for each vowel in Figure 8:

> F1 = formant 1; the bottom-most dark band for each vowel;
> F2 = formant 2; the second dark band from the bottom for each vowel; and
> F3 = formant 3; the third dark band from the bottom for each vowel.

Just as playing three notes is sufficient for producing a chord, typically the first three formants from the bottom give a vowel its characteristic sound. However, for pronunciation training F3 is not as important as F1 and F2 for judging the movements of the tongue, with one exception: the r-sound. F3 will therefore be excluded from the rest of the following discussion.

You can see in Figure 8 how F1 starts fairly low for the vowel [i], rises up as one progresses to the vowel [ɑ], and then falls again as one reaches the vowel [u]. This shows us that F1 is associated with the height of the tongue; the higher the position of the tongue, the lower the value for F1. Similarly, you can also see how F2 starts relatively high at the left of Figure 8 for the vowel [i] and continually falls as one progresses to the vowel [u]. This is because F2 is associated with tongue frontness or backness; the farther forward in the mouth the body of the tongue is when producing a vowel, the higher the value of F2. In slightly more formal terms, the following relationships hold:

> The relationship between tongue position and the first two formants.
> F1 is inversely related to tongue height.
> F2 is inversely related to tongue backness.

Note that for the vowels [u] and [ʊ], F2 almost blends into F1.

We can put this information to good use in pronunciation training. By watching the formants move up and down as learners change the position and/or shape of their tongue, they can get visual feedback about what their mouth is doing.

For the sake of completeness, it is worth noting that the value of F2 is also associated with lip rounding; the more round a vowel production is, the lower the value of F2 will be. In both English and Japanese, this is not so much an issue, since in both languages the lips are rounded only for the back vowels; lip rounding just reinforces the lowering of F2 due to the tongue moving back in the mouth. In languages where there are both round and unrounded front or back vowels, the situation can be more complex and will need more attention from the instructor and student. In remedial situations where the student is having trouble producing a low enough F2 because of trouble drawing the tongue back in the mouth, lip rounding can help compensate for it.

Again, the two relationships noted above are important for practicing vowel pronunciation, since they are the best clues to the vowel quality that learners have available. Their ears may not be reliable; until they have sufficient experience with the target language to start acquiring their own vowel inventory for the language, they will be hearing the target language in terms of their own language. The visual feedback given by the changing formants can help them overcome this limitation.

Diphthongs

The next class of sounds I will discuss is the diphthongs. To continue the musical analogy above, diphthongs are best thought of as movements; if simple vowels are sustained notes, diphthongs are slurs between notes. They are not double vowels; they are transitions from a starting position to an ending one. They are written with two vowel symbols to show this transition. For example, the diphthong in *hide* is transcribed as [aɪ] to show that its pronunciation begins at close to the same place as the simple vowel [a] ([a] is more central then [ɑ] on the IPA chart); the tongue and lips are then smoothly moved into the position for the simple vowel [ɪ] in *hid*. Again, it is the movement that identifies the vowel as a diphthong. The diphthongs are indicated in the IPA chart by arrows, as shown in Figure 9.

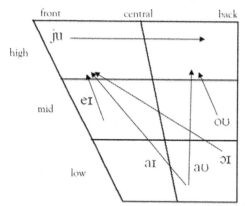

Figure 9.   The NAE diphthongs, adapted from Ladefoged (1993).

This diphthong transition between vowels can be seen in Figures 10 and 11 below. They show the pronunciation of the English diphthongs [eɪ] (*make*), [aɪ] (*hike*), [ɔɪ] (*boy*), [aʊ] (*how*), [oʊ] (*know*), and [ju] (*you*). You can see the change in the formants from the beginning of the diphthong to the end. This is due to the changing position of the tongue during the diphthong. As noted above, raising the tongue will cause F1 to fall; you can see this in [aʊ] as the tongue moves from the position for the low vowel [a] to the position for the high vowel [ʊ]. Similarly, bringing the tongue to the front of the mouth will cause F2 to raise up in the spectrogram; this can be seen clearly in [aɪ] and [ɔɪ]. These formant transitions need to be attended to when practicing diphthongs.

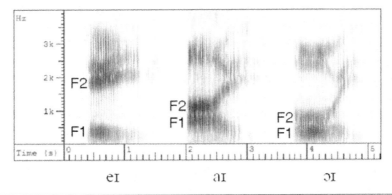

Figure 10. Wide-band spectrogram of the NAE diphthongs [eɪ], [aɪ], and [ɔɪ].

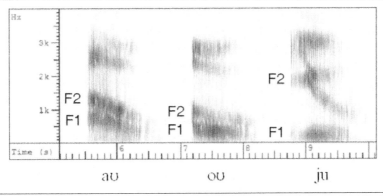

Figure 11. Wide-band spectrogram of the NAE diphthongs [aʊ], [oʊ], and [ju].

We will now turn to the visual characteristics of the consonants found in NAE, the *glides* [w] and [j], the *lateral* [l], the *rhotic* [ɹ], the *nasals* [m n ŋ], the *stops* [p b t d k g], the *fricatives* [f v θ ð s z ʃ ʒ h], and the *affricates* [tʃ dʒ]. I will begin with the class of consonants known as the glides.

Glides

The *glides* [w j] (*work, yellow*) are different from other consonants in that they are not produced by holding the mouth and lips in one steady position. They are instead transitions from one position to another, just as diphthongs are. Glides are often characterized in phonetics (e.g., Ladefoged, 1993) as the consonant counterparts of vowels—[w] is analogous to a transition from [u] to the following sound, while [j] is analogous to a transition from [i] to a following sound. This can be seen, heard, and felt when pronouncing *woo* very slowly; very little movement is required to go from [w] to [u]. The same holds true for *ye*; very little movement is required to go from [j] to [i]. Figure 12 shows that there is very little change in the formants during these words.

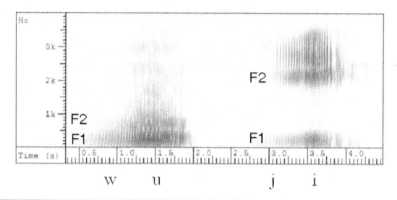

Figure 12. Wide-band spectrogram of *woo* and *ye*.

You can see the characteristic formants of the vowels [u] (low F1; low F2) and [i] (low F1; high F2) in Figure 12. You can also see from the spectrogram that there is not much change in the formats at the beginning of each word; the glides are basically a slight movement into the position for the following vowel. The initial rise in the F2 associated with the [w] in *woo* is due to the slight unrounding of the lips during the transition from [w] to [u] in this speaker's speech.

The glide transitions can be seen more clearly in words that have these glides in an initial consonant cluster. The display in Figure 13 shows a pronunciation of the words *quick* [kwɪk] and *pure* [pjur]. The change in the second formants (marked with arrows in Figure 13) can be clearly seen as it moves from the position of the glide to its position for the following vowel. In the case of *quick*, the low F2 moves from the position for [u] to the following vowel [i]; in the case of *pure*, the high F2 moves from the position of [i] to the following vowel [u]. These are the movements to look for when identifying the glides.

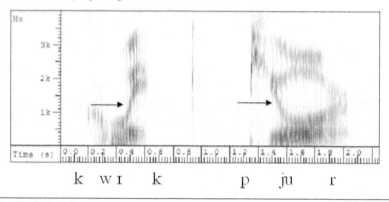

Figure 13. Wide-band spectrogram of *quick* and *pure*.

Liquids

Often l- and r-like sounds are discussed together under the umbrella term *liquids*. This is due to how fluid their pronunciation is and how much the tongue shape and placement adjusts to the sounds coming before and after. Especially in the literature on Japanese learners of English there is a long history of contrasting English [l] and [r] (Lively, Logan, & Pisoni, 1993; Miyawaki, Strange, Verbrugge, Liberman, Jenkins, & Fujimura, 1975; Takagi, 2002) because of the difficulty Japanese learners have distinguishing between the two. To complicate things, different researchers have proposed many different varieties of each sound based on how much co-articulation there is with surrounding sounds (Kent & Read, 1992, pp. 138–140)—at the very minimum, Kent and Read suggest that there are at least two major varieties of each, those found before vowels and those found after (e.g., the syllable-initial *light* and syllable-final *dark* [l]s discussed in Roach, 2004, p. 59). For the purposes of pronunciation practice, the instructor will need to decide on which words and phrases to practice, introducing as much variability in the sounds as they think the student can handle.

Despite often being classified together as liquids, there is a good reason to discuss [l] and [ɹ] separately, as in, for example, Gilbert (1993)—the way each sound is pronounced.

The Lateral. The *lateral* [l] (*like*) is, in terms of tongue positions, very similar to [d]; the primary difference is that with [l] the sides of the tongue are pulled down to let the air escape around the sides of the tongue while with the [d] the air flow is blocked off completely. This can be felt by saying [dl] slowly with no intervening vowel; the only action necessary to go from [d] to [l] is to pull down the sides of the tongue (Roach, 2004).

Like the vowels, [l] is voiced. This means it has its own characteristic formants that can be seen when it is pronounced slowly. According to Ladefoged (1993), [l] has formants at apr. 250, 1100, and 2400 Hz. The research cited in Kent and Read (1992) gives average values of 340, 1211, 2810 Hz—somewhat higher, but with similar spacing of the formants. The formants can also be seen in Figure 14, which contains examples of [l] in a *lull in*, excerpted from the longer a *lull in the action*. F1, F2, and F3 of the first [l] have been marked with small arrows.

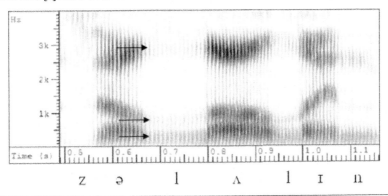

Figure 14. Wide-band spectrogram of the NAE lateral [l] in *a lull in*.

One thing you can quickly see is that the formants for [l] are much weaker than the surrounding vowel formants. This is true for all of the consonants that have clear formants. You can also see that for this speaker the formants of the [l] are in different places than the numbers cited above, being centered at approximately 300, 800 and 2900 Hz. Comparing the sets of numbers shows that the speaker-to-speaker variation in the lateral sound is large.[8] The instructor should be aware of this fact and make sure not to over-stress any given formant placement as the correct one. As long as the

---

[8]   The exact position of the formants of vowels and consonants is affected by many things—the speaker's age, the size of the speaker's head and vocal tract, the speaker's dialect, etc. See chapter 7 in Kent and Read (1992) for detailed information.

learner can be made aware of the following, they should be deemed successful in producing an adequate lateral consonant:

1. The tongue tip needs to be anchored firmly to the top of the mouth during the [l] sound. The [d] sound can be used as a good starting point.
2. The sides of the tongue need to be pulled down to let air flow out. Practicing the [dl] sequence mentioned above is a good place to start.
3. When combined with vowels, as in Figure 14, the display should show the formants for [l] as noticeably weaker than the formants for the vowels, but still well-developed.
4. Each formant for [l] should be somewhere in the same range as the numbers cited above.

The Rhotic. The *rhotic* [ɹ] (*ring*) can be, like [l], pronounced in many slightly different ways depending on where it is in the syllable and the sounds around it. However, the tongue position for English [ɹ] is even more variable than for [l]. While the shape of the tongue for [l] might change slightly due to the surrounding sounds, recent research (Espy-Wilson, Boyce, Jackson, Narayanan, & Alwan, 2000; Hashi, Honda, & Westbury, 2003) clearly shows speakers using very different tongue shapes and positions for [ɹ]. It turns out that it is not the position of the tongue that is important in the production of North American [ɹ], it is the falling third formant.

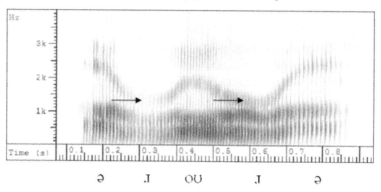

Figure 15. Wide-band spectrogram showing the fall of F3 associated with the English [ɹ] in *aurora*.

This *F3 drop* can be seen clearly in Figure 15, where the low point of the drop has been marked with arrows; it is associated with creating an air space in the mouth. This can be done by bunching the tongue up in the middle of the mouth and/or curling the tip of the tongue toward the back of the mouth. Any practice involving [ɹ] should focus on finding a tongue position that produces a good F3 drop; an explanation with clear diagrams (e.g., Gilbert, 1993, p. 12) would probably help here. How good of an [ɹ] is good enough? Again, the instructor needs to be the judge.

Stop consonants

The *stop consonants*[9] [p b p t k g] (*pie, buy, tie, die, Kai, guy*) or simply *stops*, are produced by stopping the air from flowing out of the mouth. They can be thought of as breaks in the sound between vowels and other consonants. This stopping of the air flow is very evident in the spectrogram as a white space. This space has been marked

---

[9]   Stops are sometimes referred to as *plosives* due to the sudden release of air out of the mouth when the stop is released.

with a double-headed arrow in Figure 16. You can clearly see the white vertical space, known as a *stop gap,* in between the vowel formants. This is where tongue or lips were used to stop the flow of air; no air flow means no sound is recorded or displayed.

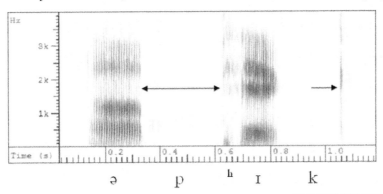

Figure 16. Wide-band spectrogram of *a pick* showing the stop gap (double-headed arrow) and release of the final consonant (right-headed arrow).

The other thing that can be seen in Figure 16 is the *aspiration* produced when the stop was released, the part of the display above the symbol [ʰ]. As implied by the use of the small h, aspiration is the same noise produced when pronouncing an *h.* How long the aspiration lasts varies widely by language and place of articulation (Cho & Ladefoged, 1999; Ladefoged & Cho, 2001; Lisker & Abramson, 1964). It usually lasts longer in English than in Japanese. Even if not specifically targeting stops during practice, the instructor should be on the look out for students producing voiceless English stops lacking aspiration. This is important because a voiceless stop without aspiration (e.g., a [p] in Spanish or Hindi) will be heard by native English speakers as a *b.* Native speakers rely on how long aspiration lasts (known as *voice onset time,* or VOT) to determine whether a [p] or a [b] was pronounced.

Another thing the instructor should keep in mind is that word-final stops often aren't released in NAE. Whereas in some dialects word-final stops are released with slight aspiration, as in Figure 16 (marked with a right-headed arrow), in NAE they often are not. Unreleased stops are difficult even for native speakers to hear, but they are even more so for students whose native language doesn't allow syllable-final stops (e.g., Japanese). If a student is having a great deal of trouble hearing the difference between, say, *trip* and *trick* ([tɹɪp], [tɹɪk]; both with unreleased final stops), the instructor may want to practice minimal pairs like these, calling attention to the slight changes that happen at the end of the vowel's formants—the end of the vowel formants will be slightly different before [p t k].

Besides the voiceless stops, there are also the voiced stops [b d g] in English. The voiced stops can be identified by a stop gap, the white vertical space in the display, the same as the voiceless stops. The stop gap can be seen in Figure 17, which shows part of the phrase *a big apple.* As with the voiceless stops, the stop gaps for [b] and [g] are clear in Figure 17. However, there is no strong voicing to be seen in the stop gap for [b] and very little for [g]. This is because although it may run against intuition, it is not actually the presence or absence of voicing that separates voiceless from voiced stops in English; it is the presence or absence of aspiration. In English voiceless stops have a fairly long period of aspiration; voiced stops typically have no voicing in the stop gap and no aspiration. (Voicing in the stop gap, known as *pre-voicing,* is common in languages like French and Spanish and is often produced by English speakers between vowels.) It can also be seen from Figure 17 that this speaker has released the [g], saying something almost resembling a *bigga apple*. Here the voicing does continue throughout the stop gap. However this extra vowel-like sound is quite natural for many speakers; as long as the instructor judges that the student's pronunciation is understandable enough, variability like this is quite acceptable.

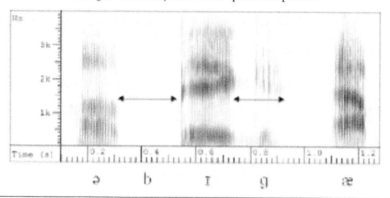

Figure 17. Wide-band spectrogram of *a big* showing the stop gap (double-headed arrows) of voiced stops.

Fricative consonants

The *fricatives* [f v θ ð s z ʃ ʒ h] (*fan, van, thing, that, sing, zip, ship, azure, hello*) are consonants that produce a large amount of frication (or *air friction*) where the air rushing out of a small space creates a hissing sound. Shushing someone ([ʃ] in English; [s] in Japanese) is a good example of a fricative sound.

English makes use of a large group of fricatives: [f v θ ð s z ʃ ʒ h] (see Ladefoged, 1993, pp. 65, 277, for discussion of the status of [h]). Fricatives differ in where in the mouth they are pronounced and in voicing. Unlike stops, the difference between voiced and voiceless fricatives is the actual presence or absence of voicing. Fricatives also differ acoustically in terms of how much noise each contains. The difference in the amount of noise produced with each can be seen in a WBS, after recording with a sampling frequency of 16kHz or even 22050Hz.

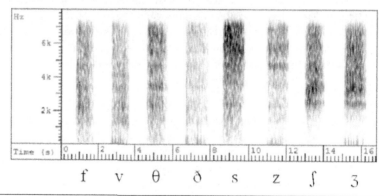

Figure 18. Wide-band spectrogram showing the noise of the English fricatives.

You can see that the noise for some fricatives covers more of the spectrogram than for others; you can also see how different parts of the different fricatives are darker. There are also formant-like horizontal bands running across the fricatives in different places. These things are evident when fricatives are recorded in isolation.

However, when recorded in running speech, fricatives, especially voiceless fricatives, are very weak compared to vowels. This makes them very difficult to see in a spectrogram. Figure 19 shows this in the phrase *a thin fish*. In running speech, the voiceless palatal fricative [ʃ] is usually clear enough to see in a spectrogram. The voiceless interdental fricative [θ], however, very often isn't. And even though voiced fricatives are in theory louder than the voiceless fricatives, some of them are often also quite difficult to see in spectrograms of phrases or sentences. In terms of pronunciation practice, this means the fricatives need to be zoomed in on during practice to magnify them, or practiced when pronounced in isolation. Having said that, for reduced speech fricatives are important in another context: when they are half of an affricate.

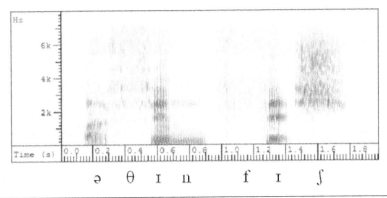

Figure 19. Wide-band spectrogram of *a thin fish* showing the noise of voiceless fricatives.

Affricate consonants

The *affricate* consonants [tʃ dʒ] (*church*, *judge*) are basically a combination of a stop and a fricative. To produce an affricate, the air is stopped in the mouth, but then the air is released out of the mouth just like a fricative. This is why the IPA symbol for an affricate is a combination of the symbols for a stop and a fricative.

English contains two affricates, [tʃ] and [dʒ]. The *stop + fricative* nature of [tʃ] can be seen in Figure 20, where the white area is again where the air flow was stopped, and the noisy portion after the white area is the frication produced when the air is released through a small area. As with the stops, Japanese and many other languages contain these sounds, and so they should not present a problem to most foreign language students. What both the instructor and student need to be able to identify is the noise caused by the fricative portion of the affricate, since this is a signature of one of the speech reductions (coalescent assimilation) to be discussed below.

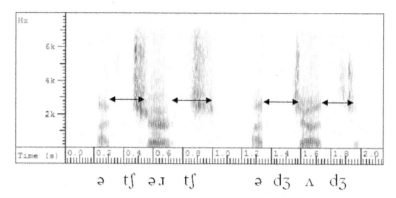

ə tʃ ə.ɪ tʃ   ə dʒ ʌ dʒ

Figure 20. Wide-band spectrogram of *a church* and *a judge* showing the English affricates (double-headed arrows).

Nasal consonants

The final class of consonants to be dealt with here is the *nasal consonants* [m n ŋ] (*sim, sin, sing*), also called *nasal stops*, or simply *nasals*. Nasals are produced by allowing the air to flow out of the nose while stopping the air flow in the mouth. You can feel this by comparing the pronunciations [b m], [d n], and [g ŋ]—while holding the lips closed to get ready to pronounce [b], you only have to let the air out of the nose to produce a [m]. The position of the lips and tongue are for all practical purposes identical; the difference lies in the lowering of the back of the roof of the mouth, called the *velum*, to allow the air to escape out of the nose. This air flow out of the nose results in a characteristic appearance in the display, as can be seen in Figure 21. Notice that like vowels, glides, [l] and [ɹ], nasals have formants, and are voiced throughout. Again, the position of the formants in the spectrogram, like for the lateral [l], vary by speaker, and the formants will be weaker than any surrounding vowels.

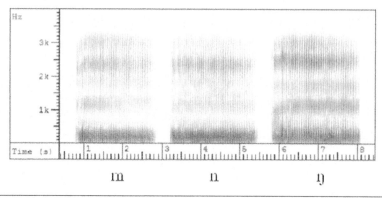

m   n   ŋ

Figure 21. Wide-band spectrogram of the English nasals showing the nasal formants.

Now that typical pronunciations of the sounds of English have been introduced, there is one more introductory topic to cover—the setup and basic use of the *WASP* software. Users who are familiar with the use of *WASP* or similar voice analysis software may wish to skip directly to the section following; those seeking more detailed instructions can refer to the Web site: http://www.meijigakuin.ac.jp/~varden/vsr/.

Setup and Recording

In order to interactively practice pronunciation using visual feedback, the instructor and student has to be able to use the software to record their voice and compare it with the native model. The steps for doing so in *WASP* will be covered here briefly; the basic procedure would be the same using any other software with the same functions. Needless to say, the larger the monitor the more detail can be seen, and the faster the PC being used the less waiting there will be while it draws the displays.

The first thing that must be done is to download and install *WASP*. *WASP* can be downloaded from its home page (http://www.phon.ucl.ac.uk/resource/sfs/wasp.htm); it can be installed by simply double-clicking on the downloaded file (as of this writing *wasp130.exe* for version 1.30). The program will also ask you if you wish to have a shortcut installed on the desktop, a recommended convenience.

Once the program is installed, the basic procedure for its setup is as follows.

1. Open up two display windows, one above the other.
2. Load or record a sample of native speech in the top display area.
3. Record the student saying the same thing in the other display area.
4. Look for portions where the displays don't match well.
5. Re-record as necessary, with the student adjusting her or his pronunciation to try to match the native speaker's.

In *WASP*, opening two windows entails opening two copies of *WASP*. The program will allow only one window at a time, but unlike most programs many copies of the program can be run at the same time. For other programs the instructor will need to refer to that software's documentation for the exact steps.

To set up two *WASP* windows:

1. Open up *WASP* by clicking on the desktop icon or selecting in from the Windows menu. Resize the window in the top half of the screen using the lower right drag handle (the lower right-hand corner). Resize it to slightly smaller than the upper half of the screen.
2. Open a second copy of *WASP*. Reposition the left upper corner of the second window exactly over the top of the first window. Then use its lower right drag handle to resize it so that both windows are the same size.
3. Move the second window to the bottom half of the screen.

The computer monitor should then look like Figure 22.

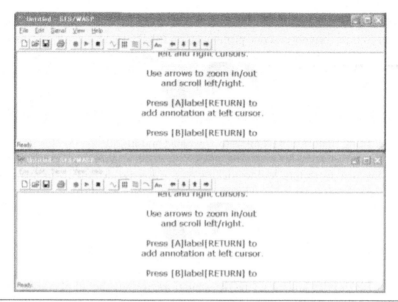

Figure 22. Two copies of WASP, open and ready for use.

For most pronunciation practice, only the speech waveform and WBS are necessary. These can be selected in the WASP toolbar, as in Figure 23.

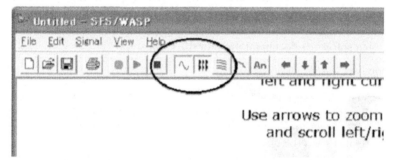

Figure 23. Selecting the waveform and wide-band spectrogram displays.

All other options can be turned off using either the toolbar or the *View* menu to maximize the viewing area in the window. The toolbar itself can also be hidden if the user doesn't mind using the menu commands instead of the toolbar buttons.

Once both windows are positioned, the instructor and student are ready to record their voices. There is a tutorial on recording into WASP under Windows XP available on the author's Web site; a quick summary of the basic procedure will have to suffice here.

There are two things affecting the quality of the recording that need to be attended to: how many times a second the computer measures the speech (the recording *sampling rate*), and how loud the person being recorded speaks into the microphone. As mentioned above, most speech reductions can be seen clearly when speech is recorded at a sampling rate of 8k. For technical reasons this lets us see all the frequencies from 0 Hz up to 4000 Hz, which includes most of the necessary information for speech sounds. The sampling rate setting is found in the Record dialog window that is opened by clicking on the Record menu command button in the toolbar; this brings up the Record dialog window. The setting is then made by selecting 8000 from the *Record Quality-Sampling Rate* pop-down menu. This lets the student to see most of the speech characteristics he'll need for practicing speech reductions.

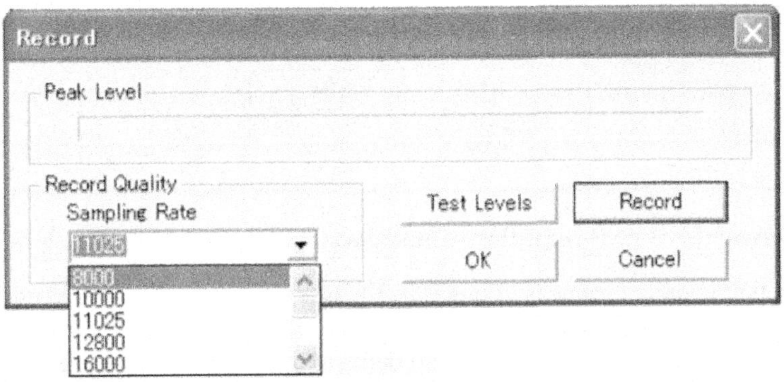

Figure 24. Setting the recording sampling rate in the Record dialog window.

The other important consideration while recording is the loudness of the speaker's voice. If the voice is too soft during recording, the recording will be both hard to hear and see. On the other hand, if someone shouts into the microphone, information about the speech quality is lost. In comparison, think of someone either whispering softly or shouting very loudly in your ear—in neither case will you understand them as well as if they are speaking in a good clear voice.

To ensure a proper recording level, Windows XP users should check the sound setting of the PC. This is one of the user settings in the control panels section. Set the sound input level to the microphone input, and the set the sound input strength to a high enough level—for all but the loudest students, this will be the maximum level.

Unfortunately, there is no direct setting in *WASP* for controlling the strength of the recording as there is in other programs. Once the PC's sound input has been set to its maximum, instructors will need to adjust the level of their voice or their student's voice either by speaking louder or softer, or by moving the microphone closer or farther away from the mouth. Speaking louder can be quite a challenge for shyer students, but thankfully there is visual feedback in the *WASP* Record dialog window to help them. To check the recording level of the voice, click on the Test Levels button in this dialog. You can then see the recording level in the Peak Level portion of the window. As the sound gets louder, the bar gets longer; as the sound gets softer, the bar will get shorter. The optimal average length for the Peak Level bar is about two-thirds of the way toward the right end, taking care not to hit the right end. Too low a level will result in a very weak recording and a light display, making it hard to see key features; too high a level will cause a loss of information due to saturating the microphone and computer circuits (again, think of someone shouting in your ear).

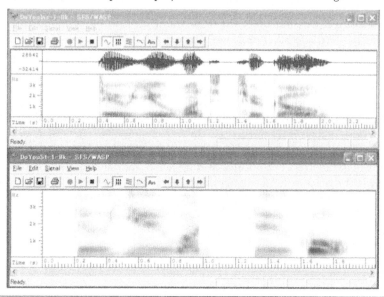

Figure 25. Setting the *WASP* recording volume level.

One final note on recording is in order. In the classroom, slowing down reduced speech when practicing can result in very unnatural-sounding speech; it is better to throw natural (i.e., fast) speech at the students to make sure they hear the correct intonation and rhythm that accompany reduced speech. However, naturally reduced speech, being quite fast, results in very short displays on the monitor since the x-axis of the *WASP* displays is time. Details can become very hard to see. Although it is not easy to produce reductions slowly with correct rhythm and intonation, it is worth practicing doing so to make sure the student can see the changes in the display that accompany mouth movements. After practicing them slowly to make sure they see the amount of detail they need, the reductions can then be practiced at a more natural pace.

Once the target phrase has been recorded into or opened up from a file in the upper *WASP* window, the student is set to record his voice into the lower window. They should repeat the recording as necessary until a clear display is achieved. Once this has been done, the computer display should look like the one in Figure 26.

Figure 26. The phrase *Do you want to go?*; native model and student recording.

Note that the recording of the student's voice in the lower window is longer than the native speaker sample in the upper window. This brings to light one more necessary skill for using phonetic software for pronunciation practice—selecting parts of a display to zoom in and out on.

To select part of the WASP display, you use the left and right mouse buttons to insert left- and right-edge cursors in the display. Then when you click on the Zoom In button in the WASP toolbar, the program will zoom in on only the part of the display between the left and right-edge cursors. This method can be used to both zoom in on a section of the display and to line up the student's speech display with the target speech display.

To line up the student's display with the target, use the following procedure:

1. Click in the top display about 1 cm to the left of the start of the speech using the left mouse button.
2. Click in the top display about 1 cm to the right of the end of the speech using the right mouse button.
3. Click on the Zoom In button to expand the selected part into the whole window.
4. Repeat the above steps with the student's recording in the bottom window.

This is not easy at first, but becomes easier and less time-consuming with practice. After adjusting the displays to line up the recordings, you should end up with something like the following. By zooming in on desired portions of the recording in this manner, you can match up the beginning of sounds, or zoom in on specific details.

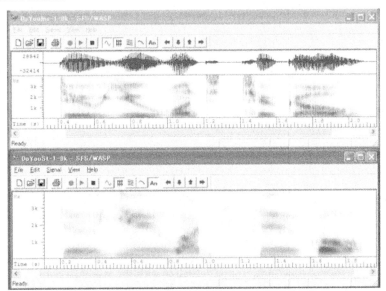

Figure 27. The phrase *Do you want to go?* with instructor and student recordings aligned.

I will now turn to the heart of this chapter: the visualization of the speech reductions commonly found in NAE.

Visualizing English Speech Reductions

In this chapter, I will introduce the visual characteristics of the following reduction processes: *schwa reduction, flapping, assimilation, and elision*. I will cover each below, with examples and notes to serve as a starting point for targeted reduction practice.

Schwa reduction

One of the most common features of at least North American casual speech is *schwa reduction*, the loss of an unstressed vowel's quality. Schwa reduction is an active, pervasive process in NAE. It also has been discussed in the Japanese EFL literature (e.g., Akita, 2002; Kondo, 1994, 1995) since vowels do not reduce in Japanese and therefore schwa reduction presents these learners with difficulty. As a concrete example of schwa reduction, although the definite article is typically pronounced [ði] before a non-low front vowel in careful speech, it usually reduces to [ðə]. This can be seen in Figure 28, showing two pronunciations of *the* excerpted from two repetitions of *The end*. The example on the left was pronounced with stress on both *the* and *end*, as when finishing reading a story; the example on the right was taken from the phrase *The ènd of the róad* with secondary stress on *end* and none on *the*.

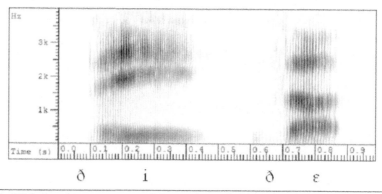

Figure 28. **Wide-band spectrogram of *the* without (left) and with (right) schwa reduction.**

For the vowel in the unreduced *the* [ði] on the left, the second formant is fairly high, much closer to F3, as is typical of the vowel [i]. In the reduced *the* on the right, the second formant is much lower, very close to F1, as is typical of the vowel [ʌ] (see Figure 8 under simple vowels above). You can also see how much shorter the vowel is in the unstressed version. In all of these reduced examples, a short, slightly weakened version of the [ʌ] in *hut* should serve as an adequate model.

As another example, in the common phrase *Do you want to go?* the vowels in *do, you,* and *to* all are pronounced in the author's dialect with the vowel [u] when stressed or in careful speech. However, they can all be reduced to schwa, giving [du jə wʌntə gou] or [də jə wʌntə gou]. In fact, the vowel quality in *do* often all but disappears, yielding something like [djəwʌnə gou]. This deletion of reduced vowels happens most often when the schwa comes right before a stressed syllable (Patterson, LoCasto, & Connine, 2003).

Besides its connection to English stress and rhythm, there is another very good reason to target schwa reduction for focused practice. The central, reduced quality of schwa makes it easy to misinterpret as a wide variety of different vowels in languages where it does not occur. As the reader may be aware, one of the major developments in the field of language acquisition has been the introduction of *perceptual magnet vowels*

(Kuhl, 1991, 1992; Kuhl et al., 1997; Minda & Smith, 2001; Sussman & Lauckner-Morano, 1995). The basic idea is that when we acquire our native language(s), we are actually learning *prototype* vowels from our caregivers—in other words, vowel templates that we use when we listen and speak. After we acquire these prototypes, they act as magnets when we are listening to someone talk. Our ear matches the vowel sounds we hear to the prototypes we learned. A vowel we hear will be drawn in to the vowel it most closely matches like it was a magnet; we will hear it as that closest vowel. Differences in pronunciation due to speaker variation, age, emotional coloring, and so forth, all but disappear. We hear the vowel that is closest to the prototype that we acquired.

This also applies when we are listening to a second or third language. The more experience we have with a language, the better we learn its vowel prototypes and the better we will be able to both distinguish and pronounce them. However, the vowel schwa, with its central location (see the vowel chart above) is open to interpretation as any vowel close to it in the vowel chart—in short, most of the other vowels. Learners of English can improve their understanding of naturally reduced English by learning how to produce and hear schwa. On the flip side, speakers of NAE often need to learn to suppress schwa reduction, since the schwas in their speech can be understood as any number of vowels in the target language.

To return to practicing NAE speech reductions, Figures 29, 30, and 31 compare the vowel quality of the vowels in the phrase *do you want to go* with no vowels reduced, with all possible schwa reductions, and with the first schwa deleted. The movement of the F2 to the position of [u] (the dips marked by arrows) can be seen in Figure 29. However, when the vowel is reduced, as in the *do, you* and *to* in Figure 30, those movements disappear, with the exception of the movement caused by the [w] since it is the consonant counterpart of [u]. In Figure 31 even the schwa has been deleted; only the transition from the [d] to the [j] is left.

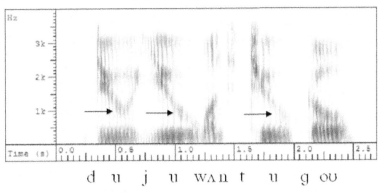

Figure 29. **Wide-band spectrogram of the phrase** *Do you want to go?* **with no schwa reduction.**

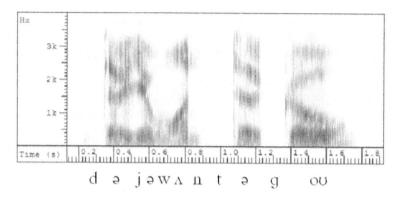

d ə jəwʌn t ə g oʊ

Figure 30. Wide-band spectrogram of the phrase *Do you want to go?* with all possible schwa reductions.

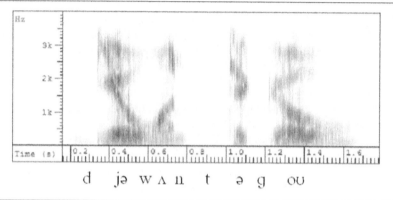

d jə w ʌ n t ə g oʊ

Figure 31. Wide-band spectrogram of the phrase *Do you want to go?* with schwa reduction and deletion of the first schwa.

Although the instructor shouldn't be overly concerned with the student perfecting schwa, since it occurs in unstressed words that often lose their prominence in speech, the learner should be made aware of the overall contribution the process makes to the reduction continuum. Once learners have gotten used to schwa reduction, they will be better equipped to move on to other reductions and changes.

Flapping

Another pervasive reduction found in NAE is what is known as *flapping*, the reduction of [t] or [d] to a quick tap of the tongue on the roof of the mouth. It is the sound found in the NAE pronunciation of *butter* and *rider*, and is represented by the symbol [ɾ]. It shows up in words where a stressed vowel is followed an unstressed syllable beginning with [t] or [d].[10]

Figure 32 gives a common example of NAE flapping. It is a WBS of unflapped *batter* and *badder* and the flapped version of both. In both pairs of words the difference in pronunciation of each pair of words disappears when flapping applies.

---

[10]   Ladefoged (1993, pp. 92–93) rightly points out that [n] can also become flapped before an unstressed vowel, producing a nasal flap—what happens in the mouth is the same.

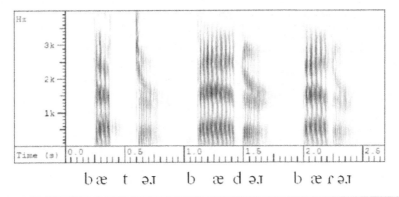

Figure 32. Wide-band spectrogram of unflapped and flapped versions of *batter* and *badder*.

Several things should be pointed out while practicing flaps:

1. The flap shows up as a stop gap (the vertical white strip) possibly accompanied by slight voicing (although it might be too short for voicing to be seen).
2. The duration of the flap is quite short, especially when compared to other NAE consonants.
3. The formants of the preceding and following vowels are largely unchanged.

While a good native-like flap may be difficult for some learners to pick up, similar sounds are present in Japanese, Spanish, Italian, and Russian. For students with those native languages, making them aware of the similar sound in their own language may help.

Assimilation

One of the other common changes in reduced speech is known as *assimilation*,[11] when one speech sound changes to become more like an adjacent sound. One of the most common assimilations in the world's languages, voice assimilation, is also found in English: The plural and third person singular suffix [z] shows up as voiceless after voiceless stops and voiced elsewhere. This happens with both nouns and verbs, in all plural and third person singular inflections. For the purposes of this chapter, voice assimilation is important in the third person singular copula. In its uncontracted form, it is pronounced [ɪt ɪz]. However, in the contracted form it is pronounced *it's* [ɪts] where the final [s] of *is* has devoiced due to the preceding voiceless [t]. This will be covered below.

Three other types of assimilations are often discussed: place of articulation assimilations, where the place in the mouth a sound is pronounced changes; manner assimilation, where a stop becomes nasalized, and so forth; and coalescent assimilations, where two sounds merge to form a new sound. This chapter will not cover place of articulation and manner of articulation assimilations, since they are often difficult to see for even the experienced speech researcher. Only coalescent assimilation will be discussed here.

---

[11]   Editors' note: For further definitions and discussion of the various terms used in this chapter to describe the reduction processes, see chapter 1 and the glossary of this book.

Coalescent assimilation of [t] and [j] happens regularly in NAE, where they combine to form the affricate [tʃ] as in *church*. In the phrases *do you* and *got you*, *do you* surfaces as [dʒʲu] in casual speech ([du ju] → [də jə] → [djə] → [dʒə]), while *got you* shows up as [gatʃu] or [gatʃə] ([gat ju] → [gatʃu]). (Note that in both cases the schwa reduction is optional.) These assimilations can be seen in Figures 33, 34, 35, and 36.

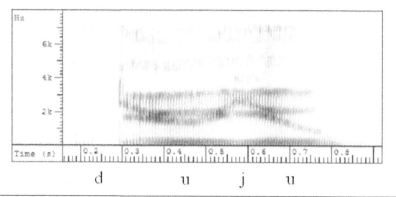

Figure 33. Wide-band spectrogram of *do you* without coalescent assimilation of [d] and [j].

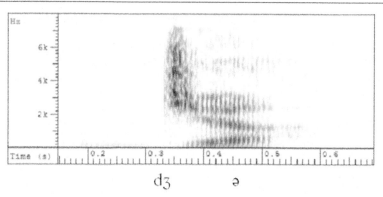

Figure 34. Wide-band spectrogram of *do you* with coalescent assimilation of [d] and [j].

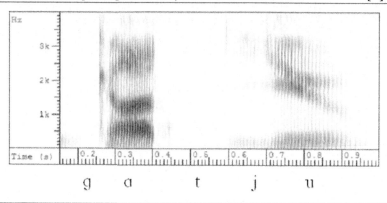

Figure 35. Wide-band spectrogram of *got you* without coalescent assimilation of [t] and [j].

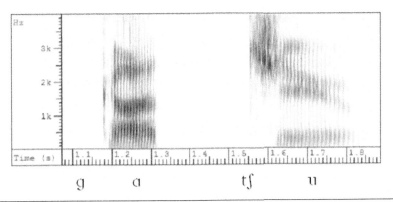

g   ɑ   tʃ   u

Figure 36. Wide-band spectrogram of *got you* with coalescent assimilation of [t] and [j].

On the right side of Figures 34 and 36, the assimilation can be clearly seen—as opposed to the distinct [t] and [j] gestures associated with careful pronunciation visible in Figures 33 and 35, a single affricate is pronounced. Note that both the place and manner of articulation have combined to produce the new speech sound: [t] is produced on the back of or just behind the front teeth, [j] is produced by pressing the tongue against the upper back teeth, and [tʃ] is produced by doing both at the same time. As for manner of articulation, while [t] is produced by stopping the air flow and [j] by letting it continually flow out of the mouth, [tʃ] is produced as an affricate, first stopping the air flow and then letting it go as a fricative.

Again, for Japanese learners of English this assimilation should not be difficult to pick up with practice, since Japanese also has the sounds [dʒ] and [tʃ].

Elision

Elisions are, as defined in Crystal (2003), the loss of a sound during speech. This happens due to speech error, but also occurs regularly in English reduced speech. Some very common examples are phrases containing the modal auxiliaries, for example, *could have, would have,* and so forth, where the [h] and [v] in *have* can be elided to produce [kʊdə], [wʊdə] (as in the familiar refrain, *coulda, woulda, shoulda*). These reductions were one of the focuses of Varden (1995), where a pre- and post test design was used to test students' improvement on recognizing these and other reductions after several weeks of focused practice. Although no statistics were generated by that pilot study, student improvement on elisions was evident in the substantial increase in correct responses by both the university and high school students involved in the study.

The phrase *Don't you?* provides a good example of an elision, and one good example of the illusion of an elision. First, the illusion of an elision is the seeming loss of the [t] in *don't you* when pronounced without coalescent assimilation (i.e., as [doʊn ju], not as [doʊntʃu]).

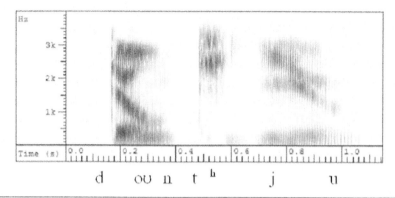

d   oʊ   n   t   ʰ   j   u

Figure 37. Wide-band spectrogram of *don't you* in careful speech.

In casual speech, it feels and sounds like the [t] is not being pronounced. However, the WBS tells a different story.

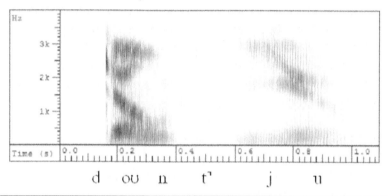

d   oʊ   n   t˺   j   u

Figure 38. Wide-band spectrogram of *don't you* showing apparent elision of the [t].

Although it feels like the [t] has been deleted, you can see how the voicing and formants associated with the nasal [n] come to a stop; there is a stop gap in the spectrogram above. This is due to stopping the air flow out of the nose. Rather than being elided, the [t] has simply been unreleased (i.e., the air hasn't been let out of the mouth). The difference in the two lies in the aspiration seen in Figure 37 labeled [ʰ], and its conspicuous absence in Figure 38 (the [˺] indicates an unreleased stop).

In contrast, both [t]s in *want to* have in actuality been elided. Figure 39 below shows it pronounced carefully, with both [t]s being released with aspiration for clarity; Figure 40 shows the reduced form of the phrase. You can see the clear stop gap (the vertical white space) for both [t]s in Figure 39, as well as the aspiration. These gaps are missing in Figure 40; no stop was pronounced. You can also see that the reduced form is shorter and more compact; the [t]s are completely gone.

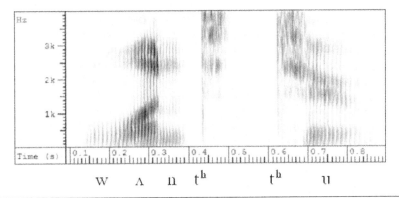

Figure 39. Wide-band spectrogram of *want to* with no reduction.

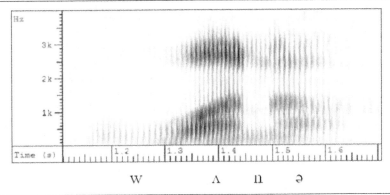

Figure 40. Wide-band spectrogram of *want to* with elision of the [t] in *want* and *to*.

Figures 41 and 42 below show the next elision, that of both the [æ] and the [d] of *and* when it is reduced to [n]. In order to see the elision of [d] better, a recording sampling rate of 16k was used to show the high-frequency noise of the [s] in *see*. You can see that the [æ] and [d] of *and* are both missing from Figure 42, leaving only [n] between the [oʊ] of *go* and the [s] of *see*. Note that although the long [æ] in Figure 41 is gone in Figure 42, the F2 still jumps up from the low F2 of [oʊ]. This is because as the tongue moves forward from [oʊ] to pronounce [n], it creates what hits the ear as [ɛ]: [goʊɛnsi].

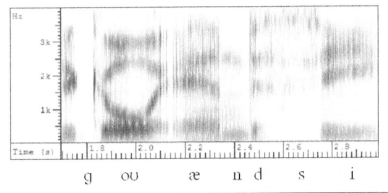

Figure 41. Wide-band spectrogram of *go and see* with no elisions.

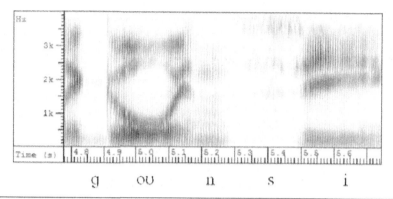

Figure 42. **Wide-band spectrogram of *go and see* with elision of [æ] and [d].**

Another example is the elision of the [ɪ] in *going* and the [t] of *to* in *going to*. By comparing Figures 43 and 44, you can see elision of both [ɪ] and [t], leaving only the nasal between the vowels. You can also see that the [oʊ] of *going* has reduced to the quality of schwa, even though it is still stressed. Also, the nasal has changed from the velar nasal [ŋ] to an alveolar [n], which can be seen as a slight change in position of the formants. And, predictably, the [u] of *to* has been reduced to schwa as well.

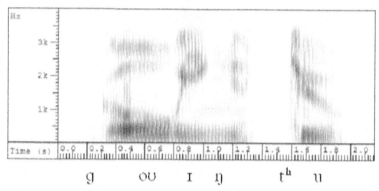

Figure 43. **Wide-band spectrogram of *going to* with no reductions.**

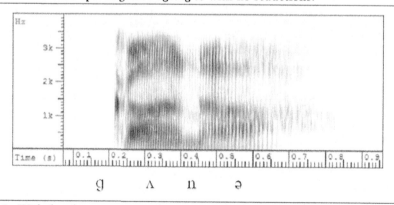

Figure 44. **Wide-band spectrogram of *going to* with elision of [ɪ] and [t], and reduction of [oʊ] and [u].**

Contractions are a subset of elisions that have been defined as the partial reduction of words and their subsequent attachment to an adjacent (usually preceding) word (Crystal, 2003). This includes both reductions of the type *I'm* for *I am* and the reduction to *wanna* from *want to*. Most EFL students are well aware that I *am* can be written *I'm*. However, they are usually completely lost when first hearing [aɪm] in natural speech. Again, in limited language contact areas like the Far East, a little practice goes a long way. Contractions of the pronoun-copula system of English will be provided here, beginning with I *am*.

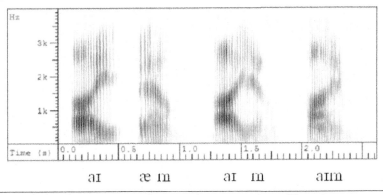

Figure 45. Wide-band spectrogram showing the contraction of I *am*.

Figure 45 contains three repetitions of I *am* in varying stages of contraction—the first as two separate words, the second as two connected syllables, and the third as a single syllable. The points worth noting here are:

1. In the first version on the left, you can see that two clearly separate syllables were pronounced ([aɪ æm]) by the two separate contours in Figure 45. In the middle version, the second syllable is connected to the first and nowhere near as strong as the unreduced one —the speaker produced a weak syllabic nasal. Finally, in the right-most version there is only one syllable visible; the [m] is now part of the one syllable.

2. In terms of the individual sounds, you can see how the sounds are blended together more and more in the increasingly reduced versions. On the left, you can see the formants change during the diphthong [aɪ] and during the movement from the second vowel [æ] to the nasal [m]. In the middle you can see how the formants change smoothly through all three sounds. On the right, you can see how the formant change for the diphthong is the only real change left.

The same two points should be made about all of the other contractions involving the copula, and any other contractions (*shouldn't*, *aren't*, etc.) that instructors wish to practice. I have personally found it useful to list the contractions on paper at the outset so that the student knows what is being discussed, but then removing the written version before beginning pronunciation practice. This helps prevent the student from falling back on the spelling or otherwise inappropriate pronunciations they may have learned and help reinforce the idea that they are learning to pronounce the single syllable they can see in the display.

Examples of the rest of the copula conjugation are given below, in the same three stages of reduction, along with notes as appropriate. Figure 46 shows the stages of reduction of *you are*. There are two things worth noting in this case:

1. Notice how the F2 formant transition for the diphthong [ju] is also reduced as we go from two separate words (the left) to two separate syllables (the middle) to a fully reduced, single-syllable word (the right).

2. Also notice the F3 transition for the [ɹ] does not lessen as the reduction progresses. However, how fast it happens does change; whereas in the unreduced and middle versions F3 drops fairly quickly at the end of the word, in the fully reduced form the F3 drop is spread out over most of the syllable. In fact, this is one reason many phoneticians (e.g., Ladefoged, 1993, p. 31) characterize this as a single vowel sound rather than as a vowel-consonant combination.

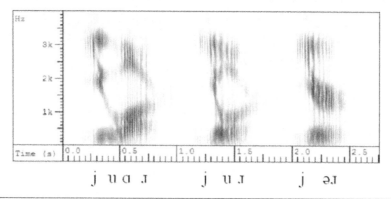

Figure 46. Wide-band spectrogram showing the contraction of *you are*.

Figures 47 and 48 show the reduction process for *he is*, and bring up the issues of recording sampling rate and zooming in mentioned earlier. The phrase in Figure 47 was recorded at a sampling rate of 8kHz, that in Figure 48 at 16kHz. As can be seen in Figure 47, recorded at a sampling rate of 8kHz, the high-frequency noise of the fricative is not visible in the display. Since this high-frequency noise is the determining characteristic of fricatives and affricates, you will need to switch to a recording sampling rate of 16kHz to see it. The formants of the vowels and other sounds are more compact at this sampling rate, but still discernible. In addition, the voicing of the [z] in the unreduced version is very light in Figure 47, but it is present. In cases like these zooming in on the sound in question quickly by selecting the sound with the cursors and hitting the Zoom In button will help tremendously.

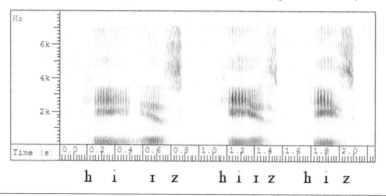

Figure 47. Wide-band spectrogram showing the contraction of *he is* recorded at 8kHz.

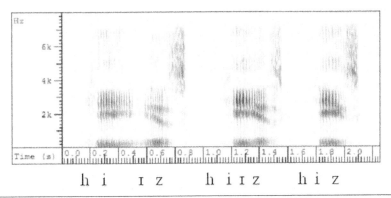

Figure 48. Wide-band spectrogram showing the contraction of *he is* recorded at 16kHz.

Figure 49 contains only the last part of *he is* to show the voicing. As you can see, there is slight voicing of the last of the [z], evidenced by the small marks around time 350 on the time scale. The instructor should not be afraid to zoom in like this to make a point; *WASP* will zoom back out with exactly the same steps that you zoom in with. Also, notice how light the voicing is in Figure 49 even when magnified. (The waveform was also turned off to give the largest possible spectrogram for the available space.) During the [z], the part of the word where the high-frequency noise is strongest, the voicing becomes very weak during the fricative. This speaker partially devoiced this fricative. Devoicing of utterance-final fricatives is a common characteristic of NAE, especially in unstressed positions of words like this (Smith, 1997).

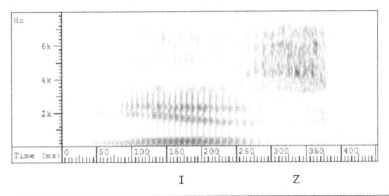

Figure 49. Wide-band spectrogram of the voicing of the [z] in *is*, magnified for clarity.

As a final example of contractions of the copula, Figure 50 shows the reduction process for *they are*. The same general comments for *are* above also apply here. However, note that the fricative [ð] (voiced *th*) is very weak compared to the following vowel; in fact, there is not much noise to be seen in Figure 50. It doesn't last very long and doesn't contain very much high frequency noise. This is natural for many native speakers. Rather than try to match something on the screen that is hard or impossible to see, the instructor and student need to be flexible and get used to zooming in on weaker sounds. Zooming in will allow *WASP* to draw a darker display for weak sounds, since it can amplify them before it draws the display.

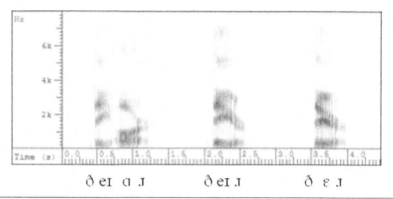

Figure 50. Wide-band spectrogram showing the contraction of _they are._

As an overview, the following points are worth being aware of while practicing these reductions.

1. Although the uncontracted forms are two-syllable productions, the fully contracted forms are one syllable only. Particularly with Japanese students, care must be taken not to insert the epenthetic vowels for which Japanese is famous.

2. The voicing assimilation in the case of _it's_ mentioned in a previous section should be spotlighted.

3. Although the vowel of _they_ is usually a diphthong in English, the corresponding reduced form often contains the simple vowel [ɛ] instead.

4. The instructor should pay attention to any student with a mother tongue doesn't contain a rhotic [ɹ] to make sure their productions contain the characteristic F3 drop for this sound.

The _coulda, woulda_ series provides one last set of good examples of these types of reductions, since the changes result in such drastically different sounds. Since the reductions are the same for all of the different reductions of this type, only the reduction of _could have_ will be presented. The following points should be noted here:

1. The fricative [v] is very hard to spot in Figures 51, 52, and 53; the high-frequency noise associated with this fricative can be light anyway, and though audible when listening to the speech, is almost impossible to see when displayed together with vowels. Again, zooming in on the unelided and elided versions will help.

2. The elision of the [h] in _have_ in Figures 52 and 53 results in flapping; its deletion, together with the [d] being attached to the following syllable, results in a stressed vowel followed by an unstressed syllable beginning with [d].

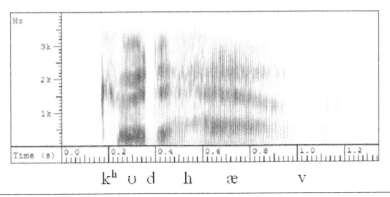

Figure 51. Wide-band spectrogram of *could have* with no reductions.

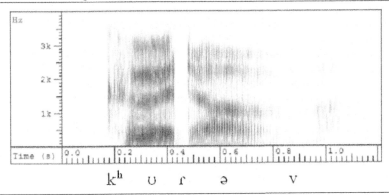

Figure 52. Wide-band spectrogram of *could have* with elision of [h] and flapping.

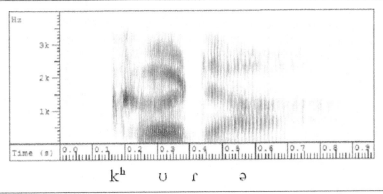

Figure 53. Wide-band spectrogram of *could have* with elision of [h] and [v], and flapping.

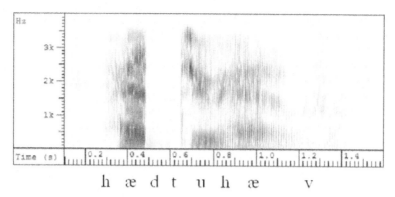

As a final example of elisions and contractions, the fairly common verbal construction *had to have* provides a good example of how much speech can vary from spelling in English. The following points should be made here:

1. This person's [h] is very weak compared to the vowels. As the vowels reduce in both quality and strength, the noise of the [h] becomes more visible; you may also see more (or less) noise with other people's speech.
2. You can see the reduction of the [æ] in *have* from Figure 54 to Figure 55—the high F2 of [æ] becomes the low F2 of [ə].
3. Similarly, you can see the reduction of the [u] in *to* from Figure 55 to Figure 56—the dip in F2 and F3 caused by pronouncing the [u] becomes a straight decrease to the F2 and F3 of [ə].
4. You can also see that the voicing of the [æ] in *had* continues during the [d], and then stops for the [t]. This can vary by speaker and by dialect.

Similar large changes in the sounds can be seen in many other reduced forms. However, it is worth noting that the dialect of this speaker doesn't make use of the very significant reductions that can occur in many east coast or southern dialects (see Brown & Hilferty, 1986a, for examples). The instructor and student alike need to be ready for the more pervasive reductions they may run into.

Figure 54. Wide-band spectrogram of *had to have* with no reductions.

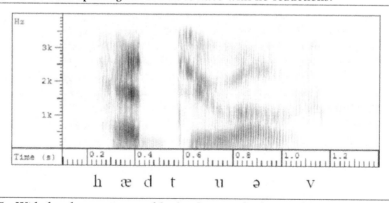

Figure 55. Wide-band spectrogram of *had to have* with elision of [h] and reduction of [æ].

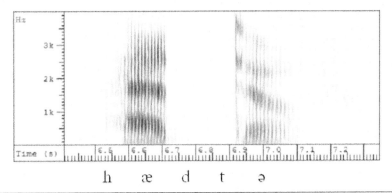

Figure 56. **Wide-band spectrogram of** *had to have* **with elision of [h] and [v], and reduction of [æ].**

Summary

This chapter has covered the basics of using the free software *WASP* for pronunciation training in NAE reduced speech. By paying attention to the changes in the computer displays that the program provides, the instructor and student can get valuable feedback on the position and movements of the parts of the mouth that occur in both unreduced and reduced speech. It is hoped that enough information and background has been provided to help a motivated instructor coach students in the natural pronunciation of English that they must deal with in order to understand and produce conversational English. It is not easy and does entail a great deal of learning, but for the instructor willing to put in the effort it can be very rewarding. I would add that, in both teaching and learning, we as instructors need to share with our students a message that is all too often lacking in foreign language classes in Japan—to err is to learn. We can help send that message by being patient with both ourselves and our students as we undertake a task like this.

Acknowledgements

The author wishes to thank Mark Connolly and Mike Mathis for providing valuable feedback on a draft of this chapter. Thanks also go to Professor Tsutomu Sato and the other members of the Audiovisual Research Section of the Japan Association for Language Education and Technology for introducing me to the topic, and for their kind comments at a presentation given in January 2005. All errors and shortcomings, of course, remain my own. Finally, I would like to dedicate this chapter to my late father, who passed away at the age of 79 during the final preparation of the manuscript.

How should connected speech

be taught in Japanese?

On Casual Speech:
How It Differs From Fast Speech[1]

NOBUKO HASEGAWA
Kanda University of International Studies, Makuhari, Japan

This chapter investigates the properties of phonological casual speech (CS) by examining several such processes of Japanese in comparison with fast speech (FS) processes. The chapter shows that CS processes are quite different in nature from FS processes, though the terms casual *and* fast *have often been used interchangeably in literature. More specifically, CS processes are indifferent to the mere speed of speech but sensitive to the sociological context such as intimacy, formalness, familiarity, and so forth. They apply only to lexically specified items and phrases, and their application affects lexical, morphological, and syntactic aspects of the entire sentence; thereby, a kind of concordance across different components of grammar is observed with respect to casualness. Thus, this chapter should be of most interest to applied linguistics researchers generally, and those Japanese language teachers, researchers, materials developers, and testers who want to understand, teach, and develop materials or tests for teaching continuous speech in Japanese.*

In the literature on casual speech, casualness and the rate of speech are often interchangeably used to refer to certain phonological processes that take place in *relaxed* or *casual* speech context.[2] For example, Zwicky (1972), one of those who first paid attention to such processes, attempting to define characteristics of casual speech, mentions, "in general, causal speech is fast, and it is stylistically marked as intimate, informal, and the like" (p. 607). He further goes on to say that "casual speech

---

[1]   This chapter is based on my earlier paper, Hasegawa (1979), where I attempted to motivate the formal distinction between fast speech (FS)processes and casual speech (CS) processes. Though I maintain the basic line of discussion laid out in the previous version, showing how different these two types of processes are, the main purpose of the present chapter is shifted more toward the description of CS processes, minimizing the theoretical discussion on how these two processes are to be treated in grammar. The descriptions provided are to be taken as *generalized statements* that may facilitate the better understanding of Japanese everyday speech and provide foundations for more extensive theoretical research in the future. Thus, the phonological rules provided simply express *intuitive* generalizations of the processes in question and the use of technical features and alphabets is intended to be minimal. For example, phonological strings, which are basically alphabetic transcriptions of items, do not necessarily represent their exact phonemic or phonetic representations. Nonetheless, the discussion presupposes the basic knowledge of the morpho-phonology of Japanese. See McCawley (1968), Shibatani (1990), Tsujimura (1996), Vance (1987), and so forth.

[2]   Editors' note: See chapter 1 for much more on these distinctions.

Hasegawa, N. (2006) On casual speech: How it differs from fast speech. In J. D. Brown, & K. Kondo-Brown, (Eds.), *Perspectives on teaching connected speech to second language speakers* (pp. 169–187). Honolulu, HI: University of Hawai'i, National Foreign Language Resource Center.

processes… seem to be constrained to be phonetically natural. In the extreme case, they can be explained as the inevitable result of increasing speed of speech: the articulators simply cannot achieve their targets in the time available" (1972, p. 608).

The tendency for the terms *causal* and *fast* to often be confounded in literature seems to have to do with the fact that languages whose linguistic phenomena have been most closely studied do not often involve grammatical processes that are sensitive to notions such as formalness, intimateness, familiarity, vulgarness, and so forth.[3]

The primary purpose of this chapter is to describe various casual speech (CS) processes, in comparison to fast speech (FS) processes, of the Tokyo dialect of Japanese, which exhibits not only phonological but also lexical, morphological, syntactic processes operating on such *sociological* notions much more clearly than English or other popularly examined languages.[4] It will be shown that, unlike FS processes, CS phonological processes share interesting characteristics with the processes of other components of grammar, that is, the lexicon, morphology, and syntax, which are also sensitive to sociological notions.

To make the discussion simple, I would like to set the primary distinction between FS and CS processes to be whether a process is sensitive to the rate of speech; if so, the process is a FS process, if not, it is a CS process. According to this primary criterion, I will first examine two FS processes, providing a generalization that holds for these processes. Then, I will introduce several CS processes, which, though they are quite prevalent in everyday conversation situations, have not been extensively discussed in literature. In Hasegawa (1979), I took up three CS processes: nasal syllabicization, vowel fusion, and contraction. In what follows, however, I will not only elaborate them with more examples but also introduce several more processes in order to explicate the general properties of CS processes in more detail. Through the examination of these processes, it is seen that CS processes exhibit distinctive characteristics regarding what determines the application or non-application of these processes; they are sensitive to and very much dependent on sociological notions and lexical information. Then in the section below on Casual Speech Processes in Grammar, the nature of sociological and lexical conditioning of CS processes is further explored across the different components of grammar, namely, the lexicon, morphology, and syntax. It is revealed that CS processes, or rather processes that refer to *sociological* factors, often exhibit *concordance* effects and the application or choice of a certain CS process in one component requires or induces the application of CS processes of other components.

Fast Speech Processes

In this section, two processes are taken up, which are sensitive to the rate of speech: high vowel devoicing (HVD) and vowel degemination and lengthening (VD&L). These processes are observed in even slow or careful speech; however, they apply much more freely and across word-boundaries in fast speech. Incidentally, their applications are neutral to sociological factors and are not specific to particular lexical items or grammatical structures.

---

[3]   In spite of the above quotes, Zwicky seems to acknowledge that casualness is different from fastness, since he mentions "casual speech need not be fast" (1972, p. 607).

[4]   In what follows, the term *sociological* is used to refer to notions like *formal, informal, polite, intimate, familiar, vulgar,* and so forth.

High vowel devoicing (HVD)[5]

One of the distinctive properties of the phonological structure of Japanese is the existence of devoiced vowels, most probably the high vowels /i/ and /u/, which occur when they appear between devoiced consonants or at the end of a word preceded by a devoiced consonant. Typical examples are given below, where devoiced vowels are marked with a dot beneath a vowel, that is, [i̥] [u̥].

(1) a. ki̥setu̥ 'season'
   b. si̥kasi̥ 'but'
   c. su̥kosi̥ 'a little'
   d. hi̥totu̥ 'one'
   e. yaku̥soku̥ 'promise'
   f. utu̥ku̥sii 'beautiful'
   g. tisi̥ki 'knowledge'
   h. usotu̥ki̥ 'liar'

Though the exact characterization of this process is not very simple in slow or careful speech—being affected by accent patterns, the position and type of the vowel in question in relation to other vowels nearby, and so forth—this process is generalized and simplified in a fast speech context, which is something like (2).[6]

(2) High vowel devoicing (HVD)
   [+vowel, +high] → [−voice] / [−voice] ___ {[−voice] or pause}

In fast speech, word or phrasal boundaries are often obscured and the effect of this rule is observed across such boundaries as long as they are within one phonological phrase.[7] Thus, this rule predicts that the [−voice] vowel at the end of a word would be affected by the presence of a [+voice] sound in the following word in fast speech. This in fact is the case as seen in (3).

(3) a. ki̥setu ga 'season-NOM'
   b. su̥kosi dake 'only a little'
   c. yaku̥soku da 'promise copula'
   d. ti̥si̥ki̥kaikyu: 'intelligentsia'
   e. to:kyo: e iku hi̥to 'the person going to Tokyo'
   f. to:kyo: e iku basu̥ 'the bus going to Tokyo'
   g. /ti̥kuti̥ku/ 'itchy' → ti̥ku̥ti̥ku̥ suru 'be itchy'

The final [−voice] vowels of (1a), (1c), and (1e) in slow or careful speech get voiced being followed by a voiced consonant of the adjacent phrase, which is shown in (3a), (3b), and (3c), respectively. Similarly, the consecutive occurrences of /i/ in (1g) get

---

[5] Editors' note: Also see Toda on *museika* or *devoicing* in chapter 11 and Sakai and Igashima on *vowel devoicing* in chapter 12 of this book.

[6] For example, when more than one syllable or mora with a high vowel takes place consecutively, as in (1g), not all high vowels may undergo devoicing in slow speech. Thus, though the first and final /i/'s in /tisiki/ also meet the condition for devoicing, they tend to retain their voicing quality and only the medial /i/ undergoes devoicing in slow speech. This seems to be due to the accent on the first mora and the fact that devoicing often applies to alternating moras. In fast speech, however, all the /i/ in /tisiki/ can be devoiced. See Vance (1989) for more extensive discussion on HVD in slow speech.

[7] Here, I would like to remain intuitive about what constitutes a phonological phrase in FS, taking it loosely to be any string of words that can be uttered without a pause. Miyara (1980) defines it in terms of where a particle occurs, which he argues marks the end of the phrase. This definition seems too narrow for FS processes, since a sequence of a noun phrase with a particle and a verb or of two noun phrases seems to constitute a phonological phrase, being subject to FS processes. See the section on VD&L for concrete examples.

devoiced as in (3d), and the voicing quality of /u/ of /iku/ 'go' depends on what consonant follows it as shown in (3d) and (3e). As for (3g), even if the /u/s in /tikutiku/ tend to retain the [+voice] quality in slow speech, they get devoiced in FS, particularly if a predicate that starts with a voiceless consonant follows the word.

The above shows that HVD, which may be confined within a word or even suppressed in a slow or careful speech, applies across word boundaries and irrespective of syntactic configurations if the rate of speech is fast enough for a phonological phrase to be so extended. Note that, even if the number of devoiced vowels increases due to the rate of speech, it does not necessarily give the impression that the speech is *degraded* or becomes *casual* or informal.[8] Therefore, it seems to be safe to maintain that HVD is purely conditioned by phonological environments and speed of speech.[9]

Vowel degemination and lengthening (VD&L)

Japanese has five short vowels, /i, e, a, o, u/, and corresponding long vowels, /i:, e:, a:, o:, u:/, in both underlying (phonemic) and surface (phonetic) levels, which makes a distinction between *obasan* 'aunt; middle aged woman' and *oba:san* 'grandmother; old woman,' for example.[10] However, some long vowels are apparently created by two identical short vowels, as is clear from the examples /kai+in/ → [kai:n] 'member;' /aku+un/ → [aku:n] 'devil's luck;' and /mono+oki/ → [mono:ki] 'storeroom,' which are given rise to through morphological combination of two morphemes. There are some cases where no obvious phonetic distinction is observed between the pairs of a long vowel at base and a derived long vowel; celebrated examples include [su:ri] 'mathematical principle' and [su+uri] 'vinegar vendor,' [sato:+ya] 'sugar salesman' and [sato+oya] 'foster parent.' This process of bringing two identical vowels into one long vowel across morphological boundaries may be stated as (4), which degeminates two identical vowels and changes them into a longer vowel.

(4) Vowel degemination and lengthening (VD&L)

$$V_i \quad + \quad V_i \quad \rightarrow \quad V_i:$$
$$[\alpha \text{ long}] \quad [\beta \text{ long}] \quad [\alpha+\beta \text{ long}]$$

---

[8] For example, as the speed of the speech of announcers, conference presenters, and so forth, gets accelerated under the pressure of running out of time, the number of occurrences of devoiced vowels would increase without altering sociological contexts.

[9] When the rate of speech accelerates, high vowels may even drop entirely, when they occur between identical voiceless sounds, in particular between /k/s.

  (i) a. /takaku keru/ → takakkeru 'kick high'
     b. /usuku kiru/ → usukkiru 'slice thinly'
     c. /kaku kami/ → ?kakkami 'paper to write on'

This process is active word-internally across morpheme boundaries as seen in the following examples:

  (ii) a. /oNgaku+kai/ → oNgakkai 'music concert'
     b. /kutiku+kan/ → ku̥ti̥kkan 'destroyer'
     c. /matu+take/ → mattake 'matsutake mushroom'

Given (i) and (ii), this process may appear to be another instance of FS processes; however, there are ungrammatical cases such as (iii).

  (iii) a. /uku koppu/ → *ukkoppu 'the cup that floats'
     b. /siku kami/ → *sikkami 'paper to spread'
     c. /kaki komu/ → *kakkomu 'fill out'

Careful examinations are called for to determine the exact nature of this process.

[10] Not every linguist agrees with this statement and there have been debates over how many *vowels* there are in Japanese at the phonemic level, and whether a long vowel is an independent vowel with the feature [+long] or a sequence of two identical short vowels. We will not get into these issues and simply assume what is stated above to be a reasonable description of Japanese for the purpose of this chapter. See Hattori (1960), McCawley (1968), Shibatani (1990), and Vance (1987) for relevant discussion.

In fast speech context, this process operates beyond a word level and applies across words and phrases:

(5) a. /akai ie/ → akaːe 'ADJ-N; red house'
    b. /uti isogu/ → utiːsogu 'V-V; shoot too soon'
    c. /toːkyoː ni iku/ → toːkyoː niːku 'PART (DAT)-V; go to Tokyo'
    d. /hon-ga aru/ → hon gaːru 'PART (NOM)-V; books exist'
    e. /taroː ni inu o yaru/ → taroː niːnu o yaru
       'between two NPs (PART (DAT)-N); give Taro a dog'
    f. /hako o oku/→ hakoːːku 'N-PART (ACC)-V; put a box'
    g. /toːkyoː o tazuneru/ → toːkyoːː tazuneru 'N-PART (ACC); visit Tokyo'

The environments above are syntactically diverse and the parts that undergo (4) are not necessarily structurally close, for example, a subject and a predicate in (5d), an indirect object and a direct object in (5e). Note that (4) does not simply make a long vowel, but obscures the distinction of vowels, preserving the original moraic length. Thus, (5f), where identical three vowels take place consecutively, and (5g), where a long vowel and a short vowel of the same kind are next to each other, end up exhibiting an *extra-long* vowel that is (at least, psychologically) three times as long as a short vowel, namely [oːː].

The two FS processes above, namely HVD and VD&L, are not confined to fast speech and they are quite freely triggered word internally even in slow or normal speech. Thus, what FS context does is to *extend* or *generalize* the domain of the application, from within a word or across morphemes to across words and phrases. In other words, these processes are phonologically *natural*—HDV is a voicing assimilation process that affects the voice quality of less sonorous vowels and VD&L is a kind of lenition process by which the effort to utter two identical vowels separately is reduced. Note, incidentally, that the extension of the domain of the application does not indicate any obvious change in the *sociological* level or stylistic context. Conversely, when the situation requires the speech to be extremely careful, for example, when an adult teaches a new word to a child, the application of these rules may be suppressed. Furthermore, they are sensitive primarily only to *phonological* environments and blindly apply irrespective of lexical items or syntactic configurations if the speed of speech is fast enough.

Casual Speech Processes

In what follows, I will examine five different types of casual speech processes, where each has some variants. I consider them to be CS processes, since, based on our primary distinction between FS and CS, their application is not affected by the rate of speech. They apply when the context of speech is *casual* or *informal* enough.

Nasal syllabicization (NS)[11]

We will observe two NS processes in this sub-section, which are quite prevalently observed even in slow speech and in *casual writing*, such as intimate letters, diaries, and text messages. The first process we will examine involves /ni/ and /no/, which become a syllabic (or moraic) nasal [N] (ん in writing), dropping the vowels /i/ and /o/, respectively, for example, /iku no da/ → [ikuN da] (行くんだ) 'it is that (I) go.' The other process is observed when the verb involves /r/ at the end and is followed by

---

[11] Editors' note: Also see Toda on *moraic nasalization* in chapter 11 and Sakai and Igashima on moraic nasal /N/ in chapter 12 of this book.

a lexical item that starts with /n/. Then, the /r/ gets assimilated into the /n/, becoming a syllabic nasal [N], for example, /yar-anai/ → [yaNnai](や<u>ん</u>ない) '(I will) not do.'

Nasal syllabicization (NS) with /no/ and /ni/

When *no*, either as a sentence final nominalizer (NM), as in (6a), or as a genitive or possessive particle (GEN), as in (6b), occurs before a copula, /o/ in *no* drops and the remaining /n/ is syllabicized into [N]. Note that the copula always starts with a voiced alveolar sound, either /d/ as in *da, desu* 'present,' *datta, desita* 'pas,t, *daro:, desyo:* 'tentative,' *de* 'connective,' or /n/ as in *ni* 'adverbial/connective,' *nara* 'provisional.' Similarly, the connective form of the copula, *ni*, becomes syllabic [N] if it is followed by the predicate *nar-u* 'become,' as in (6):

> (6) a. /kuru no nara/ → kuru N nara
>   come NM COP-if 'if it is that … come…'
>   b. /taro: no da/ → taro: N da
>   Taro GEN COP-pres. '(it) is Taro's.'
>   c. /gakusya ni naru/ → gakusya N naru
>   scholar COP-connec. 'become a scholar'
>   d. /genki ni naru/ → genki N naru
>   well COP-connec. 'get well'

These changes are apparently related to the identity of the place of articulation of /n/ of *no* and *ni* and the following consonant, /d/ or /n/, of the copula and *nar-u* 'become.' Thus, the process itself is natural in articulation; however, this process is different from the FS processes seen in the above, in the sense that it does not take place if /n/ or /d/ that follows after the *no* or *ni* in question is not a part of the copula or the predicate *nar-u*, which accounts for the unacceptability of (7).[12]

> (7) a. /kimi no namae/ → ?*kimi N namae
>   you GEN name 'your name'
>   b. /go hiki no neko/ → ?*go hiki N neko
>   five-Cl GEN cat 'five cats'
>   c. /go tsu: no tegami/ → ?*go tsu: N tegami
>   five-Cl GEN letter 'five letters'
>   d. /yuka ni neru/ → ?*yuka N neru
>   floor onto lie 'lie on the floor'
>   e. /o:saka ni nigeru/ → ?*o:saka N nigeru
>   Osaka to escape 'escape to Osaka'
>   f. /to:kyo: ni dake/ → *to:kyo: N dake
>   Tokyo in only 'only in Tokyo'
>   g. /haha-ni desu/ → *haha N desu
>   mother-to COP '(it) is to my mother'

The phonological environments in (6) and (7) are basically identical—*ni* or *no* is followed by an alveolar sound. However, only (6) exhibits NS, not (7). It is thus apparent that the application of NS is lexically specified as to what grammatical categories *ni, no*, and the items that follow them should be, that is, the *no* that is NM

---

[12] (Some of) the outputs in (7) may sometimes be observed in *very* fast speech in casual context. Even so, there is a clear difference in acceptability between (6) and (7); the NS in (6) is allowed even in slow speech and casual writing. This is particularly true in the case of the NM *no*, such as (6a). On the other hand, the syllabicized forms in (7) would never take place in slow speech, let alone in writing.

or GEN can be syllabicized only when it is followed by the copula, and the copula *ni* when it is followed by the predicate *nar-u* 'become.'[13]

The sociological conditioning of NS is not very strong and the syllabicized form [N] may occur even in a fairly formal or polite expression, regardless of the rate of speech. For example, the use of the honorific form, *irassyar-u*, which tends to mark the speech careful, is possible in place of *ku-ru* in (6a) with the syllabicized N, that is, [irassyaru N nara].[14] However, the opposite is not quite true. The occurrence of the full form does not seem appropriate or likely in vulgar utterances such as (8), even if the speech is slow.

(8) Teme: ga yatta {??no/ N} daro:
you-vul NOM did NM COP-tentative 'It was that you did it (wasn't it ?)'

The occurrence of the lexical item *teme:* 'you' in (8), which is the vulgar form of the second person pronoun, only used among gangsters and the like or by male speakers with extreme rage, forces the entire string to be marked as *vulgar*.[15] Under such circumstances, NS seems to be obligatory, forcing the use of the casual form [N]. The fact observed in (8) that the phonological CS process *must* apply when the utterance involves an item that marks the speech *informal* or *vulgar* clearly indicates that CS processes are triggered not by the rate of speech but by *sociological* factors in a given speech context. We will come back to this property of CS processes in the Section below on Casual Speech Processes in Grammar.

The following is a formalization of this rule, which is equipped with all the lexical information discussed above.

(9) Nazal Syllabicization (NS) with /no/ and /ni/[16]
{/no/, /ni/} → N / _____ {/n/, /d/}
where /ni/ = copula, /no/ = NM or GEN; and {/n/, /d/} = COP or *nar-u*

Nasal syllabicization (NS) with /r/

Another instance where a syllabicized nasal [N] takes place in casual speech is when a verb involves word-final /r/ and an item starting with /n/ follows it. There are at least four cases that fall under this process: the negative predicate with the sequence of /-rVnai/, the polite imperative of the form /-r{i/e} nasai/, the present tense verb

---

[13] There are some exceptions and some head nouns in fixed usages, if they start with an alveolar sound, can undergo this process, affecting the preceding GEN *no*.
　　(i) a. /kimi no tokoro/   →   kimiN tokoro 'your place'
　　　　 b. /anata no tame/   →   anataN tame 'for the sake of you'
　　　　 c. /heya no naka/   →   heyaN naka 'inside of the room'
　　These examples sound much better than (7a)–(7c), which also involve the genitive *no*.

[14] The polite form of the copula is *de gozaimasu*, whose occurrence marks the speech as quite polite and careful in the present day Tokyo dialect. To use it in place of *da* in (6b) seems to block NS, unless the rate of speech is *very* fast, that is, [taro: n de gozaimasu] is allowed only in fast speech.

[15] *Teme:* in (8) is an output of Vowel fusion (VF), which will be discussed in a separate section below.

[16] The NM *no* at the end of a sentence can be syllabicized into [N] even if no alveolar sound follows. Examples follow.
　　(i) a. /kita no/   →   kita N 'came?'
　　　　 b. /aw-u no/ →   aw-u N 'meet?'
　　These forms, though apparently related to (9), are sub-standard in the Tokyo dialect and seem only possible by young female speakers in tag question context.

ending /-ru/ followed by the negative imperative *na*, and the sequence of /-ru/ and the NM *no*. Let us start with the first case:[17]

(10)a. /hasir-anai/ → hasiN-nai 'not run'
   b. /wakar-anai/ → wakaN-nai 'not understand'
   c. /tomar-anai/ → tomaN-nai 'not stop'
   d. /sir-anai/ → *ʔsiN-nai 'not know'
   e. /kure-nai/ → kuN-nai 'not give (me)'
   f. /tari-nai/ → taN-nai 'not sufficient'
   g. /wasure-nai/ → *wasuN-nai 'not forget'
   h. /kari-nai/ → *kaN-nai 'not borrow'
   i. /ori-nai/ → *oN-nai 'not get down'

The NS takes place in (10a)–(10f) (except [10d]), where a vowel between /r/ and /n/ is deleted and the /r/ is assimilated into the /n/ but retains the syllabic property that the deleted vowel has possessed. This may be roughly formalized as follows:[18]

(11) Nasal Syllabicization (NS) with /r/
   rV → N / _____ n

This process applies only to designated lexical items, that is, when a consonant stem verb that ends with /r/ is followed by the negative *-anai* form, as exemplified in (10a)–(10c), though there are some marginal cases such as (10d). The grammaticality of (10e)–(10f) may be taken to be evidence for allowing (11) to apply also to vowel stem verbs, where the vowel that is subject to deletion is the stem of the verb itself. However, (10e)–(10f) seem rather exceptional to the extent that there are a number of verbs in this class that cannot undergo this process, as the ungrammaticality of (10g)–(10i) indicate. These well-formed syllabicized nasal forms are observed even in slow speech, though they tend to give a *childish* or *wheedling* tone to the speech.

The same phonological process is also triggered by the polite imperative *-nasai*, the strong negative imperative *-na*, and the NM *no*:

(12)a. /hasir-i nasai/ → hasiN nasai '(you'd better) run'
   b. /tomar-i nasai/ → tomaN nasai '(you'd better) stop'
   c. /kari nasai/ → *kaN nasai '(you'd better) borrow'
   d. /ori nasai/ → *oN nasai '(you'd better) get down'
   e. /ire nasai/ → *iN nasai '(you'd better) put in!'
   f. /wasure nasai/ → *wasuN nasai '(you'd better) forgot'

(13)a. /kure-ru na/ → kureN na 'Don't give (me)'
   b /kari-ru na / → kariN na 'Don't borrow'
   c. /hasir-u na/ → hasiN na 'Don't run!'
   d. /tomar-u na/ → tomaN na 'Don't stop'
   e. /wasure-ru na/ → wasureN na 'Don't forget'
   f. /ori-ru na/ → oriN na 'Don't get down!'

---

[17] The fixed expressions whose etymological derivations involve the same lexical items also undergo this process. For example, the adjectives in (i) that are derived from a verb that ends with /r/ with the negative predicate /anai/ have the casual form that is derived from the same process.
   (i) a. tsumaranai (< tsumar-anai) → tumaNnai 'uninteresting, boring'
       b. tamaranai (<tamar-anai) → tamaNnai 'unbearable'
[18] This is an abbreviated formalization of what is seen in (10), where more than two phonological processes may be involved, namely vowel deletion, the linking of the floating mora slot to /r/, and nasal assimilation.

Nasai takes the connective form of the verb and, according to rule (11), this process is to be relevant when the connective form takes /ri/ or /re/ at the end. As seen in (12), however, (11) applies basically only to consonant stem verbs that end with /r/, the same restriction that have been observed in (10). In contrast, the negative imperative *na*, which follows the present tense marker –(*r*)*u*, triggers this process much more generally. As seen in (13), irrespective of the source of /r/, whether it is part of a verb stem or of the present tense marker *-ru*, *na* gives rise to the syllabicized [N] in place of /ru/.

The NM *no*, which takes the indicative form of a verb, including the present tense form, behaves similarly to the negative imperative *na*, as seen in (14). That is, when it follows a verb with the present tense that ends with /ru/, irrespective of the origin of /r/, the NM *no* can trigger the process (11).

> (14) a. /kure-ru no/ → kureN no 'give (me)(?)'
> b. /tomar-u no/ → tomaN no 'stop(?)'
> c. /kari-ru no nara/ → kariN no nara → kariN nara 'if (you) borrow'
> d. /hasir-u no da/ → hasiN no da → hasiN da 'it is that (I will) run'
> e. /wasure-ru no nara/ → wasureN no nara → wasureN nara 'if (you) forget'
> f. /ori-ru no da/ → ?oriN no da → oriN da 'it is that (you) get down'

What is of particular interest is (14d)–(14f). When the NM *no* is followed by the copulative, *da*, *nara*, and so forth, it can also undergo another NS process, namely, the NS process (9) discussed in the previous subsection. This means that there should be two consecutive [N]s derived, one by (11) and the other by (9). If this results, the two [N]s are amalgamated into a single [N] and in fact, the final form sounds more natural than the intermediate form, where only the /ru/ part is syllabicized.

There in fact is another output form that corresponds to the input form of (14c)–(14f), namely, only (9) applies but (11) is suppressed, for example, [kariruN nara] for (14c), [hasiruN da] for (14d), and so forth. These forms are more natural than the intermediate forms in (14). This seems to mean that the NS of the NM *no*, (9), is more prevalent, more neutral, and less marked than the NS of /ru/, (11), and that there is some hierarchy or concordance among casual rules and, if the one that is more marked applies, the less marked one is preferably applied as well, but the opposite may not hold. This fact, as briefly touched upon in relation to (8), strengthens the hypothesis that the application of CS processes is dictated by *sociological* factors not by the rate of speech.

Note that, even when its sociological condition is met, the NS in (11) cannot apply to a string that merely satisfies the phonological environment of (11), unless the lexical condition is also satisfied.

> (15) a. /yari-nareru/ → *yaN-nareru 'get used to doing'
> b. /hasiri-nikui/ → *hasiN-nikui 'hard to run'
> c. /harunasan/ → *haNnasan 'Mt. Haruna'

These examples are all strongly ungrammatical. None of them meet the lexical requirements of (11), i.e., /r/ must be a part of the verbal system and /n/ must be either the negative –(*a*)*nai*, the polite imperative *-nasai*, the negative imperative *-na*, or the NM *no*.

Vowel fusion (VF)

As compared to NS, the process to be discussed here, which I call *vowel fusion* (VF), takes place under much more restricted sociological conditions. Primarily in men's vulgar or unrefined speech only, /ai/, /oi/, and /ae/ are fused into a long vowel [e:].[19] Observe the following:

(16) a. /nai/ → ne: 'not'
   b. (verb)-/tai/ → (verb)-te: 'want to (verb)'
   c. /takai/ → take: 'tall, high'
   d. /sugoi/ → suge: 'great'
   e. /omae/ → ome: 'you'
   f. /atarimae/ → atarime: 'of course'

VF is observed basically only in the above items: the negative *nai* 'not' as in (16a); the commonly used adjectives that end with /ai/ and /oi/, such as the desiderative *-tai* 'want to' in (16c), and other adjectives like (16c), (16d), and /hayai/ → [haye:] 'fast,' /umai/ →[ume:] 'delicious,' /kusai/ → [kuse:] 'smelly,' and so forth; and some fixed expressions such as (16e) and (16f). The occurrences of these outputs may vary and some are quite prevalent, such as (16d), and others may not, such as (16e).

This process apparently eases the pronunciation of two distinct vowels in sequence, making it a long vowel with the place of articulation somewhere in between the two vowels.[20] For example, /ai/, which is the combination of /a/ [+back, –front, –high, +low] and /i/ [–back, +front, +high, –low], is changed into [e:], whose features are a mixture of the two vowels: [–back, –front, –high, –low] with the additional feature [+long]. The conversion of /oi/ and /ae/ into [e:] has basically the same effects. This process is formalized as (17) below, though this formalization may not reflect the fusing effects of the features of the two vowels.

(17) Vowel fusion (VF)
   { ai / oi / ae} → e: / [consonant] _____

VF never applies across words or phrases, as (18a)–(18c) show, even in fast speech or by merely accelerating the rate of speech. Furthermore, its application is restricted to certain lexical items, such as (16). Thus, (18d)–(18g), though they involve /ai//oi//ae/ word-internally, do not undergo VF.

(18) a. /ore ga iku/ → *ore ge:ku 'I(vulgar) go.'
   b. /ore mo iku/ → *ore me:ku 'I(vulgar) go, too.'
   c. /yokohama-eki/ → *yokohame:ki 'Yokohama station'

---

[19]   VF can be regarded as a rule in a *social* dialect in the sense that it is much more frequently observed in the speech of certain social groups, such as gangsters, the scum of the streets among the Tokyo dialect speakers, and of the speakers of certain regional dialects. For example, the affirmative exclamation /hai/ 'yes' can be fused into [hee], which may not necessarily be *vulgar* in a dialect or idiolect.

[20]   There is another process with a similar phonetic motivation, namely, the assimilation of a high vowel to the proceeding mid vowel seen in /seNsei/ → [seNse:] 'teacher' and /houhou/ → [ho:ho:] 'method.'. This process operates as a regular phonological rule, and these forms are observed even in slow and careful speech. Thus, unlike VF, this process is not a CS process. It is not an FS process, either, in view of the ungrammaticality of (i). That is, the domain of the application does not extend even if the rate of speech increases.
   i) a. /fude-ire/   →   *fude:re 'pen case'
       b. /sute-inu/   →   *sute:nu 'discarded dog'
       c. /soto-umi/   →   *sto:mi 'open sea'
       d. /ko-uta/   →   *ko:ta 'traditional song on the samisen'
       e. /katte iku/   →   *katte:ku 'buy and go'
       f. /hoN-o uru/   →   *hoNo:ru 'sell a book'

    d. /koitu/ → *ke:tu 'this man (vulgar)'

    e. /ki:roi/ → *ki:re: 'yellow'

    f. /sekai/ → *seke: 'the world'

    g. /sonae/ → *sone: 'preparation'

It is apparent that VF has a physiological or articulatory motivation; however, it seems that the sociological condition and the lexical specification are so rigid and negatively charged that the phonological motivation is never allowed to win out.

What is interesting about this process is that its effect sometimes goes beyond altering casualness, but its output is lexicalized and acquires a different meaning that is unexpected from the non-fused counterpart. For example, the humble form of the first person pronoun *temae* becomes the vulgar form of the second person pronoun [teme:] once it undergoes VF. This indicates that it is impossible and inappropriate to derive [teme:] from /temae/ by simply applying VF to the input. VF brings about not only the phonological change but also the lexico-semantic change, a characteristic that is never expected in FS processes. Furthermore, the existence of [teme:], the vulgar second person pronoun seems to suppress fusing /omae/, an informal second person pronoun, into [ome:] in vulgar speech, though the fused form [ome:] does exist as a second person pronoun, as seen in (16e), which gives a local or dialectal color to the entire speech. In the Tokyo dialect, the vulgar counterpart of *omae* is *teme:*, rather than *ome:*. We will see more instances of this sort in the section Casual Speech Processes in Grammar: The application of CS processes may affect not only phonological strings but also the *sociological* implications and meanings of the outputs as well as the entire speech.

Less sonorous vowel deletion (LSVD)

The process to be described here also involves two vowels in sequence. Unlike VF cases, however, the two vowels in question are brought together by morpho-syntactic operations. When the /e/ of the gerundive *te*-form of a verb, either /te/ or /de/, is followed by another (auxiliary-like) predicate that starts with a vowel, like *i-ru* 'exist; progressive, perfective,' *age-ru* 'give; do for the sake of someone,' or *ok-u* 'put,' the sequences of /e-i/, /e-a/, and /e-o/ obtain. Then, phonological changes take place in CS, dropping either one of the two vowels. Observe (19),[21]

    (19) a. /tabe-te iru/ → tabeteru 'be eating' 食べてる

        b. /suN-de iru/ → suNderu 'have been living' 住んでる

        c. /kai-te irassyaru/ → kaiterassyaru 'be writing (hono.)' 書いてらっしゃる

        d. /noN-de iku/ → noNdeku 'drink and go' ?飲んでく

        e. /kat-te oku/ → kattoku 'buy (in advance)' 買っとく

        f. /tsukut-te ageru/ → tukuttageru 'make (for someone)' 作ったげる

---

[21] In extremely casual context, /te-age-ru/ as in (19f) may undergo not only the deletion of /e/, the process under discussion, but the /g/ deletion and another application of the same vowel deletion, which deletes /e/, rendering the form [taru]; that is, /tsukut+te ageru/ → tukuttageru →*tukuttaeru → tukuttaru. Note that the deletion of /g/ (or /k/) is a process at work in Japanese phonology, which is responsible for deriving the past tense form of the consonant stem verbs that end with /g/ or /k/, that is, /oyog+ta/, /kak+ta/ → [oyoida], [kaita] 'swim-past,' 'write-past,' respectively. Incidentally, the same /g/ drop and the vowel drop in question are also responsible for producing [chaw-u], the casual semi-dialectal form of *chigaw-u* 'be different,' where /g/ is deleted and the resultant /ia/ is reduced to /a/ by dropping the less sonorous vowel /i/. These processes are, though they may apply rather sporadically, certainly active in the phonological structure of Japanese.

Between the two vowels brought together, the sonority or strength of the vowels in question determines which vowel drops and which stays: That is, the one higher or stronger stays and the other drops. Therefore, if the /e/, the front mid vowel, of the *te-*form is followed by *-iru* 'exist' and its variants, like *irassyar-u* 'honorific' and *i-ta* 'past,' which start with the front high vowel /i/, the more sonorous /e/ stays and the less sonorous /i/ drops. However, if the /e/ is followed by a vowel that is more sonorous such as /o/, the back mid or low vowel, or /a/, the back or mid low vowel, the /e/ drops. Note that this process, which I call Less Sonorous Vowel Deletion (LSVD), is different from VF, where the phonological features of both vowels are selectively respected and the moraic length of the two vowels is maintained as long. Furthermore, the sociological condition for this process is much freer in casual speech: Even the honorific form can undergo this process as seen in (19c) and many of these output forms appear in casual writing as shown in (19). This is particularly true with the aspectual *i-ru* 'progressive, perfective.'

Just as other processes that involve two vowels, that is, VD&L in (4) and VF in (17), LVSD has the effect of reducing the effort of producing two consecutive vowels. However, the domain of the application does not extend merely by increasing the rate of speech and it applies only to fixed lexical items, namely, *iru*, *oku*, and *ageru*. The examples in (20) are all ungrammatical since the predicate that follows the *te-*form is a wrong kind.[22]

> (20) a. /kat+te aru/ → *kattaru 'have been bought'
>   b. /kai+te asobu/ → *kaitasobu 'play by drawing'
>   d. /gaNbat+te ikiru/ → *ganbattekiru 'live with efforts'

The following is a descriptive formalization of this process.

> (21) Less sonorous vowel deletion (LSVD)
> $V_a V_b \rightarrow V_c$, where V_c is V_a, if $V_a > V_b$ in the sonority hierarchy and V_c is V_b, if $V_b > V_a$ in the sonority hierachy.
>   (V_a is /e/ of the *te-*form and V_b is the first vowel of *i-ru*, *o-ku*, *age-ru*.)

Phrase-final reduction[23]

Miyara (1980) takes up various examples of phrase final reduction that involve the particles *-wa* 'topic, contrastive' and the provisional *–(r)eba* form. Observe the following.[24, 25]

---

[22]   The ungrammaticality of (20a) is noteworthy: The use of *ar-u* 'exist' here is auxiliary-like, just as the other predicates that trigger this process.

[23]   Editors' note: Also see Toda on *contracted forms* in chapter 11 and Sakai and Igashima on *word coalescing* in chapter 12 of this book.

[24]   The descriptions given in (22)–(27) basically follow what Miyara presents in his (39), though some examples are added here. See also footnote 23.

[25]   Note that the outputs given in (22)–(27) have the counterparts that have a short vowel /a/, in place of the final long vowel /a:/; namely, [kota], [wakya] for (22), [taberya], [kakya] for (23), [yomya],[tabetya] for (24) and so forth. Some of these reduced forms appear in writing, where the short vowel version is preferred; [OK]部屋じゃ vs. ??部屋じゃぁ/?*部屋じゃあ for (27), for example. This process of shortening of a long vowel at the end of a word or a phonological phrase takes place commonly; possibly another CS process, for example, /desyo:/ → [desyo] 'copula-tentative,' (/seNsei/) → /seNse:/ → [seNse] 'teacher,' and /koNpyu:ta:/ → [koNpyu:ta] 'computer.'

(22) Complementizer or clause specifier plus *wa*
    a. /koto-wa/ → kota: e.g., /iku koto-wa nai/ → iku kota: nai 'no need to go'
    b. /wake-wa/ → wakya: e.g., /iku wake-wa nai/ → iku wakya: nai 'no reason to go'

(23) Verb stem –*(r)eba* 'provisional' → [(r)ya:][26]
    a. /tabe-reba/ → taberya: 'if ... eat'
    b. /kak-eba/ → kakya: 'if ... write'

(24) Verb stem + infinitive /-i/ or gerundive /-te/ plus *wa*[27]
    a. verb-stem+/i wa/ → verb-stem + [ya:] e.g., /yomi-wa/ → yomya: 'read'
    b. verb-stem+/{te, de} wa/ → V-stem+[{tya:, dya:}][28]
    e.g., /tabe-te wa/ → tabe-tya: 'eat'
    e.g., /sin-de wa/ → sin-dya: 'die'

(25) Demonstrative plus *wa*
    /{ko, so, a}-re wa/ → {ko, so, a} rya: '{this, that}'

(26) Adjective stem -*ku* and Nominal Adjective -*ni* plus *wa*
    a. A-stem+/ku wa/ → A-stem+ka: e.g., /yo+ku wa/
       → yoka: 'good contrastive'
    b. NomAdj+/ni wa/ → NomAdj+nya: e.g., /kantan+ni wa/
       → kantan+nya: 'easy'

(27) Two consecutive particles containing *wa*[29]
    a. de wa → dya: e.g., /heya de wa/ → heya dya: 'in the room'
    b. ni wa → nya: e.g., /taro: ni wa/ → taro: nya: 'to Taro'

As the above descriptions indicate, these reduction processes are sensitive to particular grammatical items and even if the same phonological strings obtain, unless the condition on lexical items is not met, these processes would not be triggered. Observe (28), where (a) and (b) are due to Miyara.[30]

---

[26] The provisional verb ending –*(r)eba* undergoes the /r/ drop, when it attaches to a consonant stem verb, such as kak- 'write,' which is a process that takes place regularly in Japanese phonology involving morphemes that start with /r/ including the present tense marker *-ru*, the passive *-rare*, and so forth. See McCawley (1968), Shibatani (1990), Tsujimura (1996), and Vance (1980) for discussion on morpho-phonology of Japanese in general.

[27] Miyara mentions that there is a process that involves the potential form *-re* of a verb and *ya* 'emphasis particle,' giving rise to the same effect as (24a). He presents the following examples:
    (i) a. /yom-e ya sinai/   → yomya: sinai 'cannot read'
          b. /kas-e ya sinai/   → kasya: sinai 'cannot lend'
          c. /yame-re ya sinai/ → yamerya: sinai 'cannot quit'
  However, (ia) and (ib) do not seem able to preserve the original 'potential' interpretation. They are of the same form as the output of (24a), namely, /yomi-wa sinai/ 'not read' and /kas-i wa sinai/ 'not lend,' and they only mean what these unreduced forms mean. As for (ic), the output, [yamerya:], is simply ungrammatical. Thus, I do not include this process in (24), since this process, if it exists or is attested, does not seem to be a general process in the Tokyo dialect, which this chapter is concerned about.

[28] Note that the exclamatory conjunctive expressions, /dewa/ 'then,' /sore dewa/ 'well, then' → [dya(:)], [soredya(:)], are instances of (24b), where /de/ is the gerundive form of the copula, *da*.

[29] (27a) and (27b) are not quite equal in status; that is, the occurrence of (27a) seems much freer than (27b) and the reduced form [dya:], can be used in casual writing, while [nya:] would not.

[30] As Miyara mentions, these forms may be possible in regional dialects or even in the Tokyo dialect if particular literary effects are intended. But it is clear that they are not allowed as freely as the processes in (22)–(27).

(28)a /tori wa/ → *torya: 'bird-Top'
    b. /kuruma wa/ → *kuruma: 'car-Top'
    c. /omoide wa/ → *omoidya: 'memory-Top'
    d. /kani wa/ → *kanya: 'crab-Top'
    e. /gaikoku wa/ → *gaikoka: 'foreign countries-Top'

What has been observed in the above is generalized as (29).

(29) Phonological Reduction involving /wa/, /ba/
    a. [+consonant] [+vowel, +front] wa → [+consonant] ya:
    b. [+consonant] [+vowel, +back] wa → [+consonant] a:

The example (29a) covers the processes in the above except (22a) and (26a), which involve a back vowel before /wa/ and are taken care of by (29b). The phonological changes described in (29) are actually not a single process but involve a series of independent rules, namely, the /w/ and /b/ deletion between a vowel and /a/, the glide /y/ insertion between a high vowel and /a/, and compensatory lengthening, which makes the final /a/ into /a:/. It has been claimed that each of these processes plays an independent role in Japanese phonology in general.[31] What is special about the reduction processes in (22)–(27), however, is that these processes take place as a group in casual speech, giving rise to the effects specified in (29).

More reduction processes

As we have observed, CS processes are in one way or another conditioned by lexical information and apply only to specific lexical items. The reduction or contraction processes taken up here are not exceptions, either, referring rigidly to what structures and what strings of words are subject to them. See the examples below:

(30) a. /mi-te simau/ → mitimau → mityau 'have seen'
    b. /tomat-te simau/ → tomattimau → tomattyau 'has stopped'
    c. /yoN-de simau/ → yoN-jimau → yoNjau 'have read'
    d. /kore-de simau/ → *korejimau → *korejau 'finish at this moment'
    e. /mi-te siru/ → *mitiru → *mityu 'know by seeing'
    f. /yoN-de siru/ → *yoNjiru → *yoNju 'know by reading'

(31) a. /mi-ru koto-wa/ (nai) → mikko (nai) 'it can't be the case that …
      will see…'
    b. /yom-u koto-wa/ (nai) → yomikko (nai) 'it can't be the case that …
      will read…'
    c. /mi-ta koto-wa/ (nai) → *mitakkko (nai) / *mikko (nai) '…have
      not seen…'

In (30), it is shown that the reducible string must involve the gerundive -te form of a verb and the aspectual verb sima(w)-u. Note that if /de/ is not of the -te form as seen in (30d) or the stings merely phonetically similar such as (30e) and (30f), the reduction does not take place. Likewise, as seen in (31), only the particular string of [(the present tense verb)-koto-wa nai] 'it can't be the case that …will verb…' changes into [(the infinitive verb)-kko nai]. The input structure here is syntactically complex;

---

[31] With respect to exactly what phonological processes are involved to give rise to these reduced forms, careful examinations are called for, in terms of the entire phonological structure of Japanese. To do so, however, is beyond the scope of this chapter. As noted in footnote 22, the final vowel /a/ may stay short. This may be interpreted as the non-application of compensatory lengthening or as the application of the shortening of the phrase/word final long vowel, which has been suggested in the above. See Fukui (1986), Hattori (1960), McCawley (1968), Miyara (1980), Poser (1988), Shibatani (1979), and Vance (1987) for relevant discussion.

nai 'not' is a matrix predicate that takes a sentential complement, which is headed by a formal noun *koto*, and the verb takes place inside the complement. Only to these particular strings and structures, these reduction processes apply. The following describes these processes:

(32) a. /{te, de} simaw/ → /{timaw, jimaw} → /{tyaw, jaw}/ 'have V-ed; perfective'
'where {te, de} is the gerundtive *-te* form of a verb.'
b. Verb-/(r)u koto-wa/ (nai) → Verb(infinitive)-/kko/ (nai)

These reduction forms do occur fairly frequently in ordinary conversation among intimate speakers, though they may give a childish tone to the entire conversation. In fact, the reduced forms, including the ones above and the ones discussed below in the section Phrase-Final Reduction, are extremely popular in child speech. In addition, these two processes are not at all sensitive to the rate of speech. No matter how slow the speech is, the full form would not show up in the *casual* context where these processes are chosen to apply, and conversely, no matter how fast the speech is produced, the reduced forms may never be used in a *formal* situation, where they are inappropriate. For instance, if a child asks her mother to repeat her utterance that involves the reduced forms, the mother would most probably repeat the same reduced forms with slower speed, not the non-reduced full forms.

Recall, in the section above on VD&L in relation to VF, that the application of CS processes sometimes gives rise to unexpected meanings and implications. The contraction processes under discussion here also exhibit some changes in meanings and morpho-syntactic requirements of the items involved. For instance, the process in (32b) actually involves more than phonological changes. The output [kko] requires the infinitival form of a verb, while the input /koto-wa/ takes the present tense form. In addition, the meaning of *kko (nai)* is different from the original full form; the former is closer in meaning to the expression with *hazu* 'likelihood,' as in (the present tense verb)-*hazu-ga nai* 'cannot be the case that…' than the original (the present tense verb)-*koto-wa nai*. Thus, for some reason, through the application of this process, the meanings change and the morpho-syntactic requirements on the form of the preceding verb are altered.

As for (32a), it takes place at the sequence of /te/ or /de/ and the palatalized /s/, that is, [sh] or [sʸ], in *simaw-u*. The changes from /te-sʸ/ /de-sʸ/ to /ty/ /j/ obtain if the /e/ drops and the features of the two adjacent consonants are fused; the feature [+stop] of /t/ /d/, and the [+palatal] of [sʸ] are amalgamated and produces the affricates [ty] (or [ch]) [j], which have both [+stop] and [+palatal] quality. Then, the deletion of /m/ takes place, resulting in the final form [tyaw-u][jaw-u]. What is interesting is that the choice between the two reduced forms, the intermediate and the final, is not relevant to the rate of speech or the casualness of speech, but rather idiosyncratic. For example, the intermediate forms, [timaw-u] and [jimaw-u], do not seem to be in the *active vocabulary* of many speakers of the Tokyo dialect, including myself, while the final forms, [tyaw-u] and [jaw-u], are extremely common in casual speech. Furthermore, in child speech, only the final contracted forms are exclusively used and neither the full forms nor the intermediate forms may be in their active vocabulary.

Another piece of evidence that suggests that the final form is independent in status from the input form is found in the fact that the final form can appear where the full form is not allowed. For instance, as Martin (1975) observes, the final form may take place with a stative verb, such as *ar-u* 'exist, have,' though the full form does not sound right.

(33)a. Kodomo-ga attyaw-u to nanimo deki-nai.
　　　 child-Nom have-perf.-pres.-if anything can=do-not
　　　 'I can't do anything if/because I have a child.'
　　 b. *Kodomo-ga at-te simaw-u to nanimo deki-nai.

The last case to be taken up is seen in the following. These expressions in the output are extremely common in everyday conversation.

(34)a. /ik-anaku te wa/ → ikanaku tya 'must go'
　　 b. /tabe-nake-reba/ → tabenake rya 'must eat'

The phonological processes here are basically the same as what we have seen in the section on Phrase-Final Reductions. Example (34a) is a variant of (24b), where the *te*-form of a verb is followed by /wa/, giving rise to the same /tya(:)/, and (34b) is equivalent to (23a), involving the provisional *-reba*, which gets reduced to /rya(:)/. What is special about (34) is that it involves the negative form and the output here acquires the meaning of 'obligation,' which the input full form does not necessarily have. This is because these phrases, where the gerundive form or provisional form of the negation ends an utterance, function as a conditional phrase and the consequence expression such as *naranai* 'wouldn't do' or *dame-da* 'no good' is entirely truncated. Though the non-reduced input itself may stand alone as a conditional clause, it gives the impression that the speech stops in the middle and that the consequence clause that is supposed to follow is omitted. On the other hand, with the reduced version, such an impression is clearly suppressed. This fact seems to indicate that once the sociological condition is met to trigger the CS process of the reduction in (34), it also triggers the phrasal or clausal truncation of the consequence clause in syntax. To the extent that both processes are contingent upon each other, there is no psychological need to supply what is syntactically truncated, if the phonological reduction takes place. If the input of (34) does not undergo the reduction, however, the truncation of the consequent clause must independently takes place syntactically, which seems responsible for giving rise to the impression of an unfinished speech. This is a clear example of how CS processes interact each other across the boundaries of the components of grammar, which is the topic of the following section.

Casual Speech Processes in Grammar

We have started out our discussion by assuming that FS and CS processes are different and that the difference lies primarily in whether the rate of speech is relevant to the occurrences of the processes. We have seen that CS processes, though they often seem phonologically *natural*, are insensitive to the speed of utterance production. Besides such a difference, we have observed the following common characteristics among the CS rules we have examined: (a) CS rules are more or less conditioned by lexical information and only lexically specified items are subject to them; (b) CS rules are sensitive to sociological notions; (c) the application of CS processes often brings about new or unexpected changes in meaning and/or morpho-syntactic conditions; and (d) the application of phonological CS processes may affect the application of the rules in different components of grammar. These facts seem to indicate clearly that CS processes are different in nature from FS processes.

As noted in Hasegawa (1979), these characteristics are also observed in the phenomena of other components of grammar that are sensitive to sociological factors. Japanese is known for being abundant with grammatical phenomena that refer to such notions. In this section, we will examine a few such phenomena and see how they interact with the phonological CS processes.

The lexicon is viewed as storing various idiosyncratic properties of lexical items and, if a single concept or notion is represented by different items, the differences among them would be expressed there. Take the concept of the first person singular pronoun, for example, for which English has only one item 'I' (and its case-related variants). Japanese, however, has at lease the following forms (and perhaps more) to represent this notion.

(35) a. watakusi 'formal'
    b. watasi 'general, neutral'
    c. atakusi 'formal, female, older'
    d. atasi 'general, female'
    e. boku 'general, (younger) male'
    f. ore 'informal, male'
    g. wasi 'informal, older male, regional'
    h. assi 'male, humble, specific class'

As seen above, the differences have to do with sociological context and the choice depends on the gender, age, social class, and so forth, of the speaker and under what sociological context utterances are made. Some of them are apparently phonologically related, (35a)–(35d) for example, but whatever processes there may be to relate them, outputs have a different connotation from the input.

Subject honorification (SH) may be taken as representative of a process that involves both the morphology component and the syntactic component. It is syntactically conditioned by the presence of a particular type of a subject, that is, the referent of a subject must be socially superior to the speaker (SSS).[32] The general description of this process is that when the subject is SSS, the predicate appears in the form o/go-verb(infinitive)-ni-nar-u, as in (36a), for which the morphological attachment of o/go, the conversion of verb forms, and the addition of the honorific predicate are at work, though there are quite a few lexically specified suppletive forms such as (36b)–(36e), which must take precedence over the regular form.

(36) a. kak-u 'write'   o-kaki-ni-nar-u
    b. iw-u 'say'   ?*o-iwi-ni-nar-u   ossyar-u
    c. ik-u 'go'   ??o-iki-ni-nar-u   o-ide-ni-nar-u   irassyar-u
    d. mi-ru 'see'   *o-mi-ni-nar-u   go-ran-ni-nar-u
    e. i-ru 'exist'   *o-i-ni-nar-u   irassyar-u

Note that if the conversational situation is not *formal* enough to call for honorification, SH does not have to apply, even if the syntactic condition is met. Thus, the application of this process is dependent on sociological context, just like the CS processes examined above.

Another example of a syntactic phenomenon that is sensitive to sociological context is the occurrence of $yagar$-u.[33] $Yagar$-u attaches to a predicate, giving rise to the form, verb(infinitive)-$yagar$-u, when the referent of the subject is what or who the speaker despises or has a contempt for, the opposite to the referent of a subject in SH. Thus,

---

[32]   See Harada (1977) and Hasegawa (2005) among others for descriptions and analyses of Honorification.

[33]   Due to the *unfavorable* status of this expression, the syntax and use of $yagar$-u have rarely been discussed, with the exception of Hasegawa (2005).

the syntactic condition for the *yagar-u* attachment is the same as SH, referring to a type of a subject, though the sociological conditions placed on it are the opposite. SH tends to occur when the speech context is formal and polite, while *yagar-u* is possible only when the context is casual, unrefined, or vulgar enough for the speaker to express raw and negative feelings.

What is of particular relevance to our discussion is that the occurrence or non-occurrence of these lexical, morphological, and syntactic processes are sensitive to sociological notions that affect the application of the phonological CS processes. We have already briefly witnessed such a case in (8), where the NS becomes mandatory with the presence of the vulgar form of the second person pronoun. Two more similar examples are provided here:

(37) a. {Watakusi, Ore, Sense:}-ni-wa   wakar-anai.
            I(polite), I(male, vulgar), teacher-to-Top   understand-neg
    b. ??Watakusi nya: wakar-anai.
    c. *Watakusi nya: wakaN-ne:.
    d. Ore nya: wakaN-ne:
    e. *Sense: nya: o-wakari-ni naN-ne:
(38) {Aitu, *Ano kata}-ga ki-yagaru {*no, N}   nara,
        {he(vul), that person (hon)}- NOM   come-contempt NM if
        (if that bastard is coming, …)

In (37), the sequence of /ni-wa/, which is subject to the reduction process in (27b), and *wakar-anai*, which may undergo NS with /r/ of (11) and VF (17), take place with three different types of subjects. Though the acceptability may vary depending on the context, the relationship between the speaker and the teacher, and the speaker's idiolect, it seems that the choice of the polite first person, *watakusi*, and the application of SH, which tends to mark the speech polite, do not get along with any of the CS processes in question.[34] Similarly in (38), with the predicate *yagar-u*, which indicates that the speaker despises or has contempt for the subject and marks the speech as undoubtedly vulgar, the polite form *ano kata* is inappropriate and *aitu*, the vulgar form of the third person pronoun, better suits the speech level. In such a situation, the application of NS on the NM *no* is mandatory.[35]

These examples clearly indicate that the grammatical processes that refer to *sociological* conditions exhibit a kind of *concordance* among the processes in different components. When a particular process that is charged with a certain sociological notion takes place in one component, the grammatical processes of a similar type in terms of such notions are most likely to be triggered in other components, and their applications, though optional in principle, become mandatory in order to match the sociological level set by the process. This *concordance* across different components seems to be a distinctive characteristic of CS processes.

---

[34]   For example, (37e) may be a possible utterance of an older male speaker whose educational background is limited, even when he pays respect to the teacher.

[35]   As a matter of fact, the phonological string [kiyagaru N nara] in (38) would further undergo another CS rule, resulting in [kiyagaN nara], which seems the most appropriate form in the context (38). This shortened form obtains by the application of (11) NS with /r/, which converts the verb final /r/ into the syllabic nasal [N] being followed by NM *no*, and the reduction of one N from the sequences of Ns, which is a mandatory process. This is the same phenomenon observed in (10c)–(10f).

Summary

The terms *fast* and *casual* are often interchangeably used in the study of casual speech. In this chapter, I have attempted to make the distinction between the two clearer by examining various types of CS processes. As compared with FS processes, which are typically operative purely on phonological grounds, extending their domain of application as the rate of speech increases, CS processes exhibit the following characteristics:

(39)
Lexical and structural conditions: CS processes apply only to designated lexical items under particular structural description.
Sociological conditions: CS processes apply only when the context of speech is appropriate with respect to various sociological notions, such as casualness, politeness, intimacy, the age, gender, and social class of the speaker, and so forth.
Concordance across components: CS processes may or may not apply depending on what processes are employed in other components of grammar in producing a given utterance.

Given these characteristics of CS processes, for a better understanding of CS phenomena, it seems necessary to treat CS differently from FS and to investigate them in a broader perspective, investigating exactly how CS processes in different components interact with each other and how sociological conditions are to be accounted for in grammar in general and in Japanese in particular.

Acknowledgements

I am grateful to James Dean Brown and Kimi Kondo-Brown for inviting me to contribute to this volume by revising Hasegawa (1979). I would also like to thank Ellen Kaisse, under whose guidance my previous research was done, for introducing me to this topic, and Michael Kenstowitz, an acclaimed phonologist who happens to be a 'student' of Japanese, for convincing me that revising Hasegawa (1979) would be valuable both pedagogically and theoretically. The usual disclaimers apply.

11

Focus on Form in Teaching Connected Speech

NFLRC
monographs

TAKAKO TODA
Waseda University, Tokyo, Japan

This chapter offers pedagogical suggestions concerning teaching methodologies with a focus on connected speech in Japanese. In order to find out what forms can be taught, the author classifies Japanese reduced forms into four categories with nine sub-categories. It was found that some of the phonological processes that are operative in Japanese reduced forms share similarities with those in other languages. In particular, the phonetic output due to ease of articulation seems to have universal tendencies. However, other factors that are highly language-specific such as the role of the mora and morphosyntactic constraints are also present. The chapter then discusses how to direct learners to find rules involved in Japanese reduced forms. Finally, teaching materials are presented to promote noticing and relate forms to meaning. This chapter will be of most interest to applied linguistics researchers and those Japanese language teachers, researchers, materials developers, and testers who specifically need to understand, teach, and develop materials or tests for teaching continuous speech in Japanese.

Focus on Form in Teaching Connected Speech

Both in research and teaching, spoken language has not been paid as much attention as written language. Spoken language was traditionally considered as an imperfect or inferior form of written language, and therefore did not attract a great deal of research interest. In the classroom, language instructors felt responsible to teach learners the language correctly (i.e., the ideal version) instead of the ways it was actually used.

In Japanese as a second language (JSL) and Japanese as a foreign language (JFL) teaching, there seems to be another reason why both teachers and learners have been discouraged from teaching/learning colloquial forms of the language: the myth that Japanese people always speak formally and politely. This is not the case of course; as with other languages, Japanese speakers shift their speech-style based on the circumstances. For example, a businessperson may speak formally and politely in dealing with clients during business hours, but speak informally after work when drinking with colleagues to foster a closer relationship. Foreign businesspersons often call this phenomenon *nomunication* (Japanese-English combination term, *nomu*, 'to drink,' + -*nication*, from communication). Learners who overly use formal and correct forms, may give Japanese colleagues the impression that they are unfriendly or

Toda, T. (2006) Focus on form in teaching connected speech. In J. D. Brown, & K. Kondo-Brown, (Eds.), *Perspectives on teaching connected speech to second language speakers* (pp. 189–205). Honolulu, HI: University of Hawai'i, National Foreign Language Resource Center.

unapproachable. Similarly, learners studying in Japan who wish to have close relationships with their Japanese friends or neighbors need to use colloquial language. Hence, these learners are filled with motivation to learn realistic forms of the language.

In this chapter, I will use the term *reduced forms* in a broad sense, to refer to sound changes which take place in connected speech. These include contraction, elision, assimilation, transition, and liaison. The reduced forms appear not only for socio-linguistic reasons as described above, but also for phonetic reasons, that is, ease of articulation. Speakers tend to speak with the least articulatory effort, *so ease of articulation* can be a strong motivation for the production of reduced forms. This aspect of reduced forms is universal (i.e., it occurs in any spoken language), whereas other socio-linguistic and morphosyntactic constraints are language-specific. We need, therefore, to consider stylistic, articulatory, and syntactic parameters that would affect the use of Japanese reduced forms. It is too simplistic to say that reduced forms appear in *informal speech*, as they are often referred to in Japanese classrooms. Formal speech versus informal speech (level of formality) are independent from parameters such as carefully articulated speech versus casually articulated speech (articulation), or slow colloquial speech versus fast colloquial speech (speech tempo).[1]

In the field of ESL/EFL, there has been a considerable amount of discussion on reduced forms, such as the effect of the input of reduced forms upon listeners' listening comprehension (Henrichsen, 1984; Ito, chapter 6 of this book), effectiveness of instruction (Brown & Hilferty, 1986a, 1986b, 1995, also see chapter 4 of this book), and teachers' perspectives (Rogerson, chapter 7 of this book).

In recent years, greater diversification of the learners' interests and needs has been reported in JSL/JFL, and the need to teach and learn connected speech in Japanese has also increased. The majority of Japanese native speakers (NS) living in Japan do not have a great deal of contact with L2 learners, and so they have little knowledge of the diversity of Japanese pronunciation spoken by people with different language backgrounds. This is one of the reasons L2 learners studying in Japan feel their accent is unintelligible to NS. Familiarity with accented speech spoken by non-native speakers is an important factor in determining intelligibility. This is different from ESL/EFL situations, where many native English speakers are familiar with the varieties of English spoken by people from other speech communities. This implies intelligible pronunciation in Japanese requires a higher degree of accuracy and fluency, even if the goal of phonological acquisition for L2 learners is not native level fluency. Likewise, there is little doubt that we need to teach aspects of connected speech because L2 learners' listening comprehension is negatively affected by the presence of reduced forms (as shown in Henrichsen, 1984; Brown & Hilferty, 1986b, or chapter 4 of this book; Ito, chapter 6 of this book).

Currently, however, little material is available to teach phonological aspects of the language in Japanese language classrooms. Furthermore, with regard to reduced forms, there is no unified agreement on the use of terminology such as contraction, elision, assimilation, transition, and liaison. Further study on the categorization of Japanese

---

[1]   Editors' note: Hasegawa in chapter 10 of this book discusses such connected speech forms in terms of fast speech versus casual speech; Toda examines these sorts of changes in comparison with European languages such as English or French. She points out that Japanese sound changes, like those in European languages, are activated by ease of articulation issues and that the *mora* plays an crucial role in categorizing such Japanese connected speech forms.

reduced forms is required so that such research findings can be applied to the teaching of JSL/JFL.

To those ends, the objectives of this chapter are as follows:

1. To classify Japanese reduced forms into categories so they can be referenced by instructors who wish to teach Japanese reduced forms.
2. To discuss the universal and language-specific features in connected speech and attempt to explain morphosyntactic constraints in Japanese reduced forms.
3. To offer pedagogical suggestions concerning teaching methodologies with a focus on reduced forms.

Categories of Japanese Reduced Forms

Type 1 Elision

Elision is a common phonological phenomenon observed in the formation of reduced forms within words or phrases. In English, a stress-timed language, elision is a stress-related phenomenon and so it tends to take place in the weak positions, commonly in unstressed syllables or in function words. In contrast, Japanese is a syllable-timed language with each mora having equal weight, and so elision does not occur as a function of stress.[2] In English, elision is sometimes marked orthographically with an apostrophe when it occurs across a morphological boundary as seen in *it's* 'it is' or *you're* 'you are.' Similarly, *c'est* is a reduced form of *ce est* in French, as in *C'est la vie*. 'That's life.' In Japanese, however, there is no special orthographic marking of vowel elision.

Vowel elision is observed in reduced forms of the aspectual use of the verb *-iru* 'to be' and *-iku* 'to go.' When these verbs appear as aspect marking morpheme *-te iru* and *-te iku*, [i] is eliminated. One of the main motivations for this elision is a simplification of the consecutive occurrence of vowels, when they appear across a morphological boundary. This is due to a preference for CV (i.e., light syllable) instead of CVV (i.e., heavy syllable).

> Moo sonna koto <u>shitteru</u> (shitte iru). 'I already know that.'
> Daigaku made <u>aruiteku</u> (aruite iku). 'I will walk to the university.'

The preference towards CV is also seen in the phonetic etymology of Japanese word formation. For example, *ara* 'rough' + *umi* 'sea' → *arumi* 'rough sea.' The opposite case involves situations where the CV syllable structure is maintained by the insertion of a consonant between vowels, such as *haru* 'spring' + *ame* 'rain' → *harusame* 'spring rain.' Such a phonological process is called *intrusion*. No explanation has yet been found for why it is [s] that is inserted, however.

---

[2]   Previous studies have classified languages into two broad categories: *stress-timed* and *syllable-timed*. Japanese was first classified into the latter category (Hockett, 1955). Later, a third category, *mora-timed*, was distinguished from *syllable-timed* languages (Ladefoged, 2000, p. 233). Isochrony is often referred to in the definition of the mora. However, acoustic observations have shown that the strict version of the mora hypothesis, which claims that each mora is strictly isochronous, does not capture phonetic reality.

Type 2 Contraction

The Japanese term for contraction is *shukuyakukei* 'contracted forms,' and this phonological change is characterized by a reduction of the number of morae.[3] This is one of the linguistic terms the definition of which varies remarkably: Some researchers use *shukuyakukei* to refer to elision described in Type 1 based on the fact that the number of morae is reduced in this type also, while others use it to refer to the sound changes that occur in connected speech in general. In order to avoid confusion, I would like to use *contraction* to refer to words formed by more than one morpheme by combining sounds. This process typically produces new sounds. A strict version of this coalescence would be where two phonemes merge completely and give a birth to a different phoneme. A weak version refers to a process where two phonemes influence each other and become one phoneme that adopts some of the features from both or one of the two phonemes. In this respect, the process of contraction is similar with assimilation described in Type 3.

The phonetic characteristics of Japanese contraction with palatalized consonants [tʃ] and [dʒ] seem, at first glance, similar to some reduced forms in English, such as I *betcha* (I bet you) or *Wouldja* (Would you). The palatalized consonants [tʃ] and [dʒ] in these examples are produced through mutual assimilation between the word-final alveolar stops [t] or [d] and the following palatal semi-vowel [j] in *you*. The same phonological process is observed in words with the word-initial [j] such as *not yet* [nɑtʃɛt] and *last year* [læstʃɪə] in English.

Now let us take a look at the aspectual use of the verb *-shimau* 'end up doing,' which is pronounced as [tʃau] or [dʒau] in a contracted form.

> Kyoo kekka o <u>michatta</u> (miteshimatta). 'I ended up seeing the results today.'
> Moo <u>yonjatta</u> (yondeshimatta). 'I've already read it.'

The allophonic variations of Japanese phonemes are influential for the formation of reduced forms. In Japanese phonology, /t/, /d/, /s/, and /z/ before the high vowel [i] are palatalized: for example, *miru* 'see' [mite ʃimau] → [mitʃimau] → [mitʃau] *yomu* 'read' [jonde ʃimau] → [jondʒimau] → [jondʒau]. Phonetically speaking, both [i] and [j] are [+high] and thus likely cause the palatalization of preceding consonants. This may be a universal feature, and a motivation for producing similar alternations in both English and Japanese. However, there are also some differences. J-epenthesis is required to produce [tʃ] and [dʒ] in the following examples:

> Sonna koto <u>shicha</u> (shite wa) dame. 'You are not allowed to do such a thing.'
> Kokode <u>yonja</u> (yonde wa) ikemasen. 'Reading is prohibited here.'

The neighboring sounds in these citation forms are mutually assimilated, the epenthetic [j] is absorbed into the preceding consonant and as a result, produces a similar phonetic output [tʃ] and [dʒ] to that of English reduced forms. This contraction process of *shite wa*, a conjunctive form of *suru* 'do' and *yonde wa*, a conjunctive form of *yomu* 'read' with a topic marker *wa*, is described in Shibatani (1990, p. 175):

	do-CONJ TOPIC	read-CONJ TOPIC
	ʃite wa	**jonde wa**
w → ø	ʃite a	jonde a

---

[3] Editors' note: Also see Hasegawa on *phrase-final reduction* in chapter 10 and Sakai and Igashima on *word coalescing* in chapter 12 of this book.

j → epenthesis	ʃite ja	jonde ja
e → ø	ʃitja	jondja
palatalization	ʃitʃa	jondʒa

A similar phonological process is observed in demonstratives, such as *kore wa* 'this-TOPIC' → [korja], *are wa* 'that-TOPIC' → [arja], and *sore wa* 'it-TOPIC' → [sorja]. This is also seen in other word categories. For example, conditional verb forms also show a similar pattern: *mireba* 'see-CONDITION' → [mirja], *kakeba* 'write-CONDITION' → [kakja] and *oyogeba* 'swim-CONDITION' → [oyogja]. Also, *-nakereba* 'must' is pronounced as [nakerja] and further reduced to [nakja] in its contracted form.

> Ohirugohan <u>tabenakya</u> (tabenakutewa). 'I have to eat lunch.'
> Hayaku <u>okinakya</u> (okinakereba) naranai. 'I must get up early.'

Therefore, the process described above can be further generalized as follows:

> C-e[+bilabial]a → Cja (C represents consonant, [+bilablial] represents [w] and [b])

Secondly, coalescence is another case of contraction, where two consecutive vowels are mutually assimilated and become one vowel. For example, this occurs in the combination of the conjunctive form of the verb and the aspect morpheme *-toku* (*-te oku*) (doing something for a future purpose).

> Kyoo kaimono <u>shitoku</u> (shite oku) ne. 'I'll take care of shopping today.'
> Kaze hikanai yoo ni kusuri <u>nondoku</u> (nonde oku). 'I'll take some medicine so
>   I won't catch a cold.'

Also, vowel coalescence occurs in the combination of the conjunctive form of the verb and the aspect morpheme *-tageru* (*-te ageru*) 'doing something for someone.'

> Kawari ni <u>yattageru</u> (yatte ageru) yo. 'I'll do it for you.'
> Hon <u>yondageru</u> (yonde ageru) ne. 'I'll read a book for you.'

There are at least two contrasting positions in the analysis of the above phonological changes: vowel elision of [e] in the *-te* form (Kawase, 1992; Toki, 1975) and vowel coalescence across morphological boundaries (Kubozono, 1999; Toda, 2004). Phonologically speaking, both of these interpretations are possible. However, the former position does not explicitly distinguish why the vowel elision occurs immediately after the morphological boundary in the aspect marking morpheme *-teru* (*-te iru*) and *-teku* (*-te iku*) (Type 1), when it occurs immediately before the morphological boundary in *-toku* (*-te oku*) and *-tageru* (*-te ageru*) (Type 2). Also, non-expert NS without background knowledge of phonology will almost always not recognize that [e] is deleted, largely because [e] is a part of *-te* form and thus not shown as え at the orthographic level. In fact, the reduced forms of 〜ておく／〜て あげる are written as 〜とく／〜たげる, and neither the citation nor the reduced form show え. This situation is different from the phonological process described in Type 1: The reduced forms of 〜ている／〜ていく are written as 〜てる／〜てく, and NSs are aware that the underlined い has been eliminated from the citation form.

Vowel coalescence allows us to explain the characteristics of other reduced forms in connected speech, which are otherwise not captured by simple vowel deletion. For example, *omae* 'you' → [ome:] and *kurai* 'dark' → [kure:] in rough speech by male speakers of Japanese.

Furthermore, in conjunctive use of the verbs, the same phonological alternation described in the aspect morphemes -*toku* (-*te oku*) and -*tageru* (-*te ageru*) does not take place:

> Agat<u>te o</u>riru 'going up and down' *Agat<u>tor</u>iru
> Ori<u>te a</u>garu 'going down and up' *Ori<u>tag</u>aru

The degree of bonding is not as high in conjunctive use of the verbs as that of aspect morphemes, and when two verb phrases have equal weight in the sentence, reduced forms do not occur. Those examples indicate that the formation of reduced forms is not only affected by ease of articulation, but governed by grammatical factors.

Type 3 Assimilation

Assimilation is a common phenomenon observed in many languages. One categorization of assimilation is based on its direction: Progressive assimilation is where the preceding sound affects the following sound, and regressive assimilation is where a following sound affects the preceding sound. Mutual (or reciprocal) assimilation is where the neighboring sounds in the citation forms are mutually influenced.

An example of assimilation with voiceless consonants is where *of* in *of course* is pronounced as [əf] before a voiceless stop [k] in this environment, even though it is pronounced as [əv] in the citation form. Another example of regressive voice assimilation is observed in the pronunciation of *have* in *have to*. This pattern can be explained with the following formula: [-V] [+V] [-V] → [-V] [-V] [-V] (V=voiced). There are also examples of voice assimilation, where the [-voice] feature of a segment is assimilated by the [+voice] feature of the surrounding segments. For example, the voiced *t*, or flap, in American English [t] is pronounced as [ɾ] when it appears between stressed and unstressed vowels such as *butter*, *water*, and *pretty*. This pattern can be formulated as [+V] [-V] [+V] → [+V] [+V] [+V]. Both of these formulae show the resulting forms are easier to pronounce. Voice assimilation also occurs in the word-final position in English, where the suffix -*s* in *reads* is pronounced as [z] while that in *walks* is pronounced as [s], where voiced features from the word-final consonants are carried across to the suffix -*s* as a result of progressive assimilation.

In Type 3, I would like to present four types of assimilation for Japanese: *museika* 'devoicing,' [4] *rendaku* 'sequential voicing,' *sokuon-ka* 'consonant gemination,' and *hatsuon-ka* 'moraic nasalization.'[5]

Firstly, *museika* is known as devoicing of vowels in Japanese (see Hasegawa on *high-vowel devoicing* in chapter 10 of this book). In principle, high vowels between voiceless consonants are in the phonetic environment where devoicing is possible. Vowels are not eliminated, but their [+voice] feature is assimilated to the [-voice] feature of the surrounding consonants. This phonological process is represented as [-V] [+V] [-V] → [-V] [-V] [-V]. For low sonority vowels, such as [i] and [u], losing their [+voice] feature and becoming voiceless between voiceless consonants is regarded as a natural reduction process. Although in English, voice assimilation tends to occur in consonants rather than vowels.

---

[4]   Editors' note: Also see Hasegawa on *high vowel devoicing* in chapter 10 and Sakai and Igashima on *vowel devoicing* in chapter 12 of this book.

[5]   A phonological category called tokushuhaku 'special morae' consists of /Q/ (sokuon 'first half of geminate obstruents'), /N/ (hatsuon 'moraic nasals'), and /R/ (choo'on 'the last half of long vowels'). This category is often used in phonological analyses of Japanese.

Kochira wa Kikuchi-san da. 'This is Mr. Kikuchi.'
Tsukue no ue ni oitoku ne. 'I will leave it on the desk.'

The phonetic realization of voice assimilation varies depending on speech style and how much attention is paid to the speakers' pronunciation. For example, all three vowels in Kikuchi [kikutʃi] are candidates for devoicing, but may change in the following situations: Kikuchi [kikutʃi] in careful speech, Kikuchi [ki̥kutʃi] in normal speech, and Kikuchi [ki̥kutʃi̥] in casual speech. Also, this devoicing varies considerably depending on dialects. Speakers of Western Japanese dialects do not devoice the vowels to the same degree as those of Eastern Japanese dialects.

Devoicing of vowels is determined by the phonetic environment, and the number of morae is unchanged before and after the devoicing. For this reason, the nature of voice assimilation described here is different from vowel elision in Type 1.

Secondly, *rendaku* 'sequential voicing' refers to the process where the morpheme-initial voiceless obstruents become voiced in compounds, as seen in the following examples:

Booekigaisha ni tsutometeimasu. 'I am working for a trading company.'
Atarashii benkyoozukue o kaimashita. 'I bought a new study desk.'

The underlined voiced consonants above are originally voiceless in their word-initial position, as seen below:

booeki 'trading' + *kaisha* 'company' = booekigaisha 'trading company'
benkyoo 'study' + *tsukue* 'desk' = benkyoozukue 'study desk'

In this case, the voice assimilation of the consonant is represented at the orthographical level. For example, かいしゃ 'company' is written as がいしゃ when it appears as a second half of the compound. Thus this phonological process is represented as [+C] [-C] [+C] → [+C] [+C] [+C]. From the viewpoint of speech production, it is easier to pronounce voiced consonants between two vowels. Also, sequential voicing can be regarded as a perceptual aid for listeners to perceive the compound as one meaningful unit. L2 learners' pronunciation without sequential voicing, such as *booekikaisha,* may be heard as two words by NS.[6] However, some constraints are operative in sequential voicing. Lyman's Law (1894), which states that sequential voicing does not apply when the second element contains a voiced obstruent, is also apparent in Japanese.

nama 'raw' + *tamago* 'egg' = *namatamago* 'raw egg' *namadamago

Also, there is a tendency for foreign loanwords to resist sequential voicing.

dezitaru 'digital' + *kamera* 'camera' = *dezitarukamera* 'digital camera'
*dezitarugamera

Another situation in which sequential voicing does not apply is when the two elements in the compound are in juxtaposition.

suki 'like' + *kirai* 'dislike' = *sukikirai* 'likes and dislikes' *sukigirai

---

6   In both English and Japanese, the prosodic characteristics change in the formation of compounds. The accentual rules involved in the formation of compounds are also considered as a perceptual cue for the listener to perceive the compound as a unit (Toda, 2004). However, an analysis of accentual systems is beyond the scope of this chapter.

In contrast, sequential voicing often applies when two words are in a modifying relationship or the degree of bonding is high, as shown in the following example:

> *kuwazu* 'do not eat' + *kirai* 'dislike' = *kuwazugirai* 'dislike without even having tried it'

The original meaning of this phrase is "turn up one's nose at food before eating it," but it is conventionally used for "someone who has a prejudice." Thus we can say that sequential voicing is governed by morphosyntactic constraints. These constraints share similarities with those described in Type 2, where the aspect morphemes *-toku* (*-te oku*) and *-tageru* (*-te ageru*) are contracted, but not *agatte oriru* 'going up and down' and *orite agaru* 'going down and up.'

Lyman's Law is also sensitive to the structure of the compound. Let us take *edo* 'the old name for Tokyo,' *taiko* 'drum,' and *matsuri* 'festival,' as examples. The compound with left branch structure is [[Edodaiko]matsuri] 'festival of Edo drums' and sequential voicing applies in the initial voiceless stop in /**taiko**/. On the other hand, the right-branching compound is [Edo[taikomatsuri]] 'drum festival in Edo.' In this example, the initial voiceless stop in *taiko* does not undergo sequential voicing. In other words, sequential voicing applies to compounds with left-branching structure, and it does not apply to those with right-branching structure.

Thirdly, the phonetic values of the special consonantal morae are predictable in terms of assimilation with the consonants that follow them. Thus, this process is called regressive assimilation. Phonetically speaking, /Q/ is realized as [p], [t], [k], [s], [ʃ], or [tʃ]; /N/ as [n], [m], or [ŋ] depending on the environment. For example, /hoN/ 'book' can be realized as [hom] or [hon] as a part of compounds; *hombako* 'bookcase' and *hondana* 'bookshelf.' The phoneme /N/ also occurs before a vowel or semi-vowel and at the word-final position, such as *ten-in* 'shop keeper' and *gen-in* 'cause,' and they are realized as an allophonic uvular nasal [N]. Thus, the following forms do not occur: *ten-nin* or *gen-nin*. Instead, it is more natural to pronounce them as [tẽːN] or [gẽːN]. A similar situation is observed in sentences such as,

> Hon o yomimasu. 'I read a book.'
> Pan o tabemasu. 'I eat a bread.'

Before an object particle [o], /N/ is realized as a uvular nasal [N] in carefully articulated speech (e.g., [hoN] 'book,' [paN] 'bread'), and as a nasalization of vowels in casually articulated speech (e.g., [hõː], [pãː]).

Furthermore, I will describe some related assimilation processes: Examples with /Q/ and /N/, *sokuon-ka* 'consonant gemination' and *hatsuon-ka* 'moraic nasalization,' respectively. The former process occurs most frequently with [k]: This phonological process is present in Sino-Japanese compounds, such as *sentakki*, *sankakkei*, and *suizokkan*, where the last consonant in the first component of the compound assimilates to the initial consonant of the second component of the compound, *sentaku-ki* 'washing machine,' *sankaku-kei* 'triangle,' and *suizoku-kan* 'aquarium,' respectively. Knowledge concerning the gemination of consonants can help L2 learners to understand the word structure of the compound. Gemination can also be observed in native Japanese words:

> Kyoo wa kinoo yori attakai (atatakai) ne. 'It is warmer today than yesterday.'
> Dokka (dokoka) e ikimashita ka. 'Did you go anywhere?'

As a result of consonant assimilation, [tt] and [kk] are produced.[7] However, such consonant clusters are not permitted in Japanese phonology, and so *sokuon-ka* 'gemination' takes place: The first half of geminate consonants is phonemically described as /Q/, and it is regarded as having the weight of one mora. Thus the rhythm in the word is unchanged. Both *atatakai* and *attakai* are considered to have five morae, and likewise, both *dokoka* and *dokka* to have three morae. The timing organization of geminated consonants is challenging for L2 learners whose L1 does not have such rhythmic structure. Geminate consonants, however, appear across the morphological boundary in English, as seen in *cat tail* or *rock cake*. L2 learners can apply such L1 knowledge, in order to make this phonologically challenging L2 feature easy (Toda, 1994, 1996, 2003a).

The phonological process called *hatsuon-ka* 'moraic nasalization' is similar to *sokuon-ka* 'gemination' described above, in that the number of morae remains unchanged after the reduction process takes place.[8] For example, the possessive particle *no* in *Taro no da* 'It's Taro's' is reduced to *Taro n da* by the following alveolar consonant [d] in the copula *da* 'to be.' Similarly, the translative case particle *ni* in *Isha ni natta* 'I became a doctor' could be reduced to *Isha n natta*. There is a phonotactic sequence restriction in Japanese that does not allow consonant clusters such as [nd] or [nn]. Therefore, the first consonant becomes the moraic nasal /N/. The moraic nasals in Japanese are seen as having the weight of one mora. That is to say the temporal duration of the two-moraic copula *noda* is considered the same as its reduced counterpart *nda*, which also has two morae, and so there is no reduction in the number of morae resulting from this regressive assimilation.[9]

> Eki no chikaku ni sunderu n̲ (no) de benri desu. 'It is convenient as I live near the station.'
> Ano eega ga mitakatta n̲ (no) desu. 'I wanted to see that movie.'

It is not only in particles such as *no* and *ni* that regressive assimilation is observed in verbs with the /r/ phoneme in the stem.[10] In the following examples, the moraic nasal appears in the verb before the negative suffix *-nai* 'not':

> Nani ittanoka waka̲n̲nakatta (waka̲ra̲nakatta). 'I could not understand what has been said.'
> Konna mono innai (i̲ra̲nai). 'I do not want such a thing.'

The motivation for the regressive assimilation shown in the above examples seems primarily to be ease of articulation: both /n/ and /r/ are alveolar consonants and the articulatory movements of the tongue are simplified by the process of regressive assimilation because the contact of the tongue with the alveolar ridge is reduced from twice to once. This can be formulated as follows:

n, rV → N/-n

---

[7] The fact that the vowel between the voiceless stops in the same place and manner of articulation is eliminated is similar to elision (Type 1). However, eliminating the vowel is not the main motivation of this process, but is a result of the process of consonant assimilation.

[8] Editors' note: Also see Hasegawa on *nasal syllabicization* in chapter 10 of this book.

[9] The occurrence of [n] in a consecutive position is avoided: For example, the concessive particle *noni* 'even though' is not reduced to *nni*. Similarly, *Kaban no naka* 'in the bag' is not reduced to *kaban n naka*, instead, it is further reduced and pronounced as *kaban naka*.

[10] Japanese /r/ is an alveolar flap [ɾ], and the phonetic realization is similar to the North American English *butter* [bʌɾə].

However, there are some details of this process that cannot be described just by ease of articulation. In the following section, I will demonstrate that this process is not entirely phonetic, but also governed by morphosyntactic constraints. According to Shibatani (1990, p. 176), the vowel preceding the negative suffix *nai* drops when it follows *r*. The resulting sequence of *rn* then undergoes assimilation and becomes *nn*, for example, *siranai* → *sinnai* 'don't know,' *kurenai* → *kunnai* 'don't give (me),' *wakaranai* → *wakannai* 'don't understand.' This rule, however, does not fully explain why the reduction does not take place in some negative verb forms. For example,

> *irenai* → **innai* 'I do not put'
> *okurenai* → **okunnai* 'I do not become late'

While Shibatani's description of regressive assimilation makes no reference to verb groups, it seems necessary to take verb categories into consideration, as they affect the operation of regressive assimilation. Japanese regular verbs are classified into two categories based on how they conjugate. One group of verbs is called *godan* 'five-step' or *-u* verbs. For example, verbs with /r/-final stems are *wakar-u* 'to know/understand,' *hashir-u* 'to run,' and *kir-u* 'to cut.' Regressive assimilation with the negative suffix *nai* takes place in these examples. The other group of verbs is called *ichidan* 'one-step' or *-ru* verbs. These verbs may include /r/ in the stem such as *ire-ru* 'to put,' *okure-ru* 'to be late,' and *taore-ru* 'to fall down.' Regressive assimilation does not take place in *-ru* verbs.[11] Therefore, morphosyntactic constraints are operative, and we cannot say that all the vowels preceding the negative suffix *nai* are dropped when it follows *r*.

Another example in which this process is observed is the potential suffix:

> Konna ni takusan taber<u>an</u>nai (taber<u>are</u>nai). 'I cannot eat so much.'

The moraic nasal appears in the potential suffix *-rare* 'can,' which is used for *ichidan* 'one-step' or *-ru* verbs, as follows:

> *Taberarenai* → *taberannai* 'I cannot eat'
> *Oshierarenai* → *oshierannai* 'I cannot teach'

However, the moraic nasal does not appear in the potential form *-rare* 'can,' which is used for *godan* 'five-step' or *-u* verbs.[12]

> *kaerenai* → **kaennai* 'I cannot go home'
> *hairenai* → **hainnai* 'I cannot enter'

As shown above, assimilation is a process by which features of a phoneme change in order to make pronunciation easier, and in this respect, it can be regarded as a universal feature common to all spoken languages. Detailed observation, however, reveals that some morphosyntactic constraints specific to Japanese are involved.

Type 3 includes examples of voice assimilation, namely, *museika* 'devoicing' and *rendaku* 'sequential voicing' in Japanese. I also described the processes of regressive assimilation concerning special morae, namely, *sokuon-ka* 'consonant gemination' and *hatsuon-ka* 'moraic nasalization.' It is important to note that the acquisition of timing

---

[11]   If regressive assimilation takes place in *-ru* verbs as well as *-u* verbs, the resulting forms will merge as seen in the following examples:
> *iranai* →   *innai* [I do not need]
> *okuranai*   →   *okunnai* [I do not send]

[12]   The moraic nasal appears in the negative form for *godan* verbs:
> *kaeranai* →   *kaennai* [I do not go home]
> *hairanai* →   *hainnai* [It does not fit]

control to produce the phonological contrasts between short/long segments is essential for the acquisition of this aspect of connected speech (Toda, 2003b).

Type 4 Transition

Transition refers to characteristics that appear in the linking of connected speech. Historically speaking, *renjo* 'liaison' describes the *n*-insertion in Sino-Japanese words when the initial sound of the second element is a vowel or glide. This phenomenon is observed in words such as *ten-noo* 'emperor' or *kan-non* 'deity of Mercy.'

Liaison is regarded as one type of transition, whereby a silent final consonant is pronounced when it is followed by a vowel-initial word. In British English, [r]-linking can be seen in examples such as *there is* [ðɛər ɪz] and *far away* [fɑːr əwei]. In French, for example, when the definite plural article *les* [le] is followed by *hommes* 'person,' it is pronounced as [lezɔm]. In both languages, sounds that are not produced in citation forms are pronounced in a clause or sentence.

Another type of transition is a close transition, as seen in the following examples:

Nihong<u>o o o</u>shiete kureta n desu. '(He) taught me Japanese.'
Denwabang<u>oo o o</u>shiete kudasai. 'Please give me your telephone number.'

The underlined vowels are in close transition in connected speech, and vowels in consecutive positions are pronounced as a long vowel [oː] without a pause.

Summary: Patterns in Japanese reduced forms

In the above subsections, I classified Japanese reduced forms into four categories and nine sub-categories. Hence, the following patterns can be observed in Japanese reduced forms:

Type 1: Elision

Vowel elision (e.g., -teru, -teku)

Type 2: Contraction

Palatalization (e.g., -kya, -cha)
Vowel coalescence (e.g., -toku, -tageru)

Type 3: Assimilation

Vowel devoicing (e.g., [ki̥ku̥tʃi̥])
Sequential voicing (e.g., booekigaisha)
Consonant gemination (e.g., a<u>tt</u>akai)
Moraic nasalization (e.g., waka<u>nn</u>ai)

Type 4: Transition

Liaison (e.g., ten-<u>n</u>oo)
Close transition (e.g., Nihong<u>o o o</u>shieta)

As mentioned above, these categories are not completely independent, for example, consonant gemination (Type 3) involves vowel elision (Type 1), and contraction (Type 2) has elements of assimilation (Type 3). For the categorization of Japanese reduced forms, the concept of mora plays an important role: Type 1 and Type 2 involve a reduction in the number of morae when undergoing phonological change, whereas in Type 3 and Type 4, the number of morae remains unchanged.

The universal tendency for phonemes to assimilate to neighboring sounds for ease of articulation is apparent throughout the above discussion. However, language-specific constraints are also present in the formation of Japanese reduced forms, which are challenging for L2 learners.

Teaching Japanese Reduced Forms

There is no doubt that L1 phonology has a very powerful influence upon both L2 speech perception and production. As a result, phonological acquisition, such as discrimination of phonemes, segmentation, and prosodic structures (e.g., mora-timing, accentual system, and intonation) are challenging for most Japanese learners. Thus, my view is that explicit instruction is needed in the areas of phonetics and phonology in L2. This is not to claim that teaching linguistic forms and structures explicitly in a traditional sense is essential for phonological acquisition. However, implicit instruction, which makes no reference to forms or rules concerning Japanese phonology, may not give learners enough opportunity to notice the differences in L1 and L2 phonology.[13]

Acoustic features that are perceived as distinctively different by NSs may not be salient for L2 learners. For example, most L2 learners find the distinction of the following examples extremely difficult in both perception and production.

> Kono kamera <u>mottete</u> (motte ite). 'Please hold this camera.'
> Kono kamera <u>mottette</u> (motte itte). 'Please take this camera with you.'

The difference in the above examples may not seem salient for L2 learners (i.e., single/geminate stops), but they are different phonetically, semantically, and syntactically. In the former, the combination of the conjunctive form of the verb *motte* 'to have/hold' and the aspectual use of the verb *-iru* 'to be' is *motte(i)ru*, and its request form is *mottete* 'please hold this camera and stay here.' Whereas in the latter, *-iku* 'to go' is appended to *motte(i)ku*, whose request form is *mottette* 'please take this camera and go.' The distinction between these two sentences is difficult for Japanese learners both at the level of speech perception and production. I will discuss this issue further in the context of relating forms with meaning.

In one way of facilitating L2 phonological acquisition, L2 learners first need to notice the differences between L1 and L2 phonology, and then acquire the ability to monitor and adjust their pronunciation. Also, learners are more likely to acquire forms with communicative need and, therefore, it is important to relate forms with the meaning in context. The suggestions I have made in teaching Japanese pronunciation to facilitate L2 phonological acquisition in Toda (2001, 2004) are based on the approach called "focus on form" (Long, 1991; Long & Robinson, 1998). In the teaching of reduced forms, materials are provided for instructors to direct learners' attention to particular forms of the target language in order to promote noticing and mapping their meaning in context. Learners should be directed to find rules, rather than just memorize sets of rules given by instructors.

In this section, I would like to address the following questions in the teaching of L2 phonology in relation to teaching of reduced forms in Japanese:

---

[13] DeKeyser (1998) discusses an important question of what kinds of form are amenable to formal instruction and claims that "(I)t is rather uncontroversial that pronunciation is relatively immune to all but the most intensive forms-focused treatments, whereas large amounts of vocabulary can be acquired with very little focus on form" (p. 43).

1. How to deal with L1 transfer
2. How to relate perception and production
3. How to direct learners to find rules
4. How to promote noticing and relate forms to meaning

How to deal with L1 transfer

Various factors affect learners' phonological acquisition of L2. From the viewpoint of contrastive analysis, it may be assumed that features that are similar to the learner's native language will be easy for him/her, and those that are different will be difficult (Lado, 1957). On the other hand, the acquisition of an L2 category that is similar to the existing L1 category may be more difficult than the acquisition of categories that differ from L1. This is because L2 phonemes that are similar to L1 may be categorized as in the L1 category and replaced by those in L1 that learners are familiar with, but in fact may be acoustically quite different (Flege, 1987). In addition to the differences and similarities between L1 and L2, the typological markedness at relative degrees of difficulty is an explanation for the problems in learners' phonological acquisition of L2 (Eckman, 1977). Hence, we need to take these issues into consideration when teaching Japanese phonology.

The implications for pedagogy are that we need to treat problems due to L1 transfer, and those caused by typological markedness and complexity of L2 structure separately in the classroom. Therefore, two sections are provided in Toda (2004). Section 1 deals with instructions for the Japanese sound system. In this section, we deal with features that are language-specific and typologically more complex, which are difficult irrespective of learners' language backgrounds. Lessons can be taught in the classroom with learners from different language backgrounds. Section 2 deals with problems in phonological acquisition caused by L1 transfer (English, Korean, and Chinese).

As described in the previous section, Japanese reduced forms share similarities with those in other languages, and some phonological processes are universal. However, language-specific rules are also involved in the formation of Japanese reduced forms, and those aspects need to be learnt as a part of Japanese grammar. Therefore, the difficulties involved in the acquisition of reduced forms are not specific to L1 phonology, rather, they are common to learners with different L1 backgrounds. For this reason, I included a chapter on Japanese reduced forms in Section 1.

How to relate perception and production

Generally speaking, it is believed that perceptual ability precedes acquisition of speech production. However, findings in second language acquisition research show that speech perception and production are closely related, but not mirror images of one another. From a pedagogical point of view, perceptual acquisition does not have to strictly precede acquisition of speech production, and so teachers do not have to wait until learners have achieved perceptual acquisition before they start teaching production. In fact, pronunciation practice often enhances L2 learners' listening comprehension. However, this is not to say that perception of phonological distinctions is not essential, as lack of ability in speech perception implies that the learner may not able to hear phonologically relevant elements in the input. Also, lack of ability in speech perception negatively affects the development of L2 learners' self-monitoring skills.

At the beginning of the lesson, it is suggested that learners listen and transcribe the reduced forms. Instructors can check whether or not learners have the phonological knowledge and if they are able to perceive and transcribe the reduced forms correctly.

How to direct learners to find rules

The majority of Japanese reduced forms teaching in pronunciation-focused classrooms seems to begin by presenting learners with the citation forms and demonstrating how they change when they are reduced. Teachers may consciously or subconsciously try to order the presentation from easier forms to more difficult forms (i.e., presentation of a simple structure before a more complex structure). I have questions regarding this approach: In real life situations, learners hear reduced forms pronounced by NSs without any indication of their citation forms. Why present citation forms first? Also, if noticing is an important part of L2 acquisition, the most contextually salient form should be the least difficult to notice. Then why try to present a set of rules from easier ones to more difficult ones?

The following way is suggested to direct L2 learners to discover rules instead of learning a set of rules presented by a teacher. This method uses a focus on form approach, where an input flood consisting of multiple examples of the reduced forms in context is provided to learners. From this, it is hoped that learners will attain an awareness of the necessity of the forms and begin the acquisition processes through noticing.

1. Input flood and noticing: Learners listen to many examples that contain reduced forms. Learners notice the speech style used in the examples (e.g., using the plain form instead of the -desu or -masu form).
2. Categorizing: Learners make a list the reduced forms used in the examples. Learners categorize reduced forms into groups according to similar patterns (e.g., -teru and -teku).
3. Finding rules: In 2 and 3, learners are dealing with lists of the reduced forms, but at this stage, they are able to find more general rules themselves (e.g., elision of [i]).

CDs and worksheets are provided in Toda (2004) to be used in class for each of the stages suggested above.

How to promote noticing and relate forms to meaning

In this section, I would like to further discuss the promotion of noticing and the relation of forms to meaning in order to facilitate L2 phonological acquisition.

Firstly, L2 learners' acquisition is better promoted when linguistic structure is presented in context. Using an illustrated picture is one way to relate forms to meaning in context, as shown in Figures 1 and 2. [14]

Secondly, L2 learners' acquisition is facilitated when they are engaged in activities. For example, learners are asked to pronounce the following sentences and choose the corresponding pictures to indicate what reaction will follow the utterances in Figures 3 and 4.

---

[14]   Figures 1 through 4 are from Toda (2004) by the 3A Corporation; they are reprinted by permission.

Figure 1.   Konna ni takusan taberannai (taberarenai).
            'I can't eat so much.'

Figure 2.   Nani ittanoka wakannakatta (wakaranakatta).
            'I couldn't understand what has been said.'

Figure 3.   Kono kamera mottete.
            'Please hold this camera.'

Figure 4.   **Kono kamera mottette.**
            'Please take this camera with you.'

Through this exercise, learners notice that the characteristics of L2 phonology, which at first may not seem salient (i.e., single/geminate stops), can actually make differences to the meaning and also to the reaction they will get following these utterances. This exercise is then followed by authentic-like role-playing. The following topics can be used to stimulate learners to have conversations using reduced forms:

1. It is too hot to work today. Invite your colleague to finish work early and go have beer with you.
2. You are organizing a birthday party for your friend next week. Invite several friends to take part and discuss what you need to buy in advance to prepare for the party.
3. You are going to see a popular movie next Saturday. Discuss with your friends whether or not you should buy an advance discount ticket before Saturday.

As a suggestion for teaching, these role-plays have been used as collaborative activities with NS volunteers. They participated in the communicative role-play, recorded the conversations, and gave comments to L2 learners. In these role-plays, some learners became aware that they were not able to use the reduced forms in conversations, even though they thought they knew the forms. Other learners became aware that they were able to use reduced forms quite comfortably in the tasks, but found problems in their overall speech styles. For example, using *hai* 'yes' or *iie* 'no,' when the use of their informal counterparts, *un* or *uun*, respectively, would be preferable. Co-occurrences of *hai* 'yes' or *iie* 'no' with some reduced forms are perceived as a sudden style shift by NS volunteers, and therefore, socio-linguistically inadequate. The activities of using reduced forms in authentic contexts may prompt learners to consciously recognize their problems. Such collaborative work in producing output promotes L2 acquisition.

Finally, learners discussed issues from real life situations with NS volunteers. For example,

1. I heard that a big earthquake is supposed to hit Tokyo soon. I would like to talk about what you can do to prepare for the earthquake.
2. I have put on some weight recently. I would like to ask a friend who seems to have lost weight how she became slim.

The final result is that the practice level has shifted from *authentic-like* to *authentic* communication.

Conclusion

In this chapter, I have classified Japanese reduced forms according to their phonological characteristics into four categories with nine sub-categories. Those categories should prove useful as a reference for instructors who wish to teach Japanese reduced forms.

Some of the phonological processes seen in Japanese reduced forms share similarities with those in other languages. In particular, ease of articulation of phonetic output seems to be universal. However, some factors that are highly language-specific, such as the role of the mora and morphosyntactic constraints, are also present in the formation of Japanese reduced forms. This indicates that the phonological changes involved in the formation of reduced forms cannot be analyzed just in terms of surface level phonetic alternations due to ease of articulation. A deeper consideration of grammatical factors is also necessary.iew

Finally, I offered pedagogical suggestions concerning teaching methodologies with a focus on reduced forms. In this chapter, I was not able explore the aspects of effectiveness and the timing in formal instruction. Further discussion of these topics in the future will help in understanding reduced forms instruction.

12

NFLRC
monographs

Learning About Sound Changes
in Spoken Japanese:
The Development of
CALL Materials[1]

TAKAKO SAKAI
University of Tsukuba, Japan

YU IGASHIMA
Helsinki, Finland

Learners of the Japanese language often have difficulty in hearing and understanding the sound changes that occur in spoken Japanese. The aims of this chapter are to examine how to effectively study sound changes and how to develop CALL materials that allow for individual differences in learner aspirations and cognitive learning style. The materials cover the moraic nasal sound, word coalescing, and vowel devoicing, which are difficult but important to learn. In addition to stressing the importance of fostering in the learner a conscious awareness about sound changes, based on empirical research of how learners perceive difficult sound changes and teaching experience, this chapter outlines the principles behind the development of the materials and the contents, and also discusses learner evaluations of the materials. Thus, this chapter should be of most interest to applied linguistics researchers generally and Japanese language teachers, researchers, materials developers, and testers who specifically need to understand, teach, and develop materials or tests for teaching continuous speech in Japanese.

The Sound Changes in Spoken Japanese

There are many features of spoken Japanese that make listening comprehension difficult for learners of the Japanese language. In this chapter, we focus on one particularly troublesome characteristic—sound changes in spoken Japanese. While it is easy to recognize the word こんにちは /konnichiwa/ [konɲitɕiwa] 'hello, how is

---

[1] Editors' note: Sakai and Igashima provide examples of CALL materials developed on the bases of recent empirical research. The CALL materials focus on three phonological processes discussed in both chapters 10 and 11: *moraic nasal* (e.g., がんばんなさい/ganbannasai/), *word coalescing* (e.g., 食べちゃった/tabechatta/), and *vowel devoicing* (e.g., うつくしい /utsukushii/).

Sakai, T., & Igashima, Y.. (2006) Learning about sound changes in spoken Japanese: The development of CALL materials. In J. D. Brown, & K. Kondo-Brown, (Eds.), *Perspectives on teaching connected speech to second language speakers* (pp. 207–230). Honolulu, HI: University of Hawai'i, National Foreign Language Resource Center.

your day?' if it is pronounced clearly, different speakers may pronounce the word in a variety of ways, such as [kontɕa], [ntɕa], or [tɕiwa:].

Although the learner will be familiar with some grammatical patterns and vocabulary, when known words are pronounced in a different way, they are likely to be either misunderstood or not understood at all. For instance, in a case of misunderstanding that happened to an advanced-level student, he heard 入んなよ hainnayo/ [hainnajo] 'come in,' in this case from 入りなよ /hairinayo/, but mistook the words as 入るなよ /hairunayo/ [haiɾɯnajo] 'don't enter,' which is of course the complete opposite in meaning. The cause of this misunderstanding is the moraic nasal sound /N/, which is a sound change from the standard pronunciation. If he had known the rules concerning which sounds can be changed to the moraic nasal, he would have been able to correctly comprehend what he heard.

Another example of sound changes in Japanese speech relates to *devoiced vowels*: the phenomenon where the closed vowels /i/ and /u/ tend to be devoiced when they are both preceded and followed by voiceless consonants. Although this phenomenon is extremely common in spoken Japanese, few learners notice this kind of sound change.

If learners of Japanese study the system of sound changes, not only will their listening ability improve, but also their speaking ability, as they will be able to pronounce Japanese more naturally. However, while it is necessary to provide instruction concerning the systematic sound changes in spoken Japanese, there has been little opportunity to cover the topic in traditional Japanese listening comprehension and conversation classes (Ford-Niwa, 1996; Kawaguchi, 1984).

Even if the issue of sound changes does come up occasionally due to examples appearing in listening materials, teachers rarely attempt to cover the topic systematically. The prime reasons for the general failure to provide systematic instruction about sound changes would seem to be that teachers have not fully appreciated the importance of covering the topic and because there are few effective methods and materials.[2]

Differences in first language (L1), cognitive learning style, and educational background influence listening ability and which methods of practicing pronunciation are effective. While L1 effects are well-recognized (Hirose, 2003), clearly, cognitive learning style also has a major impact on listening ability. Examples of cognitive learning style would include whether the learner has good or poor memory for phonological information and whether the visual support of seeing the written word is necessary to retain phonological information (Sakai, 1997). Similarly, educational background can vary greatly, ranging from correspondence courses that provide no aural/oral training at one extreme to cases where the learner is simply exposed to the Japanese conversation around them. Given these factors, which mean that the content and the amount of study material required varies from learner to learner, individual study may be more effective than group study. Computer-Aided Language Learning (CALL) is particularly suitable for self-study.

Over the last few years, various kinds of CALL materials have been developed in the area of foreign language education, with many studies advocating the effectiveness of

---

[2]   Japanese textbooks dealing with sound changes include Tomisaka (1997) and Toda (2004).

using CALL materials.[3] In this context, we have been developing CALL materials as a tool for learning about the system of sound changes in spoken Japanese. In outlining the development of these materials, this chapter will introduce some survey results that are related to sound changes that are difficult for learners of Japanese to hear, and discuss how to incorporate the subject within the Japanese language class. The chapter also describes the principles underlying the development of the CALL materials and the concepts behind the content, as well as presenting the reactions of learners who have used the materials. Finally, some pedagogical suggestions are proposed for teaching about the system of sound changes.

How Do Learners of Japanese Hear Sound Changes?

Target sound changes

While there are various kinds of sound changes in Japanese, this chapter will focus on the sound changes involving moraic nasal, word coalescing, and vowel devoicing, which are particularly important for learners of Japanese. Awareness of these sound changes is necessary because learners of Japanese frequently fail to catch them completely or to hear them correctly, and this has serious implications. These sound changes have been singled out for special attention based on the results of surveys with learners of Japanese and based on teaching experience.

(1) Sound changes to moraic nasal /N/[4]
Certain sounds, such as *ni, na, ra, ri, ru, re*, change to the nasal sound /N/.
example: 赤になる /akaninaru/ [akaɲinaʁɯ] 'become red'
→ 赤んなる /akannaru/ [akannarɯ]

(2) Word coalescing[5]
When certain sounds follow each other, the following consonant becomes a semi-vowel and the two sounds coalesce.
example: 来てしまった /kiteshimatta/ [kɲiteɕimaʔta] 'I've come'
→ 来ちゃった /kichatta/ [kɲitciaʔta]

(3) Vowel devoicing[6]
The close vowels (/i/ and /u/) tend to be devoiced (pronounced without moving the vocal chords) when they are both preceded and followed by voiceless consonants. Parentheses around these syllables indicate that the final vowel is devoiced.
example: (く)(つ)(し)た /k(u)ts(u)sh(i)ta/ [kɯ̥tsɯ̥ɕi̥ta] 'socks'

There are considerable variations in the frequency of sound change forms depending on the setting and the speaker. There are also large differences based on morphological context. The Corpus of Spontaneous Japanese (CSJ; National Institute for Japanese Language) is a large-scale database of spoken Japanese, with tagged annotation for use in researching the phonetic and phonological variation in spontaneous speech. One of the corpus tags is the W-tag for speech errors,

---

[3]   The following Web site offers information about sound changes: Nagoya University Educational Centre for International Students, Japanese-language Education Media & Systems Lab "OWL" http://opal.ecis.nagoya-u.ac.jp/%7Ejems/jemstop-j.htm

[4]   Editors' note: Also see Hasegawa on *nasal syllabicization* in chapter 10 and Toda on *moraic nasalization* in chapter 11 of this book.

[5]   Editors' note: Also see Hasegawa on *phrase-final reduction* in chapter 10 and Toda on *contracted forms* in chapter 11 of this book.

[6]   Editors' note: Also see Hasegawa on *high vowel devoicing* in chapter 10 and Toda on *museika* or *devoicing* in chapter 11 of this book.

corruptions, and reduced or incorrect pronunciations, and research into sound changes utilizing this tag has made considerable progress providing valuable insights for education.

Table 1[7]. **Word coalescing frequencies for /de/ and /wa/ as a function of part of speech and speech type**

part of speech of /de/	speech type	N /de wa/	N /ja/	% coalesced
case particle	APS	1,311	11	0.8%
	SPS	389	19	4.7%
auxiliary verb	APS	653	256	28.2%
	SPA	327	471	59.0%

notes: APS = Academic Presentation Speech; SPS = Simulated Public Speaking.
This Table is based on a Table at the website of the Corpus of Spontaneous Japanese: http://www2.kokken.go.jp/~csj/public/6_2.html

Table 1 presents frequency data related to the word coalescing phenomenon where /de/ and /wa/ merge to become /ja/. The Table clearly highlights the differences in the frequency of /ja/ coalescences according to function of part of speech and speech type, where, in contrast to less than 5% for the case particle, the frequency for the auxiliary verb is 59% within simulated public speaking (Maekawa, 2004).

Similarly for sound changes involving the moraic nasal, as in the phenomenon of substituting the particle /no/ with the nasal /N/, while the incidence is low, at less than 1%, when /no/ is the case particle, approximately half the cases involving the auxiliary verb undergo this change. This is obviously related to speech style and spontaneity because the frequency falls as the speaking style becomes more formal but rises as the level of spontaneity increases.

As suggested by Sakurai (1989) among others, while the governing principles are rather complex, there are marked individual and regional differences in the incidence of vowel devoicing, even with considerable variation within the same individual.[8] Byun (2004) examined the utterances of 15 native Tokyo dialect speakers aged between 18 and 36 and found that their average devoicing rate in Japanese was 96%. The devoicing of vowels is clearly related to the speed of speaking, as devoicing is more frequent when speaking is faster.

Figure 1 shows the influence on close vowel devoicing of speaking rate. The four speaking rate conditions are based on normalized individual data. This figure shows that as the speaking rate increases, the frequency of devoicing also increases, and this is particularly so for the close vowel /i/.

---

[7]   ©2005 National Institute for Japanese Language; reprinted by permission from Yoneyama and Maekawa (2004).
[8]   Conditions under which vowel devoicing occurs:
Sakurai (1989) cites two principles and two tendencies governing the incidence of vowel devoicing in standard speech. Principle 1: When the mora /ki/, /ku/, /si/, /su/, /ti/, /tu/, /hi/, /hu/, /pi/, /pu/, and /shu/ come immediately in front of a CV mora with the vowel /a/, such as /ka/, /sa/, /ta/, /ha/, and /pa/. Principle 2: When the mora /ki/, /ku/, /si/, /su/, /ti/, /tu/, /hi/, /hu/, /pi/, /pu/, and /shu/ come immediately in front of a breath stop and the accent on the mora is low. Tendency 1: When the mora /ka/ and /ko/ in the word initial position have a low accent and the next mora is the same sound with a high accent. Tendency 2: When /ha/ and /ho/ in the word initial position with a low accent is followed by a mora that included the vowels /a/ or /o/.

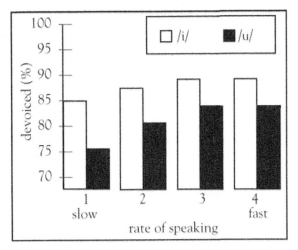

note: This figure is based on a Table at the website of the
Corpus of Spontaneous Japanese:
http://www2.kokken.go.jp/~csj/public/6_2.html

Figure 1.   Effect of speaking rate upon close vowel devoicing.

Looking at the movie *Sen to Chihiro no Kamikakushi* (Studio Ghibli; released under the English title *Spirited Away*), Hirakata (2003b) investigated the relationship between the age of the characters and sound changes, analyzing for each character the frequency of sound changes, such as word coalescing and the moraic nasal sound. The study found that while the incidence of the moraic nasal sound was high for all characters regardless of age, there were differences in the distribution of sound changes among the various character types, with certain character groups being more associated with certain sounds changes.

The survey results in this chapter clearly indicate that learners of Japanese are being exposed to various kinds of sound changes quite frequently, which they must hear and interpret. The findings about the conditions under which sound changes are likely to occur also provide useful insights for building a firm foundation for hearing sound changes and developing learning materials.

The next section introduces a study of word coalescing and moraic nasal changes, as well as a survey of vowel devoicing that was conducted to investigate how learners hear and interpret spoken Japanese that includes these sound changes.

Learners of Japanese—Hearing word coalescing and moraic nasal

This section looks first at a study of word coalescing and the moraic nasal sound aimed at learners of Japanese conducted by Igashima, Sakai, and Hirakata (2001). The purpose of the study was to discover what kinds of sound changes are difficult for learners to catch and to investigate the relationship between two aspects of the comprehension process, namely, whether learners are able to hear sound changes and whether they are able to guess from the changed sound what the unchanged pronunciation should be.

Method

Participants. Eighteen intermediate and seventeen advanced learners participated.

Materials and procedures. Conversations were created and recorded to include various examples of word coalescing and moraic nasal sounds. Two kinds of tests were conducted in which the participants listened to conversations. The task in Test a was designed to investigate whether sound changes were being heard or not. In Test A, the participants had to write down the sound changes within brackets.

After the responses for Test a were collected, Test B was given, which included a task designed to see if the participants could guess from the sound change what the unchanged pronunciation should be. In Test B, the participants had to write down the unchanged pronunciations next to the sentences that were presented in Test A.

Test A

たばこを (   ) とは思うんだけど、なかなか　(   ) んだよね。
tabako o (   ) to wa omoun dakedo, nakanaka (   ) n dayo ne.

Test B

たばこを (すわなきゃいい) とは思うんだけど、なかなか　(<u>やめらんない</u>) んだよね。
tabako o (suwanakya ii   ) to wa omoun dakedo, nakanaka (yamerannai   ) n dayo ne.
        (   )   (   )

(English translation was not provided in the original: 'I know it is better not to smoke, but it is difficult to stop.')

Results

In Test A, many participants wrote down the unchanged pronunciation rather than the sound change that was actually presented, for example, writing down いちにち /ichinichi/ 'one day' for いちんち /ichinchi/ [iɕintɕi], and それは /sore wa/ 'that …' for そりゃ /sorya/ [soʁja]. As these are words that the learners would be familiar with, it would seem that the words were being processed without conscious awareness of the changed sound.

Table 2 summarizes one part of the results from Tests a and B. There were 35 participants in total, and the figures in the Table show the number of learners giving the correct and incorrect answers for each of the seven paired items, separately given for the Tests a and B. The first column lists the correct answers for these items. Clearly, there were large differences in terms of the participants' ability to correctly hear the same sound change, in /te shimau/ becoming /chau/, according to the surrounding words and inflections. While it is not possible to comment about whether the learners had simply acquired the sound change, it should be kept in mind that the level of difficulty is influenced by a number of factors, such as the appropriateness of the vocabulary for the learner's level, the complexity of the combined forms, and the speed of speech.

Figure 2 presents the test results as a function of learner level and shows that the advanced learners scored higher on both Test a and B compared to the intermediate learners. The advanced learners were better than the intermediate learners in terms of both their ability to hear the sound changes and to guess at what the unchanged pronunciation would be. Moreover, looking carefully at the relationship between Tests a and B, the advanced learners were clearly better than the intermediate learners at correctly writing the unchanged pronunciation in Test B, when presented with the transcription of the sound change although the sound had not been correctly heard in Test A. That is, advanced learners had a greater ability to guess at the unchanged pronunciation, when they knew what the sound change was, even though they had not been able to catch the sound change itself.

Table 2. Correct responses as a function of context for the word coalescence /chau/

| | test A: correct | | test A: incorrect | | |
	test B: correct	test B: incorrect	test B: correct	test B: incorrect	total
/nigechatta/ [ɲigettɕaʔta] 'he escaped' A: nigechatta B: nigeteshimatta	13	3	9	10	35
/kaetchatta/ [kaeʔtɕaʔta] 'he returned' A: kaetchatta B: kaetteshimatta	7	0	15	13	35
/tsukuttekurechau/ [tsɰ̥kɰ̥ʔtekɯʁetɕaɯ] 'he made it (for me)' A: tsukuttekurechau B: tsukuttekureteshimatta	7	3	11	14	35
/nigetakunattchaʔta/ [ɲigetakɰna ʔtɕaʔta] 'he wants to escape' A: nigetakunatchatta B: nigetakunatteshimatta	7	2	10	16	35
/kichau/ [kɲitɕaɯ] '(before) they come' A: kichau B: kiteshimau	6	2	12	15	35
/iyannatchau/ [ijanna ʔtɕaɯ] 'it's disgusitng' A: iyannatchau B: iyannatteshimau	1	0	14	20	35
/tsubushichawanaito/ [tsɯbɯɕitɕawanaito] 'should crush it' A: tsubushichawanaito B: tsubushiteshimawanaito	1	0	11	23	35

note: There were 35 participants in total, and the figures represent the number of learners giving the correct answer.

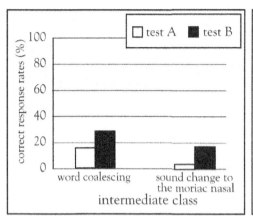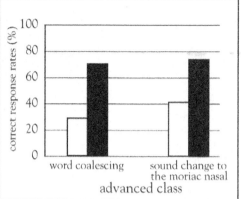

Figure 2.   Correct response rates for word coalescing and the moraic nasal sound in Tests A and B as a function of Japanese language proficiency level.

Learners of Japanese—Hearing vowel devoicing

Next, we turn to a survey of vowel devoicing in speech that was conducted by Hirakata (2003a) with advanced level learners of Japanese from China. The purpose of the study was to investigate whether vowel devoicing would be detected while watching a real news broadcast, what kinds of hearing errors would occur, and the relationship to the level of vocabulary.

Method

Participants. Fifteen learners from China who have passed level 1 of the Japanese Language Proficiency Test participated.

Materials and procedures. Monologues delivered by a female newscaster appearing in the news program "World Business Satellite." The participants were first given a vocabulary list, and after confirming the vocabulary, they viewed the program. Comprehension was checked for each sentence. After the overall content was understood, there was dictation for the sections that contained examples of devoicing. This dictation was repeated until the learners were satisfied that they had transcribed the sounds.

Results

For some words, there were few hearing errors even with devoicing of the vowels. These were words that are frequently heard in daily life.

However, there were many cases of new words or words that are less familiar not being caught, even though the participants had previously studied the words on the vocabulary lists. This highlights the fact that studying words on lists is very different from using them in context. The learners were also frequently unaware of having misheard the words and would only realize their mistakes when they were pointed out.

Examples of how the words were incorrectly heard (see Table 3) suggest that the learners were not processing the words as pronunciations, but rather were selecting words from their own vocabularies that they believed to be appropriate from the sentence contexts.

Table 3. Examples of hearing errors for vowel devoicing

1.「火付け役となった」[çi̥tsu̥kejakʷtona?ta] 'became the instigator'	
√ ひつけやくとなった	h(i)t(u)ke yak(u) to natta
しつけやくとなった	shituke yaku to natta
しつけやとなった	shituke ya to natta
2.「ヒット数を誇る」 [çi̥?tosu̥:ohʷkoʁu̥] 'proud of the number of hits'	
√ ヒットすうをほこる	h(i)tto suu wo h(o)koru
一つを誇る	hitotu wo hokoru
ひとつを起こる	hitotu wo okoru
3.「はじき出す」 [hḁdʑikni̥dasu̥] 'calculate'	
√ はじきだす	h(a)jiki das(u)
カジキだ	kajiki da
かじきだす	kajiki dasu
はじきだ	hajiki da

note: "√" indicates a correct response.

Sound changes happen with considerable frequency in Japanese conversation, but if the learner is not aware of these sound changes, even though the words are ones they know, misunderstandings or complete comprehension failures will occur. Compared to the sound of the teacher's voice or prepared listening comprehension tapes normally used in the classroom, conversation in the real world is much faster and often includes background noises (Takefuta, 1984, p. 242). In particular, because the frequency of devoicing is much higher as the speaking rate increases, a learner will often fail to hear or mishear words in authentic materials (or sources that are closer to natural conversation), even though the words are known by the learner. Thus, learners need to study by practicing listening not just at the word level, but also at the sentence level with recordings that are similar to natural conversations. Given the necessity of teaching learners of Japanese about the existence of sound changes and having learners study the nature of these sound changes, the next section will address the issues involved in teaching about sound changes.

Learning Content and Methods for Sound Changes

Although there is little empirical research investigating the actual state of teaching about sound changes in the Japanese language classroom and its effectiveness, one study by Hirakata, Igashima, and Sakai (2002) has looked at learning for sound changes and compared differences in listening ability prior and subsequent to the lessons. The participants in the study were 71 students attending university advanced-level listening comprehension classes. Teaching about sound changes was introduced as a regular element of the listening comprehension class, with about 10 minutes devoted to it each week over 11 classes. The teaching included explanations about the rules governing sound changes, listening practice for these, as well as listening practice for authentic conversations extracted from a TV drama. In a survey prior to the lessons, the majority of participants stated that they had never received instruction about sound changes. Comparing scores on a test prior to the lessons and on a retention test given 3 months after completing the 11 sessions, the study found a clear learning effect, with the rate of correctly hearing sound changes increasing from 45% to 67%. On a questionnaire about the instruction for sound changes, many learners commented that, in addition to providing valuable listening practice, the lessons had been useful for speaking and that their pronunciation had improved. This suggests that learning materials that also include pronunciation practice are beneficial for learners.

When actually teaching about the sound changes in spoken Japanese, it is important to provide comprehensive coverage of the topic. The list shown in Table 4 gives the content presented to the learners, tackling various aspects of sound changes. This list is for the learning materials related to vowel devoicing.

Table 4.   Learning contents for vowel devoicing

- Explanation about what vowel devoicing is.
  The explanations also cover the conditions under which vowel devoicing is likely to occur.
- Comparing the sounds of the words pronounced with devoicing and without.
- Prediction exercises about whether visually presented words are devoiced or not, and, for unchanged pronunciations, how the word would sound if it were devoiced.
- Listening comprehension for devoiced pronunciations at the word level.
- Classification of words with devoicing that are difficult to distinguish.
  This is a focused exercise dealing with words that are particularly likely to be misheard, and so lead to serious misunderstandings.
  example:

規則	/kisoku/	[kɲi̥sokw̥]	'regular' vs
不規則	/fukisoku/	[fw̥kɲi̥sokw̥]	'irregular'
科学的	/kagakuteki/	[kagakw̥tekɲi̥]	'scientific' vs
非科学的	/hikagakuteki/	[çi̥kagakw̥tekɲi̥]	'non-scientific'

  Listening at both the word and sentence levels
- Guessing at devoiced sounds within sentences, based on contextual meaning.
- Encouraging the learners to pronounce the words with devoicing (word level and sentence level)

Although the learning materials for word coalescing are quite similar, with many tasks in common, the word coalescing materials also need to provide explanation and exercises relating to morphological variations. More specifically, the materials deal with three kinds of word coalescing, /-eba/, /+wa/, and /-te shimau/, with exercises targeting the relationship between sound changed forms and unchanged pronunciations. For instance, it is important for learners to be able to judge, based on sentence context, whether はなしゃわかる /hanasha wakaru/ [hanaɕawakaɾw] is a word coalescing form of /hanashi wa wakaru/ 'understand the conversation' or /hanaseba wakaru/ 'will understand if speak about it.'

Because there are also many similar sounding words, such as 聞いちゃう /kiichau/ [kɲiːtɕaw] "he's heard,' 切っちゃう /kittchau/ [kɲi̥ʔtɕaw] 'he's cut it,' 来ちゃう /kichau/ [kɲi̥tɕaw] 'he's come,' and 着ちゃう /kichau/ [kɲi̥tɕaw] 'he's wearing it,' it is important to practice differentiating between them. Multiple versions of this kind of differentiation exercise are needed because the difficulty of the task increases markedly as the complexity of the surrounding vocabulary and inflections increases.

Finally in this section, we describe the instruction about sound changes that we have been incorporating within our language classes. This instruction takes about 10 minutes during a 75-minute period once a week for a listening comprehension class for advanced-level Japanese learners. The instruction covers various sound change topics, such as the moraic nasal sound, word coalescing, vowel devoicing, and vowel merging/dropping. Here, we outline the contents of the classes covering the moraic nasal sound. Erlam (2003) examined the effects of deductive and inductive instruction on the acquisition of direct object pronouns in French as a second language and observed higher scores for several post-tests with the deductive instruction group. We have placed particular emphasis on devising a study plan that, rather than simply providing information about sound changes, actively draws on both deductive and inductive methods in order to make the learners *consciously aware* of sound changes as detailed in the Appendix. As noted above, some sound changes are heard and produced without conscious awareness that the sound is being changed. Many of these cases involve words that are frequently encountered on a daily basis. Given that exercises that foster an inductive awareness of sound changes in the learner are effective in leading them to appropriate use of sound changes, our target has been to cultivate conscious awareness, by employing exercises that require the learner to seek out the rules by themselves from multiple examples. We have also devised exercises that encourage the learners to move beyond the conscious rules to be able to inductively apply them, through exercises that build and extend their growing understanding of the rules governing sound changes. The combination of exercises that involve deductive and inductive processing help the learners to develop a firm awareness of the sound changes in spoken Japanese.

This section has discussed some of the practical aspects in teaching about the sound changes that were dealt with in the previous section on how learners of Japanese hear sound changes. There are, however, various restrictions that are unavoidably associated with group-oriented teaching in the classroom. In the next section, we describe how we have developed CALL materials about sound changes for self-study.

The Development of CALL Materials for Sound Changes

The advantages of CALL for learning about the sounds of a language

There are increasingly more Web sites that provide CALL materials for learning Japanese online.[9] The advantages of using CALL for learning about the sounds of a language include,

- Because the amount of time available is limited, it is difficult to devote sufficient time to the systematic study of sound changes within language classes. There are also few materials that focus on sound changes. CALL materials that cover the sound changes in Japanese systematically are suitable for self-study and can aid effective learning.

- Because the learning content required, as well as the learner's cognitive learning style, may vary from individual to individual, it is not effective to use learning materials developed for self-learning in a class for everyone. Thus, it is desirable to develop CALL materials that offer considerable freedom in terms of how they are used so that the learners can select content that is most suited to their needs and cognitive learning styles.

- The results of a questionnaire completed by learners (Hirakata, 2002) indicate that learners want to be able to hear different kinds of voices, in addition to that of the teacher. With CALL materials, it is easier to present learners with a wide range of different speaking voices, varying in terms of gender and age, which the learner can easily listen to repeatedly. It is simple to supplement the materials, by mixing different elements, such as using different voices or different exercise

---

[9]   The following Web site offers the list of Japanese language online materials http://www.manythings.org/japanese/ (produced by Kelly, C.)

drills. It is also possible to store large quantities of speech data for different voices and exercise drills, and to randomize the order in which these are presented.

We are confident about the value of learning about the sounds of a language with CALL materials and have been developing materials that draw on the positive advantages of this medium.

Principles underlying the creation of the CALL materials for sound changes

Awareness of the learner's knowledge about sound changes

Based on the survey results, some knowledge is often acquired in an unconscious manner from familiarity with words like /ichinchi/ and /wakannai/, rather than from a set of rules. However, it is important for learners to be consciously aware of the rules that govern sound changes, so that they can apply that knowledge to other words. When the learners are conscious of the rules, they will have greater success in correctly hearing and interpreting unfamiliar words that involve sound changes. It is important to provide learners with materials that allow them to learn in a systematic fashion by presenting comprehensible rules and by practicing the application of these through sound recognition exercises.

Connecting sound and meaning at all levels

We are attempting to employ three kinds of exercises in an integrated manner: listening exercises that focus on target sounds; exercises that create connections between sound and meaning by listening to simple sentences; and exercises that link the processes of guessing and comprehension for naturally flowing conversations. By activating both bottom-up and top-down processing, the possibility of access based on available information increases, which enhances learning (see Figure 3).

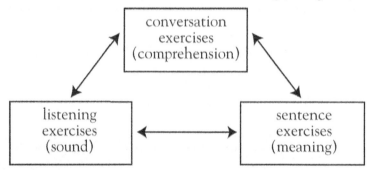

Figure 3.   Relations between the exercises and comprehension.

Familiarity with various voices

Our materials present a rich variety of recordings, so that learners are able to listen to the same words and sentences being pronounced by different kinds of voices in terms of age and gender. In addition to having the learners actually experience the variety in the sound changes, this also helps them to become familiar with the range of variation.

Exercises that establish connections with pronunciation

In order to improve the listening ability of learners it is not enough to rely solely on exercises that only involve listening to the sounds. It is also important to create exercises that aid the learner in establishing firmer phonological representations of the target sounds by having the learner practice pronouncing the sound changes him/herself. Accordingly, we have created exercises that encourage the learner to pronounce the sound change forms, in order to improve listening ability from the two perspectives of speaking and listening.

By working through the CALL materials, learners come to recognize the rules that underlie sound changes. And, by becoming completely familiar with the target sounds, they are able to catch sound changed forms in spoken language that they were not able to hear before. Moreover, by repeating the process of practical listening in following the exercises, learners gain the ability to guess immediately at what the unchanged pronunciation would be. Thus, we are seeking to establish connections to the meaning of sounds heard in comprehension and so improve listening ability.

Outline of the Materials

Study content

Our materials cover the three types of sound changes in word coalescing, the moraic nasal, and vowel devoicing, as these changes are very important for learners to be able to recognize. The three topics are further classified into different types based on context, such as /-ba/, /+wa/, and /-te shimau/, which are used and explained in the materials. Rather than explain the sound change forms in specialist terms, the materials present a clear example of the target sound change, which is used as a referent label for that sound change form.

Material level

We believe that it is essential to learn about sound changes at every level of studying Japanese, from beginner through to advanced levels, in order to improve listening comprehension for Japanese. Accordingly, we have established for the materials two levels of difficulty in terms of vocabulary and sentence patterns, so that they may be used by a broad spectrum of learners. The material levels are based on the question levels of the Japanese Language Proficiency Examinations (1994), with the low-level materials corresponding to levels 3 and 4 of the examinations, and the high-level materials reflecting the examination levels 1 and 2 in terms of vocabulary, sentence patterns and orthography. In creating the exercises, we have paid particular attention to the level of difficulty and have employed various techniques to adjust the level across the materials. For example, the low-level exercises covering sound changes related to verbal inflections are made easier by including adverbs before target sound changes, whereas the high-level exercises consist of short sentences without adverbs that require the learner to recognize the target forms from the sound change only.

Content structure

The learning materials are structured into three sections: introduction, explanation and exercises. However, it is not necessary for the learner to follow this order, because the materials have been created so that the learner can start studying from any section according to their objectives.

Introduction. Learners using the materials for the first time would start from the introduction section. Our prime objectives in creating the introduction sections have been to provide clear explanations about the kinds of sound change forms covered in the materials and to determine which topics the learner is already familiar with and which aspects need to be studied.

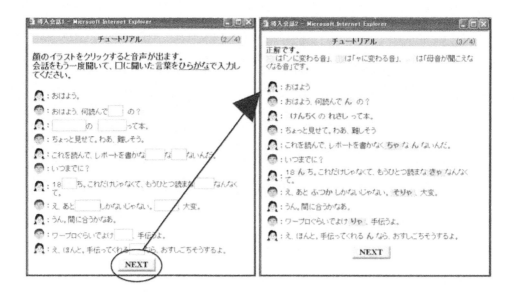

Figure 4.   Tutorial example: After inputting their answers in the blank boxes within the conversation, the learner would click on the 'next' button to see the correct answers displayed with color-coding, as in the screen shot on the right.

Explanation. Explanation is provided for all topics. The learner is free to refer back to this section at any time, such as when struggling to hear a particular target sound or understand some part of the exercises.

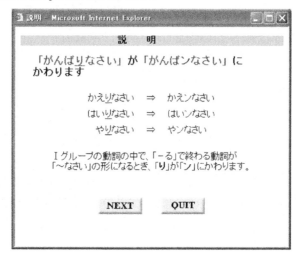

Figure 5.   Explanation example.

Exercises. Various kinds of exercises are provided, reflecting different levels of difficulty, ranging from basic exercises to more practical practice exercises. This is the main component of the materials. There are two kinds of questions, either multiple-choice style questions or dictation questions, depending on the content. The exercise questions are presented one at a time and feedback on whether a response is correct is given for each question. More details concerning the content of the exercises are given below.

Types of exercises

Recognition exercises. Exercises to check whether the learner can hear the target sound changes and to make them aware of the sound change forms. Presenting the same scene with examples of sound changes and unchanged pronunciations helps the learner recognize the differences in the sounds by allowing them to repeatedly compare the different versions.

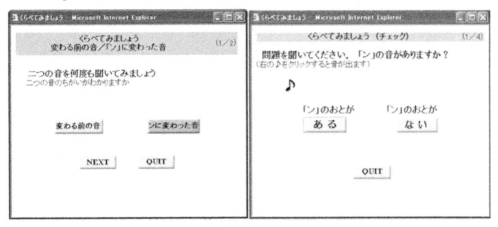

Figure 6.   Recognition exercise example: The '♪' symbol indicates a sound file, which can be played by clicking on the symbol. The panel on the left presents sound files for both the unchanged and changed sounds, which the learner can listen to and compare repeatedly. The panel on the right presents a sound file to check if the learner is able to detect whether a sound changed form is present or absent.

Checking exercises. These are exercises consisting of one word dictation to check that the learner's understanding of the rules for the sound changes, together with exercises that involve predicting what the sound change forms will become. These exercises also include listening to words that include sound change forms, dictating the unchanged sound, as well as making selections from multiple-choice answers.

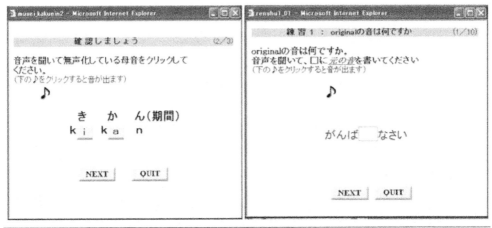

Figure 7.   Checking exercise examples: These checking exercise examples relate to devoicing and the moraic nasal. In the checking exercise in Panel A, after listening to the sound file, the learner should click on the vowel which was devoiced. In the checking exercise in Panel B, after listening to the sound

file, the learner should guess from the heard sound change what the unchanged sound should be and input that in the blank box.

Basic exercises. These basic exercises include word-level exercises as well as listening exercises for slightly longer units. Other variations include listening to sentences and selecting the unchanged pronunciation from multiple-choice answers. In addition, other exercises include multiple items, such as 帰んの? /kaenno/ [kaenno] 'Do you go back home?' versus 帰んないの? /kaennaino/ [kaennaino] 'Don't you go back home?'

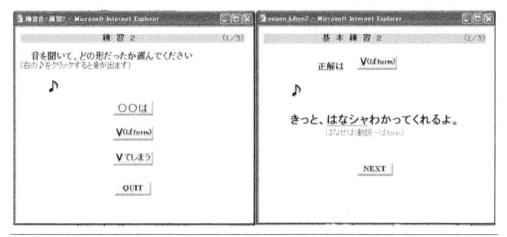

Figure 8.   Basic exercise example: This basic exercise example focuses on word coalescing. After listening to the sound file in the panel on the left, the learner should select the correct grammatical pattern involved in the sound change. When the learner makes a correct selection, the program provides feedback as in the panel on the right by presenting a transcription of the sentence, together with unchanged grammatical pattern, so that the learner can listen again while reading the transcription.

Figure 9.   Basic exercise example: This checking exercise example relates to devoicing and the moraic nasal. After listening to the sound file in the panel on the left, the learner should select the unchanged sound. When the learner makes a correct selection, the program provides feedback as in the panel on the right by presenting a transcription of the sentence, together with unchanged sound, so that the learner can listen again while reading the transcription.

Applied exercises. The applied exercises are more practical than the basic exercises. These include exercises for distinguishing sound changes related to sentence patterns and exercises for distinguishing similar sounds; examples follow.

Vowel devoicing

ちょっと見てて	/chotto mitete/	[tɕoʔtomɲitete]	'watch for a while'
ちょっと見てきて	/chotto mitekite/	[tɕoʔtomɲitekɲi̥te]	'go and have a look'
ちょっと見てって	/chotto mitette/	[tɕoʔtomɲiteʔte]	'watch a bit, then go'

Word coalescing: Conjugation practice

買っちゃう	/katchau/	[kaʔtɕaɯ]	'I'll buy it'
買っちゃおう	/katchao/	[kaʔtɕao]	'I think I'll buy that'
買っちゃえば	/katchaeba/	[kaʔtɕaeba]	'buy it, then'

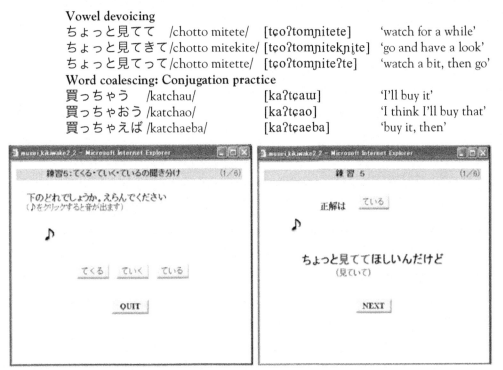

Figure 10. Applied exercise examples: This basic exercise examples focuses on word coalescing. Again, after listening to the sound file in in the panel on the left, the learner should select the correct verbal inflection involved in the sound change. When the learner makes a correct selection, the program provides feedback as in the panel on the right by presenting a transcription of the sentence, together with the correct verbal inflection, so that the learner can listen again while reading the transcription.

Conversation exercises. Conversation exercises include activities that target whether the learner is able to catch sound changed forms in the flow of natural conversation and whether they are able to immediately guess at what the unchanged pronunciation would be. After first understanding the conversational setting, the learners listen to the whole conversation (as many times as desired). Then, they write down the unchanged pronunciations in blanks at each turn in the conversation. The learners are provided with feedback about whether the response is correct for each question and can proceed to the next question when they have answered correctly.

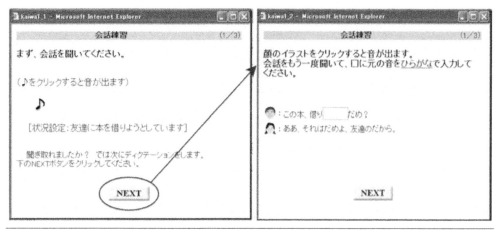

Figure 11. Conversation exercise example: In the conversation exercise, the learner would first read a sentence setting the situation for the conversation and then listen to the sound file in in the panel on the left. After listening to the conversation, the learner then enters the unchanged pronunciation into blank box in the conversation displayed in in in the panel on the right.

Pronunciation exercises. These are exercises that help learners not only to recognize sound changes, but also to develop a deeper knowledge of sound changes by having the learners pronounce the sound changes themselves. Single sentences containing sound changes are presented visually. First, the learners listen to a model voice saying the sentence and then pronounce the sentence at the same time, following along with the recording. This exercise can be repeated until the learners are able to speak the sentence matching the speech of the model voice. The materials currently do not allow the learners to record their own speech and compare this to the model.

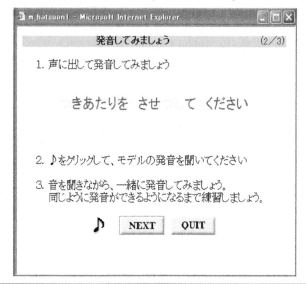

Figure 12. Pronunciation exercise example: This pronunciation exercise for vowel devoicing is designed to promote conscious awareness of the sound change. After reading aloud a sentence transcription, where devoiced vowels are indicated as faint characters, the learner can repeatedly practice saying the sentence, by shadowing along with a model voice.

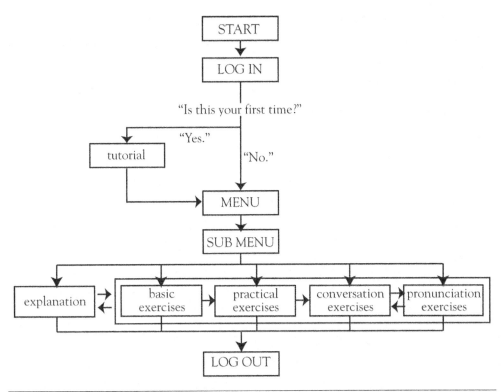

Figure 13. Flowchart for using the CALL materials.

In the next section, we present the results of a survey which investigated the learning effects of using the developed CALL materials and report on learner evaluations of the materials.

Evaluation of the CALL Materials

Survey about the materials

Method

Participants. Lower-intermediate level learners participated. Group A consisted of 6 learners; group B, of 19 learners.

Materials and procedures. The target of the study was moraic nasal sounds, as outlined above.

Group A	Each learner worked on an individual computer and worked through the materials totally on a self-study basis.
Group B	The materials were projected onto a screen in the classroom and were used for teacher-directed learning in a group setting.

Pre-test and post-test

Listening test The learners listened to a conversation containing examples of the moraic nasal sound and then made selections from multiple-choice answers to match what the speaker said.

Dictation test The instructor read (twice) simple sentences that contain moraic nasal sounds, and the learners were to write down the unchanged pronunciations within brackets.

Group A took a second retention test 1 week after completing the materials and individual interviews.

Results

As Figures 14 and 15 show, the correct response rate increased in the post-test compared to the pre-test for both groups, which indicates the effectiveness of the learning materials. Figure 14 shows pretest correct response rates for the recognition of moraic nasal sounds within spoken language and clearly indicates that the level of recognition was very low, at only 21%, for learners who had just completed beginner-level courses. In particular, the results for the dictation test indicate that while both groups could hear the moraic nasal sound, many learners were unable to correctly reply with what the unchanged pronunciation should be; clearly, their awareness of these sound changes was insufficient. The correct response rate was especially low when the moraic nasal sound was part of a verbal inflection, such as /kuru no wa / [kɯrɯnowa] '(the one) who comes' →/kun no wa/ [kɯnnowa] and /magaranai/ [magaɾanai] 'don't bend' →/magannai/ [magannai].

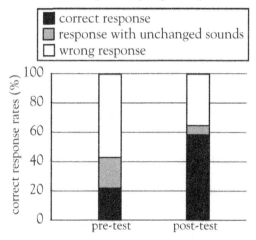

Figure 14. Correct response rates on the dictation test for the moraic nasal sound as a function of test time.

In particular, while the learning in Group B took place within a limited amount of time during a class period, there were learning effects for acquiring knowledge about the moraic nasal sound and for becoming more familiar with the sounds through using the materials. Looking also at the different test items, there was clearly a large improvement for the dictation questions. The dictation exercise required both hearing for the moraic nasal sound and being consciously aware of information about the moraic nasal sound. Accordingly, these results demonstrate the effects of acquiring knowledge about the moraic nasal sound and of becoming familiar with hearing the nasal sound due to the materials.

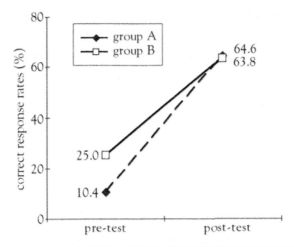

Figure 15. Combined correct response rates for the listening and dictation tests for Groups A and B as a function of test time.

It is clear that the high correct-response rates observed in the post-test were matched in the retention test conducted 1 week later for Group A. This suggests that, rather than simply repeating exercises about sound changes in spoken language over and over, activities of first acquiring conscious knowledge about sound changes and then doing adequate listening practice for the sounds enhance listening comprehension ability may be more beneficial.

Evaluations of the interview survey

After the learners in Group A had completed the second listening test, individual interviews were conducted concerning the usability and the style of the materials, and the learners were asked about various aspects of the materials, such as the usability of the materials, the appearance of the displays, the quality of the sound, and the level of difficulty for the questions. The following evaluations were received:

In terms of usability, good evaluations were received from almost all the learners. This may reflect the fact that all the current participants had experience in inputting Japanese and the fact that the materials had been created to only require mouse clicks and simple Japanese input.

Almost all evaluations were positive regarding both the volume and the quality of the recordings. One possible cause of some negative evaluations regarding the sound was that some learners felt the male voices were sometimes difficult to hear. Sound quality is related to file size and, in turn, depends on compressions rates for the data.

In terms of the screen displays, almost everyone gave positive evaluations, suggesting that these were appropriate. Responses about the explanation screen displays also indicated that these were appropriate in terms of content and length.

While most respondents expressed the view that the level of the exercises was appropriate, some learners commented that the word level exercises and the content of the conversations were easy. In terms of the number of exercise questions, most respondents wanted more applied exercises and conversation exercises, remarking in support of these requests that the randomizing function is particularly good for practice, that the exercises are helpful for consolidating understanding, and that basically the materials improved listening ability.

In particular, there were positive evaluations indicating that it was particularly beneficial to be able to listen to various voices. Rather than expressing concern over background noise on the recordings, learners were actually asking for more authentic recordings with background noises and voices speaking at different speeds, which would seem to be important factors for improving listening comprehension.

In summary of these points,

- It is clear that conscious awareness about the sound changes in spoken language was initially lacking in the beginning and intermediate learners who participated in the present study.

- In order to achieve improvements in listening comprehension by learning about the sound changes in spoken language, it is important to provide clear phonological explanations and ample opportunities to become familiar in listening to the sound changes. Clear learning effects were obtained for the "CALL materials for learning about sound changes" examined in this study.

- In terms of how to use the materials, it is clear that learning effects can be obtained not only by using the materials for self-study, but also by using them in class.

- If systematic phonological knowledge input is provided and there is sufficient listening practice with the materials, then the learner can achieve clear improvements in listening ability by working through the materials covering moraic nasal sounds just once.

- Positive evaluations of the materials were universally received from the learners, with the only negative comments suggesting that the applied and conversation exercises were too short. The materials will be supplemented in the future by adding a new function to save study histories for the CALL user. This will make it easier to see how learners actually use the materials, which will be particularly important in identifying the exercise questions that learners use most frequently, in order to further enhance the materials.

Pedagogical Suggestions for the Sound Changes in Japanese

After taking a few of the sessions about sound changes, one Japanese language student remarked, "I thought I was poor at listening to Japanese because I didn't know enough Japanese words, but now I realize that a lot of the time it was because I wasn't catching the sound changes." This is certainly the first step towards conscious awareness of the sound changes. In general, learners are not that interested in the sounds of the language, and we cannot really expect learners to notice sound change forms by themselves. It is crucial for teachers to start to move learners towards a conscious awareness of the sounds of the language and how these can vary. Learners who have acquired only the spoken language, like native speakers and young learners, are usually able to hear and interpret sound changes unconsciously. In such cases, it is useful to utilize their ability to perceive sound changes by making the learner consciously aware in a systematic manner of the rules that they have unconsciously acquired, so they can apply that knowledge to the next stage. Approaches to learning about sound changes will vary according to the leaner: Some learners may learn to understand the differences in the sounds by listening over and over again, some learners may find it easier to hear the sounds when they can see the words, while some learners may prefer to learn by also pronouncing the sounds themselves, and still other learners may want to have detailed rules. It is therefore important to provide materials wherein the learners can select both the amount and content of learning to meet their own personal needs and cognitive learning styles.

Although the CALL materials for learning about sound changes introduced in this chapter were developed to achieve these objectives, they can also be used effectively in classroom settings, either for teacher-guided learning or teacher-supervised self-learning. In such cases, the teacher can provide helpful feedback to the learner concerning the selection of appropriate content and in checking on pronunciations in speaking exercises. As the survey by Hirakata, Igashima, and Sakai (2002) noted, learners want to experience a wide range of voices, and our materials can be used as a rich resource of recordings, allowing learners to hear the same content being spoken by various voices, ranging from children to older people and from males to females. A particular feature of our materials is the fact that learners are able to easily listen repeatedly to the important parts.

One issue for future development will be to extend the coverage of sound changes. Once learners actually become consciously aware of the sound change forms tackled in the present materials and realize that their listening ability has improved, they are likely to ask about what other kinds of sound changes exist. We plan to extend our materials by developing systematic explanations, various voices, and various kinds of exercises to cover other sound changes in Japanese, such as vowel merging, vowel dropping, and consonant doubling, so that learners can start to acquire knowledge about these forms, too, without having to wait for the teacher to introduce the topics.

Finally, we would like to comment on comprehension strategies. Broadly speaking, comprehension can be divided into bottom-up processing (working from smaller units of words and phrases and moving to larger units of sentences) and top-down processing (where, in contrast, priority is on the whole). Although dealing with sound changes would appear to be primarily a bottom-up kind of strategy, in reality, both bottom-up and top-down processing often operate together in comprehension. When learners encounter words that they do not understand, they will use top-down strategies to guess about the uncertain words and to predict where the conversation is going, by activating their grasp of the themes and of the large meanings in the overall conversation, their background knowledge, and grammatical and lexical knowledge about the other words in the sentence. As one component of this kind of holistic listening comprehension, we would like to stress that it is important for learners to also be able to apply their knowledge for sound changes when trying to interpret words that have not been heard clearly. To this end, we have been seeking to integrate learning about sound changes as part of the learner's total listening ability for spoken Japanese.

Acknowledgements

We would like to express our gratitude to Yukiko Hirakata, who has collaborated in our earlier studies, for her comments and advice in the preparation of this chapter. We would also like to thank Dr. Terry Joyce for his help in checking the English in the chapter.

Appendix: Class plan for the moraic nasal sound

1. Have the learner listen to sentences including various kinds of sound changes. For advanced-level students, it is also possible to use extracts from natural sources. Between 15 and 20 instances are appropriate for the target sound changes.

2. Have the learner complete blank-filling dictation exercises for target sections.

3. Encourage the learner to think about how s/he tackles the listening task above: Did s/he hear the target sound (a) as an unchanged pronunciation or (b) as the sound changed form?

4. Have the learner listen again, this time writing down the alternative form. That is, (a) write the unchanged pronunciation if hearing the sound change and (b) write down the sound change form, if the unchanged pronunciation is heard.

5. Have the learner categorize or group the sound changes.

6. Have the learner speculate about what kinds of rules govern the sound changes. If possible, it is advisable to do this in groups, because key elements in developing conscious awareness are the ability to convey one's understanding to others and monitoring of what is not fully understood.

7. Based on perceived rules, have the learner create conversations with words that the learner thinks can undergo the sound changes. After discussing which examples work and which do not, provide the learner with systematic rules.

NFLRC
monographs

Why Second Language Learners of Japanese Need to Learn Difficult Minute Sounds in Connected Speech

YUKARI HIRATA
Colgate University, New York

Learners of Japanese have difficulty in distinguishing the length of vowels and consonants in Japanese (e.g., ka-ko vs. ka-k-ko). In traditional pronunciation training, these word pairs are presented in isolation. This chapter argues that the ability to distinguish these minute sounds in isolated words is different from the ability to distinguish them in connected speech. Three experimental studies are presented: (a) native English speakers learning to perceive Japanese vowel and consonant length in isolation versus in connected speech; (b) native Japanese speakers producing vowel length contrasts with varied speaking rates; and (c) native Japanese speakers perceiving those vowel length contrasts. These studies highlight the importance of the connected speech context for second language learners as they learn to perceive difficult speech sounds. Hence, this chapter will be of central interest to applied linguistics researchers as well as Japanese language teachers, researchers, materials developers, and testers.

Native English Speakers' Difficulty in Perceiving Japanese Length Contrasts

This chapter focuses on native English speakers' difficulty in perceiving certain minute sounds in Japanese, that is, Japanese length contrasts.[1] Both vowel and consonant length are *phonemic* in Japanese, that is, whether a vowel or consonant is short or long can change the meaning of words. For example, *ka-ko* with short vowels and consonants means 'past,' and *ka-k-ko* with a long word-medial consonant means 'parenthesis,' while *ka-do* with short vowels and consonants means 'corner,' and *ka-a-do* with a long vowel means 'card.' The difference between these pairs of words is mainly durational, and is reflected in the number of *moras*.[2] The mora is a unit similar

---

[1] Editors' note: For more on the general literature related to reduced forms in Japanese, see chapters 10, 11, and 12.

[2] In this chapter, Japanese words are transcribed with hyphens dividing moras. For example, *ka-k-ko* has three moras and the first part of long *k* counts as one mora. See Vance (1987) for more details about moras.

Hirata, Y. (2006) Why second language learners of Japanese need to learn difficult minute sounds in connected speech. In J. D. Brown, & K. Kondo-Brown, (Eds.), *Perspectives on teaching connected speech to second language speakers* (pp. 231–243). Honolulu, HI: University of Hawai'i, National Foreign Language Resource Center.

to the syllable, but duration sensitive: *ka-ko* (two moras); *ka-k-ko* (three moras); *ka-do* (two moras); *ka-a-do* (three moras). The acoustic difference between short and long vowels is quite small. For example, a long vowel in *ka-a-do* might be 150–200 milliseconds (ms) longer than a short vowel in *ka-do* when spoken carefully in isolation. The quality of short and long vowels is almost identical (Kondo, 1995; Tsukada, 1999; Ueyama, 2000), unlike the English vowels in *heat* versus *hit*. Previous research shows that native English speakers, who do not use such length contrasts in their native language, have difficulty acquiring them (Han, 1992; Landahl & Ziolkowski, 1995; Landahl, Ziolkowski, Usami, & Tunnock, 1992; Oguma, 2000; Toda, 1997).[3]

The traditional method of teaching these difficult length contrasts has been to carefully present these pairs of words in isolation (e.g., *ka-ko* and *ka-k-ko*), and ask students which word they have heard. This careful method makes sense, given that the only difference is one of duration and that the difference is so small. This traditional method of teaching usually persists even when new computer technology is introduced. Kawai and Hirose (2000) used automatic speech recognition technology to provide learners of Japanese with feedback on the vowel duration of their production of the Japanese word pair, *ka-do* versus *ka-a-do*. The criterion used for the automatic feedback was native Japanese listeners' categorical boundary of absolute duration between the short and long vowels of these words in isolation. Although this training method might be useful at an initial stage of learning, the ability gained might not generalize to the same distinction for words spoken in sentences. This hunch comes from my own experience in teaching native English speakers these difficult length contrasts. When I present word pairs such as *ka-do* and *ka-a-do* carefully in isolation and ask students to tell me which one they have heard, they are almost always able to answer correctly. However, they become less confident when the words are presented in sentences, not to mention when we are engaged in actual conversation!

In this chapter, I first present an experimental study (study 1) which indicates that the learner's ability to perceive Japanese length contrasts differs when words are presented in isolation and when the same words are presented in connected speech context (Hirata, 2004b). Throughout this chapter, I use "connected speech context" to mean a natural speech context larger than words in isolation. The speech materials I used were not conversational or casual speech but naturally read utterances. I do not focus on details of the sound changes that take place in connected speech (e.g., how the Japanese intervocalic /g/ is realized as a voiced velar fricative when spoken in a sentence or at a rapid rate). However, having shown that the learner's ability is consistently lower in connected speech context than in isolation, I argue that it is very important to teach Japanese length contrasts in connected speech context. Second, I provide data on the duration of Japanese vowels spoken by native Japanese speakers in connected speech at varied speaking rates (study 2; Hirata, 2004c). These results provide insight into why learners of Japanese might have difficulty in perceiving vowel length contrasts. Finally, I present data on native Japanese speakers' perception of Japanese vowel length (study 3; Hirata & Lambacher, 2004). The results of this study indicate that native speakers often determine vowel length using perceptual cues *outside* the target word, thus highlighting further the importance of using connected speech context.

---

[3]   Editors' note: Also see chapter 11 of this book.

Study 1: Japanese Learners' Perception in Citation Versus Connected Speech

Questions

In this first study, native English speakers were trained to perceive Japanese length contrasts, and their ability was tested before and after training (Hirata, 2004d). In the pretest and posttest, the same words were presented in two contexts: one presented in citation form (word context) and the other presented in connected speech (sentence context). Two types of training were given: *word training*, which provided only words in citation form, and *sentence training*, which provided the same words in connected speech context. The questions addressed are

1. Does the perceptual ability of native English speakers differ in the two contexts?
2. Are there differential effects of the two types of training?

Method

Participants

Three groups of participants were recruited: a control group (n = 18), a word-training group (n = 18), and a sentence-training group (n = 17).[4] They were all monolingual native speakers of American English (aged 19–25) who had no previous experience with Japanese. They were not exposed to Japanese outside this experiment. Native English speakers with no previous experience with Japanese were chosen because the study aimed to identify the precise effects of the two contexts and two types of training without the interference of learning experience outside the study.

Procedure

At the beginning of the experiment, all participants were instructed in Japanese length contrasts and how to identify the number of moras in a word (e.g., that *ka-do* contains two moras while *ka-a-do* contains three moras). The control group took only a pretest and, after a 4-week interval, a posttest. Both of the tests had a word test (i.e., words presented in citation form) and a sentence test (i.e., words presented in sentences). The word-training group took the pretest, participated in 10 sessions of word training (over roughly 3 weeks), and then took the posttest. The sentence-training group took the pretest, participated in ten sessions of sentence training (over roughly 3 weeks), and then took the posttest.

Training

Training materials were 489 words spoken in both citation form (word training) and in sentences (sentence training). Words were of one to six moras, and the training task was to identify the number of moras in a given word. There were a total of 10 training sessions, and each consisted of six blocks of 10 trials, with the same words used in both word and sentence training in the same order. The task for word-training participants was to click the number of moras in each word after it was heard through headphones. If a participant gave the correct answer, the training program responded with "Correct!" and displayed both the test word and the answer (e.g., *ha-de* [two moras]). If the participants gave an incorrect answer, the program responded

---

[4]   Editors' note: Because of the small sample sizes in the three studies summarized in this chapter, readers are cautioned to interpret the results carefully.

with "Sorry..." gave the same information as above, and then required the participant to listen to the word three additional times.

For sentence training, each word was spoken embedded within a carrier sentence. Each block had a different carrier sentence. For each word, the carrier sentence was displayed on the computer screen with the training word omitted, for example, *Zuibun ___ desu ne.* 'It's very ___, isn't it?' as the participant heard the full sentence, *Zuibun hade desu ne.* The task for the sentence-training participants was to identify the number of moras in the inserted word (e.g., two moras for *ha-de*). The feedback system was the same as that in word training.

Testing

The testing materials were completely different from those used in training. The goal was to examine the participants' generalized ability to perceive Japanese length contrasts and not to see how much they remembered from the training materials. The task for the pretest and posttest was the same as that for training, except that participants received no feedback on their responses during the tests. The pretest and posttest contained identical sets of materials, but the order of stimuli was randomized. Each test had word and sentence components for each participant. The word and sentence tests contained the identical sets of 60 words. The only difference was that they were presented in isolation versus in sentences. The order of word and sentence tests was randomized across participants.

Results

Word versus sentence contexts

Figure 1 shows the overall results for the three groups on the pretest and posttest. The percent correct test scores were consistently lower for the sentence than the word context (the lower vs. upper panels of Figure 1) [$F(1, 50) = 311.40, p < 0.001$]. The mean test scores for all tests for all groups were 35.8% for the sentence, and 57.0% for the word test. Another interesting result related to the context was that the amount of pretest-posttest improvement in the two contexts significantly differed [$F(1, 50) = 18.57, p < 0.001$]. The improvement was significantly less for the sentence (11.4%) than the word context (18.1%). This means that even when one can accurately perceive the number of moras in words presented in isolation, this does not guarantee that the same words will be perceived accurately in the sentence context.

Trained versus control groups

There was no significant improvement made by the control group, which did not participate in training. In contrast, significant improvement was observed for the trained groups (word training and sentence training) from the pretest to the posttest [$F(2, 50) = 9.53, p < 0.001$]. In the word context (the upper panel of Figure 1), the word-training group improved by 30.1%, and the sentence-training group improved by 25.4%. Both trained groups improved in the sentence context as well (the lower panel of Figure 1), although the amount of improvement was less (14.5% for the word-training group; 20.4% for the sentence-training group). These results indicate that both types of training helped improve participants' perception of Japanese moras, enabling them to detect short versus long consonants and vowels.

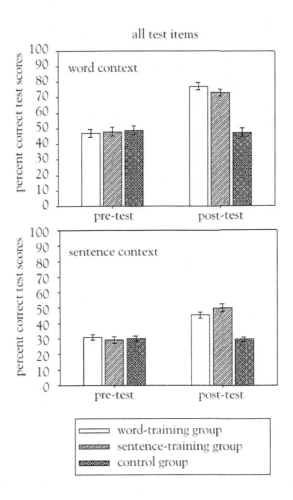

all test items

note: The error bars represent one standard error from the mean. Reprinted with permission from Yukari Hirata, *The Journal of the Acoustical Society of America*, 116, 2384 (2004). Copyright 2004, Acoustical Society of America.

Figure 1.   Mean percent correct scores on all test items on the pretest and posttest for word-training, sentence-training, and control groups

Word- versus sentence-training groups

One important question addressed in this study was whether there was a differential effect of the two types of training. The posttest score of the word-training group was slightly higher than that of the sentence-training group in the word context (77.1% vs. 73.3%), but this difference was not significant [tD (5, 33) = 1.17, $p > 0.05$]. In the sentence context, the mean posttest score of the sentence-training group was slightly higher than that of the word-training group (49.7% vs. 45.3%), but this difference was not significant [tD (5, 33) = 1.39, $p > 0.05$]. However, an interesting result emerged when looking at the gap between the scores of the word and sentence contexts for each group. The difference score (word context minus sentence context) was significantly greater for the word-training group (31.9%) than for the sentence-training group (23.6%) [tD (5, 33) = 3.05, $p < 0.05$]. This means that the group that heard only isolated words had a greater discrepancy between the scores of the two contexts than the group that heard only sentences. This suggests that, given training in only one context, the degree of generalization to the untrained context was greater for the sentence-training than the word-training participants.

A subset of words used in the pretest and posttest were found to be more difficult than the other types of words. In particular, the word type "combination," in which there was one long vowel and one long consonant within a word, for example, *ka-a-pe-t-to* 'carpet' (five moras) or two long vowels, for example, *ke-e-se-e* 'formation' (four moras) proved most difficult [$F(3, 150) = 360.32$, $p < 0.001$]. As seen in Figure 2, the test scores in this word type were consistently lower than the overall test scores in Figure 1. For this word type, the trained groups also showed significant improvement while the control group did not. Again, the difference score (i.e., the gap between the two contexts) of the word-training group (28.9%) was significantly higher than that for the sentence-training group (15.7%) [$tD (1, 33) = 2.84$, $p < 0.01$]. The word-training group's ability to generalize to the sentence context was smaller than the sentence-training group's ability to generalize to the word context. These results taken together indicate that sentence training is more advantageous if our ultimate goal is to train learners to perceive difficult sounds in connected speech context.

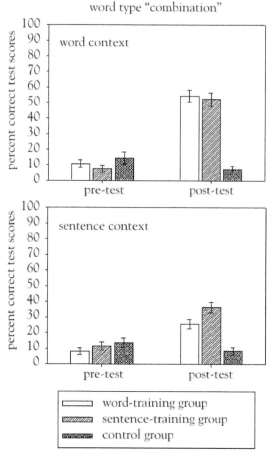

note: The error bars represent one standard error from the mean. Reprinted with permission from Yukari Hirata, *The Journal of the Acoustical Society of America*, 116, 2384 (2004). Copyright 2004, Acoustical Society of America.

Figure 2.   Mean percent correct scores on word type "combination" at pretest and posttest for word-training, sentence-training, and control groups

Discussion

Study 1 revealed that the ability of nonnative listeners to identify Japanese length contrasts differs when words are spoken in isolation and when the same words are spoken in connected speech context. That listeners were less accurate in connected speech contexts intuitively makes sense, but why is it the case? What mechanism is involved in processing speech in the two contexts? Many participants in the sentence training in the above experiment commented that, given that they were not used to hearing a fluent stream of spoken Japanese, it was extremely hard for them to extract the target words from the carrier sentences. Training with connected speech might have given these participants some of the skill needed for segmenting a stream of speech into words and segments. The participants in the word-training group, who heard words only in citation form, however, did not have the chance to acquire this skill.

Sentence-training participants also commented on the rate at which the sentences were spoken. The fact that sentences varied in speaking rate even slightly, presented difficulties for participants. Speaking rate is one important factor that might have contributed to the differential performance between the two contexts. The issue of speaking rate was thus the focus of the next study.

Study 2: Physical Duration of Vowels at Different Speaking Rates

Questions

Long vowels are longer than short vowels by definition, but what happens when speaking rate changes? Are long vowels always longer than short vowels, regardless of the speaking rate? Do native speakers of Japanese reliably produce the distinction between short and long vowels when the vowels are spoken at different speaking rates? If not, how are native speakers of Japanese able to hear the distinction? If no acoustic dimension reliably corresponds to vowel length, is it not too much to ask nonnative speakers to learn to distinguish short and long vowels? Previous studies examined the duration of Japanese vowels and found the duration ratio of short and long vowels to be 1:2.4–3.2 (Han, 1962; Tsukada, 1999; Ueyama, 2000). However, very little was known as to whether this ratio holds true at varied speaking rates. In this section, I summarize the results of a recent experiment, which analyzed acoustically short and long vowels in Japanese (Hirata, 2004c).

Method

Participants

Four native Japanese speakers (two males and two females) with a mean age of 31 (range: 24–35) participated in this study. The four participants were from Ibaraki, Gifu, Nagano, and Aichi prefectures and reported speaking standard Japanese.

Procedure

The four native Japanese speakers produced pairs of two- and three-mora words, which included short and long vowels, spoken in a carrier sentence at slow, normal, and fast speaking rates. Prior to recording, written instructions were given to the participants for producing three speaking rates. The "normal" rate was defined as a tempo that is "relaxed and comfortable" for the speaker. The "slow" rate was defined as the "slowest tempo possible that the speaker could produce" while keeping a sentence flowing together (i.e., without inserting breaks between words). The "fast" rate was defined as the "fastest tempo possible without making an excessive number of errors."

Target words were both nonsense words (e.g., *me-me*, *me-e-me*, and *me-me-e*)[5] and real words (e.g., *ka-do* 'corner' vs. *ka-a-do* 'card,' and *ri-ka* 'science' vs. *ri-ka-a* 'liquor'). All words had a pitch accent on the first syllable. Thus, for each vowel there was an accented vowel pair as in *ka-do* and *ka-a-do*, and an unaccented vowel pair as in *ri-ka* and *ri-ka-a*. Duration of vowels (e.g., *a* vs. *a-a* in the above example pairs) was measured using acoustic analysis software.[6] A total of 1,440 vowel tokens were measured.

Results

Duration of vowels

The mean duration was 84 ms for short vowels and 198 ms for long vowels (in real words), yielding a ratio of 1: 2.36, similar to those found in previous studies. Figure 3 shows the distribution of duration for short and long vowels spoken at all three rates. The upper panels show duration of vowels in the accented position (e.g., in *ka-do* and *ka-a-do*), and the lower panels show duration of unaccented vowels (e.g., in *ri-ka* and *ri-ka-a*). For both accented and unaccented vowels, there is a considerable amount of durational overlap between the range of short and long vowels. Note that a vowel whose duration is within the range of 60 to 240 ms can be either short or long. The mean duration of short versus long vowels for each speaking rate was 123 versus 306 ms for the slow, 75 versus 178 ms for the normal, and 55 versus 110 ms for the fast rates. The duration distinction was quite clear within each rate, but as one can see from these mean values, the mean slow short vowel (123 ms) was *longer* than the mean fast long vowel (110 ms). Effects of speaking rate were also seen in the ratios of short vs. long vowels: The ratios were smaller for the fast rate (1: 2.0) than for the normal (1: 2.4) and the slow rates (1: 2.5).

These results might partially explain why nonnative speakers have difficulty in learning Japanese vowel length contrasts. According to the results above, when the vowels are spoken slowly, listeners need to detect a durational difference of 183 ms (306 minus 123 ms) on average. However, the task becomes much more difficult for fast speech, as they then need to detect a very small difference of only 55 ms (110 minus 55 ms). The fact that the ratio between the short and long vowels becomes smaller for the fast rate might also add to the difficulty.

---

[5]   The only exception in this set of nonsense words was *ma-ma*, which is a real word meaning 'mom.'

[6]   Editors' note: For more on software for analyzing speech characteristics, see chapter 9 of this book.

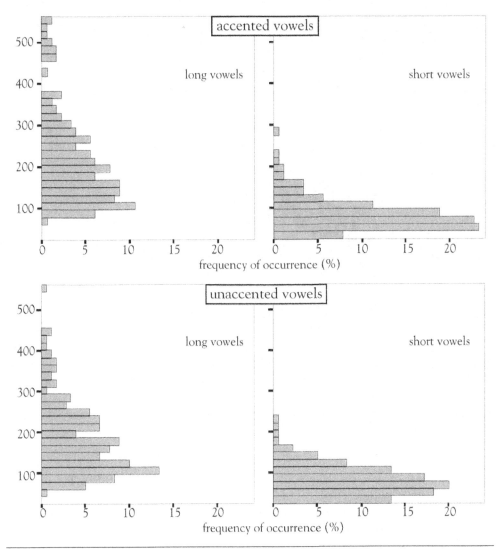

Figure 3. Distributions of vowel durations in milliseconds in real words spoken at three rates across four speakers

Vowel-to-word duration ratios

To investigate whether there is any invariant acoustic property corresponding to each of the short and long vowels, further analysis was conducted. For each word produced, the proportion of the target vowel to the entire word was calculated. For example, the duration of the vowel *o* relative to the duration of the word *ka-to*, and the duration of the long vowel *o-o* relative to the duration of the word *ka-to-o* were calculated separately. The results showed that the mean vowel-to-word ratio was 0.29 for short vowels, and 0.46 for long vowels. This means that, on average, the short vowels occupied 29% of the word duration, and the long vowels occupied 46% of the word duration. A subset of production (nonsense words) is plotted in Figure 4. In this figure, a clear boundary of 0.38 distinguished the two categories with high accuracy across all three rates. Taken together, we can conclude that the proportion of the vowel to the entire word is a good indicator of the two vowel categories, even when speaking rate variations yield a considerable overlap between the absolute duration of short and long vowels. This implies that native Japanese speakers produce the vowel length distinction clearly and reliably.

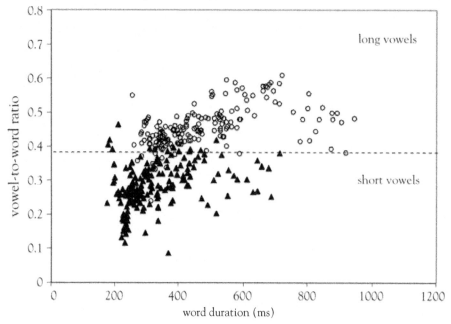

note: White circles represent tokens for long vowels, and dark triangles represent tokens for short vowels.

Figure 4.   Ratios of vowel to word duration plotted against word duration (results from nonsense words)

Discussion

Study 2 provides some explanation for why learners of Japanese might face difficulty in perceiving Japanese length contrasts. Vowel duration varies and overlaps considerably across rates. In particular, short vowels spoken slowly can be longer than long vowels spoken quickly. In addition, the duration difference between the short and long vowels is smaller for faster rates. One implication for teaching is that providing only vowel contrasts in citation form (which are carefully spoken in isolation) might not be optimal because in the real world learners of Japanese must deal with connected speech spoken at various speaking rates. Study 2 also indicates that the durations of short and long vowels produced by native Japanese speakers are clearly organized and separated from each other in terms of the ratio of the vowel to the word. This assures us that detecting vowel length is not an unreasonable task for learners of Japanese.

Study 3: Native Japanese Speakers' Perception in Connected Speech

The next question addressed in this chapter is how native Japanese speakers perceive vowel length in connected speech. It is known that the primary perceptual cue used to distinguish Japanese short and long vowels is their duration (Fujisaki, Nakamura, & Imoto, 1975). It is not known, however, what role the surrounding speech (i.e., speech *outside* the target vowels) plays in connected speech. In particular, study 3 investigates the role of the carrier sentence in native speakers' perception of vowel length (Hirata & Lambacher, 2004). Study 3 consists of two experiments.

Experiment 1

Method

In Experiment 1, one group of 20 native Japanese listeners identified the vowel length of two and three mora words, for example, *ma-ma, ma-a-ma, and ma-ma-a*, in a carrier sentence *Sokowa* ___ *to kaite arimasu* ('___ is written there') spoken at slow and fast speaking rates (intact condition). These stimuli were a subset of those used in Study 2. Thus, the duration of short and long vowels was clearly separate within each speaking rate, but there was overlap between the slow short vowels and fast long vowels.

For the second group of 20 native Japanese listeners, the target words were excised from the carrier sentence (excised condition). Thus, the second group heard the same target words as those in the intact condition, but without the carrier sentence. Any difference in identification accuracy between the two groups would indicate the role of the carrier sentence: If the accuracy in the excised condition is lower, we can say that listeners needed the carrier sentence to accurately identify the vowel length.

Results

The percent correct identification for the excised condition was 69.5%, significantly lower than that for the intact condition (98.1%) [$F(1, 38) = 181.5, p < 0.001$]. This result indicates that listeners were often unable to accurately identify the vowel length without the carrier sentence while the same words were almost perfectly identified with the original carrier sentence.

Experiment 2

The above result demonstrates that surrounding connected speech provides listeners with some important cue about the vowel length of the target word. However, this result did not clarify what aspect of the carrier sentence contributed to the accurate identification. Does the presence of a carrier sentence at *any* rate provide listeners with helpful context? Or, is the presence of a carrier sentence at an *appropriate* rate needed? This question was addressed in Experiment 2.

Method

Speech materials used in Experiment 2 were created from the original materials used in Experiment 1, spoken at slow and fast rates. Using acoustic analysis software, the target words (e.g., *ma-ma, ma-a-ma, and ma-ma-a*), were edited out of the original carrier sentence and embedded into a carrier sentence of another rate (mismatch condition). For example, the target word *ma-ma* that had been originally spoken in the carrier sentence at the slow rate was replaced with the word *ma-ma* that had been originally spoken in the carrier sentence at the fast rate. Thus, the speaking rate of the target word was always different from the rate of the carrier sentence. These stimuli were presented in a randomized order to a new group of 19 native Japanese speakers. If the presence of a carrier sentence, regardless of its rate, is all that matters for accurate identification of vowel length, then listeners in the mismatch condition would identify vowel length as accurately as those in the intact condition. The identification accuracy in the mismatch condition should also be higher than that in the excised condition. However, if the appropriate rate of a carrier sentence is necessary for accurate identification, having a carrier sentence with a mismatched rate would hurt identification accuracy. In this case, the identification accuracy in the mismatch condition would be lower than the intact and excised conditions.

Results

The percent correct identification score of the mismatch condition was 52.4%, significantly lower than that of the intact condition (98.1%) [$F(1, 37) = 352.3$, $p < 0.001$]. The score of the mismatch condition was also significantly lower than that of the excised condition (69.5%) [$F(1, 37) = 30.0$, $p < 0.001$]. Thus, the mismatched rate of the carrier sentence hurt the accuracy more than the absence of the carrier sentence in the excised condition. These results indicate that the carrier sentence spoken at the appropriate rate, and not just at any rate, plays an important role for high identification accuracy.

Conclusions

In study 1, the ability of beginning learners of Japanese to perceive Japanese length contrasts was found to be consistently lower when words are presented in connected speech context than in isolation. Study 1 also showed that the amount of perceptual improvement was smaller for the connected speech context than for the isolation context. As for effects of training, the participants who always heard target words in connected speech context were able to generalize their ability to isolated words. This result is consistent with that in Hirata (2004a), which tested Japanese learners before and after production training with connected speech. However, participants in the present study who heard only target words in citation form were less able to generalize their ability to connected speech context. These results counter the intuition that one must present speech materials carefully in citation form in order to teach learners difficult minute sounds. Although this method of teaching might be a suitable first step for beginning learners, the present results suggest that it is very important to teach these difficult minute sounds in connected speech context. There seems to be no guarantee that learners will automatically learn to perceive meaningful small sounds in connected speech.

Study 2 provided insight into why learners of Japanese might have difficulty perceiving Japanese vowel length contrasts. The duration of Japanese vowels spoken by native speakers varies with speaking rate, and there is significant overlap between short and long vowel categories spoken at different rates. One implication for teaching is that providing length contrasts only in citation form might not be pedagogically optimal because, in the real world, learners of Japanese will face connected speech spoken at varying rates. Acoustic analysis also revealed that vowel-to-word duration ratio is a reliable indicator of short and long vowel distinction for two and three mora words: A vowel that occupies less than 38% of the word is almost certainly a short vowel, and a vowel that occupies more than 38% of the word is almost certainly a long vowel. This suggests that the important cue to vowel length distinction is not the absolute duration of a vowel, but the duration of that vowel relative to that of the word. Training learners of Japanese with a variety of speaking rates might increase their awareness of this proportional cue.

The results of study 3 further highlight the importance of connected speech context in the perception of vowel length. Native speakers of Japanese were not always able to identify the vowel length accurately when the word was taken out of the original sentence context. Having the carrier sentence with the mismatched rate hurt the identification accuracy even more. In all three conditions (intact, excised, and mismatch), the target words were acoustically identical. These results indicate that connected speech contains important information about the rate of speech, and that native listeners use that information as a perceptual cue to vowel length distinction. In other words, native Japanese listeners often determine vowel length using perceptual cues *outside* the target word, thus underscoring the importance of connected speech context.

The above results are consistent with those in Hirata (1990a), which investigated the perception of native Japanese speakers of *consonant* length in a sentence. Hirata found that native Japanese speakers used the varied speaking rates of the sentence as a cue to consonant length distinction (*i-ta* vs. *i-t-ta*), which supports the findings in study 3. In contrast, learners of Japanese in the same experiment were unable to use the rate of speech as a cue to consonant length distinction (Hirata, 1990b). There is a clear need for a new teaching method that successfully exposes learners to connected speech yet directs their attention to the fine durational differences of vowels and consonants in Japanese. Further research in phonetics and second language pedagogy is necessary to develop such a method and assess its efficacy

Acknowledgments

The studies described in this chapter received funding from Colgate University. The author thanks Jon Bernard for helpful comments on the earlier version of this manuscript.

How should connected speech be tested?

Testing Reduced Forms

James Dean Brown
Kimi Kondo-Brown
University of Hawai'i

This chapter begins by examining some of the tests used to do research on reduced forms. These include the Bowen (1975b, 1976) Integrative Grammar Test (IGT), the Brown and Hilferty (1982, 1986a, 1986b, also see chapter 4 of this book) reduced-forms dictations, the Henrichsen (1984) variation of the IGT to test sandhi-variation, as well as the other variations developed by Matsuzawa (chapter 5 in this book) and Ito (chapter 6 of this book). The chapter then goes on to discuss classical activities used to test reduced-forms (after Ito, chapter 6 of this book) including reduced-forms read-aloud tests, reduced-forms cloze exercises, reduced-forms listen-and-repeat tests, and other reduced-forms testing ideas like partial reduced-forms dictations, reduced-forms dialog comprehension, reduced-forms dialog dictocomp, testing sentence stress, minimal contrast tests, hearing and production tests for inserted /j/ or /w/ sounds, a multiple-choice discrimination test for simple consonant transitions, and a hearing and production test for assimilations /d/ to /b/ assimilations before bilabial /p b m/. The chapter then raises the question of whether similar tests would work for other languages. The answer includes example tests for both French and Japanese connected speech. The chapter also discusses the need for communicative activities used to test reduced-forms (including the characteristics of focus-on-form sorts of activities, as well as the characteristics of communicative tests in general), as well as some ideas for other alternative forms of assessment (including portfolios, conferences, and peer-assessments or self-assessments). This chapter should be of interest to all readers interested in connected speech.

Introduction

When Brown and Hilferty (1982, 1986a, 1986b, also see chapter 4 of this book) were teaching reduced forms, they realized that one of the reasons teachers may be avoiding the teaching of reduced forms in EFL/ESL classrooms might be that nobody knows how to test them. To address this issue, this chapter will examine some of the issues involved in assessing the students' abilities to understand and use reduced forms. In the process, we will use the terms *testing* and *assessment* more or less synonymously. The reduced forms that we will consider assessing along the way will include such aspects of the pronunciation system as word stress, sentence stress and timing, reduction, citation and weak forms of words, elision, intrusion, assimilation, juncture, and contraction. We will begin the process by examining some of the

Brown, J. D., & Kondo-Brown K. (2006) Testing reduced forms. In J. D. Brown, & K. Kondo-Brown, (Eds.), *Perspectives on teaching connected speech to second language speakers* (pp. 247–264). Honolulu, HI: University of Hawai'i, National Foreign Language Resource Center.

different types of tests that have been used over the years in the published research on reduced forms. We will then offer a number of alternatives that teachers can use in their classrooms to test the various aspects of reduced speech they may be teaching (including examples in English, French, and Japanese).

Tests Used to Research Reduced Forms

Such as it is, the history of testing reduced forms probably begins with Bowen's (1975b, 1976) development of the Integrative Grammar Test (IGT). This is the first instance we have been able to find of a published call for testing reduced forms. In this case, the test was designed to assess the students' abilities to listen to isolated sentences "pronounced in normal, informal, conversational English" (p. 31), that begin with two words involved in reduction and demonstrate comprehension by writing the full form of the second word in each sentence in the blank provided.

The following are example items from the IGT (Bowen, 1976, p. 31):

A few examples are the pronunciation of /d/ in	answer
Who'*d* he been to see?	had
Who'*d* he wanna see?	did
Who'*d* he like to see?	would
or the interpretation of /əm/ in	
Give'*m* an inch and he'll take a mile.	him
Leave '*m* if they're not here in the next five minutes.	them
or the intepretation of /ət/ in	
Here '*t* the factory we're always busy.	at
Here '*t* seems like we're always behind schedule.	it
or the interpretation of /ə/ in	
Whatt*aya* want with that cat?	do
Whatt*aya* doin' with that cat?	are
Whatt*aya* done with that cat?	have

In his report on the 50-item IGT, Bowen (1976) argued for its validity by showing that it had produced well-distributed descriptive statistics and moderate to high correlation coefficients with a variety of overall proficiency measures in a wide assortment of English learning situations around the world (with many hundreds of students sampled in total). Bowen reported an equivalent forms estimate of the reliability for the IGT of .968. In addition, a K-R21 reliability estimate that we have calculated nearly 30 years later for his IGT administration results at the American University Cairo ($n = 686$; $k = 50$; $M = 29.0$; $SD = 23.23$) turned out to be .997, which is very hard to beat.

The IGT was not without controversy. Bowen's (1976) write up in the *RELC Journal* immediately drew academic fire from Coleman (1977) for not having tested a sufficient number of native speakers of English and for not considering the plight of illiterate and uneducated native speakers and non-native speakers who have acquired their English "through an unconventional learning process" (p. 92). We feel that Bowen (1977) more than adequately addressed these concerns.

Brown and Hilferty used what they called reduced-forms dictations in their research reported in Brown and Hilferty (1982, 1986a, 1986b, also see chapter 4 of this book).

An example reduced-forms dictation was shown in Brown and Hilferty (1998). Because that reduced forms dictation is copyrighted, a heavily adapted version is shown here.

To begin, the teacher should introduce the following vocabulary (key content words not involved in reduced forms), while writing it on the blackboard: *New York, Tuesday, plane ticket, sightseeing, Manhattan, Statue of liberty*. Then the teacher tells the students that he/she will read the dictation "three times: once fast, once fast, and once fast" (this typically draws a laugh from students) with the second fast reading including pauses so students will have time to write *the full forms of all the words in the dialog*. Naturally, if the teacher is a non-native speaker who is not comfortable with reading this dialog full of reduced forms, a cassette tape of another person (perhaps a native speaker of North American English) could be prepared in advance. Here is the reduced-forms dictation, as it would be read:

David: Whenerya goin' ta New York?
Alice: I'm gonna go on Tuesday.
David: Boy! I wish I were gettin' ouda here fer awhile. Ya gotcher plane ticket?
Alice: Naw. I've gotta gedit tomorra.
David: Whaddya hafta do in New York?
Alice: I gotta deliver some products, but I also wanna do sum sightseeing.
David: Where'll ya go?
Alice: I wanna gedouda Manhattan 'n see the Statue of Liberty.
David: 'kay, hav' a goo time.
Alice: Mmkay, g'bye.

And, the following would serve as an answer key where each underlined full word the students write correctly would be given one point:

David: <u>When are you going to</u> New York?
Alice: <u>I am going to</u> go on Tuesday.
David: Boy! I <u>wish I</u> were <u>getting out of</u> here <u>for</u> awhile. You <u>got your</u> plane ticket?
Alice: <u>No</u>. I <u>have got to get it tomorrow</u>.
David: <u>What do you have to</u> do in New York?
Alice: I <u>have got to</u> deliver some products, but I also <u>want to</u> do <u>some</u> sightseeing.
David: <u>Where will you</u> go?
Alice: I <u>want to get out of</u> Manhattan <u>and</u> see the Statue of Liberty.
David: Okay, <u>have a good</u> time.
Alice: <u>Okay, goodbye</u>.
50 possible (counting underlined words only)

Henrichsen (1984) used single independent sentences to test what he called sandhi-variation in one from of his test: The students heard 15 sentences with reduced forms (selected from Bowen's IGT) and were required to write down the full forms of the words they heard in each sentence. As in the IGT, the first two words in each sentence were reduced. The students were warned that each sentence would only be read one time and not repeated. Here are some of the example sentences given in Henrichsen, along with the words the scorer would be looking for as a correct answer (only the second word was scored in each sentence):

example	answer
Give them a few days and they will be back. [givəm]	them
What a nice drink of orange juice that was! [hwatənays]	a
What had he done that made the judge so angry. [hwatədiydən]	had
This has got to be the best we have every done! [ðisəzgatəbiy]	has
[*Here at head*quarters we are always busy. hıyrəʔhɛd]	at

Henrichsen did not report reliability estimates for his test, and the descriptive statistics were broken down by high and low level students, so no overall K-R21 estimate could be recreated from his results. However, for the individual groups, the K-R21 estimates we calculated for the two high-level ESL student groups turned out to be low to moderate (.40 and .68). For the native speakers and the low level ESL groups, the K-R21 estimates ranged from zero to very low (.00 to .31). In fairness to Henrichsen, we must point out that the total reliability for all ESL students combined is likely to have been higher than the estimates re-created here.

Ito (chapter 6 of this book) used a slight variation of Henrichsen's (1984) test, in which students heard 20 sentences (half based on lexical reduction and half based on phonological reduction) that they were required to write down in their full forms. Two of the words (near but not at the beginning) in each sentence were contracted or blended together. The students were warned that each sentence would only be read one time and not repeated. Here are some of the sentences adapted from Ito's Appendix B, along with the words the scorer would be looking for as a correct answer (only the words involved in a reduced form were scored):

example lexical reduced forms sentences	answer
He *doesn't* work very hard at home.	does not
We *won't* go out to dinner with our friends.	will not
They *don't* have dictionaries on their desks.	do not
She *hasn't* taught biology at the school.	has not
I *haven't* spoken to my teacher.	have not

example phonological reduced forms	
I think that *I've* never lived in a small town.	I have
I know that *he's* never worked at an automobile factory.	he has
I think that *she's* been a good friend of mine.	she has
I think that *they've* stayed at a hotel in this city.	they have
I think that *they're* buying tickets at the theater.	they are

Ito essentially had two 20-item tests, one where the items included reduced forms and one where the input was spoken clearly and precisely, for a total of 40-items. Her test appeared to work reasonably well in her study: Even though the descriptive statistics indicted high mean scores, sufficient variance was produced to result in a Cronbach alpha reliability estimate of .78. (For more information, see chapter 6; for complete directions and all the sentences used, see Ito's Appendix B.)

Matsuzawa (chapter 5 in this book) used a test in his study similar to the ones used by Henrichsen (1984) and Ito (chapter 6 of this book). He asked the examinees to write down all words they heard in listening to the 30 sentences in each of his two forms. However, spaces for the students to write the words were provided in parentheses. He decided to do the test in this way so his participants would not just focus on the reduced forms involved but would instead attempt to comprehend the entire sentence. In the example item he provided (one that tested palatalization in *did you* /dɪdʒu/), the italicized words in the second and third pair of parentheses were examined and counted correct or incorrect (only correct spellings were counted as correct).

(Where) (*did*) (*you*) (go) (Friday)?

Matsuzawa did not provide any reliability information about his tests, but he did provide descriptive statistics that indicate that his test was reasonably well centered and spreading students out fairly well ($k = 30$; $M = 14.95$; $SD = 4.43$). Based on these statistics, we were able to calculate a K-R21 estimate of the internal consistency reliability of his test, which turned out to be a moderate .63.

One other study worth mentioning here is that by Anderson-Hsieh, Riney, and Koehler (1994). They developed and used a productive test of what they called connected speech simplifications. It involved reading aloud 15 sentences adapted from a pronunciation book (Prator & Robinett, 1985). The sentences involved many instances of word boundary consonant clusters. The student output was analyzed linguistically to understand the students' linking, flapping, vowel reduction, deletion, and epenthesis abilities. While the procedure was designed to be an elicitation device rather than an assessment tool, with the addition of some way to score the output, a procedure along these lines could possibly be developed into a test of the students abilities to produce reduced forms.

Those procedures that were used as tests by researchers over the years appear to have worked reasonably well. However, they seem to lack a bit in imagination: Brown and Hilferty (1982, 1986a, 1986b) used their reduced-forms dictation and reported on it many times, and the rest of the researchers all used slight variations of the Bowen (1975b, 1976) IGT. Are there other types of tests that teachers can use in their classrooms to assess the students' abilities to understand and produce reduced forms? We will take up some of those possibilities next.

Ideas for Classroom Testing of Reduced Forms

Ito (in chapter 2 of this volume), points to a number of "classic activities such as dictation (e.g., Norris, 1995), read-aloud exercises (e.g., Celce-Murcia, Brinton, & Goodwin, 2004; Dauer, 1993), cloze exercises (e.g., Hewings & Goldstein, 1998; Kobayashi & Linde, 1984; Norris, 1995), and listen-and-repeat exercises (e.g., Gimson, 1975; Kobayashi & Linde, 1984) that have often been proposed for instruction on reduced forms." In fairness, Ito (in chapter 2 of this volume) pointed out that such classical activities "may be restricted in terms of their effectiveness in that they do not involve any meaningful communication," and suggests focus on form types of activities as an alternative.

We feel that virtually all of these "activities" can be adapted to help teachers assess their students' abilities to understand and produce the reduced forms they have learned in class (note that Cahill, in chapter 8 of this book, also supplies a number of activities that could be adapted for assessment purposes). Let's begin by considering some examples of classic activities that can be used to test reduced forms and then look at more communicative possibilities.

Classical activities used to test reduced-forms

We began listing the assessment activities in this section with the three mentioned by Ito in chapter 2 of this book: read-aloud, cloze exercises, and listen-and-repeat activities. Soon however, we realized that each of those has variations, and we began to think of other possibilities as well.

Reduced-forms read-aloud tests

One way to use read-aloud procedures to assess students' abilities to produce reduced forms would be to adapt to assessment purposes the data elicitation procedure reported in Anderson-Hsieh, Riney, and Koehler (1994). This would involve developing a passage (perhaps a dialog written to mimic spoken language would be most natural for reduced forms) with word combinations that would involve using whatever reduced forms the teacher wants to focus on and have the students read that passage aloud with the instruction that they should use as many reduced forms as possible. If their rendition of the passage were recorded on a cassette tape or digitally using the recorder program on a PDA, an mp3 player, an MD recorder, and so forth, the teacher would then be able to rate their ability to produce reduced forms by marking a copy of the original script to be used in giving students feedback on their performances. Naturally the number of correct reduced forms (from among those being tested) could become a score on the test as well.

One major disadvantage of any read-aloud assessment is that a clear-and-precise-citation-forms reading of a written text is technically not wrong. Even if students have been told to read the passage with reductions, it is a somewhat unnatural task. After all, reductions are about oral language. Perhaps having students read (in pairs) a dialog written to be like oral language is one way to at least partially mitigate this problem. Teachers will have to decide if the advantages (relatively fast way of getting students to produce language while controlling what the students will have to say) outweigh the disadvantages of using read-aloud procedures.

Reduced-forms cloze exercises

This type of assessment can take many forms, but the most common would be the cloze fill-in dictation dialog, which can be developed from any dialog that purposely uses reduced forms. The advantage of this cloze version of the reduced-forms dictation is that students may not feel quite so overwhelmed as they do with the full version because the assessment is a bit more focused such that students can listen for specific words and phrases. For example, the reduced-forms dictation shown above (adapted reported in Brown & Hilferty, 1982, 1986a, 1986b) could be further adapted such that the script would be the same, but the answer sheet would be more focused on the reduced forms of *going to, got to, have to,* and *want to* as follows:

David: Whenerya goin' ta New York?
Alice: I'm gonna go on Tuesday.
David: Boy! I wish I were gettin' ouda here fer awhile. Ya gotcher plane ticket?
Alice: Naw. I've gotta gedit tomorra.
David: Whaddya hafta do in New York?
Alice: I gotta deliver some products, but I also wanna do sum sightseeing.
David: Where'll ya go?

Alice: I wanna gedouda Manhattan 'n see the Statue of Liberty.
David: 'kay, hav' a goo time.
Alice: Mmkay, g'bye.

David: When are you ___ ___ New York?
Alice: I am ____ ____ go on Tuesday.
David: Boy! I wish I were getting out of here for awhile. You got your plane ticket?
Alice: No. I have ___ ___ get it tomorrow.
David: What do you ___ ___ do in New York?
Alice: I have ___ __ deliver some products, but I also ___ ___ do some sightseeing.
David: Where will you go?
Alice: I ___ ___ get out of Manhattan and see the Statue of Liberty.
David: Okay, have a good time.
Alice: Okay, goodbye.
14 possible (counting words in blanks only)

Reduced-forms listen-and-repeat tests

One type of reduced-forms listen-and-repeat test would involve the students listening to the teacher read each line from the following dictation and repeating it. After instruction on the reduced forms of *going to*, *got to*, *have to*, and *want to*, the teacher might choose to do this with each student and attend to (and score) only those reduced forms in bold italics in the following example (14 possible points counting words in bold italics only):

David: Whenerya **goin' ta** New York?
  [student repeats]
Alice: I'm **gonna** go on Tuesday.
  [student repeats]
David: Boy! I wish I were gettin' ouda here fer awhile. Ya gotcher plane ticket?
  [student repeats]
Alice: Naw. I've **gotta** gedit tomorra.
  [student repeats]
David: Whaddya **hafta** do in New York?
  [student repeats]
Alice: I **gotta** deliver some products, but I also **wanna** do sum sightseeing.
  [student repeats]
David: Where'll ya go?
  [student repeats]
Alice: I **wanna** gedouda Manhattan 'n see the Statue of Liberty.
  [student repeats]
David: 'kay, hav' a goo time.
  [student repeats]
Alice: Mmkay, g'bye.
  [student repeats]
14 possible (counting words in bold italics only)

Other reduced-forms testing ideas

Partial reduced-forms dictations

Another variation of the reduced-forms dictation that might prove particularly useful
for students who are having trouble dealing with full-fledged reduced-forms dictations
would be the partial reduced-forms dictation, which would provide them with a bit
more written context to work with. In a partial reduced-forms dictation, the students
would once again hear the entire dialog as follows:

David: Whenerya goin' ta New York?
Alice: I'm gonna go on Tuesday.
David: Boy! I wish I were gettin' ouda here fer awhile. Ya gotcher plane ticket?
Alice: Naw. I've gotta gedit tomorra.
David: Whaddya hafta do in New York?
Alice: I gotta deliver some products, but I also wanna do sum sightseeing.
David: Where'll ya go?
Alice: I wanna gedouda Manhattan 'n see the Statue of Liberty.
David: 'kay, hav' a goo time.
Alice: Mmkay, g'bye.

In the partial dictation, the students would only have to write in the words spoken
by one of the characters, in which case the student's answer sheet would look like
the following:

David: Whenerya goin' ta New York?
Alice: _____ .
David: Boy! I wish I were gettin' ouda here fer awhile. Ya gotcher plane ticket?
Alice: _____ . _____ .
David: Whaddya hafta do in New York?
Alice: _____ , _____ .
David: Where'll ya go?
Alice: _____ .
David: 'kay, hav' a goo time.
Alice: _____ , _____ .
25 possible (counting reduced forms in blanks only)

Such a partial dictation could even be more focused by blanking out only those words
involved in reduction, in which case the students answer sheet would look like
the following:

David: Whenerya goin' ta New York?
Alice: _____ on Tuesday.
David: Boy! I wish I were gettin' ouda here fer awhile. Ya gotcher plane ticket?
Alice: _____ . I _____ .
David: Whaddya hafta do in New York?
Alice: I _____ deliver some products, but I also_____ do _____ sightseeing.
David: Where'll ya go?
Alice: I _____ Manhattan ___ see the Statue of Liberty.
David: 'kay, hav' a goo time.
Alice: _____ , _____ .
25 possible (counting reduced forms in blanks only)

Reduced-forms dialog comprehension

To test for listening comprehension and focus the students on the meaning of what the dialog characters are saying, the teacher could read (or play a tape of) a reduced-forms dictation like the one repeatedly given above and ask comprehension questions like the following:

David: Whenerya goin' ta New York?
Alice: I'm gonna go on Tuesday.
David: Boy! I wish I were gettin' ouda here fer awhile. Ya gotcher plane ticket?
Alice: Naw. I've gotta gedit tomorra.
David: Whaddya hafta do in New York?
Alice: I gotta deliver some products, but I also wanna do sum sightseeing.
David: Where'll ya go?
Alice: I wanna gedouda Manhattan 'n see the Statue of Liberty.
David: 'kay, hav' a goo time.
Alice: Mmkay, g'bye.

1.   When is Alice going to New York?
2.   Has Alice already got her plane ticket?
3.   What does Alice have to do in New York?
4.   What does Alice also want to do in New York?
5.   Where will Alice go in New York?

Reduced-forms dialog dictocomp

In this sort of test, the students should probably hear the dialog two or three times, before picking up their pencils. They would then be asked to write down as much of the conversation as they can remember. The teacher could then grade them for the number of idea units the students managed to remember and write down.

Testing sentence stress

Sentence stress is a concept that underlies the whole notion of a stress-timed language like English and the reduced forms that result from stress timing. One way to test sentence stress would be a variation of the read-aloud test discussed above. Ask students to read aloud one or more of the following nursery rhymes while they tap the stress points:

Jack and Jill Went Up the Hill...*by Mother Goose*

> Jack and Jill went up the hill,
> To fetch a pail of water;
> Jack fell down, and broke his crown,
> And Jill came tumbling after.

Baa, Baa, Black Sheep...*by Mother Goose*

> Baa, baa, black sheep,
> Have you any wool?
> Yes sir, yes sir,
> Three bags full;
>
> One for my master,
> One for my dame,
> And one for the little boy
> That lives in our lane.

Jack be Nimble...*by Mother Goose*

> Jack be nimble,
> And Jack be quick;
> And Jack jump over
> The candlestick.

Little Miss Muffet...*by Mother Goose*

> Little Miss Muffet
> Sat on a tuffet,
> Eating of curds and whey;
> Along came a spider,
> And sat down beside her,
> And frightened Miss Muffet away.

Then grade the students for the number of rhythmically correct lines (or stress points) read and give students feedback on where they went wrong on a handout containing the nursery rhymes. It might prove useful to read the nursery rhymes aloud (or play a tape) first and allow the students some time to practice alone or in pairs.

Minimal contrast tests

After teaching low-level students how vowel dropping works in English, you can test their ability to distinguish words with dropped vowels from words without them as follows: Have the students create an answer sheet in their notebooks with the numbers 1–10 down the left side. Tell them that they will now hear 10 word pairs and that, in each pair, the vowel at the beginning of one of the words will be dropped. They are to write down a "1" if the vowel is dropped in the first word, or a "2" if it is dropped in the second word. Here are some example word pairs:

> 'round – around
> away – 'way
> okay – 'kay
> 'llot – allot
> 'llow – allow
> annoy – 'nnoy
> 'nother – another
> ahold – 'hold
> along – 'long
> awhile – 'while

For more advanced students, the same procedures can be used to test their comprehension of contrasts in phrases like the following:

> okay, I'll do it – 'kay, I'll do it
> it seems like – 'tseems like
> 'fyou like – if you like
> 'llot of people – allot of people
> 'round 10:00 o'clock – around 10:00 o'clock
> along the way – 'long the way
> awhile ago – 'while ago
> 'round the corner – around the corner
> away from here – 'way from here
> annoying guy – 'nnoying guy

Hearing and production of inserted /j/ or /w/ sounds

Prepare a test with the following words on it. Be sure to underline the vowels as shown. Remind the students that /j/ and /w/ sounds are added between vowels in some words when those vowels cross syllable boundaries. Slowly read the words to them (or play a cassette tape of them) and ask the students to circle the words where a /j/ should be inserted and underline those where a /w/ should be inserted:

easy, evaluate, archeology, habitual, appeal, earn, shear, diabetes, ear, purveyor, affiliate (v.), bear, coed, field, idea, broad, hierarchy, earn, coordinate, groan, hygiene, creak, feast, cornea, east, psychoanalysis, early, deodorize, pause, and peon.

Alternatively, you can have the students read the following words into a recording device and score them for correct /j/ and /w/ insertions (or have them read the words in pairs taking turns, while the partner checks for correct insertions of /j/ and /w/):

hear, fiery, retrieve, mower, pleasure, influence, scenario, breast, glower, bower, dour, shower, caustic, dean, rayon, Co-opt, create, bias, deceive, caution, creak, Illinoian, defeat, bread, priest, flower, fraud, heard, orient, and friend.

An alternative sort of test (like the following but without the Xs) could be used to check the students' abilities to detect inserted /j/ and /w/ sounds. Read the following words (or play a tape of them). Instruct the students that they must decide whether /j/, /w/, or *nothing* has been inserted. They should answer by making an X or check mark in the appropriate box:

word/phrase	/j/	/w/	nothing
groan			X
bias	X		
coed		X	
genuine		X	
high over	X		
creak			X
Illinoian	X		
[pause]			X
plea agreement	X		
radio announcer	X	X	
allow us		X	
toy ox	X		
easy			X
you ask		X	

Multiple-choice discrimination test for simple consonant transitions

After teaching the four different ways simple transitions occur when two consonants occur across word boundaries, the following multiple-choice reduced-forms discrimination test (naturally without the Xs) could be used to check for their understanding of the four different types of simple consonant transition. For each phrase, the students must select one of the four possible pronunciations for the consonant that ends the first word by making an X or check mark in the appropriate box:

word pairs	no change; smooth transition	become one long consonant	first consonant unreleased	first consonant unreleased glottal stop
are red		X		
bass fishing	X			
cake pan			X	
change pants	X			
credit tip		X		
fine day	X			
hot gun				X
if guys	X			
Irish lassie	X			
kick box			X	
less stress		X		
let me				X

Hearing and production of assimilations /d/ to /b/ before bilabial /p b m/

The phoneme /d/ assimilates to /b/ at a syllable boundary before the bilabial phonemes /p b m/, but not in front of other consonants and vowels. After teaching this concept, the following multiple-option reduced-forms discrimination test (naturally without the Xs) could be used to check for their understanding of the environments in which /d/ assimilates to /b/. Read the following phrases (or play a cassette tape of them) and instruct the students to decide what happens to the /d/ at the end of the first word and select whether the */d/ becomes /b/* or the */d/ remains /d/* by marking an X or check mark in the appropriate box:

phrase	/d/ becomes /b/	/d/ remains /d/
bad dog		X
bad mouth	X	
bad time		X
crowd pleaser	X	
Dad decided		X
dead person	X	
flood plain	X	
good boy	X	
good morning	X	
good point	X	
good way		X
had been	X	

had more	X	
had taken		X
had wanted		X
head back,	X	
head over		X
odd kind		X
odd man	X	
red book	X	
sad day		X
sad moment	X	
speed by	X	
speed around		X
Ted pushed.	X	

Similar tests could be developed for other sorts of anticipatory, progressive, and reciprocal assimilations that occur on English (see for instance, Avery & Ehrlich, 1992; Celce-Murcia, Brinton, & Goodwin, 2004; or Brown, forthcoming).

Would similar tests work for other languages?

Naturally, English is not the only language that uses reduced forms in its spoken versions. For example, one of the authors was a French major at the undergraduate level and was taught the concept of liaison right along with the phonemes of French.

Example tests of French reduction

With the appropriate modifications, a test of French liaison could easily be developed.

For instance, at one level, students could be asked to rewrite each of the phrases below correctly adding all appropriate dashes, contractions, and letters to make the pronunciation smooth (answer key in italics).

Ce est moi.	*C'est moi*	1 point
Je y vais.	*J'y vais.*	1 point
Je me appele Jean.	*Je m'appele Jean.*	1 point
Je en suis sûr.	*J'en suis sur.*	1 point
Que sais je?	*Que sais-je?*	1 point
Ce que le on a dit.	*Ce que l'on a dit.*	1 point
Coup de oeil.	*Coup d'oeil.*	1 point
Je ai donc du choisir.	*J'ai donc du choisir.*	1 point
Je ne ai pas trop.	*Je n'ai pas trop.*	1 point
Est ce que il y a assez?	*Est-ce qu'il y a assez?*	2 points
Est ce que il y en a assez?	*Est-ce qu' il y en a assez?*	2 points
A il un moment?	*A-t-il un moment*	3 points
		16 points total

At another level, students could be asked to examine each pair of bold-faced phrases below. In each pair, one phrase should be pronounced with a liaison. Mark the ties (e.g., **mes amis**) in the phrase that involves liaison in each pair (answer key provided).

Les pommes	Les enfants.
Nous allons demain	Nous venons demain.
Comment ca va?	Comment allez-vous?
Est-ce que **vous avez** l'heure?	Est-ce que **vous venez** souvent.
Les arbres	Les fleurs
Saint Bernard	Saint Ignace
Je **suis** content.	Je **suis** amoureux.
C'est incroyable.	C'est moi.
Des enfant…	Des bananes…
Elle **fait assez**…	Elle **fait** souvent…

Clearly then, teaching and testing reduced forms is not just about English as a second or foreign language. But perhaps it is just about European languages. Clearly that is not true as illustrated by the examples in the following section.

Example tests of Japanese reduction

The following test will measure the students' ability to hear nasal syllabicization [N] that takes place in Japanese causal speech. As seen in previous chapters (chapters 10 and 11 of this book), there are various instances of nasal syllabicization in Japanese. This test focuses on [N] that takes place (a) within a *u*-verb that ends with the /r/ phoneme in the stem before the negative suffix –*nai* [N-nai] or the imperative suffix –*nasai* [N nasai] (see chapter 10 of this book), and (b) within the potential suffix -*rare* used for a *ru*-verb before the negative suffix -*nai* [raNnai] (see chapter 11 of this book).

The examinees should be told the following: While listening to the recorded tape, complete the following casual exchanges in Japanese by choosing the item you hear. [Note: The test items will be written in Japanese only. Correct answers or what the students will hear are marked by the sharp symbol # .]

Q1. A: この問題の答えわかる？　　B: ( ) わからない。　　/wakara nai/
　　　　　　　　　　　　　　　　　 ( ) わかんない。　　#/wakan nai/

Q2. A: これ、使う？　　　　　　　B: ( ) 使わない。　　#/tsukawa nai/
　　　　　　　　　　　　　　　　　 ( ) 使んない。　　*/tsukan nai/

Q3. A: 漢字が ( ) 覚えられないよ。　/oboerare nai yo/　　　B: あたしも。
　　　　 ( ) 覚えらんないよ。　#/oboeran nai yo/　　　B: あたしも。

Q4. A: ただいま！　　　　　　　　B: ( ) おかえりなさい。　　/okaeri-nasai/
　　　　　　　　　　　　　　　　　 ( ) おかえんなさい。　　#/okaen-nasai/

Q5. A: まだ起きてんの。早く ( ) 寝なさい。　#/ne-nasai/　　B: はあい。
　　　　　　　　　　　　( ) 寝んさい。　*/ne-nsai/　　B: はあい。

Q6. A: プールの水、冷たすぎて ( ) 入れないよ。 #/haire nai yo/
　　　　　　　　　　　　　　　　　　　　　　　B: そんなに冷たい？
　　　　　　　　( ) 入んないよ。 */hain nai yo/
　　　　　　　　　　　　　　　　　　　　　　　B: そんなに冷たい？

The following items test the students' knowledge of what Hasegawa (see chapter 10 of this book) calls "Less Sonorous Vowel Deletion." The students will be asked to change the underlined *te*-form verbs before one of the auxiliary verb/-oku/, /-iru/, /-iku/, or /-ageru/ using the reduced form.

The examinees should be told the following: Make the following casual utterances more natural by rewriting the underlined predicates using the reduced form. [Note: The test items will be written in Japanese only. The answers are provided in parentheses.]

Q1.　今晩のおかずもう<u>買っておいた</u>/katte-oita/よ。
　　　　　　（買っといた/kattoita/）

Q2.　　晩ご飯用意して<u>待っている</u>/matte-iru/から、早く帰ってきてね。
　　　　　　（待ってる/matteru/）

Q3.　このクッキー、友達の家に<u>持っていって</u>/motte-itte/いい？
　　　　　　（持ってって/mottette/）

Q4.　今晩遅くなるから、先に晩御飯<u>食べていて</u>/tabete-ite/ね。
　　　　　　（食べてて/tabetete/）

Q5.　この洗濯物。外に<u>ほしておく</u>/hoshite-oku/ね。
　　　　　　（ほしとく/hoshitoku/）

Q6.　母さんが行けないんだったら、代わりに私が<u>行ってあげる</u>/itte-ageru/よ。
　　　　　　（行 ったげる/ittageru/）

The following test will check the student's ability to comprehend a paragraph-level working-class male speech, which is characterized by a frequent use of the vowel fusion (e.g., /omae/ → /om<u>ee</u>/; see chapter 10). The speech also includes many other instances of causal markers such as vowel elisions (e.g., /yatte-iru/→/yatt<u>eru</u>/), nasal syllabicization (e.g., /nonde iru no/ → /no<u>n</u> den no/), contractions/reductions (e.g., /kure-reba/→ /kurer<u>ya</u>/, /shite wa/→/shi<u>cha</u>/). It also includes instances of assimilation *rendaku* (/hito tasuke/→ /hito<u>d</u>asuke/) and transition (/ko o omou/→ /ko<u>oo</u>mou/; for more on this topic, see Toda in chapter 11 of this book).

The examinees should be told the following: Listen to the recorded monologue. The speaker is Jiro, a working-class, middle-aged man. He is talking to his friend, Satoshi, at a bar. After you listen to the tape, answer the questions below in English with as much detail as possible. [Note: Right below the Japanese transcription, the Roman letter version is provided. Answers to the questions are provided in parentheses.]

[The student will listen to the following monologue once.]

おめえ、まだ飲んでんの？そんなに飲んじゃ、体によかねえよ。

おめえんちの長男、アフリカで人助けやってんだって。てえした者じゃ
ねえか。そりゃ、親が子を思う分だけ子が親を思ってくれりゃ、問題ね
えだろうよ。でも、せん中そういかねえんだよ。子に捨てられたなんて
いっちゃいけねえよ。子が家を出てっくのはあたりめえなんだからさ。
あっちが幸せなりゃ、それでいんじゃねえか。

[The target sound changes are underlined.]

<u>Omee</u>, mada nond<u>en</u> no? Sonna ni non<u>jya</u>, karada ni yo<u>ka nee</u> yo.

<u>Omee n chi</u> no choonan, afurika de hito <u>dasuke</u> yatt<u>en</u> datte. <u>Teeshita</u> mon <u>ja nee</u> ka. <u>Sorya</u>, oya ga <u>kooomou</u> bun dake ko ga oya o omotte kurer<u>ya</u> mond<u>ee nee</u> daroo yo. Demo, yo <u>n</u> naka soo ika<u>nee n</u> da yo. Ko ni <u>s(u)terareta</u> nante <u>iccha</u> ike

nee yo. Koga ie o dete<u>kku</u> no wa atare<u>imee</u> na<u>n</u> dakara sa. A<u>cchi</u> ga shiawase na<u>rya</u>, kore de <u>in</u> <u>ja</u> <u>nee</u> ka.

1. What is Jiro's concern for Satoshi? [Jiro is concerned that Satoshi is drinking too much and it won't be good for his health.]
2. What does Jiro think of Satoshi's son? Why? [Jiro is impressed by Satoshi's son because he is helping people in Africa.]
3. What general view does Jiro have about children in relation to their parents? [If children think of their parents as much as the parents think of them, there may be no problem, but that's not how things are in this world. Also, it is natural for children to leave home.]
4. What is Jiro's advice for Satoshi about his son? [Don't say your son abandoned you. If your son is happy, it's a good thing, isn't it?]

Communicative activities used to test reduced-forms

As mentioned earlier, Ito (in chapter 2 of this book) advocated the use of focus-on-form types of activities. Here, I would like to consider the application of such activities to the testing of reduced forms. According to Ito, such activities should

*   Be communicative.
*   Be based on authentic materials (she argues that real life authentic materials are bound to contain many examples of reduced forms).
*   Be interactional (in the sense that it involves both speaking and listening, where *speaking* "involves the speaking skills that are required for meaningful communication" and *listening* is not just "'listen and fill in the blank,' but is the skill that learners need in order to communicate effectively").
*   Be tasks that include crucial reduced forms ("in which listeners must rely on specific reduced forms to comprehend the speaker's meaning. If the listener fails to understand the reduced forms, communication breakdown will occur and lead to the failure to achieve the task.").
*   Engage learners in both form and meaning.
*   Follow the principle of focus on form.

If communicative task-based teaching activities are being used to teach reduced forms, it would make sense to use such communicative task-based testing to test word stress, sentence stress and timing, reduction, citation and weak forms of words, elision, intrusion, assimilation, juncture, and contraction. To expand Ito's list a bit, Brown (2005, pp. 21–24) lists the following characteristics of a communicative test in terms of communicative test-setting requirements and bases for rating communicative performances:

*   Communicative test-setting requirements:
    Meaningful communication
    Authentic situation
    Unpredictable language input
    Creative language output
    All language skills (including reading, writing, listening, and speaking)

*   Bases for ratings:
    Success in getting meanings across
    Use focus rather than usage
    New components to be rated

An example of such an assessment task for advanced learners might have directions as in the following:

Example directions

> Listen to the message from your "boss" on the phone machine in front of you; do what your boss requests by looking at the five hotel pamphlets next to the phone; read those pamphlets and take whatever notes you need; then, leave a return message for your boss as required. You will be scored on how well you succeed in accomplishing the task and on your use of reduced forms.

Example message

> "Hi, I'm going out of town next Monday for a convention in Topeka, Kansas. Could you look at the pamphlets I sent over to you and decide which of the five hotels I should stay at? I will need a hotel that has a business center, Internet access in the rooms, and a fitness room with a bicycle machine. Also the hotel must be within walking distance of the convention center, which means no more than one-half mile, and the check out time should be no earlier than noon (or similar requirements as the test designer wishes). Let me know which hotel would be best and how it meets my needs."

Hotel pamphlets

You will also need to develop five pamphlets, one of which meets all the bosses requirements, and the other five of which either clearly do not meet those requirements in one way or the other or don't provide sufficient information to know if they do.

Examinee's job

Clearly, it is the examinee's job to look at the five *hotel pamphlets* and decide which one would best suit the boss, then leave a message on the phone machine for the boss with his/her recommendation for a hotel and in what ways that hotel meets the needs of the boss.

Scoring

The scoring of the task could be done in a variety of ways, but the focus should be on the degree of success in completing the task and on comprehension and production of reduced forms.

Obviously, though it meets the criteria listed above (from Ito, this volume, and Brown, 2005), such a task is quite involved and time consuming. To enhance its usability, it could be done in a language lab with the lab playback and recording devices substituting for a telephone answering machine. The scoring could then also be done from a central console. Computer-assisted or Internet-assisted versions of such a task would also be more efficient (for more on designing and scoring such performance tests, see Norris, Brown, Hudson, & Yoshioka, 1998, and Brown, Hudson, Norris, & Bonk, 2002).

Some other alternative forms of assessment

Other forms of pedagogically related assessment (discussed in Brown, 2005; Brown & Hudson, 2002; with examples shown in Brown, 1998) may also prove helpful like portfolios, conferences, and self- or peer-assessments. Reduced-forms *portfolios* could be useful for encouraging students to recognize reduced forms when they hear them and recognize their prevalence in native speech. Such a portfolio might take the form of a cassette or video-tape of authentic language that the students have collected form native speakers with notes and reflections on where and how the language was reduced by those native speakers. One variation might be a listening journal in which students would keep track of reduced forms they have encountered in native speech.

Reduced-forms *conferences* could be used to allow students relatively informal and private time to ask about and receive feedback on reduced forms they had encountered (and perhaps recorded in their listening journals). Such conferences could also be used to give students feedback on specific problems the teacher had noticed the students having in class with reduced forms.

Reduced-forms *peer-assessments* or *self-assessments* could be used to help students understand the sorts of things a rater would be listening for in rating their abilities to understand and use reduced forms. For example, students could be asked to perform in some way, perhaps making a presentation to the class or doing a pair work task. If categories (e.g., use of schwa, elision, juncture, progressive assimilation, reciprocal assimilation) were worked out in advance with the students and defined (say in a scoring grid that described good, moderate, and poor performance in each category), the students would better understand what was expected of them when they perform. They would then be able to rate each other in a peer-assessment mode, or if the performances were audio- or video-taped, they could do self-assessments. My experience is that the students will also want some form of teacher feedback or score, but that does not take away from the awareness-raising benefits of having them first do peer- or self-assessments.

Conclusion

Readers may have noticed that many of the test formats in this book look like exercises that a teacher might use in teaching reduced forms. That would be a correct observation. And why not? Shouldn't the tests designed to assess students' abilities to understand or produce reduced forms be the same as the activities/exercises used to teach those same topics? Put another way, shouldn't the tests used to assess students' accomplishments in a course be related to the curriculum and materials they used in attaining those accomplishments? Or put yet a third way, why should students be tested differently from the way they are taught? What would that accomplish?

Perhaps the single difference between activities/exercises and tests/assessments is that tests/assessments result in a score or some other form of feedback on the student's performances to the students themselves (and possibly to their teachers, parents, administrators, and any other interested parties).

Are reduced-forms tests different from other tests? No. Essentially what we have illustrated in this chapter is that most of the various sorts of tests that teachers have been using for years to test other aspects of language can also be used, or at least adapted with a little imagination, to test the various aspects of reduced forms (word stress, sentence stress and timing, reduction, citation, and weak forms of words, elision, intrusion, assimilation, juncture, and contraction). In short, an inability to test reduced forms is no longer a justification for not teaching them.

References

101 Languages of the World [Computer software]. (1993). Nashua, NH: Transparent Language.

Akita, M. (2002). *The developmental stages of the acquisition of schwa by Japanese learners of English*. Poster session presented at the annual meeting of the Linguistic Society of America, San Francisco.

Anderson-Hsieh, J. (1992). Using electronic visual feedback to teach suprasegmentals. *System, 20*(1), 51–62. Retrieved June 17, 2005, from Linguistics and Language Behavior Abstracts database.

Anderson-Hsieh, J. (1996). Teaching suprasegmentals to Japanese learners of English through electronic visual feedback. *JALT Journal, 18*(2), 315–325.

Anderson-Hsieh, J., Riney, T., & Koehler, K. (1994). Connected speech modifications in the English of Japanese ESL learners. *Issues and Developments in English and Applied Lingusitics, 7*, 31–52.

Avery, P., & Ehrlich, S. (1992). *Teaching American English pronunciation*. Oxford, England: Oxford University Press.

Azar, B. S. (1996). *Basic English grammar* (2nd ed.). Upper Saddle River, NJ: Prentice Hall Regents.

Bley-Vroman, R., & Kweon, S.-O. (2002). Acquisition of the constraints on *wanna* contraction by advanced second language learners: Universal grammar and imperfect knowledge. Paper presented in the University of Hawai'i Department of SLS Brownbag Series, Honolulu.

Bolinger, D. (1965). *Aspects of language*. New York: Harcourt, Brace, Jovanovich.

Bond, K. (2001). Reduced forms. *Karen's linguistic issues*. Retrieved July 6, 2003, from http://www3.telus.net/linguisticsissues/ReducedForms.html

Borden, G. J., Harris, K. S., & Rapheal, L. J. (1994). *Speech science primer: Physiology, acoustics, and perception of speech*. Baltimore, MD: Williams & Wilkins.

Bowen, J. D. (1975a). *Patterns of English pronunciation*. Rowley, MA: Newbury House.

Bowen, J. D. (1975b). An experimental integrative test of English grammar. *Working Papers in Teaching English as a Second Language, 9*, 3–17.

Bowen, J. D. (1976). Current research on an integrative test of English grammar. *RELC Journal, 7*, 30–37.

Bowen, J. D. (1977). The integrative grammar test: A further note. *RELC Journal, 8*, 94–95.

Brown, A. (1995). Minimal pairs: Minimal importance? *ELT Journal, 49*(2), 169–175.

Brown, G. (1990). *Listening to spoken English* (2nd ed.). London: Longman.

Brown, H. D. (2001). *Teaching by principles: An interactive approach to language pedagogy* (2nd ed.). Upper Saddle River, NJ: Prentice Hall Regents.

Brown, J. D. (1988). *Understanding research in second language learning.* New York: Cambridge University.

Brown, J. D. (2005). *Testing in language programs: A comprehensive guide to English language assessment.* New York: McGraw-Hill.

Brown, J. D. (Ed.). (1998). *New ways of classroom assessment.* Washington, DC: Teachers of English to Speakers of Other Languages.

Brown, J. D. (forthcoming). *Shaping students' pronunciation: Teaching the connected speech of North American English.* Unpublished manuscript, University of Hawai'i at Mānoa.

Brown, J. D., & Hilferty, A. G. (1982). The effectiveness of teaching reduced forms for listening comprehension. Paper presented at the TESOL Convention, Honolulu, Hawai'i.

Brown, J. D., & Hilferty, A. G. (1986a). Listening for reduced forms. *TESOL Quarterly, 20*(4), 759–763.

Brown, J. D., & Hilferty, A. G. (1986b). The effectiveness of teaching reduced forms for listening comprehension. *RELC Journal, 17*(2), 59–70.

Brown, J. D., & Hilferty, A. G. (1989). Teaching reduced forms. *Modern English Teaching,* January issue, 26–28.

Brown, J. D., & Hilferty, A. G. (1995). Comprehending reduced forms. In D. Nunan, & L. Miller (Eds.), *New ways in teaching listening* (pp. 124–127). Alexandria, VA: TESOL.

Brown, J. D., & Hilferty, A. G. (1998). Reduced-forms dictations. In J. D. Brown (Ed.), *New ways of classroom assessment* (pp. 324–327). Washington, DC: TESOL.

Brown, J. D., & Hudson, T. (2002). *Criterion-referenced language testing.* Cambridge, England: Cambridge University Press.

Brown, J. D., Hudson, T., Norris, J. M., & Bonk, W. (2002). *Investigating second language performance assessments.* Honolulu: Second Language Teaching & Curriculum Center, University of Hawai'i Press.

Buck, G. (1995). How to become a good listening teacher. In D. J. Mendelsohn & J. Rubin, (Eds.), *A guide for the teaching of second language listening* (pp. 113–131). San Diego, CA: Dominie.

Burns, I. (1992). Pronunciation-based listening exercises. In P. Avery & S. Ehrlich (Eds.), *Teaching American English pronunciation* (pp. 197–205). Hong Kong: Oxford University.

Byun, H.-G. (2004). Nihon zaijyuu no kankokujin nihongo gakushuusha ni okeru boin no museeka (Vowel devoicing in Korean and Japaense: The case of Korean learners of Japanese living in Japan). *Nihongo kyooiku, 122*, 12–21.

Canale. M. (1983). From communicative competence to communicative language pedagogy. In J. Richards & H. Schmidt (Eds.), *Language and communication* (pp. 2–27). London: Longman.

Carter, R., Hughes, R., & McCarthy, M.f (1998). Telling tails: Grammar, the spoken language and materials development. In B. Tomlinson (Ed.), *Materials development in language teaching* (pp. 67–86). Cambridge, England: Cambridge University.

Celce-Murcia, M., Brinton, D. M., & Goodwin, J. M. (2004). *Teaching pronunciation: A reference for teachers of English to speakers of other languages*. New York: Cambridge University.

Chaudron, C. (1983). Simplification of input: Topic reinstatements and their effects on L2 learners' recognition and recall. *TESOL Quarterly, 17*(3), 437–458.

Cho, T., & Ladefoged, P. (1999). Variation and universals in VOT: Evidence from 18 languages. *Journal of Phonetics, 27*, 207–229.

Chomsky, N., & Halle, M. (1968). *The second pattern of English*. New York: Harper & Row.

Clarey, M. E., & Dixson, R. J. (1963). *Pronunciation exercises in English*. New York: Regents.

Coleman, H. (1977). The integrative grammar test: A comment. *RELC Journal, 8*, 91–93.

Cook, H. M. (2001). Why can't learners of JFL distinguish polite from impolite speech styles? In K. R. Rose & G. Kasper (Eds.), *Pragmatics in language teaching* (pp. 80–102). Cambridge, England: Cambridge University.

Corder, S. P. (1967). The significance of learner's errors. *International Review of Applied Linguistics in Language Teaching, 5*, 161–170.

Cordry, H. V. (1997). *Dictionary of American-English pronunciation*. San Francisco, CA: Austin & Winfield.

Cranen, B., Weltens, B., de Bot, K., & Van Rossum, N. (1984). An aid in language teaching: The visualisation of pitch. *System, 12*, 25–29. Retrieved June 17, 2005, from ERIC database.

Crystal, D. (1980). *A first dictionary of linguistics and phonetics*. London: Deutsch.

Crystal, D. (1997). *A dictionary of linguistics and phonetics* (4th ed.). Cambridge, MA: Blackwell.

Crystal, D. (2003). *A dictionary of linguistics and phonetics* (5th ed.). Cambridge, MA: Blackwell.

Dalton, D., & Seidlhofer, B. (2001). *Pronunciation*. Oxford, England: Oxford University.

Dauer, R. M. (1983). Stress-timing and syllable-timing reanalyzed. *Journal of Phonetics, 11*, 51–62.

Dauer, R. M. (1993). *Accurate English: A complete course in pronunciation*. Englewood Cliffs, NJ: Prentice Hall Regents.

Dauer, R. M., & Browne, S. C. (1992). *Teaching the pronunciation of connected speech*. Paper presented at the 26th annual meeting of TESOL, Vancouver, BC (ERIC Document Reproduction Service No. ED354777).

de Bot, K. (1980). The role of feedback and feedforward in the teaching of pronunciation-an overview. *System, 8*(1), 35–45. Retrieved June 17, 2005, from Linguistics and Language Behavior Abstracts database.

de Bot, K. (1983). Visual feedback of intonation I: Effectiveness and induced practice behaviour. *Language and Speech 26*, 331–335.

de Bot, K., & Mailfert, K. (1982). The teaching of intonation: Fundamental research and classroom applications. *TESOL Quarterly, 16*(1), 70–77. Retrieved June 17, 2005, from ERIC database.

DeKeyser, R. M. (1998). Beyond focus on form: Cognitive perspectives on learning and practicing second language grammar. In C. Doughty & J. Williams (Eds.), *Focus on form in classroom second language acquisition* (pp. 42–63). Cambridge, England: Cambridge University.

Dowd, A., Smith, J., & Wolfe, J. (1998). Learning to pronounce vowel sounds in a foreign language using acoustic measurements of the vocal tract as feedback in real time. *Language and Speech, 41*(1), 1–20.

Dunkel, P. A. (1995). Authentic second/foreign language listening texts: Issues of definition, operationalization, and application. In P. Byrd (Ed.), *Material writer's guide* (pp. 95–106). Boston: Heinle & Heinle.

Eckman, F. R. (1977). Markedness and the contrastive analysis hypothesis. *Language Learning, 27*, 315–330.

Ellis, R. (1985). *Understanding second language acquisition*. Oxford, England: Oxford University.

Erickson, D. (2003). *The jaw as a prominence articulator in American English*. Poster session presented at the annual meeting of the Acoustical Society of Japan, location?.

Erickson, D. (2004, June). *On phrasal organization and jaw opening*. Poster session presented at From Sound to Sense: 50+ Years of Discoveries in Speech Research. Massachusetts Institute of Technology, Cambridge.

Erlam, R. (2003). The Effects of deductive and inductive instruction on the acquisition of direct object pronouns in French as a second language. *The Modern Language Journal, 87*(2), 242–250.

Espy-Wilson, C. Y., Boyce, S. E., Jackson, M., Narayanan, S., & Alwan, A. (2000). Acoustic modeling of American English /r/. *The Journal of the Acoustical Society of America, 108*(1), 343–356.

Excel 2002 SP2 [Computer software]. (2001). Tokyo: Microsoft.

Flege, J. E. (1987). The production of "new" and "similar" phones in a foreign language: Evidence for the effect of equivalence classification. *Journal of Phonetics, 15*, 47–65.

Ford-Niwa, J. (1996). Chokai dictation ni arawareta ayamari no bunseki [Error analysis for listening dictation]. *Tsukuba Daigaku Ryugakusei Senta Nihongo Kyoiku Ronshu [Collections of Tsukuba University Exchange Student Center Japanese Language Research Papers], 11*, 21–39.

Fujisaki, H., Nakamura, K., & Imoto, T. (1975). Auditory perception of duration of speech and non-speech stimuli. In G. Fant & M. A. A. Tatham (Eds.), *Auditory analysis and perception of speech* (pp. 197–219). London: Academic.

Fukui, N. (1986). Leftward spread: Compensatory lengthening and gemination in Japanese. *Linguistic Inquiry, 17*, 359–364.

Gatbonton, E., & Segalowitz, N. (1988). Creative automatization: Principles for promoting fluency within a communicative framework. *TESOL Quarterly, 22*(3), 473–492.

Gilbert, J. (1995). Pronunciation practice as an aid to listening comprehension. In D. J. Mendelsohn & J. Rubin (Eds.), *A guide for the teaching of second language listening* (pp. 97–112). San Diego, CA: Dominie.

Gilbert, J. B. (1984). *Clear speech: Pronunciation and listening comprehension in North American English.* New York: Cambridge University.

Gilbert, J. B. (1993). *Clear speech: Pronunciation and listening comprehension in North American English* (2nd ed.). New York: Cambridge University.

Gimson, A. C. (1962). *An introduction to the pronunciation of English.* London: Arnold.

Gimson, A. C. (1970). *An introduction to the pronunciation of English* (2nd ed.). London: Arnold.

Gimson, A. C. (1975). *A practical course of English pronunciation: A perceptual approach.* London: Edward Arnold.

Gimson, A. C. (revised by Ramsaran, S.) (1989). *An introduction to the pronunciation of English* (4th ed.). London: Arnold.

Gimson, A. C. (revised by Cruttenden, A.). (2001). *Gimson's pronunciation of English* (6th ed.). London: Arnold.

Gitlits, I. (1972). The use of visible speech apparatus in Russian schools for the deaf. *The Teacher of the Deaf, 70*(414), 298–302.

Goto, H. (1971). Auditory perception by normal Japanese adults of the sounds "l" and "r". *Neuropsychologia, 9*, 317–323.

Grant, L. (1993). *Well said.* Boston: Heinle & Heinle.

Griffee, D. T. (1993). *More HearSay: Interactive listening and speaking.* Tokyo: Addison-Wesley Japan.

Griffee, D. T., & Hough, D. (1986). *HearSay: Survival listening and speaking.* Tokyo: Addison-Wesley Japan.

Guilford, J. P., & Fruchter, B. (1973). *Fundamental statistics in psychology and education* (5th ed.). New York: McGraw-Hill.

Guillot, M. (1999). *Fluency and its teaching.* Clevedon, England: Multilingual Matters.

Gunterman, T. (1985). Strategies and methods for English teachers in Japanese high schools. In C. Wordell (Ed.), *A guide to teaching English in Japan* (pp. 125–143). Tokyo: Japan Times.

Gussenhoven, C., & Jacobs, H. (2003). *Understanding phonology.* London: Arnold.

Gussman, E. (2002). *Phonology: Analysis and theory.* Cambridge, England: Cambridge University.

Hagen, S. A. (2000). *Sound advice: A basis for listening.* New York: Pearson Education.

Hakuta, K. (1976). A case study of a Japanese child learning English as a second language. *Language Learning, 26,* 321–351.

Han, M. (1962). The feature of duration in Japanese. *Onsei no Kenkyuu [Phonetic Studies], 10,* 65–80.

Han, M. (1992). The timing control of geminate and single stop consonants in Japanese: A challenge for nonnative speakers. *Phonetica, 49,* 102–127.

Harada, S. (1976). Honorifics. In M. Shibatani (Ed.), *Syntax and semantics 5: Japanese generative grammar* (pp. 499–561). New York: Academic Press.

Hasegawa, N. (1979). Casual speech vs. fast speech. *CLS, 15,* 126–137.

Hasegawa, N. (2005). Honorifics. In M. Everaert & H. van Riemsdijk (Eds.), *The Blackwell companion to syntax* (vol. 2, pp. 493–543). Oxford, England: Blackwell.

Hashi, M., Honda, K., & Westbury, J. R. (2003). Time-varying acoustic and articulatory characteristics of American English [r]: A cross-speaker study. *Journal of Phonetics, 31*(1), 3–22.

Hattori, S. (1960). *Gengogaku no hoho* [Methods of linguistics]. Tokyo: Iwanami Shoten.

Henrichsen, L. E. (1984). Sandhi-variation: A filter of input for learners of ESL. *Language Learning, 34*(3), 103–126.

Henrichsen, L. E., Green, B. A., Nishitani, A., & Bagley, C. L. (2002). *Pronunciation matters: Communicative, story-based activities for mastering the sounds of North American English.* Ann Arbor, MI: University of Michigan.

Hewings, M. (1993a). *Pronunciation tasks: A course for pre-intermediate learners.* Cambridge, England: Cambridge University.

Hewings, M. (1993b). *Pronunciation tasks: A course for pre-intermediate learner (Teacher's book).* Cambridge, England: Cambridge University.

Hewings, M., & Goldstein, S. (1998). *Pronunciation plus—Practice through interaction.* New York: Cambridge University.

Hill, C., & Beebe, L. (1980). Contraction and blending: The use of orthographic clues in teaching pronunciation. *TESOL Quarterly, 14*(3), 299–323.

Hirakata, Y., Igashima, Y., & Sakai, T. (2002). Otohenka no kookatekina ninshiki renshu kaihatsu ni mukete [For developing an effective recognition practice of sound change]. *Nihongo Kyooiku Hoohoo Kenkyuukaishi [Japanese Language Educational Method Journal]*, 9(1), 32–33.

Hirakata, Y. (2003a). *Nihongo Gakushusha no Otohenka no Gochoukai no Chousa to Bunseki-Chugokujin gakushusha o taisho ni shita museka no goyore* [Research and analysis of the Japanese language learners' misunderstanding in listening sound changes: How Chinese students misunderstand voiceless vowel in hearing]. Report of the Grant-in-Aid for Scientific Research (C)(2001–2003), Supported by Japan Society for the Promotion of Science and the Ministry of Education, Science, Sports, and Culture. Project No. 12680296, 28–32.

Hirakata, Y. (2003b). Eiga "Sen and Chihiro no kamikakushi" niokeru otohenka no nendai, seibetsu niyoru tokucho [Analysis of how certain sounds change in speech style and how are these sounds changed by the speaker's sex and ages: Using "Spirited Away"] In T. Sakai (Ed.), *Nihongo jokyu chokai noryoku no sokute-naze kikenai no ka* [How to measure advance Japanese learner's hearing ability: Reasons for difficulties in hearing]. Report of the Grant-in-Aid for Scientific Research (C)(2001–2003) (pp. 1–91). Supported by Japan Society for the Promotion of Science and the Ministry of Education, Science, Sports, and Culture. Project No. 12680296.1–92.

Hirakata, Y., Igashima, Y., & Sakai, T. (2002). Otohenka no kokateki na ninshikirennshu ni mukete [Research on making an effective practice system for listen spoken sounds]. *Japanese Language Educational Method Journal*, 9(2), 32–33.

Hirata, Y. (1990a). Perception of geminated stops in Japanese word and sentence levels. *The Phonetic Society of Japan*, 194, 23–28.

Hirata, Y. (1990b). Perception of geminated stops in Japanese word and sentence levels by English-speaking learners of Japanese language. *The Phonetic Society of Japan*, 195, 4–10.

Hirata, Y. (2004a). Computer assisted pronunciation training for native English speakers learning Japanese pitch and durational contrasts. *Computer Assisted Language Learning*, 17(3–4), 357–376.

Hirata, Y. (2004b). Training native English speakers to perceive Japanese length contrasts in word versus sentence contexts. *Journal of the Acoustical Society of America*, 116(4), 2384–2394.

Hirata, Y. (2004c). Effects of speaking rate on the vowel length distinction in Japanese. *Journal of Phonetics*, 32(4), 565–589.

Hirata, Y. (2004d). MORA: *Good-bye, syllable! Listening training for learners of Japanese*. A CD-ROM available from yhirata@mail.colgate.edu

Hirata, Y., & Lambacher, S. G. (2004). Role of word-external contexts in native speakers' identification of vowel length in Japanese. *Phonetica*, 61, 177–200.

Hirose, Y. (2003). Recycling prosodic boundaries. *Journal of Psycholinguistic Research*, 32(2), 162–195.

Hockett, C. F. (1955). *A manual of phonology*. Indiana University Publications in Anthropology and Linguistics, Memoir 11, Bloomington, IN.

Hough, D. (1995). *Before HearSay: Basic listening for the classroom*. New York: Addison-Wesley.

Hyman, L. M. (1975). *Phonology: Theory and analysis*. New York: Holt Rinehart Winston.

Igashima, Y., Sakai, T., & Hirakata, Y. (2001). Gakushusha nitotte kikitori ga konnanna hanashi kotoba no oto hennka towa -hatsuonka.yoonka on baai- [Where are difficulties in understanding changed sounds in spoken Japanese]. *Japanese Language Educational Method Journal, 8*(2), 26–27.

IPA. (2001). *Handbook of the International Phonetic Association: A guide to the use of the international phonetic alphabet*. Cambridge, England: Cambridge University.

IPA. (2005). The international phonetic association. Reproduction of the international phonetic alphabet (revised 1983, last updated 2005). Retrieved December 1, 2005, from http://www2.arts.gla.ac.uk/IPA/ipachart.html

Ito, Y. (in press). Flapping in Japanese learners' connected speech of English. *Proceedings of the 8th Annual College-Wide Conference for Students in Languages, Linguistics and Literature (LLL) at University of Hawai'i at Mānoa*.

Iwashita, N. (2001). The effect of learner proficiency on interactional moves and modified output in nonnative-native interaction in Japanese as a foreign language. *System, 29*, 267–287.

James, E. F. (1976). The acquisition of prosodic features of speech using a speech visualizer. IRAL, *International Review of Applied Linguistics in Language Teaching, 14*(3), 227–243. Retrieved June 17, 2005, from Linguistics and Language Behavior Abstracts database.

Japanese language proficiency test: Test content specifications. (1993). Japan Foundation and Association of International Education, Japan Foundation.

Jones, D. (1972). *An outline of English phonetics*. Cambridge, England: Cambridge University.

Jones, K., & Ono, T. (2000). Reconciling textbook dialogues and naturally occurring talk: What we think we do is not what we do. *Arizona Working Papers in Second Language Acquisition and Teaching*. Tucson: University of Arizona.

Kaisse, E. M. (1985). *Connected speech: The interaction of syntax and phonology*. Orlando, FL: Academic.

Kawaguchi, Y. (1984). Hatsuon to chokai no shido -jokyureberu no mondaiten- [Guidance for pronunciation and listening: Advanced level problems]. *Wasedadaigaku gogakukenkyujo Koza Nihongo Kyoiku [Waseda University Language research center seminar Japanese language education], 20*, 37–47.

Kawai, G., & Hirose, K. (2000). Teaching the pronunciation of Japanese double-mora phonemes using speech recognition technology. *Speech Communication, 30*, 131–143.

Kawase, I. (1992). Contraction in Japanese. *Bulletin of International Center, 2*, 1–24. Tokyo: The University of Tokyo.

Kelly, G. (2003). *How to teach pronunciation*. London: Longman.

Kent, R. D., & Read, C. (1992). *The acoustic analysis of speech*. San Diego: Singular.

Kenworthy, J. (1987). *Teaching English pronunciation*. London: Longman.

Kim, H.-Y. (1995). Intake from the speech stream: Speech elements that L2 learners attend to. In R. Schmidt (Ed.), *Attention and awareness in foreign language learning* (pp. 65–83). Honolulu: Second Language Teaching & Curriculum Center, University of Hawai'i.

Kingdon, R. (1950). Teaching the weak forms. *English Teaching, 4*(8), 206–214.

Kingdon, R. (1958a). *English conversational practice*. London: Longman.

Kingdon, R. (1958b). *The groundwork of English intonation*. London: Longman.

Kirk, R. E. (1968). *Experimental design: Procedures for the behavioral sciences*. Belmont, CA: Brooks/Cole.

Kitano, K. (2001). Anxiety in the college Japanese language classroom. *The Modern Language Journal, 85*, 549–566.

Kobayashi, E., & Linde, R. (Eds.). (1984). *Practice in English reduced forms*. Tokyo: Sansyusya.

Kondo, K. (1998). The paradox of US language policy and Japanese language education in Hawai'i. *International Journal of Bilingual Education and Bilingualism, 1*, 47–64.

Kondo, Y. (1994). *Phonetic underspecification of schwa*. Paper presented at the 1994 International Conference on Spoken Language Processing, Yokohama, Japan.

Kondo, Y. (1995). *Production of schwa by Japanese speakers of English: A crosslinguistic study of coarticulatory strategies*. Doctoral dissertation, University of Edinburgh, Scotland.

Kondo-Brown, K. (2003). Heritage language instruction for post-secondary students from immigrant backgrounds. *Heritage Language Journal, 1*. Retrieved December 2003, from ftp: http://www.heritagelanguages.org/

Kondo-Brown, K. (2004). Investigating interviewer-candidate interactions during oral interviews for child L2 learners. *Foreign Language Annals, 37*, 602–615.

Kondo-Brown, K. (2005). Differences in language skills: Heritage language learner subgroups and foreign language learners. *The Modern Language Journal, 89*(4), 563–581.

Koster, C. J. (1987). *Word recognition in foreign and native language*. Providence, RI: Foris.

Krashen, S. (1987). *Principles and practice in second language acquisition*. London: Prentice-Hall International.

Kreidler, C. W. (1989). *The pronunciation of English: A course book in phonology*. Oxford, England: Blackwell.

Kreidler, C. W. (1997). *Describing spoken English: An introduction*. London: Routledge.

Kubozono, H. (1999). *Nihongo no onsei [Japanese sound]*. Tokyo: Iwanami Shoten.

Kuhl, P. (1991). Human adults and human infants exhibit a prototype effect for phoneme categories; monkeys do not. *Perception and Psychophysics, 50*, 93–107.

Kuhl, P. (1992). Infants' perception and representation of speech: Development of a new theory. In *ICSLP–92, International Conference on Spoken Language Processing* (pp. 449–456). Alberta, Canada: Quality Color.

Kuhl, P. K., Andruski, J. E., Chistovich, I. A., Chistovich, L. A., Kozhevnikova, E. V., & Ryskina, V. L. (1997). Cross-language analysis of phonetic units in language addressed to infants. *Science, 277*(5326), 684–686.

Kumaravadivelu, B. (1994). Intake factors and intake processes in adult language learning. *Applied Language Learning, 5,* 33–71.

Kweon, S.-O. (2000). *The acquisition of English contraction constraints by advanced Korean learners of English: Experimental studies on wanna contraction and auxiliary contraction.* Unpublished doctoral dissertation, University of Hawai'i at Mānoa, Honolulu.

Kweon, S.-O. (2001). The acquisition of English contraction constraints by advanced Korean learners of English: Experimental studies on *wanna* contraction and auxiliary contraction (Doctoral dissertation, University of Hawai'i at Mānoa, 2000). *Dissertation Abstracts International, 61,* 10.

Labov, W. (1969). Contraction, deletion, and inherent variabilities of the English copula. *Language, 45*(4), 715–762.

Ladefoged, P. (1993). *A course in phonetics* (3rd ed.). New York: Harcourt Brace.

Ladefoged, P. (2000). *A course in phonetics* (4th ed.). Boston: Thomson Wadsworth.

Ladefoged, P. (2001). *Vowels and consonants: An introduction to the sounds of the world's languages.* Oxford, England: Blackwell.

Ladefoged, P., & Cho, T. (2001). Linking linguistic contrasts to reality: The case of VOT. In N. Gronnum & J. Rischel (Eds.), *Travaux du cercle linguistique de Copenhague Vol. XXXI (To honour Eli Fischer-Forgensen),* 212–225. Copenhagen: C.A. Reitzel.

Ladefoged, P., & Maddieson, I. (1996). *The sounds of the world's languages.* Oxford, England: Blackwell.

Lado, R. (1957). *Linguistics across cultures.* Ann Arbor: University of Michigan.

Lambacher, S. (1999). A CALL tool for improving second language acquisition of English consonants by Japanese learners. *Computer Assisted Language Learning, 12*(2), 137–156. Retrieved June 17, 2005, from Linguistics and Language Behavior Abstracts database.

Landahl, K., & Ziolkowski, M. (1995). Discovering phonetic units: Is a picture worth a thousand words? *Papers from Regional Meetings, Chicago Linguistic Society, 31*(1), 294–316.

Landahl, K., Ziolkowski, M., Usami, M., & Tunnock, B. (1992). Interactive articulation: Improving accent through visual feedback. In I. Shinjo, K. Landahl, M. MacDonald, K. Noda, S. Ozeki, T. Shiowa, M. Sugiura (Eds.), *The Proceedings of the Second International Conference on Foreign Language Education and Technology* (pp. 283–292). Kasugai, Aichi: The Language Laboratory Association of Japan.

Lane, L. (2005). *Focus on pronunciation 1.* London: Longman.

Laroy, C. (2003). *Pronunciation*. Oxford, England: Oxford University.

Larsen-Freeman, D. E. (1976). An explanation for the morpheme acquisition order of second language learners. *Language Learning, 26*, 125–134.

Leather, J., & James, A. (1991). The acquisition of second language speech. *Studies in Second Language Acquisition, 13*, 305–341.

Lisker, L., & Abramson, A. (1964). A cross language study of voicing in initial stops. *Word, 20*, 384–422.

Lively, S. E., Logan, J. S., & Pisoni, D. B. (1993). Training Japanese listeners to identify English /r/ and /l/ II: The role of phonetic environment and talker variability in learning new perceptual categories. *The Journal of the Acoustical Society of America, 94*(3), 1242–1255.

Long, M. H. (1991). Focus on form: A design feature in language teaching methodology. In K. de Bot, R. B. Ginsberg, & C. Kramsch (Eds.), *Foreign language research in cross-cultural perspective* (pp. 39–52). Amsterdam: John Benjamins.

Long, M. H. (1991). Focus on form: A design feature in language teaching methodology. In K. de Bot, R. B. Ginsberg, & C. Kramsch (Eds.), *Foreign language research in cross-cultural perspective* (pp. 39–52). Amsterdam: John Benjamins.

Long, M. H., & Robinson, P. (1998). Focus on form: Theory, research, and practice. In C. Doughty & J. Williams (Eds.), *Focus on form in classroom second language acquisition* (pp. 15–41). Cambridge, England: Cambridge University.

Lyman, B. S. (1894). *Change from surd to sonant in Japanese compounds*. Philadelphia: Oriental Club of Philadelphia.

Machida, S. (2001). Anxiety and oral performance in a foreign language test situation. *Australian Review of Applied Linguistics, 24*, 31–50.

Madsen, H. S., & Bowen, J. S. (1978). *Adaptation in language teaching*. Rowley, MA: Newbury House.

Maekawa, K. (2003). Corpus of spontaneous Japanese: Its design and evaluation. In *Proceedings of ISCA and IEEE Workshop on Spontaneous Speech Processing and Recognition* (pp. 7–12). Tokyo.

Maekawa, K. (2004). Design, Compilation, and Some Preliminary Analyses of the Corpus of Spontaneous Japanese, In K. Maekawa & K. Yoneyama, (Eds.), *Spontaneous speech: Data and analysis* (pp. 87–108). Tokyo: The National Institute for Japanese Language.

Martin, S. (1975). *A reference grammar of Japanese*. New Haven, CT: Yale University Press.

McCawley, J. (1968). *The phonological component of a grammar of Japanese*. The Hague: Mouton.

Minda, J. P., & Smith, J. D. (2001). Prototypes in category learning: The effects of category size, category structure, and stimulus complexity. *Journal of Experimental Psychology: Learning, Memory, and Cognition, 27*(3), 775–799.

Miyara, S. (1980). Phonological phrase and phonological reduction. *Papers in Japanese Linguistics, 7*, 79–121.

Miyawaki, K., Strange, W., Verbrugge, R., Liberman, A., Jenkins, J., & Fujimura, O. (1975). An effect of linguistic experience: The discrimination of [r] and [l] by native speakers of Japanese and English. *Perception & Psycholinguistics, 18*(5), 331–340.

Moh-Kim, T. (1997). Building fluency: A course for non-native speakers of English. *English Teaching Forum, 35*(1), 26–37.

Molholt, G. (1990). Spectrographic analysis and patterns in pronunciation. *Computers and the Humanities 24*(1–2), 81–92. Retrieved June 17, 2005, from ERIC database.

Mori, J. (2002). Task design, plan, and development of talk-in-interaction: An analysis of a small group activity in a Japanese language class. *Applied Linguistics 23*, 323–347.

Morley, J. (1979). *Improving spoken English.* Ann Arbor: University of Michigan.

Morley, J. (1987). *Improving spoken English: An intensive personalized program in perception, pronunciation, practice in context.* Ann Arbor: University of Michigan.

Morley, J. (1991). The pronunciation component in teaching English to speakers of other languages. *TESOL Quarterly, 25*(3), 481–520.

Murphy, J. (1991). Oral communication in TESOL: Integrating speaking, listening, and pronunciation. *TESOL Quarterly, 25*(1), 51–76.

Nagle, S., & Sanders, S. (1986). Comprehension theory and second language pedagogy. *TESOL Quarterly, 20*(1), 9–26.

Naiman, N. (1992). A communicative approach to pronunciation teaching. In P. Avery & S. Ehrlich (Eds.), *Teaching American English pronunciation* (pp. 163–171). Hong Kong: Oxford University.

Negishi, R. (1999). Nihongo gakushuusha he no shuuyakukei shidoo no meyasu: Nihonjin ni yoru hyooka to shiyoo-ritsu o fumaete [A standard for the teaching of contracted forms to learners of Japanese: Based on the evaluation and conversational use of native speakers]. *Nihongo kyooiku [Japanese Language Education], 102,* 30–39.

Neri, A., Cucchiarini, C., Strik, H., & Boves, L. (2002). The pedagogy-technology interface in computer assisted pronunciation training. *Computer Assisted Language Learning, 15*(5), 441–467.

Nilsen, D. L. F., & Nilsen, A. P. (1973). *Pronunciation contrasts in English.* Englewood Cliffs, NJ: Prentice Hall Regents.

Nishi, K., & Kewley-Port, D. (2005, May). *Training Japanese listeners to identify American English vowels.* Poster session presented at the 149th Meeting of the Acoustical Society of America. Vancouver, BC, Canada.

Norris, J. M., Brown, J. D., Hudson, T., & Yoshioka, J. (1998). *Designing second language performance assessments.* Honolulu: Second Language Teaching & Curriculum Center, University of Hawai'i Press.

Norris, R. W. (1993). Teaching reduced forms: An aid for improving lower-level students' listening skills. *Fukoka Women's Junior College Studies, 46*, 49–56.

Norris, R. W. (1995). Teaching reduced forms: Putting the horse before the cart. *English Teaching Forum, 33*, 47–50.

Nunan, D. (1991). *Language teaching methodology.* Hertfordshire, England: Prentice Hall International.

Obendorfer, R. (1998). *Weak forms in present-day English.* Oslo: Novus.

Odlin, T. M. (1978a). *Contraction in ESL: A case study in variable rules.* Unpublished master's thesis, University of Texas at El Paso.

Odlin, T. M. (1978b). Variable rules in the acquisition of English contraction. *TESOL Quarterly, 12*(4), 451–458.

Oguma, R. (2000). Perception of Japanese long vowels and short vowels by English-speaking learners. *Japanese-Language Education Around the Globe, 10*, 43–55.

Ohara, Y., Saft, S., & Crookes, G. (2001). Toward a feminist critical pedagogy in a beginning Japanese-as-a-foreign-language class. *Japanese Language and Literature, 35*, 105–133.

Ohta, A. S. (1999). Interactional routines and the socialization of interactional style in adult learners of Japanese. *Journal of Pragmatics, 31*, 1493–1512.

Okamura, A. (1995). Teachers' and non-teachers' perception of elementary learners' spoken Japanese. *The Modern Language Journal, 79*, 29–40.

Omaggio Hadley, A. (2001). *Teaching language in context* (3rd ed.). Boston, MA: Heinle & Heinle.

Orion, G. F. (1988). *Pronouncing American English: Sounds, stress, and intonation.* New York: Newbury House.

Patterson, D., LoCasto, P. C., & Connine, C. M. (2003). Corpora analyses of frequency of schwa deletion in conversational American English. *Phonetica, 60*(1), 45–69.

Pennington, M. C. (1990). Acquiring proficiency in English phonology: Problems and solutions for the Japanese learner. *Nagoya Gakuin Daigaku Foreign Language Education Bulletin, 16*, 1–19.

Pennington, M. C. (1996). *Phonology in English language teaching.* New York: Longman.

Peterson. P. (1991). A synthesis of methods for interactive listening. In M. Celce-Murcia (Ed.), *Teaching English as a second or a foreign language* (pp. 106–122). Boston, MA: Heinle & Heinle.

Pike, K. L. (1945). *The intonation of American English.* Ann Arbor: University of Michigan.

Porter, D., & Roberts, J. (1987). Authentic listening activities. In M. Long & J. Richards (Eds.), *Methodology in TESOL: A book of readings* (pp. 177–187). New York: Newbury House.

Poser, W. (1988). Glide formation and compensatory lengthening in Japanese. *Linguistic Inquiry, 19*, 494–503.

Prator, C .H., & Robinett, B. W. (1995). *Manual of American English pronunciation* (4th ed.). New York: Thomson Learning.

Richards, J. (1983). Listening comprehension: Approach, design, procedure. *TESOL Quarterly, 17*(2), 219–240.

Richmond, E. B., Barrett, C. E., & Kraul, D. R. (1979). Yes, you can learn foreign language pronunciation by sight! *Audiovisual Instruction, 24*(1), 48–49. Retrieved June 17, 2005, from ERIC database.

Roach, P. (2004). *English phonetics and phonology: A practical approach.* Cambridge, England: Cambridge University.

Rogerson, P., & Gilbert, J. B. (2001). *Speaking clearly: Pronunciation and listening comprehension for learners of English.* Cambridge, England: Cambridge University.

Rosetta Stone Language Software [Computer software]. (2005). Harrisonbug, VA: Farfield Language Technologies.

Rost, M. (1991). *Listening in action: Activities for developing listening in language teaching.* New York: Prentice Hall.

Rost, M. A., & Stratton, R. K. (1978). *Listening in the real world: Clues to English conversation.* Tucson, AZ: Lingual House.

Rost, M. A., & Stratton, R. K. (1980). *Listening transitions: From listening to speaking.* Tucson, AZ: Lingual House.

Ruipérez, G. (2001). Web assisted language learning (WALL) and learning management systems (LMS) in virtual centres for foreign languages. *International Journal of English Studies, 2*(1), 81-96.

Saito, H., & Beecken, M. (1997). An approach to instruction of pragmatic aspects: Implications of pragmatic transfer by American learners of Japanese. *The Modern Language Journal, 81,* 363–377.

Saito, Y. (1986). The mora phonemicization of short syllables with a sonorant onset in spoken Tokyo Japanese. *Journal of Japanese Language Teaching, 60,* 205–220.

Sakai, T. (1997). Nihongo shutoku tekisei tesuto no saikento –chokaku joho shori wo chushin ni- [Reconsidering the Japanese Language Aptitude Test (1) on Anditory Information Processing]. *Bungeigengo kenkyu Gengohen Tukubadaigaku [Tsukuba University Literature and Linguistics Research, Linguistics Series], 32,* 17–30.

Sakai, T. (2003). *Nihongo jokyu chokai noryoku no sokute -naze kikenai no ka* [How to measure advanced Japanese learner's hearing ability: Reasons for difficulties in hearing]. Report of the Grant-in-Aid for Scientific Research (C)(2001–2003), (pp. 1–91). Supported by Japan Society for the Promotion of Science and the Ministry of Education, Science, Sports, and Culture. Project No. 12680296.

Sakurai (1989) *Kyotsuugo no hatsuon de chuui subeki kotogara* [Matters in the pronunciation of standard language that deserve attention], *Nihongo akusento jiten* [Dictionary of Japanese accents]. Tokyo: Nihon Housou Kyoukai Shuppan.

Schmidt, R. (1990). The role of consciousness in second language learning. *Applied Linguistics, 11,* 129–158.

Schmidt, R. (1992). Psychological mechanisms underlying second language fluency. *Studies In Second Language Acquisition, 14*, 357–385.

Schmidt, R. (1995). Consciousness and foreign language learning: A tutorial on the role of attention and awareness in learning. In R. Schmidt (Ed.), *Attention and awareness in foreign language learning* (pp. 1–63). Honolulu: Second Language Teaching & Curriculum Center, University of Hawaiʻi.

Shavelson, R. J. (1996). *Statistical reasoning for the behavioral sciences* (3ʳᵈ ed.). Boston: Allyn & Bacon.

Sheeler, W. D., & Markley, R. W. (1991). *Sound and rhythm: A pronunciation course* (2ⁿᵈ ed.). Englewood Cliffs, NJ: Prentice Hall Regents.

Sheldon, A., & Strange, W. (1982). The acquisition of /r/ and /l/ by Japanese learners of English: Evidence that speech production can precede speech perception. *Applied Psycholinguistics, 3*, 243–261.

Shibatani, M. (1990). *The languages of Japan.* Cambridge, England: Cambridge University.

Shockey, L. (2003). *Sound patterns of spoken English.* Malden, MA: Blackwell.

Siegal, M. (1996). The role of learner subjectivity in second language sociolinguistic competency: Western women learning Japanese. *Applied Linguistics, 17*, 356–382.

Šimáčková, S. (1997). Flapping in nonnative English: A process or a rule? *Working Papers in Linguistics, 29*, 33–51. University of Hawaiʻi at Mānoa.

Šimáčková, S. (2000). Prosodically motivated allophonic processes in the speech of Czech learners of English. Doctoral dissertation, University of Hawaiʻi at Mānoa. *Dissertation Abstracts International, A: The Humanities and Social Sciences, 60*, 11.

Smith, C. L. (1997). The devoicing of /z/ in American English: Effects of local and prosodic context. *Phonetica, 25*(44), 471–500.

Snow, B. G., & Perkins, K. (1979). The teaching of listening comprehension and communication activities. *TESOL Quarterly, 13*(1), 51–61.

Sommers, A. H. (1977). *Modern phonology.* Baltimore: University Park.

Stenson, N., Downing, B., Smith, J., & Smith, K. (1992). The effectiveness of computer-assisted pronunciation training. *CALICO Journal, 9*(4), 5–19.

Sussman, J. E., & Lauckner-Morano, V. J. (1995). Further tests of the "perceptual magnet effect" in the perception of [i]: Identification and change/no-change discrimination. *The Journal of the Acoustical Society of America, 97*(1), 539–552.

Swain, M. (1983). Communicative competence: Some roles of comprehensible input and comprehensible output in its development. In S. Gass & C. Madden (Eds.), *Input in second language acquisition* (pp. 235–253). Rowley, MA: Newbury House.

Takagi, N. (2002). The limits of training Japanese listeners to identify English /r/ and /l/: Eight case studies. *Journal of the Acoustical Society of America, 111*(6), 2887–2896.

Takefuta, Y. (1984). *Hiaringu no kodokagaku* [The behavioral science of hearing]. Tokyo: Kenkyusha Shuppan.

Tanaka, N. (1988). Politeness: Some problems for Japanese speakers of English. *JALT Journal, 9*(2), 81–102.

Temperly, M. (1987). Linking and deletion in final consonant clusters. In J. Morley (Ed.), *Current perspectives on pronunciation* (pp. 59–82). Washington, DC: TESOL.

Teschner, R. V., & Whitley, M. S. (2004). *Pronouncing English: A stress-based approach with CD-ROM.* Washington, DC: Georgetown University.

Toda, T. (1994). Interlanguage phonology: Acquisition of timing control by Australian learners of Japanese. *Australian Review of Applied Linguistics, 17*(2), 51–76.

Toda, T. (1996). *Interlanguage phonology: Acquisition of timing control and perceptual categorization of durational contrast in Japanese.* Unpublished doctoral dissertation, The Australian National University, Canberra.

Toda, T. (1997). Strategies for producing mora timing by non-native speakers of Japanese. In Daini Gengo Shuutoku Kenkyuukai (Ed.), *Acquisition of Japanese as a second language* (pp. 157–197). Tokyo: Bonjinsha.

Toda, T. (2001). Focus on form in teaching pronunciation. In *Proceedings of the Annual Meeting of the Society for Teaching Japanese as a Foreign Language* (pp. 151–156). [in Japanese]

Toda, T. (2003a). *Second language speech perception and production: Acquisition of phonological contrasts in Japanese,* Lanham, MD: University Press of America.

Toda, T. (2003b). Acquisition of special morae in Japanese as a second language. *Journal of Phonetic Society of Japan, 7*(2), 70–83. [in Japanese]

Toda, T. (2004). *Komunikeeshon no tame no nihongo hatsuon lessun* [Japanese pronunciation exercises for communication]. Tokyo: 3A Corporation.

Toki, S. (1975). The contracted form as it occurs in educational TV programs. *Journal of Japanese Language Teaching, 28,* 55–66.

Tokuda, N. (Ed.). (2002). Special Issue on ICALL, *Computer Assisted Language Learning, 15*(4), 319–327.

Tomisaka, Y. (1997). *Nameraka nihongo kaiwa* [Successful communication in Japanese]. Tokyo: ALC.

Tomlin, R. S., & Villa, V. (1994). Attention in cognitive science and second language acquisition. *Studies in Second Language Acquisition, 16,* 183–203.

Trager, E. C. (1982). *The PD's in depth.* Culver City, CA: ELS.

Trager, E. C., & Henderson, S. C. (1956). *The PD's: Pronunciation drills for learners of English.* Culver City, CA: ELS.

Tsujimura, N. (1996). *An introduction to Japanese linguistics.* Oxford, England: Blackwell.

Tsukada, K. (1999). *An acoustic phonetic analysis of Japanese-accented English.* Unpublished doctoral dissertation, Macquarie University, Sydney.

Ueyama, M. (2000). *Prosodic transfer: An acoustic study of L2 English vs. L2 Japanese.* Unpublished doctoral dissertation, University of California at Los Angeles.

Underhill, A. (1994). *Sound foundations.* Oxford, England: Heinemann.

Ur, P. (1987). *Teaching listening comprehension.* Cambridge, England: Cambridge University.

Vance, T. J. (1987). *An introduction to Japanese phonology.* New York: State University of New York.

Vardanian, R. M. (1964). Teaching English intonation through oscilloscope displays. *Language Learning, 14,* 109–117.

Varden, K. (1995). Teaching "fast speech" reductions in the classroom: Initial results of a study in progress. *Meiji Gakuin Review, 92,* 33–57.

Vogt, W. P. (1999). *Dictionary of statistics and methodology: A nontechnical guide for the social sciences* (2nd ed.). Thousand Oaks, CA: Sage.

Weinstein, N. (1982). *Whaddaya say?* Culver City, CA: English Language Services.

Weinstein, N. (2001). *Whaddaya say? Guided practice in relaxed speech* (2nd ed.). London: Longman.

Wells, J. C. (2000). *Longman pronunciation dictionary* (2nd ed.). Harlow: Pearson Education.

Wilson, W., & Barnard, P. (1992). *Fifty-fifty.* Englewood Cliffs, NJ: Prentice-Hall.

Yamada, Y., & Moeller, A. J. (2001). Weaving curricular standards into the language classroom: An action research study. *Foreign Language Annals, 34,* 26–33.

Yoneyama, Y., & Maekawa, K., (Eds.). (2004). Spontaneous speech: Data and analysis *Proceedings of the 1st Session of the 10th International Symposium.* Tokyo: The National Institute for Japanese Language.

Yorozu, M. (2001). Interaction with native speakers of Japanese: What learners say. *Japanese Studies, 21,* 199–213.

Yoshimi, D. R. (2001). Explicit instruction and JFL learner's use of interactional discourse markers. In K. R. Rose & G. Kasper (Eds.), *Pragmatics in language teaching* (pp. 223–244). Cambridge, England: Cambridge University.

Young-Scholten, M. (1994). On positive evidence and ultimate attainment in L2 phonology. *Second Language Research, 10,* 193–214.

Zwicky, A. M. (1972). On casual speech. In P. M. Peranteau, J. N. Levi, & G. C. Phares (Eds.), *Papers from the eighth regional meeting Chicago Linguistic Society* (pp. 607–615). Chicago, IL: Chicago Linguistic Society.

Glossary of Selected Terms
Related to the Content of This Book

Terms indicating very common characteristics such as place and manner of phonemes and their allophones are not included.

anticipatory assimilation (sometimes called *regressive assimilation*) —a process whereby one phoneme is influenced by the phoneme that follows it, for example, /n/ to /m/ assimilation occurs in words like *sunbeam* /sʌmbim/ in English.

assimilation – a process whereby one phoneme is changed into another because of the influence of a nearby phoneme. For example, in Japanese, the place name made up of the two words *shin* and *bashi* is pronounced (and even spelled in Roman characters) as *Shimbashi*; assimilation can occur in several ways depending on the direction in which phonemes influence each other (see *anticipatory assimilation*, aka, *regressive assimilation*; *progressive assimilation*, aka, *lag* or *perseverative assimilation*; and *reciprocal assimilation*, aka, *coalescent assimilation*).

blending – linguistic dictionaries typically define this term as the combining of parts of two words to form a third word as in *smoke* + *fog* = *smog*, or *Spanish* + *English* = *Spanglish*; however, Hill & Beebe (1980, p. 300) used this term in a completely novel way to refer to a process whereby the word boundary between two words in a *spoken* sequence is obscured in contrast to *contraction* which is generally used to refer to such sequences that occur in both spoken and written forms.

blurred utterances (see synonym *connected speech*, and definitions for *reductions* and *reduced forms*)

casual speech (CS; see contrast in definition of *fast speech*, FS, and full explanation in chapter 10) – "CS processes are indifferent to the mere speed of speech but sensitive to the sociological context such as intimacy, formalness, familiarity, and so forth. They apply only to lexically specified items and phrases, and their application affects lexical, morphological, and syntactic aspects of the entire sentence; thereby, a kind of concordance across different components of grammar is observed with respect to casualness" (definition taken directly from chapter 10)

citation form (also see *weak form*) – the dictionary or clear pronunciation of a word used when that word is stressed or pronounced in isolation; this pronunciation may be quite different from the *weak form* pronunciation(s) of the same word used when it is found in a unstressed positions. For example, the citation form for *and* is /ænd/ in NAE, while the same word in *Bread and butter* can be pronounced /æn/ or /n̩/ in connected speech (i.e., /brɛdænbʌɾɾ/ or /brɛdn̩bʌɾɾ/).

close juncture (see synonym *close transition*)

close transition (also see *transition* and *open transition*) – refers to those pronunciations wherein the connection between successive sounds is *close*, that is, without a break. For example, in *nitrate* and *night rate*, the connections between /t/ and /r/ are different; the former demonstrates a *close transition* and the latter an *open transition*.

coalescent assimilation – (see synonym *progressive assimilation*)

coarticulations (also see *assimilation*) – overlapping in the articulation of adjacent phonemes

colloquial speech (see synonym *connected speech*)

connected speech (also sometimes referred to as *casual speech*, *colloquial speech*, *fast speech*, *informal speech*, and *relaxed speech*) – analysis of the continuous chains in normal spoken language and conversation as compared with the typical linguistic analysis of individual phonemes analyzed in isolation including but not restricted to the processes of word stress, sentence stress and timing, reduction, strong and weak forms of words, elision, intrusion, assimilation, transition (juncture), liaison, and contraction.

contracted forms (also see *phrase-final reduction* and *word coalescing*, and full explanation in chapter 11) – "The Japanese term for contraction is *shukuyakukei* 'contracted forms,' and this phonological change is characterized by a reduction of the number of morae. This is one of the linguistic terms the definition of which varies remarkably..." (definition taken directly from chapter 11).

contraction – a way of showing the reduced characteristics of spoken language in written language (often used to write dialogue in a way that shows its spoken flavor), for example, *can't, I've, she's, they'll, we're, you'd*, and so forth.

deletion (see synonym *elision*)

elision (sometimes called *deletion* or *omission*) – a process of elimination or dropping of phonemes (vowels or consonants) that would be present in the citation form of a word or phrase. For example, in citation form *chocolate* is pronounced /tʃakələt/, but in connected speech, NAE speakers would be much more likely to drop the middle vowel as in *chocolate* /'tʃaklət/. Elision can also occur at word boundaries as in the last consonant in the word *old* in *He's a good ol' boy* where it is pronounced /ol/, while in citation form it would be /old/, or elsewhere.

ellipsis – deletion of entire words in *connected speech*, for example, the following phrase has three instances of ellipsis: *Wanna go with?* [(Do you) *want to go with* (us)?]

fast speech (FS; see contrast in definition of *causal speech*, CS, and full explanation in chapter 10) – In Japanese, processes related primarily to the quickness of speech, including *high vowel devoicing* (HVD) and *vowel degemination and lengthening* (VD&L; definition adapted from chapter 10).

formants (see *wide-band spectrograms*) – the frequencies of sound in vowels that are resonating in the mouth; shown as dark horizontal bands marked F1, F2, and F3 in *wide-band spectrograms* (definition adapted from chapter 9).

freeware – software that is made available without charge

high vowel devoicing (HVD; also see *museika* or *devoicing,* and *vowel devoicing,* and examples in chapter 10) – "one of the distinctive properties of the phonological structure of Japanese is the existence of devoiced vowels, most probably the high vowels, /i/ and /u/, which occur when they appear between devoiced consonants or at the end of a word preceded by a devoiced consonant" (definition taken directly from chapter 10).

informal speech (see synonym *connected speech*)

intrusion – a process that involves inserting phonemes within or between words, for example, within words, many NAE speakers insert a /t/ between the /n/ and /θ/ in *month* /mʌntθ/, or between /n/ and /ʃ/ as in *bunch* /bʌntʃ/, or between /l/ and /s/ as in *false* /falts/; or they insert a /p/ between /m/ and /f/ as in *comfort* /kʌmpfərt/; or they insert a /k/ between /ŋ/ and /st/ as in *gangster* /geŋkstər/ or between /ŋ/ and /θ/ as in *length* /lɛŋkθ/; between words, speakers of some dialects of NAE insert an /r/ in environments like *China and Japan,* which would then be pronounced something like *Chin'r and Japan* or /tʃainərəndʒəpæn/.

juncture (see synonym *transition*)

lag (see synonym *progressive assimilation*)

liaison – one specific type of *transition,* wherein a sound is introduced at the end of one word if the following word begins with a vowel, e.g., in French, the plural article *les* is typically pronounced /le/ with the *s* silent when the following word begins with a consonant as in *les parents* (the parents) pronounced /leparã/; however, when the following word begins with a vowel as in the word *enfants* (children), the *s* is pronounced as a /z/ creating a liaison to the next word with the ensemble pronounced /lezãfã/

linking – connections between words across word boundaries; in NAE these occur in connected speech in different ways between consonants and consonants (e.g., *top person* /tapːʌrsən/, *hot cake* /haʔˀkeik/), consonants and vowels (e.g., *skip it* /skɪpɪt/, *half hour* /hæfaur/), and vowels and vowels (e.g., *blue ink* /bluwɪŋk/, *be able* /bijebl̩/)

mora (also see *special morae*) – linguistic unit that identifies the sense of "phonic (*hyouon*) time-units" or "time-lengths" in Japanese speech, or put another way, the smallest metrical time unit equal to a short syllable

moraic nasalization (also see *nasal syllabicization,* and full explanation in chapter 11) – In Japanese, "*hatsuon-ka* 'moraic nasalization' is similar to *sokuon-ka* 'gemination' in that the number of morae remains unchanged after the reduction process takes place. For example, the possessive particle *no* in *Taro no da* 'It's Taro's' is reduced to *Taro n da* by the following alveolar consonant [d] in the copula *da* 'to be'" (definition taken directly from chapter 11).

museika (also see *high-vowel devoicing* and *vowel devoicing,* and full explanation in chapter 11) – process of "devoicing of vowels in Japanese... In principle, high vowels between voiceless consonants are in the phonetic environment where devoicing is possible. Vowels are not eliminated, but their [+voice] feature is assimilated to the [-voice] feature of the surrounding consonants" (definition taken directly from chapter 11).

narrow-band spectrogram – a graph that shows the different frequencies that a sound contains; especially useful when looking at the harmonics of a sound (definition adapted from chapter 9)

nasal syllabicization (NS) (also see *moraic nasalization* and full explanation in chapter 10) – includes two processes in Japanese, "which are quite prevalently observed even in slow speech and in *casual writing*, such as intimate letters, diaries, and text messages. The first process we will examine involves /ni/ and /no/, which become a syllabic (or moraic) nasal [N] (ん in writing), dropping the vowels /i/ and /o/, respectively, for example, /iku no da/ → [ikuN da] (行くんだ) 'it is that (I) go.' The other process is observed when the verb involves /r/ at the end and is followed by a lexical item that starts with /n/. Then, the /r/ gets assimilated into the /n/, becoming a syllabic nasal [N], for example, /yar-anai/ → [yaNnai](やんない) '(I will) not do.'" (definition taken directly from chapter 10).

omission (see synonym *elision*)

open juncture (see synonym *open transition*)

open transition (also see *transition* and *close transition*) – refers to those pronunciations where there is a slight break in the continuity of pronunciation. For example, consider *nitrate* and *night rate*; the connection between /t/ and /r/ is different in the two (the former demonstrates a close transition and the latter an open transition).

palatalization – one sort of reciprocal assimilation that occurs in NAE connected speech when the /t/, /d/, /s/, or /z/ phonemes are followed by a /j/ phoneme and combine to become /tʃ/, /dʒ/, /ʃ/, or /ʒ/, respectively, for example, /t/ followed by /j/ combines to become /tʃ/ as in *what you*: /wat ju/ to /watʃu/.

perseverative assimilation (see synonym *progressive assimilation*)

phrase-final reduction (also see *contracted forms* and *word coalescing*, and full explanation in chapter 10) – in Japanese, reduction processes that may involve the phonological changes of such items as particles *-wa* 'topic, contrastive' and the provisional *-(r)eba* form (e.g., /koto-wa/→ kota:, /mi-reba/ → 'mirya'; definition adapted from chapter 10).

pitch trace – a graph of the pitch of a speaker's voice as it goes up and down (definition adapted from chapter 9)

progressive assimilation (sometimes called *lag* or *perseverative assimilation*) involves a phoneme being influenced by the phoneme that precedes it, as is the case in the NAE example of the effect of the voiceless /t/ on the pronunciation of *s* as a *voiceless* /s/ in *cats*, as compared to the influence of voiced /g/ on the pronunciation of *s* as a *voiced* /z/ in *dogs*.

reciprocal assimilation (sometimes called *coalescent assimilation*) occurs when two phonemes mutually influence each other, for example, in the NAE phrase *That you?* in continuous speech, the /t/ phoneme combines with /j/ across word boundaries to become a third sound /tʃ/.

reduced forms (also see *blurred speech, reduction,* and *reductions*)—the forms that are manifested in *connected speech* as a result of the process of *reduction.* Two example *reduced forms* might be written as *I'm* and *Whatcha say?* They are both parts of *connected speech,* one accomplished by *contraction* and the other by *assimilation,* and at the same time, they are two different *reduced forms.*

reduced speech (see synonym *connected speech*)

reduction (also see *blurred utterances, reductions,* and *reduced forms*) – the processes that occur in *connected speech,* in which phonemes of the language are changed, minimized, or eliminated in order to facilitate pronunciation.

reductions (also see *blurred utterances, reduction,* and *reduced forms*) – used as a synonym with *reduced forms,* that is, the forms that are manifested in *connected speech* as a result of the process of *reduction.* Two example *reduced forms* might be written as *I'm* and *Whatcha say?* They are both *reductions* formed by the process of *reduction* in *connected speech,* one accomplished by *contraction* and the other by *assimilation,* and at the same time, they are two different *reduced forms.*

regressive assimilation (see *anticipatory assimilation*)

relaxed form of words (see synonym *weak form*)

relaxed speech (see synonym *connected speech*)

sandhi forms (also see *assimilation*) – refers generally to phonological changes that are applied when adjacent grammatical forms are joined

schwa – the phonetic name for the neutral vowel /ə/; schwa often occurs in NAE in unstressed syllables

schwa reduction (see *schwa*)—one of the most common features of NAE connected speech in which many vowels in unstressed syllables become schwa /ə/, for example, the *citation form* of *ago* is pronounced /ago/, but when it occurs in an unstressed syllable in connected speech as in *years ago* /jirz əgo/, /a/ is reduced to /ə/⬚

sentence stress (also see sentence timing)—the stress or pattern of stress groups in a sentence (or utterance, since they are typically oral)

sentence timing (also see sentence stress)—the pattern of stress or syllable timing in the stress groups in a sentence (or utterance)

sequential voicing (see full explanation and examples in chapter 11) – In Japanese, "*rendaku* 'sequential voicing' refers to the process where the morpheme-initial voiceless obstruents become voiced in compounds" (definition taken directly from chapter 11).

sociological notions (especially in chapter 10) – for purposes of this book, social, and group influences on language particularly with regard to connected speech, including notions like level of formality, politeness, familiarity, vulgarity, and so forth.

special morae (also see *mora,* and full explanation in chapter 11) – In Japanese, a "phonological category called tokushuhaku 'special morae' consists of /Q/ (sokuon 'first half of geminate obstruents'), /N/ (hatsuon 'moraic nasals'), and /R/ ('choo'on 'the last half of long vowels'). This category is often used in phonological analyses of Japanese" (definition taken directly form chapter 11).

spectrogram – a combination of the information presented by the waveform and pitch trace. "The waveform shows us how the loudness of the sound (the y-axis) changes over time (the x-axis), while the pitch trace shows us how the frequency (the y-axis) changes over time (the x-axis). The spectrogram presents all of this information at once using a third axis, the darkness of the picture (the z-axis); it shows us how the frequency (the y-axis) and loudness (the z-axis, or darkness) both change over time (the x-axis)." (definition taken directly from chapter 9).

stress-timed languages—those languages that tend to give each *stress group* approximately the same weight, for example, English (wherein the utterance *When'll 'Tom be coming 'back?* would be timed in two stress groups *When'll 'Tom* and *be coming 'back* of about equal weight.

strong form of words (see synonym *citation form*)

syllable – in spoken language, the smallest distinctive unit made up of a single continuous sound formed by a vowel or diphthong, or by either these with one or more consonants before, after, or on both sides of it, or a syllabic consonant.

syllable-timed languages – those languages that tend to give each *syllable* approximately the same prominence, for example, Japanese (wherein *arigato gozaimasu* 'thank you very much' is broken up into the following syllables, or *mora: a ri ga to o go za i ma su* each with approximately the same weight) and French (wherein an utterance like *Il est très fatigué* 'He is very tired' would be pronounced in six syllables of approximately equal weight as follows: *Il est très fa ti gué*).

transition (sometimes called *juncture*) – the processes whereby neighboring phonemes are connected (also see *close transition* and *open transition*).

vowel devoicing (also see *high vowel devoicing museika* or *devoicing*, and full explanation in chapter 12) – in Japanese, "The close vowels (/i/ and /u/) tend to be devoiced (pronounced without moving the vocal chords) when they are both preceded and followed by voiceless consonants" (definition taken directly from chapter 12).

waveform – graph that shows "how the loudness of the sound (the y-axis) changes over time (the x-axis)" (definition taken directly from chapter 9).

weak form (also see *citation form*) – the pronunciation of a word when it is unstressed in connected speech, especially in contrast to the *citation* form; depending on the meaning being expressed, the phonological environment, and level of formality involved, the weak form may be quite different from the *citation form* (see *citation form* entry for examples).

wide-band spectrograms (also WBS) – graph that clearly shows when phonemes start and stop, in contrast to narrow-band spectrograms; WBSs also have one other very useful feature: the dark horizontal bands that are marked F1, F2, and F3 (these are the *formants* of the vowels, the frequencies of sound that are resonating in the mouth; definition adapted from chapter 9).

word coalescing (also see *phrase-final reduction* and *contracted forms*, and full explanation in chapter 12) – In Japanese, "When certain sounds follow each other, the following consonant becomes a semi-vowel and the two sounds coalesce" (definition taken directly from chapter 12).

word stress—the organization of stressed *syllables* in a word in terms of prominence.

About the Contributors

Editors

JAMES DEAN ("JD") BROWN is a professor in the Department of Second Language Studies at the University of Hawai'i at Mānoa. He has spoken and taught courses in places ranging from Brazil to Yugoslavia, and has published numerous articles and books on language testing, curriculum design, program evaluation, and research methods.

KIMI KONDO-BROWN is an associate professor in the Department of East Asian Languages at the University of Hawai'i at Mānoa where she teaches in the MA and PhD programs, particularly in Japanese pedagogy and research methodology. She has authored numerous articles in journals such as *The Modern Language Journal*, *Language Learning*, *Foreign Language Annals*, *Language Testing*, *International Journal of Bilingual Education and Bilingualism*, and *Linguistics and Education*.

Authors

ROBERT CAHILL has been teaching high school, college, and business English in Japan for 20 years. He is currently teaching at Yokohama Shodai High School and has developed curricula for business, tourism, and computer-related courses. He has been preparing students for homestays for the last 15 years and has consequently become more and more interested in materials relating to connected speech and speaking strategies. He has also had the opportunity to work with many bilingual students and uses graded readers and an English-language video library to teach writing skills. He has an MEd from Temple University.

NOBUKO HASEGAWA is currently teaching linguistics at the Graduate School of Language Sciences, Kanda University of International Studies. She also serves as Director of the Center for Language Sciences there, leading research projects on theoretical and applied linguistics. She received her PhD in Linguistics from University of Washington and has published an introductory textbook on Japanese linguistics and various articles on theoretical linguistics. Her recent research interest lies not only in theoretical linguistics but also in language development and teaching English to young children.

ANN HILFERTY has recently joined the Boston Public Schools as a literacy coach with high school teachers. She is also participating in a research project on adult literacy with the National Center for the Study of Adult Learning and Literacy (NCSALL) at Harvard University. Prior to her work with the public schools, Ann enjoyed a career in teaching and administration at the college level in Boston, Nigeria, and the People's Republic of China. She administered and taught in programs in composition, ESL, and methods of teaching ESL. Ann has co-authored a textbook on methods of teaching ESL, and has published articles on teaching ESL and Applied Linguistics. She received her EdD from Harvard University. Her current research interest is the adult acquisition of second language reading.

YUKARI HIRATA is currently teaching Japanese language and culture and language acquisition at Colgate University. Her research interests are in the acquisition of second language speech, acoustic phonetics, experimental phonetics, and Japanese as a second language. She has published articles in the *Journal of Phonetics*, *Journal of the Acoustical Society of America*, *Phonetica*, *Computer Assisted Language Learning*, and *Phonetic Society of Japan*. She is currently working on a project supported by the National Science Foundation examining the effects of speaking rate on native English speakers' acquisition of Japanese vowel length contrast. She received her PhD in Linguistics from the University of Chicago.

YU IGASHIMA taught a Japanese language course for graduate-level foreign students attending the Japan-Indonesia Science and Technology Forum in Japan until 2002. While she was a student at the Yokohama National Graduate School, she conducted research into the development of Japanese language abilities in both Japanese children living abroad and in foreign children living in Japan. She is also interested in the use of technology, such as computers and the Internet, for teaching the Japanese language. Currently, she is continuing her research into the development of CALL resources for improving listening abilities.

YASUKO ITO is a recent doctoral graduate from the Department of Second Language Studies at the University of Hawai'i at Mānoa. She also has an MA in Education and M.S. in Applied Linguistics, and has taught academic English as well as undergraduate courses in second language acquisition and second language pedagogy. Her working experience also includes teaching Japanese and working as a university course evaluator. Her academic interests are teaching of listening and speaking, second language acquisition, second language phonology and syntax, and psycholinguistics.

TAKASHI MATSUZAWA works for a U.S.-based multinational company in Japan. He received an MEd in TESOL with a certificate in Teaching Japanese as a Second Language from Temple University Japan. He has taught several English courses at his company, including Reduced Forms, Vocabulary Learning, and Workshop for English Teleconference, aimed at helping his subordinates and peers to improve communications in English. He is interested in studying practical learning issues of English for Japanese learners. He is currently working on a paper on an issue of learning Japanese. He hopes to teach English or Japanese as his future career.

MOANA ROGERSON (ROSA) is currently working in International Education with the University of Oregon and AHA International. While earning degrees in International Studies and Italian from the University of Oregon, Moana had the opportunity to study in Italy. She returned to live in Italy after graduation where she learned firsthand the real challenges of second language acquistion. Moana earned her master's degree in Second Language Acquisition from the University of Hawai'i and has taught English as a second language at universities in Oregon and Hawai'i. Her primary area of interest is in developing authentic teaching materials that address reduced forms and naturally occurring language patterns and pronunciation.

TAKAKO SAKAI is currently teaching Japanese as a second language at the Foreign Student Center of the University of Tsukuba, Japan. She is one of the authors behind the seven volumes of *Situational Functional Japanese*, a series of Japanese language textbooks aimed at foreign students. She has also developed computer software covering drills for listening comprehension and software for Japanese language proficiency testing. Her current research interests include looking at how to improve learners' listening abilities and her ongoing research into assessing Japanese language proficiency.

TAKAKO TODA is a professor at Waseda University, Tokyo, where she is currently teaching phonetics and phonology in the Graduate School of Japanese Applied Linguistics. She also coordinates pronunciation courses at the Center for Japanese Language. She received her PhD in Linguistics from the Australian National University in 1996. Her major research interests are first and second language speech perception and production. Her major publications include *Second Language Speech Perception and Production: Acquisition of Phonological Contrasts in Japanese* (2003; Lanham, MD: University Press of America), *Communication no tame no Nihongo Hatsuon Lesson* (2004; Tokyo: 3A Corporation [in Japanese]), and *Japanese Pronunciation Lesson* (2004; Seoul: Nexus Press [in Korean]).

J. KEVIN VARDEN (PhD Linguistics; University of Washington, Seattle) is an associate professor in the Center for Liberal Arts at Meiji Gakuin University, Tokyo/Yokohama. He has taught a variety of linguistic and EFL classes, currently including A History of the Japanese Language and a seminar series on laboratory phonology. His duties include helping administer the university's general education EFL program, as well as heading a research project creating multi-media EFL study materials. Research interests involve both theoretical linguistics (the phonology/phonetics interface) and more recently the use of technology for teaching natural speech.

*****
NATIONAL FOREIGN LANGUAGE RESOURCE CENTER
University of Hawai'i at Mānoa

NFLRC Monographs

Monographs of the National Foreign Language Resource Center present the findings of recent work in applied linguistics that is of relevance to language teaching and learning (with a focus on the less commonly-taught languages of Asia and the Pacific) and are of particular interest to foreign language educators, applied linguists, and researchers.
Prior to 2006, these monographs were published as "SLTCC Technical Reports."

PRAGMATICS AND LANGUAGE LEARNING volume 11 KATHLEEN BARDOVI-HARLIG CÉSAR FÉLIX-BRASDEFER ALWIYA S. OMAR *(Editors)*	This volume features cutting-edge theoretical and empirical research on pragmatics and language learning among a wide-variety of learners in diverse learning contexts from a variety of language backgrounds (English, German, Japanese, Persian, and Spanish) and target languages (English, German, Japanese, Kiswahili, and Spanish). This collection of papers from researchers around the world includes critical appraisals on the role of formulas in interlanguage pragmatics and speech-act research from a conversation-analytic perspective. Empirical studies examine learner data using innovative methods of analysis and investigate issues in pragmatic development and the instruction of pragmatics. 430 pp.
2006	ISBN(10): 0–8248–3136–5 ISBN(13): 978–0–8248–3136–3 $30.
CORPUS LINGUISTICS FOR KOREAN LANGUAGE LEARNING AND TEACHING ROBERT BLEY-VROMAN & HYUNSOOK KO *(Editor)*	Dramatic advances in personal-computer technology have given language teachers access to vast quantities of machine-readable text, which can be analyzed with a view toward improving the basis of language instruction. Corpus linguistics provides analytic techniques and practical tools for studying language in use. This volume provides both an introductory framework for the use of corpus linguistics for language teaching and examples of its application for Korean teaching and learning. The collected papers cover topics in Korean syntax, lexicon, and discourse, and second language acquisition research, always with a focus on application in the classroom. An overview of Korean corpus linguistics tools and available Korean corpora are also included. 265 pp.
2006	ISBN 0–8248–3062–8 $25.

NEW TECHNOLOGIES AND LANGUAGE LEARNING: CASES IN THE LESS COMMONLY TAUGHT LANGUAGES

CAROL ANNE SPREEN
(Editor)

In recent years, the National Security Education Program (NSEP) has supported an increasing number of programs for teaching languages using different technological media. This compilation of case study initiatives funded through the NSEP Institutional Grants Program presents a range of technology-based options for language programming that will help universities make more informed decisions about teaching less commonly taught languages. The eight chapters describe how different types of technologies are used to support language programs (i.e., Web, ITV, and audio- or video-based materials), discuss identifiable trends in e-language learning, and explore how technology addresses issues of equity, diversity, and opportunity. This book offers many lessons learned and decisions made as technology changes and learning needs become more complex. 188 pp.

2002   ISBN 0–8248–2634–5 $25.

AN INVESTIGATION OF SECOND LANGUAGE TASK-BASED PERFORMANCE ASSESSMENTS

JAMES DEAN BROWN,
THOM HUDSON,
JOHN M. NORRIS,
& WILLIAM BONK

This volume describes the creation of performance assessment instruments and their validation (based on work started in TR# 18). It begins by explaining the test and rating scale development processes and the administration of the resulting three seven-task tests to 90 university level EFL and ESL students. The results are examined in terms of (a) the effects of test revision; (b) comparisons among the task-dependent, task-independent, and self-rating scales; and (c) reliability and validity issues. 240 pp.

2002   ISBN 0–8248–2633–7 $25.

MOTIVATION AND SECOND LANGUAGE ACQUISITION

ZOLTÁN DÖRNYEI
& RICHARD SCHMIDT
(Editors)

This volume — the second in this series concerned with motivation and foreign language learning — includes papers presented in a state-of-the-art colloquium on L2 motivation at the American Association for Applied Linguistics (Vancouver, 2000) and a number of specially commissioned studies. The 20 chapters, written by some of the best known researchers in the field, cover a wide range of theoretical and research methodological issues, and also offer empirical results (both qualitative and quantitative) concerning the learning of many different languages (Arabic, Chinese, English, Filipino, French, German, Hindi, Italian, Japanese, Russian, and Spanish) in a broad range of learning contexts (Bahrain, Brazil, Canada, Egypt, Finland, Hungary, Ireland, Israel, Japan, Spain, and the US). 520 pp.

2001   ISBN 0–8248–2458–X $25.

STUDIES ON KOREAN IN COMMUNITY SCHOOLS

DONG-JAE LEE,
SOOKEUN CHO,
MISEON LEE,
MINSUN SONG,
& WILLIAM O'GRADY
(Editors)

The papers in this volume focus on language teaching and learning in Korean community schools. Drawing on innovative experimental work and research in linguistics, education, and psychology, the contributors address issues of importance to teachers, administrators, and parents. Topics covered include childhood bilingualism, Korean grammar, language acquisition, children's literature, and language teaching methodology. 256 pp.

[in Korean]

2000   ISBN 0–8248–2352–4 $20.

A FOCUS ON LANGUAGE TEST DEVELOPMENT: EXPANDING THE LANGUAGE PROFICIENCY CONSTRUCT ACROSS A VARIETY OF TESTS

THOM HUDSON
& JAMES DEAN BROWN
(*Editors*)

2001

This volume presents eight research studies that introduce a variety of novel, non-traditional forms of second and foreign language assessment. To the extent possible, the studies also show the entire test development process, warts and all. These language testing projects not only demonstrate many of the types of problems that test developers run into in the real world but also afford the reader unique insights into the language test development process. 230 pp.

ISBN 0–8248–2351–6 $20.

A COMMUNICATIVE FRAMEWORK FOR INTRODUCTORY JAPANESE LANGUAGE CURRICULA

WASHINGTON STATE
JAPANESE LANGUAGE
CURRICULUM
GUIDELINES COMMITTEE

2000

In recent years the number of schools offering Japanese nationwide has increased dramatically. Because of the tremendous popularity of the Japanese language and the shortage of teachers, quite a few untrained, non-native and native teachers are in the classrooms and are expected to teach several levels of Japanese. These guidelines are intended to assist individual teachers and professional associations throughout the United States in designing Japanese language curricula. They are meant to serve as a framework from which language teaching can be expanded and are intended to allow teachers to enhance and strengthen the quality of Japanese language instruction. 168 pp.

ISBN 0–8248–2350–8 $20.

FOREIGN LANGUAGE TEACHING & MINORITY LANGUAGE EDUCATION

KATHRYN A. DAVIS
(*Editor*)

1999

This volume seeks to examine the potential for building relationships among foreign language, bilingual, and ESL programs towards fostering bilingualism. Part I of the volume examines the sociopolitical contexts for language partnerships, including:

• obstacles to developing bilingualism
• implications of acculturation, identity, and language issues for linguistic minorities.
• the potential for developing partnerships across primary, secondary, and tertiary institutions

Part II of the volume provides research findings on the *Foreign language partnership project* designed to capitalize on the resources of immigrant students to enhance foreign language learning. 152 pp.

ISBN 0–8248–2067–3 $20.

DESIGNING SECOND LANGUAGE PERFORMANCE ASSESSMENTS

JOHN M. NORRIS,
JAMES DEAN BROWN,
THOM HUDSON,
& JIM YOSHIOKA

1998, 2000

This technical report focuses on the decision-making potential provided by second language performance assessments. The authors first situate performance assessment within a broader discussion of alternatives in language assessment and in educational assessment in general. They then discuss issues in performance assessment design, implementation, reliability, and validity. Finally, they present a prototype framework for second language performance assessment based on the integration of theoretical underpinnings and research findings from the task-based language teaching literature, the language testing literature, and the educational measurement literature. The authors outline test and item specifications, and they present numerous examples of prototypical language tasks. They also propose a research agenda focusing on the operationalization of second language performance assessments. 248 pp.

ISBN 0–8248–2109–2 $20.

SECOND LANGUAGE DEVELOPMENT IN WRITING: MEASURES OF FLUENCY, ACCURACY, & COMPLEXITY

KATE WOLFE-QUINTERO, SHUNJI INAGAKI, & HAE-YOUNG KIM

In this book, the authors analyze and compare the ways that fluency, accuracy, grammatical complexity, and lexical complexity have been measured in studies of language development in second language writing. More than 100 developmental measures are examined, with detailed comparisons of the results across the studies that have used each measure. The authors discuss the theoretical foundations for each type of developmental measure, and they consider the relationship between developmental measures and various types of proficiency measures. They also examine criteria for determining which developmental measures are the most successful and suggest which measures are the most promising for continuing work on language development. 208 pp.

1998, 2002   ISBN 0–8248–2069–X $20.

THE DEVELOPMENT OF A LEXICAL TONE PHONOLOGY IN AMERICAN ADULT LEARNERS OF STANDARD MANDARIN CHINESE

SYLVIA HENEL SUN

The study reported is based on an assessment of three decades of research on the SLA of Mandarin tone. It investigates whether differences in learners' tone perception and production are related to differences in the effects of certain linguistic, task, and learner factors. The learners of focus are American students of Mandarin in Beijing, China. Their performances on two perception and three production tasks are analyzed through a host of variables and methods of quantification. 328 pp.

1998   ISBN 0–8248–2068–1 $20.

NEW TRENDS & ISSUES IN TEACHING JAPANESE LANGUAGE & CULTURE

HARUKO M. COOK, KYOKO HIJIRIDA, & MILDRED TAHARA
(Editors)

In recent years, Japanese has become the fourth most commonly taught foreign language at the college level in the United States. As the number of students who study Japanese has increased, the teaching of Japanese as a foreign language has been established as an important academic field of study. This technical report includes nine contributions to the advancement of this field, encompassing the following five important issues:

- Literature and literature teaching
- Technology in the language classroom
- Orthography
- Testing
- Grammatical versus pragmatic approaches to language teaching 164 pp.

1997   ISBN 0–8248–2067–3 $20.

SIX MEASURES OF JSL PRAGMATICS

SAYOKO OKADA YAMASHITA

This book investigates differences among tests that can be used to measure the cross-cultural pragmatic ability of English-speaking learners of Japanese. Building on the work of Hudson, Detmer, and Brown (Technical Reports #2 and #7 in this series), the author modified six test types that she used to gather data from North American learners of Japanese. She found numerous problems with the multiple-choice discourse completion test but reported that the other five tests all proved highly reliable and reasonably valid. Practical issues involved in creating and using such language tests are discussed from a variety of perspectives. 213 pp.

1996   ISBN 0–8248–1914–4 $15.

LANGUAGE LEARNING STRATEGIES AROUND THE WORLD: CROSS-CULTURAL PERSPECTIVES

REBECCA L. OXFORD
(*Editor*)

1996, 1997, 2002

Language learning strategies are the specific steps students take to improve their progress in learning a second or foreign language. Optimizing learning strategies improves language performance. This groundbreaking book presents new information about cultural influences on the use of language learning strategies. It also shows innovative ways to assess students' strategy use and remarkable techniques for helping students improve their choice of strategies, with the goal of peak language learning. 166 pp.

ISBN 0–8248–1910–1 $20.

TELECOLLABORATION IN FOREIGN LANGUAGE LEARNING: PROCEEDINGS OF THE HAWAIʻI SYMPOSIUM

MARK WARSCHAUER
(*Editor*)

1996

The Symposium on Local & Global Electronic Networking in Foreign Language Learning & Research, part of the National Foreign Language Resource Center's *1995 Summer Institute on Technology & the Human Factor in Foreign Language Education*, included presentations of papers and hands-on workshops conducted by Symposium participants to facilitate the sharing of resources, ideas, and information about all aspects of electronic networking for foreign language teaching and research, including electronic discussion and conferencing, international cultural exchanges, real-time communication and simulations, research and resource retrieval via the Internet, and research using networks. This collection presents a sampling of those presentations. 252 pp.

ISBN 0–8248–1867–9 $20.

LANGUAGE LEARNING MOTIVATION: PATHWAYS TO THE NEW CENTURY

REBECCA L. OXFORD
(*Editor*)

1996

This volume chronicles a revolution in our thinking about what makes students want to learn languages and what causes them to persist in that difficult and rewarding adventure. Topics in this book include the internal structures of and external connections with foreign language motivation; exploring adult language learning motivation, self-efficacy, and anxiety; comparing the motivations and learning strategies of students of Japanese and Spanish; and enhancing the theory of language learning motivation from many psychological and social perspectives. 218 pp.

ISBN 0–8248–1849–0 $20.

LINGUISTICS & LANGUAGE TEACHING: PROCEEDINGS OF THE SIXTH JOINT LSH-HATESL CONFERENCE

CYNTHIA REVES, CAROLINE STEELE, & CATHY S. P. WONG
(*Editors*)

1996

Technical Report #10 contains 18 articles revolving around the following three topics:

- Linguistic issues — These six papers discuss various linguistic issues: ideophones, syllabic nasals, linguistic areas, computation, tonal melody classification, and *wh*-words.
- Sociolinguistics — Sociolinguistic phenomena in Swahili, signing, Hawaiian, and Japanese are discussed in four of the papers.
- Language teaching and learning — These eight papers cover prosodic modification, note taking, planning in oral production, oral testing, language policy, L2 essay organization, access to dative alternation rules, and child noun phrase structure development. 364 pp.

ISBN 0–8248–1851–2 $20.

ATTENTION & AWARENESS IN FOREIGN LANGUAGE LEARNING RICHARD SCHMIDT *(Editor)*	Issues related to the role of attention and awareness in learning lie at the heart of many theoretical and practical controversies in the foreign language field. This collection of papers presents research into the learning of Spanish, Japanese, Finnish, Hawaiian, and English as a second language (with additional comments and examples from French, German, and miniature artificial languages) that bear on these crucial questions for foreign language pedagogy. 394 pp.

1996   ISBN 0–8248–1794–X $20.

VIRTUAL CONNECTIONS: ONLINE ACTIVITIES & PROJECTS FOR NETWORKING LANGUAGE LEARNERS MARK WARSCHAUER *(Editor)*	Computer networking has created dramatic new possibilities for connecting language learners in a single classroom or across the globe. This collection of activities and projects makes use of e-mail, the internet, computer conferencing, and other forms of computer-mediated communication for the foreign and second language classroom at any level of instruction. Teachers from around the world submitted the activities compiled in this volume — activities that they have used successfully in their own classrooms. 417 pp.

1995, 1996   ISBN 0–8248–1793–1 $30.

DEVELOPING PROTOTYPIC MEASURES OF CROSS-CULTURAL PRAGMATICS THOM HUDSON EMILY DETMER & J. D. BROWN	Although the study of cross-cultural pragmatics has gained importance in applied linguistics, there are no standard forms of assessment that might make research comparable across studies and languages. The present volume describes the process through which six forms of cross-cultural assessment were developed for second language learners of English. The models may be used for second language learners of other languages. The six forms of assessment involve two forms each of indirect discourse completion tests, oral language production, and self-assessment. The procedures involve the assessment of requests, apologies, and refusals. 198 pp.

1995   ISBN 0–8248–1763–X $15.

THE ROLE OF PHONOLOGICAL CODING IN READING *KANJI* SACHIKO MATSUNAGA	In this technical report, the author reports the results of a study that she conducted on phonological coding in reading *kanji* using an eye-movement monitor and draws some pedagogical implications. In addition, she reviews current literature on the different schools of thought regarding instruction in reading *kanji* and its role in the teaching of non-alphabetic written languages like Japanese. 64 pp.

1995   ISBN 0–8248–1734–6 $10.

PRAGMATICS OF CHINESE AS NATIVE & TARGET LANGUAGE GABRIELE KASPER *(Editor)*	This technical report includes six contributions to the study of the pragmatics of Mandarin Chinese: • A report of an interview study conducted with nonnative speakers of Chinese; and • Five data-based studies on the performance of different speech acts by native speakers of Mandarin — requesting, refusing, complaining, giving bad news, disagreeing, and complimenting. 312 pp.

1995   ISBN 0–8248–1733–8 $15.

A BIBLIOGRAPHY OF PEDAGOGY & RESEARCH IN INTERPRETATION & TRANSLATION

ETILVIA ARJONA

This technical report includes four types of bibliographic information on translation and interpretation studies:

- Research efforts across disciplinary boundaries — cognitive psychology, neurolinguistics, psycholinguistics, sociolinguistics, computational linguistics, measurement, aptitude testing, language policy, decision-making, theses, dissertations;
- Training information covering program design, curriculum studies, instruction, school administration;
- Instruction information detailing course syllabi, methodology, models, available textbooks; and
- Testing information about aptitude, selection, diagnostic tests.

115 pp.

1993   ISBN 0–8248–1572–6 $10.

PRAGMATICS OF JAPANESE AS NATIVE & TARGET LANGUAGE

GABRIELE KASPER
(*Editor*)

This technical report includes three contributions to the study of the pragmatics of Japanese:

- A bibliography on speech act performance, discourse management, and other pragmatic and sociolinguistic features of Japanese;
- A study on introspective methods in examining Japanese learners' performance of refusals; and
- A longitudinal investigation of the acquisition of the particle *ne* by nonnative speakers of Japanese.

125 pp.

1992, 1996   ISBN 0–8248–1462–2 $10.

A FRAMEWORK FOR TESTING CROSS-CULTURAL PRAGMATICS

THOM HUDSON
EMILY DETMER
& J. D. BROWN

This technical report presents a framework for developing methods that assess cross-cultural pragmatic ability. Although the framework has been designed for Japanese and American cross-cultural contrasts, it can serve as a generic approach that can be applied to other language contrasts. The focus is on the variables of social distance, relative power, and the degree of imposition within the speech acts of requests, refusals, and apologies. Evaluation of performance is based on recognition of the speech act, amount of speech, forms or formulæ used, directness, formality, and politeness. 51 pp.

1992   ISBN 0–8248–1463–0 $10.

RESEARCH METHODS IN INTERLANGUAGE PRAGMATICS

GABRIELE KASPER
& MERETE DAHL

This technical report reviews the methods of data collection employed in 39 studies of interlanguage pragmatics, defined narrowly as the investigation of nonnative speakers' comprehension and production of speech acts, and the acquisition of L2-related speech act knowledge. Data collection instruments are distinguished according to the degree to which they constrain informants' responses, and whether they tap speech act perception/comprehension or production. A main focus of discussion is the validity of different types of data, in particular their adequacy to approximate authentic performance of linguistic action. 51 pp.

1991   ISBN 0–8248–1419–3 $10.